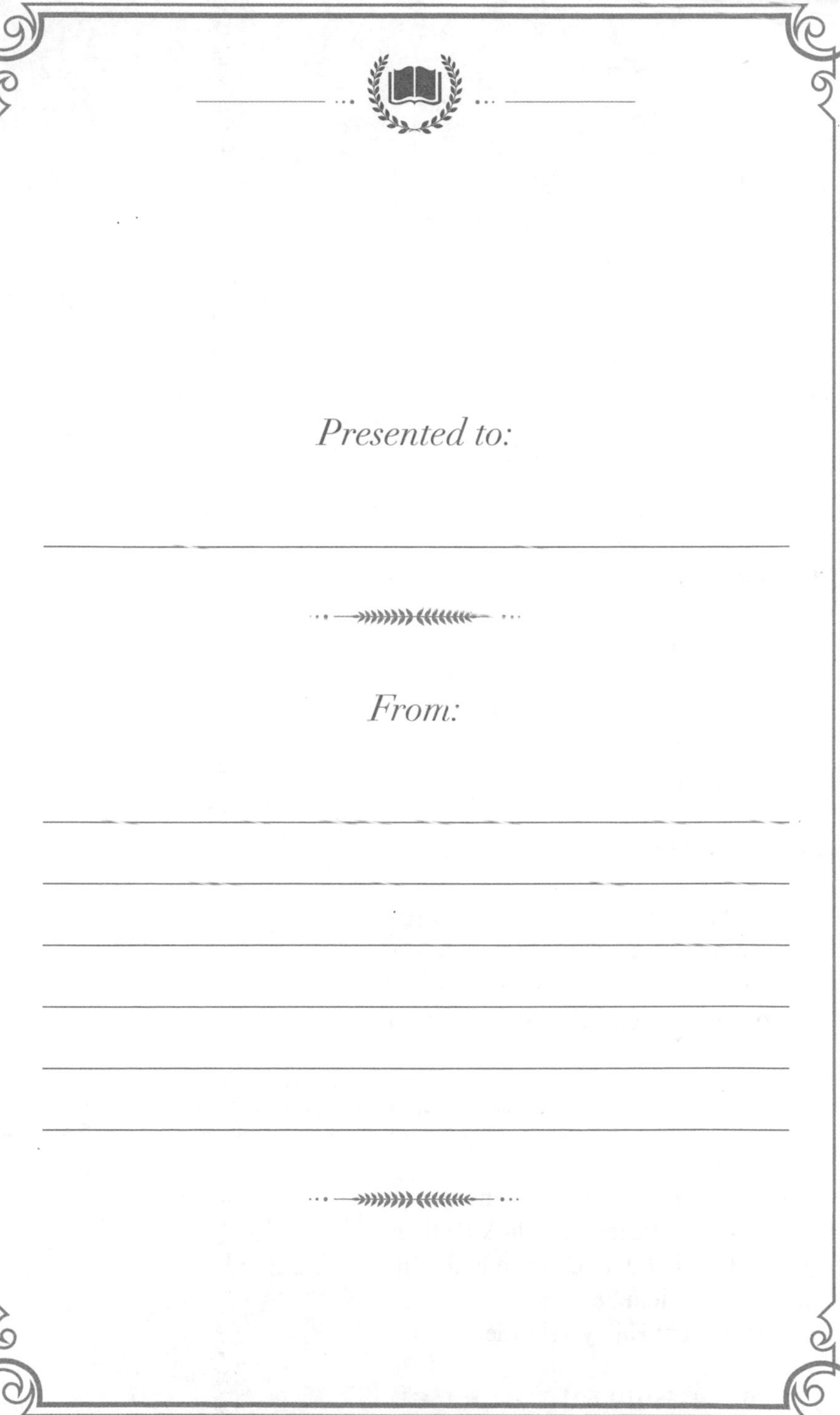

Presented to:

From:

Triumphant Truth

Published by Amazing Facts, Inc.
P.O. Box 1058
Roseville, CA 95678
916-434-3880
afbookstore.com

Content Manager: Curtis Rittenour
Writers: Curtis Rittenour, Mark Kellner,
Laurie Lyon, Cosmin Ritivoiu
Copyeditor: Michelle Kiss
Graphic design: Haley Trimmer

ISBN: 978-1-58019-601-7

TRIUMPHANT TRUTH

28 ESSENTIAL BELIEFS OF THE REMNANT

A Daily Devotional

Table of Contents

It usually happens without thinking.

A runner wins a race and, within milliseconds of crossing the finish line, throws up her arms in the air as a celebration of victory. Researchers have discovered that this nonverbal display of joy happens in cultures around the world. And even blind athletes, who have never seen others do it, will reflexively lift up their arms in triumph.

The Bible often talks about God's victory on behalf of His people. After they crossed the Red Sea, the children of Israel sang, "I will sing to the LORD, for He has triumphed gloriously!" (Exodus 15:1). When the Israelites later fought against the Amalekites, the Bible explains, "So it was, when Moses held up his hand, that Israel prevailed; and when he let down his hand, Amalek prevailed" (Exodus 17:11).

That's why as Christians we shouldn't be lifting up our arms as a boast of our spiritual strength, as if we alone gained the victory. Followers of God know that it is only through Christ and His sustaining power that we triumph over the forces of evil. And nothing more clearly reveals Christ than the Bible truth. Indeed, King David sang, "My hands also I will lift up to Your commandments, which I love, and I will meditate on Your statutes" (Psalm 119:48).

It's for this reason that Amazing Facts publishing has created *Triumphant Truth,* the daily devotional you now hold in your hands. Our goal is to provide you a daily opportunity to reflect on the fundamental beliefs of God's remnant church. Each essential teaching within, whether on the doctrine of the sanctuary or the Sabbath, is presented over the course of a couple weeks to help you more deeply consider the important Bible truths for these end times.

Someday, when the truth about God's character is made known to the world, His saints will raise their arms in victory, acknowledging they overcame "by the blood of the Lamb" (Revelation 12:11). The apostle also wrote, "I saw something like a sea of glass mingled with fire, and those who have the victory over the beast, over his image and over his mark and over the number of his name, standing on the sea of glass, having harps of God" (Revelation 15:2).

These overcomers sing, "Great and marvelous are Your works, Lord God Almighty! Just and true are Your ways, O King of the saints!" (verse 3). Like the Israelites at the Red Sea, we will shout the praises of God, and raise our arms in victory, for truth has finally triumphed!

Pastor Doug Batchelor
President, Amazing Facts

The Holy Scriptures

1

Beliefs Matter

"You shall know the truth, and the truth shall make you free" (John 8:32).

For 29 years, Hiroo Onoda, an Imperial Japanese Army officer, refused to believe World War II was over. When he was sent to the Philippines in late 1944, his last order was to keep fighting until given further orders. After Japan surrendered, Onoda and several others who had also been trained in guerrilla tactics remained hidden on Lubang Island. They built bamboo huts, stole food from villages, patched their uniforms, and kept their guns in working order.

Leaflets were dropped from planes explaining that the war had ended, but Onoda and his comrades believed it was enemy propaganda. They continued to evade search parties until, one by one, the men died or surrendered. Not until 1974 did Lieutenant Onoda change his mind. It took a delegation from the Japanese government and his own brother to finally convince him to lay down his weapons.

God has sent messages from heaven asking us to surrender our lives to Christ. The Bible provides the truth of the gospel, but many refuse to study Scripture and think it is useless material or even distorted propaganda. But within the pages of this sacred book, we learn that Jesus was victorious over Satan at the cross of Calvary.

Hiroo Onoda reminds us that what you believe matters and shapes your life. Throughout this devotional, we'll learn about 28 basic Bible teachings—beliefs that matter, change you, and show God's great love for you. Satan has attempted to make you believe in fallacies that will keep you fighting useless battles that will eventually lead you to death.

Take time every day to study the Word of God and believe its contents. Read the Bible for yourself, become acquainted with Christ who is "the way, the truth, and the life" (John 14:6). Don't trust the propaganda of the devil. And when you know the truth for yourself, the Bible promises that it will set you free.

Apply It:

Make a commitment to read a portion of the Bible every day.

Dig Deeper:

Psalm 119:15; John 17:17; 2 Timothy 3:15–17

Nature Speaks

"Since the creation of the world His invisible attributes are clearly seen, being understood by the things that are made, even His eternal power and Godhead, so that they are without excuse" (Romans 1:20).

Have you ever looked up into the star-studded heavens on a moonless night away from the city lights? How many stars could you see with the naked eye? You know there are *billions* of stars, but you might be surprised to know that even on the darkest nights you can see just 4,550 stars.

Still, something about looking up at the stars brings wonder and humility to the soul. The immense universe above often stuns city dwellers when they take their first venture out into the country. Grab a pair of 50-mm binoculars and the number of visible stars shoots up to around 217,000. Look through a three-inch telescope and observe a jaw-dropping 5.3 million stars! Our own Milky Way Galaxy alone is believed to have about 300 billion stars.

Just by observing the wonders of Creation—like the countless stars in the night sky—humanity can learn something of its Designer. The poet-king David wrote, "The heavens declare the glory of God; and the firmament shows His handiwork. Day unto day utters speech, and night unto night reveals knowledge" (Psalm 19:1, 2).

Learning about God in nature is called "general revelation" and should not be considered a useless pursuit. Christ often explained Bible truths through this "second book." Consider that the very foundation of the Scriptures is laid on this first verse: "In the beginning God created the heavens and the earth" (Genesis 1:1).

When you study the stars, you are seeing a part of creation that has been untouched by human sin. You get a glimpse of God's power just by looking up into the heavens. Billions of twinkling lights truly show us that God is love.

Apply It:

Go outside on a clear night sometime this week, look up into the sky, and observe God's love for you in the wonders of the heavens.

Dig Deeper:

Job 12:7–10; Psalm 96:11, 12; John 1:3

A Closer Look

"God, who at various times and in various ways spoke in time past to the fathers by the prophets, has in these last days spoken to us by His Son, whom He has appointed heir of all things, through whom also He made the worlds" (Hebrews 1:1, 2).

The first microscope was not intended to be a scientific instrument by its creator, but more of a novelty. The Romans used glass in the first century to make objects appear larger, and the Italian Salvino D'Armate later created the first eye glass in the thirteenth century. But the first person to create a compound microscope (two lenses used together in a hollow tube) was a Dutch spectacle maker, Zacharias Jansen, in the 1590s. Magnification was only around 9 times, and images were blurry.

It was a Dutch scientist, Anton van Leeuwenhoek, who took the microscope to a whole new level. He painstakingly polished more than 550 lenses to create a superior instrument with a magnifying power of 270x. Van Leeuwenhoek made many biological discoveries with his new microscope and drew pictures of things never before observed by the naked eye, including bacteria, yeast plants, and blood corpuscles in capillaries.

As we seek to more clearly understand God, we must admit that our vision is blurred by sin. Though we can observe many of His qualities in the natural world, there is much more we may discover through a closer look at the Bible. The Word of God, both the Old and New Testaments, brings God up close and is a specific revelation. First through prophets, and then even more clearly "in these last days ... by His Son", we may read the Scriptures and see the truth about God's love for lost humanity.

The Bible is like a microscope, giving us a superior picture of God. When we peer deeply into this special revelation, we learn much more about sin, the great controversy, and the plan of salvation. The Scriptures magnify eternal truths beyond what our human minds can comprehend and bring the messages from heaven to a whole new level.

Apply It:

Using a concordance, look up all the words in the Bible under "Scripture" (and "Scriptures"). Prayerfully reflect on the purpose of God's Word.

Dig Deeper:

Daniel 10:21; John 10:35; Acts 18:24

The Focal Point

"[Jesus] said to them, 'O foolish ones, and slow of heart to believe in all that the prophets have spoken! Ought not the Christ to have suffered these things and to enter into His glory?' And beginning at Moses and all the Prophets, He expounded to them in all the Scriptures the things concerning Himself" (Luke 24:25–27).

It is considered the world's most recognizable painting. Leonardo da Vinci's *The Last Supper* was commissioned by the Duke of Milan in 1495 and covers the end wall of the dining hall at the monastery of Santa Maria delle Grazie in Milan, Italy. It portrays the reaction of the disciples after Jesus announced that one of them would betray Him.

There are many speculations about hidden secrets within the painting, but what is plainly seen, thanks to da Vinci's use of lighting and perspective, is that the central figure is Christ. Not only is Jesus the highlight of *The Last Supper,* He is literally the focal point of the painting. Indeed, Leonardo employed a perspective that made the Savior's face the very center of the piece.

Just as da Vinci's masterpiece has suffered over the centuries (once barely escaping total destruction by an Allied bomb in 1943), it reminds us of the life and scope of the Holy Scriptures. Over the centuries, the Bible has taken a beating, yet it survives today as the Book of all books—the most widely distributed piece of literature of all ages.

And as our text above reveals, the central figure, the focal point of all the Bible, is Jesus Christ. In every chapter, through every story and figure, the Savior is the center of attention. The Scriptures describe Christ as "the Alpha and the Omega, the Beginning and the End, the First and the Last" (Revelation 22:13).

The central truth of the Bible is not the interesting stories, the history of Israel, or beautiful poetry. If we would rightly understand God's Word, we must turn our eyes upon Jesus and look full into His wonderful face.

Apply It:

Study a copy of *The Last Supper* and then read John 13. Ask yourself, "Am I making Jesus the central figure of my life?"

Dig Deeper:

John 12:21; Romans 16:25–27; 2 Corinthians 3:14

The True Author

"The Spirit of the LORD spoke by me, and His word was on my tongue" (2 Samuel 23:2).

Authors sometimes take on a pen name (*nom de plume*), which is a pseudonym used on the title page of their literary work. Samuel Langhorne Clemens used the aliases Mark Twain and Sieur Louis de Conte for different writings. Benjamin Franklin used the pen name Mrs. Silence Dogood, and C.S. Lewis wrote as Clive Hamilton.

There are different reasons why authors use pen names. Sometimes a writer wants to use a more distinctive name or even disguise his or her gender. In some cases, authors use a pseudonym to protect themselves from retribution for their writing.

When it comes to the authorship of the Bible, the writers of Scripture did not try to conceal or elevate themselves. Neither did Bible writers claim to make up the content of their messages. They acknowledged God as their divine source. Isaiah attributes his book to a vision from the Lord (1:1), as do many other writers, including Amos, Micah, and Habakkuk.

More specifically, writers often identified the work of God through the Holy Spirit in giving them messages. Ezekiel said, "The Spirit entered me when He spoke to me, and set me on my feet; and I heard Him who spoke to me" (Ezekiel 2:2). In the New Testament, Paul explained, "The Holy Spirit spoke rightly through Isaiah the prophet to our fathers" (Acts 28:25).

God has made Himself known in the Bible through the Holy Spirit. Through the hands of about forty human authors, the Lord has communicated heavenly truths over a period of around 1,500 years. Because the true source of the Scriptures came through the inspiration of the Holy Spirit, we may know that the real author of the Bible is God.

Apply It:

Carefully read (or sing) the words to the hymn "Give Me the Bible" and then carry its message with you throughout the day.

Dig Deeper:

Nehemiah 9:30; Micah 3:8; Romans 1:1, 2

God-Breathed

"All Scripture is given by inspiration of God, and is profitable for doctrine, for reproof, for correction, for instruction in righteousness, that the man of God may be complete, thoroughly equipped for every good work" (2 Timothy 3:16, 17).

It's been called the "kiss of life" and has saved countless people who have stopped breathing. Mouth-to-mouth resuscitation was first publicly advocated by an English physician, William Hawes, in the mid-1700s. For a year, he paid a reward to anyone who brought him the body of someone who had drowned (within a reasonable amount of time). He eventually set up the Royal Humane Society with training and life-saving apparatus, mostly in ports and coastal towns where the risk of drowning was highest.

Insufflations, also called "rescue breaths," force air into a person's respiratory system. Cardiopulmonary resuscitation (CPR) training recommends first checking for circulation (a pulse), then checking for breathing, and then, if necessary, performing mouth-to-mouth resuscitation. Many organizations recommend the use of a pocket mask to minimize the risk of cross infection. Breathing for someone else can save a life.

God first breathed the breath of life into Adam at Creation. But there is another type of breathing that describes how writers of the Holy Scriptures worked. Today's Bible verse says, "All Scripture is given by inspiration of God." The Greek word for this process is *theo-pneustos* and means "God-breathed." The Word of God is "profitable" because God Himself breathed life into it.

Even though revelations were written down in human language, they are still God's messages. It was not so much that the words were inspired; rather, the writers were inspired. These men did not flip on a digital voice recorder to capture God's exact words. Writers often did write God's exact words, but in most cases, they wrote in their own language what they saw or heard through the power of the Holy Spirit. Through God's life-giving Spirit, we have received in the Bible life-saving truths.

Apply It:

Watch a short video (or read a short description) on how to conduct CPR. Then pray for the Holy Spirit to use you to save others, both physically and spiritually.

Dig Deeper:

Exodus 4:14-16; Numbers 23:5; Deuteronomy 18:18

Just Like Us

"Elijah was a man with a nature like ours, and he prayed earnestly that it would not rain; and it did not rain on the land for three years and six months" (James 5:17).

He was the only U.S. president who reached the Oval Office without first winning election as president or vice president. Gerald Ford, the 38th President of the United States, never aspired to be the man in the White House. His only desire was to reach the top of the Congressional hierarchy as Speaker of the House.

Ford had served for eight years as House Minority Leader when scandals began to plague Vice President Spiro Agnew. After Agnew resigned, President Richard Nixon (who was beginning to feel the heat of Watergate) asked congressional leaders who should be Agnew's successor. They gave him no choice but Ford, who eventually replaced Nixon as president when Watergate blew up. "I have not sought this enormous responsibility, but I will not shirk it," Ford said when he took up the reigns.

Ford's words capture the attitude of the writers of the Bible. Those who were chosen to be God's spokesmen often did not aspire to be authors of the Word of God. The Lord did not commission angels to write the Scriptures, but ordinary yet God-fearing people with, as today's text states, "a nature like ours." Indeed, King David, one of the most prolific writers of the Old Testament, committed serious sins.

Bible writers often worked under difficult circumstances to present God's messages. Gerald Ford could relate. He wrote: "History and experience tell us that moral progress comes not in comfortable and complacent times, but out of trial and confusion." That's certainly true when it comes to the inspiration of the Bible, a light that shines brightly through humble people like you and me.

Apply It:

Ask yourself, "Am I resistant to the Word of God?" Read what happened to God's written word from the prophet Jeremiah in the days of King Jehoiakim. (See Jeremiah 36.)

Dig Deeper:

Numbers 22–24; Habakkuk 1; Jonah 1:1–3; 4:1–11

Entirely Trustworthy

"All these things happened to them as examples, and they were written for our admonition, upon whom the ends of the ages have come" (1 Corinthians 10:11).

"Listen, my children, and you shall hear of the midnight ride of Paul Revere." Henry Wadsworth Longfellow's popular poem about a Boston silversmith and American patriot has been read to most grade-school children, but many don't realize it's sprinkled with myths that are more of a product of late nineteenth century nationalism.

The poem suggests Revere rode alone, but the truth is that there were two other primary riders—William Dawes and Samuel Prescott. Most scholars agree that there were as many as forty riders who carried the warning through northern and eastern Massachusetts. It is also unlikely that he cried out, "The British are coming," since all the people considered themselves British. He probably called out, "The Regulars are coming," meaning the British army.

Some believe that the historical records found in the Bible have been sprinkled with myths. Yet the Bible itself claims to be inspired by God (2 Timothy 3:15) and affirms heaven's guidance in choosing its content. God told men to write a factual history of His dealing with Israel (e.g., Numbers 33:1, 2). Luke wrote an accurate account about Jesus "that you may know the certainty of those things in which you were instructed" (Luke 1:4). Bible writers were directed by the Lord to present history in a way that would lead people to salvation.

Even the biographies of Scripture reveal evidence of inspiration by not covering up the weaknesses of major characters like Abraham, Moses, or Paul. Failures of Israel's kings are plainly, openly described. Bible writers understood all historical narratives as historically accurate and spiritually relevant. There are no degrees of inspiration in the Bible; it is absolutely the authentic Word of God.

Apply It:

Read the apostle Paul's warnings to us about the Israelites' failures in 1 Corinthians 10:1–13. Which historical example do you most need to hear?

Dig Deeper:

John 10:31; Romans 15:4; 2 Peter 2:6

Accurate Truths

"The Word became flesh and dwelt among us, and we beheld His glory, the glory as of the only begotten of the Father, full of grace and truth" (John 1:14).

He never intended to initiate an avalanche of science-fiction literature, but a simple misunderstanding sparked a theory that wouldn't die for decades. In 1877, Italian astronomer Giovanni Schiaparelli was mapping the surface of the planet Mars. He called the dark and light areas he observed as "seas" and "continents." Then he labelled what he thought were channels using the Italian word "canali."

Schiaparelli's peers translated this word as "canals" and launched a theory that these had been created by intelligent life on the Red Planet. U.S. astronomer Percival Lowell mapped out hundreds of these "canals" and published three books on the supposed artificial structures that were supposedly built to carry water. Lowell influenced another writer, H. G. Wells, to create his famous *The War of the Worlds,* which describes Martians invading Earth. NASA has since assured that there are no alien-made channels crisscrossing Mars.

Some critics claim that the Bible is filled with errors. They believe the copied manuscripts changed over the centuries and cannot be trusted. It is true that scholars have found minor variations made by copyists, but the essential truths have not changed. Archaeology has proven that many supposed errors were misunderstandings on the part of translators—somewhat like Schiaparelli's peers—who were unfamiliar with biblical customs.

In the same way that Jesus "became flesh and dwelt among us," the Bible was given to us in the language of humanity so that we could understand divine truth. But people are limited in their ability to perceive heavenly realities. Despite efforts to destroy the Bible, it has been miraculously preserved and still accurately reveals God's perfect will for our lives.

Apply It:

Some words change meaning over time. Look up a few of these words in the King James Version and then study a Bible dictionary or commentary for their modern meaning: "carriages" in Acts 21:15, "charger" in Mark 6:25, and "leasing" in Psalm 4:2.

Dig Deeper:

Psalm 25:5; Daniel 8:12; 1 Thessalonians 2:13

It Is Written

"Man shall not live by bread alone, but by every word that proceeds from the mouth of God" (Matthew 4:4).

Less than three of every ten Americans say they trust the federal government to do the right thing. When a national election survey first asked citizens this question in 1958, 73 percent said they could trust the government just about always or most of the time. In recent years that number has plunged to three percent for "just about always" and 16 percent for "most of the time."

In 1964, the numbers were at an all-time high of 77 percent. But within a decade—a time that included the Vietnam War, civil unrest, and the Watergate scandal—trust had dropped by more than half. Though trust rebounded in the 1980s, it began falling again after the 9/11 terror attacks. The war in Iraq, economic uncertainty, and even Hurricane Katrina played a role. Interestingly, younger people are slightly more trusting of the government today.

Jesus had absolute trust in the government of heaven. When faced with His own crisis with the devil, Christ turned to a resource that never let Him down—the Word of God. The revelation of divine truth in the pages of Scripture were so essential to His life that He compared the Bible to our need for daily food.

The trustworthiness of the government of Israel and the spiritual leaders of God's people had fallen to an all-time low when the Messiah came to earth—so much so that the rulers of the time did not even recognize that their long-awaited Deliverer stood among them!

Christ believed in the authority of the Word of God. He set it above human traditions and public opinion. Jesus pleaded with the Jews to study the Scriptures carefully (Matthew 21:42). In a time when trust in institutions is low, we can have a sure foundation in the Bible.

Apply It:

Read through how Jesus handled temptations from the devil in Matthew 4:1–11 and adopt His strategy as your own.

Dig Deeper:

Psalm 119:160; Luke 10:26; John 5:39

The Spirit Leads

"We have received, not the spirit of the world, but the Spirit who is from God, that we might know the things that have been freely given to us by God" (1 Corinthians 2:12).

The Dutch national museum made an embarrassing discovery a few years ago. One of the most prized possessions in their collection was a moon rock. During the Apollo trips to the moon, more than 840 pounds of rock were collected, and some were given as gifts by U.S. ambassadors to different countries around the world.

The prime minister of the Netherlands received one such gift and, when he died in 1988, the rock was donated to the museum. Everyone thought the rock was authentic, and it was even insured for half-a-million dollars. But researchers at the Free University of Amsterdam had their doubts and began extensive testing. They finally concluded that the rock was a piece of petrified wood worth about $70. No one knows how the switch was ever made.

The Word of God is compared to a solid rock (Matthew 7:24) and is even better than fine gold (Psalm 19:10). But how does one truly know they possess heavenly truth? It comes only through the influence of the Holy Spirit, who alone can reveal God's messages. A casual reading of the Word will not open the divine teachings to a reader. The apostle Paul explained that "no one knows the things of God except the Spirit of God" (1 Corinthians 2:11).

One way the Spirit leads us to believe in the Bible is through predictive prophecy. When prophets foretell the future (see Daniel 2) through the guidance of the Holy Spirit, we grow to trust the Scriptures. "And so we have the prophetic word *confirmed*..." (2 Peter 1:19, emphasis added).

We are helpless in knowing truth and may actually be holding on to things that are worthless. The Holy Spirit is the One who guides us and helps us test and know the teachings of the Bible. "God has revealed them to us through His Spirit. For the Spirit searches all things, yes, the deep things of God" (1 Corinthians 2:10).

Apply It:

Make a commitment to always pray for the Holy Spirit to guide you before reading the Bible.

Dig Deeper:

Isaiah 8:20; Matthew 16:13–17; 1 Corinthians 12:3

Miracles of Beauty

"Have you entered the treasury of snow, or have you seen the treasury of hail?" (Job 38:22).

The Vermont winter was the perfect place for Wilson Bentley to practice his favorite hobby. While a teenager, he began experimenting with the newly discovered medium of photography to take pictures of his favorite subject—the snowflake. He successfully constructed a contraption to attach his camera to his microscope and captured his first picture in 1885, and he never looked back.

Over the course of 46 years, the Vermont farmer took more than 5,000 snow-crystal images on glass photographic plates. He lived his entire life in the same farmhouse, in the same town, using the same equipment he built as a teenager. Bentley's photographs showed up in many publications for decades, giving the world a better look at the beauty of snowflakes.

It is said that no two snowflakes are alike. Yet in all this incredible variety, the six-sided pattern of snow crystals never changed. The symmetrical structures, when carefully observed, all have the same basic configuration. Unity and diversity are combined by the Creator—giving us a powerful illustration of the Bible.

Many critics superficially read the Holy Scriptures and say that the diversity of stories, poetry, and history make up nothing more than a "jumbled" conglomeration of ancient material. Yet when the Spirit of God illumines the humble mind, it brings to light hidden truths and divine patterns that reveal—from Genesis to Revelation—the plan of salvation.

What may appear to some students of the Scriptures to be a collection of disconnected stories about Israel, strange prophecies, and history is really a unified whole revealing to us the God of love. Through Spirit-inspired writers, the Lord revealed a revelation of His plan to redeem people from sin. Look closely and you will see a beauty that many overlook.

Bentley called snowflakes "tiny miracles of beauty." Every verse of Scripture could be described in the same way.

Apply It:

Study pictures of snowflakes. If you are able, observe some with your naked eye or with a magnifying glass. Then reflect on the symmetry and beauty of the Scriptures.

Dig Deeper:

Job 38:29; Psalm 33:6; 1 Corinthians 1:18

The Indestructible Word

"The grass withers, the flower fades, but the word of our God stands forever" (Isaiah 40:8).

Have you ever watched a baby use a book? They don't usually hold it open with their hands and carefully turn pages. No, the book usually goes straight into their mouths. Paper books are a favorite for many babies since they crinkle and crunch. But pages can potentially turn into soggy pieces that could choke a toddler. That's why some companies actually create tear-resistant and waterproof books made of durable material, which can be chewed on and even thrown into a wash machine if needed.

One of the strongest evidences that the Bible is truly the Word of God is that it is indestructible. It has suffered more vicious attacks than any other book in all of history because it claims to be God's Word.

During the early church, the Roman emperor Diocletian tried to suppress the spread of Christianity and, according to Eusebius, "Royal edicts were published everywhere, commanding that the churches be leveled to the ground and the Scriptures destroyed by fire." During this time, if a person was discovered to have a copy of the Bible and failed to surrender it to be burned, they would be killed.

Diocletian eventually boasted, "I have completely exterminated the Christian writings from the face of the earth!" Yet when Constantine next ruled, he wanted copies of the Bible in every church. Since all Bibles had supposedly been destroyed, he offered a reward for any copy of the Word of God. Within 24 hours he had fifty copies of the Bible brought to him.

During the Middle Ages, the Roman Church burned thousands of copies of the Bible. The Frenchman Voltaire, who died in 1778, also attempted to destroy the Scriptures. Even though efforts have been made to refute, overthrow, demolish, and burn the Bible, "the word of our God stands forever."

Apply It:

Take a Bible in your hands and prayerfully thank God that you not only own a copy of the Scriptures, but that it is an everlasting source of truth.

Dig Deeper:

Matthew 24:35; John 12:48; 1 Peter 1:24, 25

Preserved Forever

"The words of the Lord are pure words, like silver tried in a furnace of earth, purified seven times. You shall keep them, O Lord, You shall preserve them from this generation forever" (Psalm 12:6, 7).

Imagine brushing away dirt from an ancient piece of pottery and finding an inscription that mentions the name of a Bible character whose existence has been questioned by critics of the Bible. Archaeology has repeatedly affirmed the historical reliability of God's Word even though some scholars argue that the record of the Bible cannot be trusted.

One of the earliest archaeological finds relating to the Bible is a large, black basalt rock called the Moabite Stone. Discovered in 1868, this three-foot-three-inch tall stele commemorates the successful revolt of the king of Moab against Israelite control. It provides information not explained in the Bible about the role of Omri (1 Kings 16:21–28) in regaining control over this kingdom.

In 1935, James Starkey discovered 21 ostraca (fragments of clay pottery with writing) in excavations at Lachish, a city in the lowland of Judah. They were a series of letters written during the time of Nebuchadnezzar's sieges and indicate the writer's hopes for help from Egypt. The Lachish letters provide some of the last words of Judah as it tried to survive the attacks of Babylon. The city finally fell, as did Jerusalem.

One of the greatest manuscript discoveries that affirms the accuracy of the Bible was the Dead Sea Scrolls in 1948. They date back a century before the time of Jesus and contain all of the Old Testament books (except Esther). Compared to later manuscripts, they show the incredible preservation of the biblical text.

Historical artifacts have proven many times over that the Bible is accurate and true. Manuscript evidence supporting the Bible has also shown the Scriptures to be the best-documented book in the ancient world.

■ Apply It:

Read or watch an account of the discovery of the Dead Sea Scrolls and learn how these manuscripts affirm the careful transmission of the Bible through the ages.

■ Dig Deeper:

Jeremiah 34:1–7; John 7:17; 2 Timothy 2:15

The Trinity

2

Knowing God

"This is eternal life, that they may know You, the only true God, and Jesus Christ whom You have sent" (John 17:3).

You'd really like to get to know someone better, but alas, you're unsure how to jumpstart a conversation. Maybe you feel awkward, shy, or just inexperienced at getting better acquainted with a special someone. Never fear, there are mountains of questions online that will give you a place to start!

Relationship gurus have crafted hundreds of questions that you can ask people you have just met, such as: If you didn't have to sleep, what would you do with the extra time? What hobby would you get into if you had more time and money? How do you relax after a hard day at work?

Then there are questions that go deeper and help you to really get to know a person. For instance: In what situation would you feel most out of place? What was the best compliment you've ever received? What gets you fired up? What do you tell yourself most often?

When it comes to knowing God, many people shrug off the whole notion of getting acquainted with a "higher power" that seems too far away. After all, God is transcendent and beyond human comprehension, so why try? Yet the Bible teaches that eternal life comes from *knowing* God.

Is this even possible?

The good news is that God has already started the conversation. The Lord understands our predicament and took the initiative to communicate with humanity. Even when Adam and Eve first sinned in the beginning, God pursued them in Eden. "And they heard the sound of the Lord God walking in the garden in the cool of the day ..." (Genesis 3:8).

Even though we will forever be learning about God, He has shown Himself to us so that we may enter into a meaningful relationship with Him and truly know Him.

Apply It:

Write a letter to God. Tell the Lord how much you would like to know Him better. Open up your heart to God like you would to a good friend.

Dig Deeper:

Matthew 22:37; 1 Corinthians 2:6–12; 1 John 5:20

Seeing God

"Blessed are the pure in heart, for they shall see God" (Matthew 5:8).

It all started at the Oregon Caves National Monument in 1938. Harold Graves ran a photo services shop in Portland and was an avid photographer. On his trip to the park he ran into a fellow camera buff, William Gruber, who had two cameras strapped together. Gruber was attempting to duplicate the stereoscope photos that were common in the nineteenth century.

William Gruber wanted to produce three-dimensional color slides that could be looked at in a new hand-held viewer. Graves offered his services and, by the next day, the two friends had struck a deal to produce View-Master. Their product, which was introduced at the 1939 New York World's Fair, featured views of scenic attractions from around the country. View-Master eventually focused their product on children, and it was later voted by *Time* as one of the best toys of the century.

Though stereo-photography has been around since 1838, and the first 3D film came out in 1915, there is something that far exceeds even the best virtual reality experiences available today. It is the accurate view of the true Master of the universe. But seeing God takes more than a headset. It must involve the heart.

Today's text explains that people who will see God are "pure in heart." This means we must be open to the Holy Spirit and willing to obey God. The Bible explains, "If anyone wills to do His will, he shall know concerning the doctrine, whether it is from God or whether I speak on My own authority" (John 7:17). If you would *know* God, you must be willing to obey God.

Most people in Jesus' time on earth failed to see that He was the Son of God. "He came to His own, and His own did not receive him" (John 1:11). They refused to submit themselves to the Holy Spirit, who spoke through the Scriptures. They didn't need better technology to study the divine; they needed an open heart to view eternal realities—not virtual realities.

Apply It:

Earnestly pray for God to purify your heart that you might see Him more clearly.

Dig Deeper:

Matthew 11:27; 1 Corinthians 1:20, 21; Hebrews 12:14

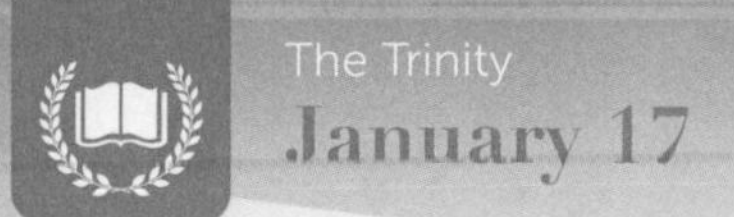

January 17

Believing is Seeing

"Without faith it is impossible to please Him, for he who comes to God must believe that He is, and that He is a rewarder of those who diligently seek Him" (Hebrews 11:6).

Many scientists, cosmologists, and even some agnostics agree that our universe appears as if it was designed for life. The foundation and location of our solar system and planet are in a delicate balance for us to live on Earth. For instance, the "habitable zone" of the earth's orbit around the sun is very narrow. If it were slightly closer or slightly farther away, a stable water cycle would be impossible. We would either freeze to death or die from unbearable heat.

The surface gravity on Earth is perfect to sustain life. If it were stronger, the atmosphere would contain too much methane and ammonia and kill us. If it were weaker, our planet wouldn't be able to retain enough water. The atmosphere is finely calibrated in its ratio of oxygen to nitrogen. Even our moon helps sustain life on Earth. The moon stabilizes the earth's orbit and rotation, preventing a more dramatic wobbling effect.

While there are thousands of evidences for the existence of God, none of them *proves* God. The Lord has chosen to reveal Himself through nature and the Bible, general and special revelation, but He encourages us to believe (see John 3:16). All the amazing design we see in our universe points to a Designer, and all the fine-tuning of the elements on our planet so that life can exist indicates that there must be a Fine-tuner.

Yet the Lord, in respecting our freedom of choice, allows us to doubt or believe that life is the result of chance or intentional purpose. In order to truly see the God of creation, there is a necessary element called faith. Joshua challenged Israel to "choose for yourselves this day whom you will serve" (Joshua 24:15). The Bible teaches that unless we choose to believe, we cannot see the Designer who made all that we observe.

Apply It:

Go for a walk in nature this week and look for patterns of design, believing that God exists and rewards those who diligently seek Him.

Dig Deeper:

Psalm 19:1; John 1:9; Romans 1:20

Invisible Attributes

"Since the creation of the world His invisible attributes are clearly seen, being understood by the things that are made, even His eternal power and Godhead, so that they are without excuse" (Romans 1:20).

Why would a brave police officer risk his life by leaning over a balcony and handcuffing himself to a woman who was about to jump to her death? Why would an 82-year-old barber bring a chair out into a park and offer to cut hair for homeless people for free? Why would softball players carry an injured batter for the other team to home plate so she could score?

Another evidence for the existence of God comes from what is called the "moral" argument. If you look at every culture in the history of humanity, all of them have had some sort of law. Every civilization throughout the ages has had some sense of right and wrong. Even the Bible explains, "For when Gentiles, who do not have the law, by nature do the things in the law, these, although not having the law, are a law to themselves" (Romans 2:14). When someone does a random act of kindness, people sit up and take notice.

Where does the essence of right and wrong come from, if not from a holy God who upholds the universe by laws? The apostle Paul spoke of the Godhead—the Father, Son, and Spirit—and explained that even without the Bible, people can recognize God's "invisible attributes" (Romans 1:20)—that is, His characteristics such as love and justice.

People may still choose to not believe in the existence of God because they think His existence lacks scientific proof. Paul says such unbelievers have evidence but choose to "believe the lie" (2 Thessalonians 2:11) and so they "are without excuse" (Romans 1:20). Ultimately, everyone may know, by looking at our world, that in the presence of tragedy there is kindness that comes from above.

By the way, after the police officer handcuffed himself to the woman who was about to jump to her death, he threw away the key. Do you know that God loves you so much that Jesus came to die in your place? He was willing to throw away His own life to save you from certain death.

Apply It:

Choose to do a random act of kindness today without telling anyone about it.

Dig Deeper:

Psalm 14:1; Ecclesiastes 3:11; Romans 1:25

January 19

The Names of God

"Let them praise the name of the LORD, for His name alone is exalted; His glory is above the earth and heaven" (Psalm 148:13).

When it comes to naming babies, some unusual choices have been picked out by parents and confirmed by government records. You expect to hear about babies named Sophia, Jackson, Olivia, and Lucas—but you'll also find names like Happy, Famous, Beauty, and Success.

Then there are parents who love certain locations in the world so much that they have picked the name of a city or country for their child's name—including Tokyo, Nazareth, Arabia, and Zealand. Some have even added a touch of royalty to their child, scrunching together names like Sirjames, Kingjosiah, and Siranthony.

You probably won't learn much about the babies above through their names, although you might learn a few things about their parents. But when it comes to the names of God in the Bible, you will discover the different qualities of His character. During the time the Bible was written, names were important and revealed the character of a person.

The Hebrew names *El* and *Elohim* tell us about God's divine power and reveal Him as a strong and mighty One (Genesis 1:1; Exodus 20:2). *El Elyon* means "God Most High" and emphasizes His exalted status (Genesis 14:18–20). *Adonai* is the name "Lord" and describes the ruling power of God (Isaiah 6:1). These names show us the majestic character of God.

Other names for God reveal His desire to be in a relationship with His people. For instance, *El Shaddai* means "God Almighty" and presents Him as the source of comfort and blessing (Exodus 6:3). The name *Yahweh,* strictly speaking, is a proper name for God. It's often translated as Jehovah or LORD with capital letters. It teaches us that God is present and near to those who call on His name.

Apply It:

Can you think of any other names for God in the Bible? Use a Bible dictionary or look online and discover a few more names for the Lord.

Dig Deeper:

Exodus 20:7; Psalm 7:17; Acts 2:21

God's Mighty Arms

"The Lord said to Moses, 'Has the Lord's arm been shortened? Now you shall see whether what I say will happen to you or not'" (Numbers 11:23).

Kirill Sarychev is built like a moose. He broke the world record in 2015 in the raw bench press with a stunning lift of 738.5 pounds. The six-foot six-inch tall powerlifter from Russia weighs around 375 pounds. He also set a world record in 2016 in the raw three-lift powerlifting competition by hoisting a total of 2,386.5 pounds. Sarychev began his powerlifting career at the age of fifteen.

In describing the attributes of God, the Bible doesn't leave out qualities that are above and beyond human strength. For example, the Lord is omniscient (all-knowing). Job writes, "Do you know how the clouds are balanced, those wondrous works of Him who is perfect in knowledge?" (Job 37:16). He is the "Alpha and Omega" and knows the beginning from the end (Revelation 1:8).

God is omnipresent and transcends all space. The Bible says, "There is no creature hidden from His sight, but all things are naked and open to the eyes of Him to whom we must give account" (Hebrews 4:13). God is eternal and not bound by time. David writes, "Before the mountains were brought forth, or ever You had formed the earth and the world, even from everlasting to everlasting, You are God" (Psalm 90:2).

God is also omnipotent (all-powerful) and nothing is impossible for Him. There are more than forty references in Scripture describing the Lord's strong arms. Speaking of God's salvation to Jerusalem, the Bible says, "The Lord has made bare His holy arm in the eyes of all the nations; and all the ends of the earth shall see the salvation of our God" (Isaiah 52:10). God's arms represent His omnipotent strength.

When you are afraid, never forget that you are safe in your Father's arms. "The eternal God is your refuge, and underneath are the everlasting arms" (Deuteronomy 33:27).

Apply It:

Picture God's strong and safe arms wrapped around you as you pray and thank Him for His power and protection.

Dig Deeper:

Exodus 6:6; Psalm 98:1; Isaiah 59:1

Ruler Over All

"The king's heart is in the hand of the Lord, like the rivers of water; He turns it wherever He wishes" (Proverbs 21:1).

History has seen its share of mad monarchs who have created grief for humanity. Caligula, the infamous emperor of Rome (AD 12 to 41) certainly is near the top of the list of men who wielded authority in cruel and sometimes eccentric ways. Zhengde, emperor of China (1491 to 1521), could also dispatch subjects he didn't like with quick brutality. Ivan the Terrible (1533 to 1584) took pleasure in torturing the nobility of Russia to keep them in line. He even murdered his own son in a fit of rage.

Still, the craziest king in all history literally went mad for seven years. The Bible describes what happened to Nebuchadnezzar, a proud Babylonian king who thought he was God. "Is not this great Babylon, that I have built for a royal dwelling by my mighty power and for the honor of my majesty?" (Daniel 4:30). While these words were still on his lips, he suddenly became mad and behaved like an animal.

At the end of seven years, the Scripture records that Nebuchadnezzar's senses returned and he humbly praised God. "His dominion is an everlasting dominion, and His kingdom is from generation to generation. ... He does according to His will in the army of heaven and among the inhabitants of the earth. No one can restrain His hand" (Daniel 4:34, 35).

Nebuchadnezzar left us a fitting description of the sovereignty of God. While many earthly rulers have attempted to hold absolute authority over their kingdom with cruelty, there is only One who is truly the sovereign head of all the universe, the Lord God of heaven. No one rules over God. "Whatever the Lord pleases He does, in heaven and in earth, in the seas and in all deep places" (Psalm 135:6).

Unlike the cruel tyrants of human history, we can trust in the sovereignty of God. Someday all the universe will agree, "Great and marvelous are Your works, Lord God Almighty! Just and true are Your ways, O King of the saints!" (Revelation 15:3).

Apply It:

Who was the best king in all Bible history and what qualities of this ruler were like God?

Dig Deeper:

1 Chronicles 29:11, 12; Psalm 29:10; Proverbs 16:4

Chosen to Live

"Just as He chose us in Him before the foundation of the world, that we should be holy and without blame before Him in love" (Ephesians 1:4).

It was the deadliest mass shooting committed by an individual in U.S. history. On the night of October 1, 2017, 64-year-old Stephen Paddock opened fire from the Mandalay Bay Hotel into a crowd of concertgoers on the Las Vegas Strip in Nevada. Over ten minutes, Paddock indiscriminately fired nearly 1,100 rifle rounds—killing 58 people and injuring 851 others, before he ended his own life.

Some people believe God randomly kills people. They think the Lord has chosen some people to be in heaven and others to burn in hell. In a misunderstood view of the word "predestined," they conclude that the Lord has indiscriminately picked who will live forever and who will die. It makes God out to be sadistic and hides the truth that the Lord wants everyone to be saved.

The apostle Paul wrote that God "predestined us to adoption as sons by Jesus Christ to Himself, according to the good pleasure of His will" (Ephesians 1:5). The verb *to predestinate* means "to determine beforehand" and "to set apart." People hearing Paul's letter believed that their future was predestined by stars and planets. So it was good news to know that God had a better plan for them.

The truth is that God "desires all men to be saved and to come to the knowledge of the truth" (1 Timothy 2:4). His plan is *inclusive*, not arbitrarily *exclusive*. The Lord is "not willing that any should perish but that all should come to repentance" (2 Peter 3:9).

Jesus died for everyone and "whoever believes in Him should not perish but have everlasting life" (John 3:16). While God has made possible the gift of salvation for everyone and has chosen each of us, we may choose to reject His offer. The lost are not randomly chosen by God to go to hell; they walk away from eternal life by their own free will.

Apply It:

God has chosen you, but have you chosen Him? If you have not accepted Jesus' gift of salvation, why not ask Him into your life now?

Dig Deeper:

Joshua 24:15; Romans 8:29, 30; Ephesians 1:11, 12

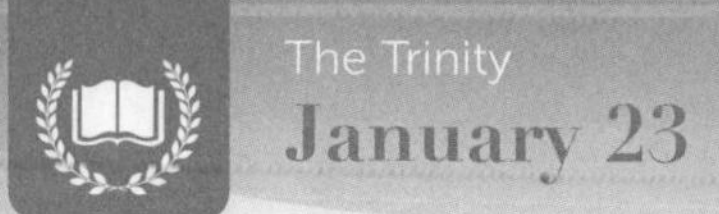

Three in One

"There is one God and one Mediator between God and men, the Man Christ Jesus" (1 Timothy 2:5).

Conjoined twins are identical twins whose bodies are physically connected. It's an extremely rare occurrence and, sadly, half are stillborn with another third dying within 24 hours of their birth. Modern surgery has made it possible to separate many conjoined twins. While some cases are quite simple, others are life-threatening because of shared vital organs.

One of the most famous pairs of conjoined twins was Eng and Chang Bunker, who were born in 1811 in Thailand (Siam). They moved to the United States and traveled with P.T. Barnum's circus; they were called the "Siamese twins," a term that came to be used for conjoined twins.

There is a connection in the Godhead that is not an accident of nature. The oneness of God is a concept humans have tried to grasp for millennia. How could God be three distinct persons and still be one? The Bible clearly presents to us a monotheistic view of God. "Hear, O Israel: The Lord our God, the Lord is one!" (Deuteronomy 6:4). The Hebrew word for "one" can mean to unite or unify.

The Scriptures affirm a plurality within the Godhead. At creation, the Bible says, "Let *Us* make man in *Our* image, according to *Our* likeness" (Genesis 1:26, emphasis supplied). Some verses distinguish the Spirit of God from God. At creation, "The Spirit of God was hovering over the face of the waters" (Genesis 1:2).

Each member of the Trinity is fully divine, including Jesus of whom Paul writes, "For in Him dwells all the fullness of the Godhead bodily" (Colossians 2:9). The clearest presentation of the three separate beings of the Godhead was at the baptism of Jesus, when Christ [the Son] had the dove [the Holy Spirit] descend on Him as God [the Father] spoke words of affirmation to Jesus. (See Matthew 3:16, 17.)

A triune God, who is three in one, is a concept difficult to understand but presented in the Bible as the nature of the One who loves us. By faith we may accept this truth even though it is beyond our understanding.

Apply It:

Think of examples of unity and diversity in the natural world that illustrate the oneness of God. For instance, the human body is made up of many parts but is still one body.

Dig Deeper:

Isaiah 48:16; Zechariah 14:9; 2 Corinthians 13:14

Eternal Love

"I and My Father are one" (John 10:30).

A couple from Texas ended life together the same way they began their relationship 62 years earlier—holding hands. Thomas and Delma Ledbetter died less than ninety minutes apart in a nursing home where they were brought when both of them became ill. Staff pushed their two beds together and Thomas reached over and grabbed his wife's hand.

Their two daughters said their parents loved to travel the country and go camping together. Tom first held Delma's hand on their first date. They never wanted to be apart. Family members shared, "Their love was a testimony to many, and was surely a match made in heaven."

There's an even deeper bond of unity within the Godhead. While Jesus was dying on the cross, He cried out, "My God, My God, why have You forsaken Me?" (Mark 15:34). Christ suffered from a broken heart when sin separated Him from the Father. Sin breaks our connection with God as Jesus experienced when He willingly took our sins upon Himself and died in our place. Christ's separation from His Father killed Him.

We have little comprehension of how the death of Jesus affected the reciprocal love relationship within the Godhead. For all time the Father, the Son, and the Spirit had been united. They were co-eternal, co-existent, and expressed unselfish love and devotion far beyond what we can understand. John writes that Jesus "was in the beginning with God" (John 1:2).

Father, Son, and Spirit are all divine and are all God. Human organizations put final authority into the hands of one person—a president or chairperson. The Godhead share their divine qualities while each is still completely God. Together they are one in authority and purpose. The love between a devoted husband and wife only gives us a tiny glimpse of the loving relationship that exists within the Trinity.

Apply It:

Think about a happily married couple who exhibit the qualities of loving oneness.

Dig Deeper:

Isaiah 42:1; 1 Corinthians 12:12; 1 John 4:8

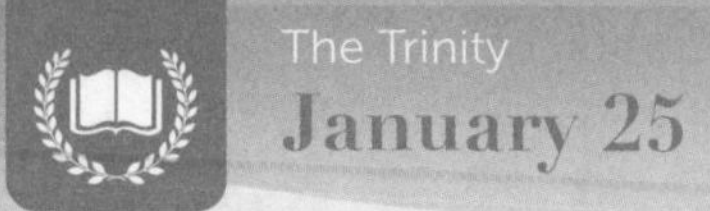

Teamwork in the Trinity

"When the Helper comes, whom I shall send to you from the Father, the Spirit of truth who proceeds from the Father, He will testify of Me" (John 15:26).

In an incredible feat of teamwork that occurred during a 2010 Oklahoma vs. Oklahoma State football game, Broderick Brown displayed self-sacrifice when he tried to intercept a pass from Landry Jones that led him out of bounds. Instead of just letting the ball go, Brown leapt up in the air and over the sideline, then—before touching ground out of bounds—tipped the ball back onto the field toward teammate Shaun Lewis, who caught it in bounds.

It's not just sports teams that understand the importance of working closely with others. Businesses know that valuing fellow employees increases the opportunities for collaboration. It requires building trust, respecting differences, and having a common goal. As Brown displayed in his quick move at the edge of the field, it also requires setting aside self for the greater good. You can go much further as a team than anyone could go alone.

The epitome of collaboration and cooperation is seen in the Godhead. Each member of the Trinity is part of the other—while at the same time having separate roles. God the Father is the source of all power, Jesus serves as a mediator to humanity, and the Holy Spirit—who knows the "deep things of God" (1 Corinthians 1:10)—distributes the blessings of heaven.

We see this perfectly demonstrated in the coming of Jesus. Gabriel's testimony to Mary shows the three members of the Godhead working together. God's angel told Mary, "The Holy Spirit will come upon you, and the power of the Highest will overshadow you; therefore, also, that Holy One who is to be born will be called the Son of God" (Luke 1:35). All three worked in harmony in order for Christ to be born. In a winning play, salvation came to our world.

Apply It:

Pray that just as Christ is in the Father that He will be in your heart today (John 14:20).

Dig Deeper:

John 15:26; 2 Corinthians 5:19; Colossians 1:27

Focused Power

"The kingdom of God is not in word but in power" (1 Corinthians 4:20).

If you need to cut a piece of paper, you simply pick up a pair of scissors and get to work. But what if you need to cut through a piece of steel four inches thick? Easy. Just use water. We're not talking about using a garden hose. A $50,000 waterjet cutter is an industrial tool capable of cutting through thick steel.

Waterjet cutting requires a continuous stream of highly pressurized water (up to 90,000 psi) and can cut through a wide variety of materials—including wood, rock, and metal. It works especially well on materials that are heat sensitive. Unlike metal cutters, a waterjet never gets dull.

When you focus water under enough pressure, you can cut steel. Laser cutters use focused light beams and can also cut through steel. Imagine what would happen if the Godhead came together and focused their work on a single project? Actually, in the courts of heaven and in the councils of the Trinity, a plan was laid for the salvation of humanity, a plan that required all the focused energy of the triune God.

Though each member of the Godhead is involved in redeeming humanity, the focus of Scripture is on Jesus who "has redeemed us from the curse of the law" (Galatians 3:13). Like the focused power of a waterjet cutter, the cross is a highly focused revelation of God's love. Through the blood of Christ, we see the intense love of the Father and the unrestrained power of the Holy Spirit.

Isaiah explains, "But your iniquities have separated you from your God" (Isaiah 59:2). Sin created a thick and nearly impenetrable barrier between ourselves and God. The hardness of our hearts seemed impossible to pierce. But an instrument of torture—the cross of Calvary—became the means to cut through sin. Like a focused beam of energy, the love of the Godhead poured itself out to lost humanity, slicing through the thick wall of sin separating us from God.

Apply It:

Sing (or read the lyrics) of the hymn *There Is Power in the Blood.* Then thank God for the cross that cuts through sin and sets you free.

Dig Deeper:

Romans 1:16; 1 Corinthians 1:30; Hebrews 12:2

The Father

3

Two Gods?

"I watched till thrones were put in place, and the Ancient of Days was seated; His garment was white as snow, and the hair of His head was like pure wool. His throne was a fiery flame, its wheels a burning fire; a fiery stream issued and came forth from before Him. A thousand thousands ministered to Him; ten thousand times ten thousand stood before Him" (Daniel 7:9, 10).

Thanks to William Shakespeare, the legacy of Richard III, the last Yorkist king of England, will always be remembered in a dark and twisted way. The reputation of this misunderstood monarch was portrayed in Shakespeare's play *King Richard III* as a tyrannical ruler.

The hunchbacked Richard supposedly threw his two nephews, Edward and Richard, into the Tower of London and later had them murdered. But no evidence has been found to back up this cold-blooded story, and even the murders themselves are questioned. Historians thought people made up the fact that Richard III had a crooked back, which made him look more like a monster. Actually, in 2012, his remains were found and it was confirmed that he did have scoliosis.

A much greater smear campaign has been waged against God the Father, the great King of the universe. The devil himself has tenaciously worked to present a distorted view of God. By exaggerating certain parts of the Bible, such as the story of Uzzah in 2 Samuel 6, Satan has tried to create division in the Bible over a supposedly cruel God of the Old Testament and a kind God, represented by Jesus, in the New Testament.

But the Scriptures do not describe two separate pictures of God, one of vengeance and one of mercy. The Old Testament is filled with descriptions that affirm a God of grace and compassion. Both Daniel and Moses were given glimpses of the Majesty of heaven, yet when Moses asked to see God's glory, he was shown the Lord who is "merciful and gracious, longsuffering, and abounding in goodness and truth, keeping mercy for thousands, forgiving iniquity and transgression and sin" (Exodus 34:5–7).

Apply It:

Have you ever been misunderstood or maligned? Think about how God the Father must feel when His children view Him as a tyrant.

Dig Deeper:

Psalm 86:5; Jonah 4:2; 2 Corinthians 5:19

A Deeper Look

"[Moses] said, 'Please, show me Your glory' " (Exodus 33:18).

It was an accident. Wilhelm was working one day in his lab in Wurzburg, Germany, when something strange occurred across the room. The physicist was testing whether cathode rays could pass through glass when he noticed a glow coming from a nearby chemically coated screen. He theorized that some type of radiation was moving through space. The year was 1895, and Wilhelm Conrad Röntgen had just discovered the X-ray.

Röntgen tested his theory, with the help of his wife, by capturing the first image of the bones in her hand and her wedding ring. When he began to lecture and show the rays' ability to photograph bones within living flesh, the discovery captured the attention of the scientific community. Just a few weeks later, an X-ray was used to find a bullet in the leg of a Canadian patient.

Moses wanted to see God more closely, but the Lord told him, "You cannot see My face; for no man shall see Me, and live" (Exodus 33:20). But the Lord covered Moses in the cleft of a rock and passed by, allowing him to view His back. After giving Moses the Ten Commandments, the Lord once more passed before him and proclaimed, "The LORD, the LORD God, merciful and gracious, longsuffering, and abounding in goodness and truth, keeping mercy for thousands, forgiving iniquity and transgression and sin, by no means clearing the guilty" (Exodus 34:6,7).

Moses did not need to see an X-ray picture of God to learn of His deeper character qualities. Greater than the Lord's mighty power is His genuine compassion for fallen humanity. Though guided by justice and unwilling to blindly pardon the guilty, the revelation of God in the Old Testament uncovers a heart that *longs* to forgive.

When David was in deep distress, he said, "Please let us fall into the hand of the LORD, for His mercies are great; but do not let me fall into the hand of man" (2 Samuel 24:14). With deeper vision may we also see our Father's mercy.

Apply It:

Using a concordance, count the number of times the word "mercy" is used to describe God in the Old Testament.

Dig Deeper:

Psalm 145:9; Luke 6:36; Hebrews 4:16

A Generous Offer

"Behold, the days are coming, says the Lord, *when I will make a new covenant with the house of Israel and with the house of Judah—not according to the covenant that I made with their fathers ... which they broke"* (Jeremiah 31:31, 32).

The oldest treaty ever signed by the United States is the 1783 Treaty of Paris. It ended the American Revolution and established the United States as free sovereign and independent states. On September 3, representatives from the British Empire and the United States signed a document that set very generous boundaries for the latter.

America's allies, France and Spain, hoped the United States would be a small and weak nation, so the American negotiating team, led by John Jay, Benjamin Franklin, and John Adams, dealt directly with London. Instead of receiving a small parcel of land between the Atlantic and the Appalachians, the British gave the new state all the land up to the Mississippi River—including fishing rights in Canada. This enabled the United States to grow westward and eventually become a major continental power.

The Bible often referred to covenants, most often describing a formal relationship agreement between God and Israel (e.g., see Exodus 19:3–6). What's impressive about the different covenants in Scripture—which theologians love to debate—is the fact that God keeps making conditional agreements with humanity even after they are repeatedly broken. Instead of throwing His mighty hands up in the air, the Lord keeps pursuing His people.

Covenants demonstrate God's deep love and His interest in lost souls; they show how eager the Lord is to redeem and have a lasting relationship with His children. His covenant with Noah reveals a personal God who cares about the welfare of people. His covenant with Israel as a nation was to promise to bless them if they would obey Him.

While the "old" covenant was with the nation of Israel, God's "new" covenant is offered to individual believers in Christ. We see this clearly expressed in Hebrews 8:8–11, where the provisions and conditions of both are the same. But the choice to become a new person is up to you.

Apply It:

Have you accepted God's generous offer of salvation? He promises to bless you if you humbly seek Him.

Dig Deeper:

Genesis 3:15; Exodus 19:5–8; Hebrews 8:8–11

God Is Love

"You saw how the Lord *your God carried you, as a man carries his son, in all the way that you went until you came to this place"* (Deuteronomy 1:31).

"It's okay. Just give him another kiss, Daddy." These words came from a four-year-old boy as he watched his father trying to resuscitate his newborn brother. The baby had been born in the car on the way to the hospital and was not breathing. As the father frantically followed the instructions of the emergency operator speaking through his cell phone, the boy and his mother watched in amazement.

When the baby started breathing, the father wrapped him in his shirt and waved at the officer who was arriving on the scene. To the adults who were present, the father had performed a delicate, lifesaving task, but to the four-year-old boy, the father was simply expressing his love.

When the Israelites escaped Egyptian slavery, Moses saw that their experience was the expression of a Father's love. The deliverance of the Israelites from a life of slavery was not just an attempt at providing temporary relief. It was the beginning of a close bond that would "establish" all God's followers "as a holy people to Himself" (Deuteronomy 28:9). This bond would show how God would bring all His human children "everlasting joy" (Isaiah 51:11).

To many people, God seems to hold Himself aloof. In actuality, the Old Testament provides many portraits of the Father's affection. In Hosea, God yearningly says, "When Israel was a child, I loved him. ... I taught Ephraim to walk, taking them by their arms. ... I drew them with gentle cords, with bands of love. ... I stooped and fed them" (Hosea 11:1, 3, 4).

God loves "with an everlasting love" (Jeremiah 31:3). He is not satisfied with token kisses and rote hugs. Instead, He wants to be closely involved in our daily lives.

Apply It:

Give a family member an extra hug or expression of love.

Dig Deeper:

Psalm 8:3–4; Psalm 18:1–2; Psalm 22:24

Our Forgiving God

" 'Return to Me,' says the Lord of hosts, 'and I will return to you' " (Zechariah 1:3).

There is a good reason it has been nicknamed "The River of No Return." The treacherous Salmon River flows through 425 miles of rugged terrain in central Idaho, with a watershed of 14,000 square miles. Between its headwaters and confluence with the Snake River, it drops a whopping 7,000 feet. The magnificent granite-walled canyons are deeper than the Grand Canyon. The river's average discharge is over 11,000 cubic feet *per second!*

When Lewis and Clark first crossed the continental divide in 1805, they ventured down to look at the Salmon River for an easier route west but immediately realized it was too rough to navigate. Early explorers could raft down the river, but they could not return upstream because of the tremendous current. It was a one-way trip with no return.

Many have viewed the God of the Old Testament in the same way—treacherous and without mercy. *If you step over the wrong line just once, you are sent on a one-way trip with no return.* God has been viewed as harsh, vengeful, and unforgiving. Yet a closer look at the Hebrew Bible reveals otherwise.

David—the man who committed the double sins of adultery and murder—often cried out, "Have mercy upon me, O God" (Psalm 51:1). He believed that God—of the Old Testament—was merciful and forgiving. "As the heavens are high above the earth, so great is His mercy toward those who fear Him; as far as the east is from the west, so far has He removed our transgressions from us" (Psalm 103:11, 12).

David saw the most forgiving river in the universe that flowed from the throne of God. "There is a river whose streams shall make glad the city of God" (Psalm 46:4). Though we may fail, God offers to forgive us and invites us to return to Him. When we do, only our sins take a one-way trip, never to be seen again.

Apply It:

Think of the most peaceful river you've ever visited while you sing or read the lyrics to the hymn *Shall We Gather at the River.*

Dig Deeper:

Isaiah 1:18; Daniel 9:9; Micah 7:18, 19

The Faithful God

"O Israel, you will not be forgotten by Me!" (Isaiah 44:21).

He was a young adult whose father died in battle. Now he had a son of his own, still an infant or perhaps a toddler. And, he couldn't walk. He lived in Lo Debar, a place so desolate its name means "without pasture." In an agrarian society such as ancient Israel, a town without a pasture was worthless.

For Mephibosheth, son of Jonathan and grandson of King Saul, it was far from the wealth and privilege his father and grandfather enjoyed. And Lo Debar was far removed from the splendor of Jerusalem, his former home.

He was a forgotten man, known perhaps to his neighbors, but probably not well. They may not have known how he was crippled when a nurse dropped the very young Mephibohsheth while fleeing Jerusalem after Saul and Jonathan died in battle, the king falling on his own sword. The years saw Israel's attention focused on David.

But David remembered Jonathan, who saved his life when he was on the run from a vengeful monarch. So when things settled down, King David asked, "Is there not still someone of the house of Saul, to whom I may show the kindness of God?" (2 Samuel 9:3). Ziba, a former servant of Saul, told David about Jonathan's son.

And Mephibosheth went from being forgotten to being favored, from living in a nowhere land to dining at the king's table, and inheriting all of his grandfather's lands.

Just as David remembered Jonathan, so God remembers His people—His "Israel," the church today. In very intimate terms, God tells us, "Can a woman forget her nursing child, and not have compassion on the son of her womb? Surely they may forget, yet I will not forget you" (Isaiah 49:15).

God sent Jesus to redeem the people He created, and He promises that He will never forget us when we cry out to Him. Even if we stray from the path of righteousness, God will bring us back when we repent. He's a God who remembers because He unconditionally loves you.

Apply It:

Resolve to share God's love today with someone who might feel they have been forgotten.

Dig Deeper:

2 Samuel 9:1–13; Isaiah 41:9–10; Leviticus 26:40–42

Father of Us All

"In this manner, therefore, pray: Our Father in heaven, hallowed be Your name" (Matthew 6:9).

Sonora Dodd deeply admired her father, a Civil War vet and hardworking farmer. Just after the war, William Smart married Elizabeth Harris—and the couple had five children. When Elizabeth died, Smart married Ellen Cheek (who already had three children by a previous marriage). The family continued to grow, and the couple had six more children.

By 1891, Smart had four children from his first marriage (one died), three step children, and six children from his second marriage. In 1889, the family moved near Spokane, Washington. That same year, Ellen passed away during childbirth. William was left alone to raise and care for all these children—from newborn to 19 years old.

William's daughter, Sonora, admired her father's dedication and, after hearing of the first Mother's Day, suggested to local authorities that they declare the first official Father's Day. By 1910, her idea gained traction and, in 1916, President Woodrow Wilson visited the Father's Day observances in Spokane. In 1972, it became a permanent national observance on the third Sunday of each June.

Perhaps we could choose an earlier date for Father's Day. Moses first spoke of God as Father when he said to the Israelites, "Is He not your Father, who bought you? Has He not made you and established you?" (Deuteronomy 32:6). Through the plan of redemption, God adopted Israel as His child. Isaiah stated, "Now, O Lord, You are our Father" (Isaiah 64:8). Malachi agreed, "Have we not all one Father? Has not one God created us?" (Malachi 2:10).

In the New Testament, Paul distinguished God the Father from Jesus when he said, "There is one God, the Father, of whom are all things ... and one Lord Jesus Christ" (1 Corinthians 8:6). Jesus often spoke of His Father and encouraged us to address God as "our Father" when in prayer. Even more than an earthly father, there is much to admire in our heavenly Father, the One who knows all that we need (Matthew 6:32).

Apply It:

What admirable qualities do you see in your earthly father or someone who was like a father to you?

Dig Deeper:

Isaiah 63:16; Malachi 1:6; John 14:9

Not Complicit

"Say to those who are fearful-hearted, 'Be strong, do not fear! Behold, your God will come with vengeance, with the recompense of God; He will come and save you' " (Isaiah 35:4).

In 2017, one of the most popular online dictionaries declared that its word of the year was *complicit*. This word basically means that someone enabled an illegal or wrongful action or failed to stop it. The website, along with other news agencies, said that the spike in Internet searches for this word was understandable given recent events. They cited reports of corrupt politicians, sex scandals, irresponsibility toward the environment, and the tolerance of hate speech. All of these events had one thing in common: Multiple people were responsible.

In the Old Testament, God was keenly aware of the importance of justice, unwilling to be complicit in human injustice. This importance comes from the Father's own character. Moses recognized this when he sang, "All His ways are justice, a God of truth and without injustice" (Deuteronomy 32:4).

Many have taken offense to the picture of God in the Old Testament because they feel that He is harsh. It is likely that those who misunderstand the judgments of God in the Old Testament are unfamiliar with the atrocities that were tolerated in the ancient Near East. God was deeply concerned about cults that performed human sacrifices, nations that oppressed the weak, and religions that mistreated women.

In speaking of those who have no one to defend them, God said, "I will surely hear their cry" (Exodus 22:23). David describes God as a "father of the fatherless, a defender of widows" (Psalm 68:5). God said, "I will contend with him who contends with you, and I will save your children" (Isaiah 49:25). We may know that, as a loving Father, God acts on behalf of the victims.

Apply It:

Pick up a piece of trash that you did not throw on the ground and throw it away.

Dig Deeper:

Psalm 106:34–38; Exodus 34:7; Psalm 79:9, 10

The Biggest Giver

"For God so loved the world that He gave ..." (John 3:16).

Imagine being able to give $1 million to your favorite charity. But that's only a drop in the bucket for some of America's biggest philanthropists. In 2017, the ten largest donations totaled $10.2 billion, more than double from the $4.3 billion in 2016. At the top of the list is Bill Gates, co-founder of Microsoft, who gave $4.6 billion with his wife to the Bill & Melinda Gates Foundation—which focuses on global development, health, and education.

Many of the large gifts go to universities to help with student scholarships. Others focus on housing, science, improving the criminal-justice system, medical research, and nature conservation. But as you glean through the list of names including Mark Zuckerberg and Michael Dell, you will not find money being donated to deal with the problem of sin.

While charitable gifts have their place in helping with many of the results of sin, only one solution can remedy the root problem. The plan for saving humanity from eternal death began before the earth was even created. The Bible speaks of the plan for Jesus to be our Savior as "foreordained before the foundation of the world" (1 Peter 1:20). Only divinity could rescue humanity.

God is a great giver. It is in His very nature to give. At Creation, we see the Godhead working together to provide a beautiful world to Adam and Eve (Genesis 1:1, 2, 26). In the cradle of Bethlehem, we see the Father offering to humanity the greatest gift ever given. But it is at Calvary that we most clearly see the giving heart of God torn open to its greatest depths.

When Jesus died for our sins, it was not to convince God to love us. Christ gave His life to show just how much the Father cares for lost people. "For God so loved the world" reveals to us the soul of a Father who was willing to give up His most precious Son in order to redeem us from the curse of sin. For "God was in Christ reconciling the world to Himself" (2 Corinthians 5:19).

Apply It:

Can you think of someone in the Bible who demonstrated God's giving heart by their actions?

Dig Deeper:

Genesis 22:8; Matthew 11:27; John 16:25–28

The Father's Kiss

"I say to you that likewise there will be more joy in heaven over one sinner who repents than over ninety-nine just persons who need no repentance" (Luke 15:7).

Years ago, on a Sunday afternoon in New York City, a small band of Christians stood on a busy street singing hymns and offering their testimony to the passersby who would listen. At the edge of the crowd stood a thin, rough-looking man whose appearance suggested his better days were behind him.

"We're going to pray now," the man leading the street meeting said. "Do you need a prayer? If so, raise your hand."

Tom Lucas did just that. "I was without a tooth in my head or a prayer in my heart. I needed help," he would later say.

Some of the outdoor worshipers spoke with Tom and helped him find a rehabilitation program, where he confronted his addictions to drugs and alcohol, got a set of dentures, and found salvation. For years afterwards, he worked as a substance abuse counselor, helping those in whose path he once trod.

That group is a small representation of the God who loves us, as Jesus demonstrated time and again. Christ explained, "The Son of Man has come to seek and to save that which was lost" (Luke 19:10). So also, "The Son of Man did not come to be served, but to serve, and to give His life a ransom for many" (Matthew 20:28).

The parable of the lost son, found in Luke 15, especially expresses the heart of our heavenly Father. The turning point in the story is when the son comes to his senses about the character of his father. "He arose and came to his father. But when he was still a great way off, his father saw him and had compassion, and ran and fell on his neck and kissed him" (Luke 15:20).

Wealthy men, such as the father in this story, didn't run to their children in those days. It was too undignified—especially in light of a son who had disgraced the family name. But this father was different. Even when the son was attempting to apologize, the father was showing affection on his returned prodigal. Such is the compassion of our heavenly Father toward us when we turn to Him.

Apply It:

Who in your community needs a tangible reminder of God's love? Stretch out a hand of kindness this week to that person.

Dig Deeper:

Mark 5:35–43; John 11:1–45; Romans 2:4

A Better Father

"A father of the fatherless, a defender of widows, is God in His holy habitation" (Psalm 68:5).

Norbert Wiener was a child prodigy in the field of mathematics. He attended graduate school at Harvard University and played an important role in furthering the field of cybernetics. However, his family life was less than ideal. His father was severe and mostly absent. As Norbert grew older, his father took over his education and pushed him to the point of emotional breakdown. However, Wiener recovered from his traumatic interactions with his father and went on to live a successful life.

God has given all earthly fathers freedom. They can succumb to Satan's temptations and choose to inflict incredible pain on their children. This can happen through direct abuse, unreasonable demands, or complete neglect. However, God will not only hold them responsible, He is also working to adopt every person into His superior care. In multiple ways, God seeks to woo us back to Himself. "No one can come to Me unless the Father who sent Me *draws* him" (John 6:44, emphasis added).

The most direct way is that we can begin interacting with God as we would with an earthly father. This could mean listening to His voice in Scripture and nature, watching for His providential movements, or saying "Our Father in heaven" (Matthew 6:9). However, it is likely that God is also working to connect us with other members of His family who can help us in the healing process. The Bible states that "the sweetness of a man's friend gives delight by hearty counsel" (Proverbs 27:9).

The Bible promises that God will be a Father to those who have no father. Hosea reminds us, "In You the fatherless finds mercy" (14:3). Even Jesus said, "I will not leave you orphans; I will come to you" (John 14:18). When your earthly father fails you, know that you have a heavenly Father who will never fail you.

Apply It:

Do you know someone who needs the guidance of a father or mother in their life? Pray for them and encourage them.

Dig Deeper:

John 19:25–27; John 16:27; James 1:17

The Son

4

Serpent Removal

"I will put enmity between you and the woman, and between your seed and her Seed; He shall bruise your head, and you shall bruise His heel" (Genesis 3:15).

Do you have ophidiophobia? Nothing strikes fear in the heart of many Americans like snakes (51 percent to be exact). It's even greater than the fear of public speaking (40 percent). So what do you do if you find a snake inside your house? Never fear—call a snake-removal professional! Animal control people suggest you don't drive the snake into hiding but try to open a door and use a broom to gently herd it outside. Or you can put a bucket over it until someone removes it for you.

The devil actually presented himself as a snake in the Garden of Eden when he deceived Eve and led the world into sin and death. Jesus called him "a murderer from the beginning" (John 8:44). In fact, the first gospel promise is illustrated with a snake. The Lord promised to put into the heart of the woman (the church) and her Seed (Christ) a hatred for the snake (Satan) and his seed (his followers).

The "Seed" was not clearly explained when first given to Adam and Eve. After this cryptic picture of salvation was presented, humanity looked for a coming Savior to rescue them from the venomous attacks of their enemy. The Old Testament Scriptures constantly pointed forward to the Messiah. Isaiah said a "virgin shall conceive and bear a Son" (Isaiah 7:14). Micah predicted, "You, Bethlehem Ephrathah, ... out of you shall come forth to Me the One to be Ruler in Israel" (Micah 5:2).

When Christ came, He forever sealed Satan's doom. On Calvary, the head of the serpent was crushed. Someday Satan "who deceived them" will be "cast into the lake of fire" (Revelation 20:10) and be forever destroyed. We will never have to fear this snake again.

Apply It:

Read another snake story in the Bible in Numbers 21:4–9. How is it that the Israelites were to look at a serpent and live?

Dig Deeper:

John 3:14; 2 Corinthians 5:21; Revelation 12:9

Healer of Broken Hearts

"He heals the brokenhearted and binds up their wounds" (Psalm 147:3).

Broken heart syndrome, also known as stress cardiomyopathy, is a temporary weakening of the heart's left ventricle, which causes it to balloon out and impairs the pumping action. On an EKG, it can look exactly like a heart attack, but unlike a heart attack, it isn't caused by the blood vessels being blocked. Broken heart syndrome can be caused by the unexpected death of a loved one, losing a large amount of money, or some other sudden catastrophe. Strangely, sometimes this condition can even be caused by such positive situations as a surprise party or winning a lot of money.

While broken heart syndrome generally reverses itself within days or weeks, the broken hearts we acquire by living in a sinful world are more challenging to treat. That's one of the specific reasons Jesus came to our planet—to heal our broken hearts by bringing us hope.

Quoting from Isaiah's prophecy regarding the Messiah, Christ stated early in His earthly ministry: "The Spirit of the LORD is upon Me, because He has anointed Me to preach the gospel to the poor; He has sent Me to heal the brokenhearted" (Luke 4:18).

Jesus suffered the most intense pain our world can inflict. He was betrayed by a friend for a mere pittance. Although innocent, He was beaten and horribly mistreated during His trial. During His torturous execution, He was mocked and ridiculed, and He was forsaken by most of His own disciples. No wonder the prophecy described Him as "despised and rejected by men, a Man of sorrows and acquainted with grief" (Isaiah 53:3).

Is your heart broken today? Jesus has perfect empathy toward your pain, and through His sacrifice He offers you healing and peace. "He was wounded for our transgressions, He was bruised for our iniquities; the chastisement for our peace was upon Him, and by His stripes we are healed" (Isaiah 53:5). Have you accepted His compassionate offer?

Apply It:

Read Isaiah 53:4, and then thank Jesus for daily carrying your grief and sorrow, and ask Him to bring healing to your wounded heart.

Dig Deeper:

Psalm 31:24; Psalm 34:18; Hebrews 12:2

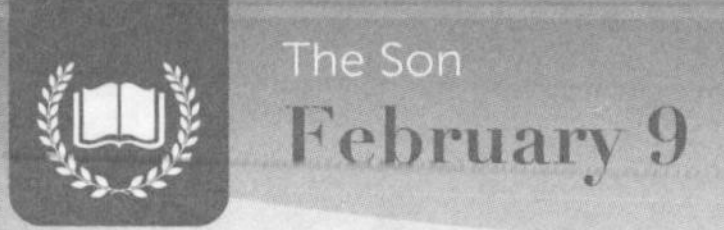

Uncovering the Clues

"He vigorously refuted the Jews publicly, showing from the Scriptures that Jesus is the Christ" (Acts 18:28).

He broke the record for the "most portrayed literary human character in film and TV." The popular fictional sleuth of Victorian and Edwardian England was almost called Sherrinford. The British author, Sir Arthur Conan Doyle, masterfully portrays Sherlock Holmes as a detective known for his sharp observation, forensic science, and logical reasoning. He has been so popular that many have believed him to be a real person.

The investigator of Scripture will discover, after carefully studying clues in the Old Testament, that the promised Messiah is no fictional character, but Jesus Christ. Only in the Son of Mary do we find the fulfillment of the prophecies made to the patriarchs of the Old Testament.

For instance, Matthew traces the genealogy of Jesus back to Abraham and calls him "the Son of Abraham" (Matthew 1:1). The apostle Paul agrees that Jesus fulfills the promise to Abraham. "Now to Abraham and his Seed were the promises made. He does not say, 'And to seeds,' as of many, but as of one, 'And to your Seed,' who is Christ" (Galatians 3:16).

Even the Messianic title Son of David was applied to Jesus. When entering Jerusalem during the Passover, the multitudes who followed Him shouted, "Hosanna to the Son of David!" (Matthew 21:9). Peter preached this truth at Pentecost after the resurrection. "Men and brethren, let me speak freely to you of the patriarch David. ... Therefore, being a prophet, and knowing that God had sworn with an oath to him that of the fruit of his body, according to the flesh, He would raise up the Christ to sit on his throne" (Acts 2:29, 30).

Study the Scriptures for yourself and you will conclude that the data unquestionably identifies Jesus as the Son of God, the Savior of the world. But remember, "A man can receive nothing unless it has been given to him from heaven" (John 3:27).

Apply It:

Study several Old Testament prophecies about the coming Messiah (Micah 5:2; Isaiah 7:14; Psalm 22:1) and see if you can find their New Testament fulfillment.

Dig Deeper:

Psalm 34:20; Isaiah 53:4–8; Zechariah 12:10

Perfect Timing

*"When the fullness of the time had come,
God sent forth His Son"* (Galatians 4:4).

Timing can be critical. Take the Earth's rotation, for instance, which, at the equator, measures 1,037 miles per hour. Amazingly, just a 10 percent increase in speed would cause us to lose about two hours per day—which would wreak havoc with our circadian rhythm, triggering health problems in humans and other creatures. Due to greater centrifugal force, we would weigh less, which could result in weaker bones. And the faster rotation would mean less sunlight each day, initiating climate changes with negative impacts on both animals and plants—including food crops.

In the spiritual realm, timing is just as crucial. Jesus arrived on our planet at just the right moment and in perfect sync with the Old Testament prophecies regarding the coming of the Messiah. According to Daniel's 70-week prophecy, the Messiah would appear 69 weeks after "the going forth of the command to restore and build Jerusalem" (Daniel 9:25) in 457 BC. Since a day in prophecy equals a literal year (Ezekiel 4:6; Numbers 14:34), the 69 weeks represent 483 literal years—which ended in AD 27, the very year Jesus was baptized and began His earthly ministry.

Jesus acknowledged this time prophecy at the start of His ministry when He said, "*The time is fulfilled,* and the kingdom of God is at hand" (Mark 1:15, emphasis added).

From there, the prophecy goes into even more astonishing detail, specifying the exact year of Christ's death. "Then he shall confirm a covenant with many for one week; but in the middle of the week He shall bring an end to sacrifice and offering" (Daniel 9:27). Halfway through the 70th week—the last seven years of the prophecy—as predicted, Jesus died on the cross, ending the sacrifices and offerings of the sanctuary service that had all pointed forward to this momentous event.

The perfect timing and coordination of this divine rescue operation should exponentially boost our faith in God's Word and in the identity of Jesus as our Savior.

Apply It:

List three ways in which God's timing has brought blessings to your life.

Dig Deeper:

Romans 5:6; Romans 13:11; Ephesians 1:10

A Predicted Betrayal

"Even my own familiar friend in whom I trusted, who ate my bread, has lifted up his heel against me" (Psalm 41:9).

It was a creative effort to demoralize the troops, but most American soldiers in the South Pacific found it entertaining to listen to Japanese propaganda broadcasts during World War II. Tokyo Rose, a name given to several English-speaking women, read anti-American scripts to discourage soldiers, but often in a manner that undermined the broadcasts' intent.

Iva Toguri, a Los Angeles native, became stranded in Japan during the war while visiting relatives. She couldn't receive help from her family back home since they were placed in internment camps, so she took a part-time job as a typist at Radio Tokyo and was then recruited to speak on *The Zero Hour.* She was later convicted of treason when she tried to return to the United States, but the evidence against her was slim and she was eventually pardoned.

Thirty pieces of silver became evidence enough to convict the heart of a man known for the greatest betrayal in history. Jesus' own disciple, Judas Iscariot, turned his back on Christ (John 18:2). The Old Testament foretold this disloyal act and even indicated the price of the betrayal (Zechariah 11:12).

Jesus knew Judas would turn his heel against Him and connected his duplicity with prophecy. "I do not speak concerning all of you. I know whom I have chosen; but that the Scripture may be fulfilled, 'He who eats bread with Me has lifted up his heel against Me' " (John 13:18).

But don't let Judas' treasonous act demoralize your faith. The sad commentary on this treacherous act is actually an affirmation of the reliability of the Scriptures, confirming that Christ is the Son of God.

Apply It:

Read 1 Peter 3:15, 16, and think of three ways you can speak up for Christ.

Dig Deeper:

Jeremiah 17:10; Matthew 10:32, 33; 2 Peter 2:1

The Real Messiah

"I am the resurrection and the life. He who believes in Me, though he may die, he shall live. And whoever lives and believes in Me shall never die. Do you believe this?" (John 11:25, 26).

A preacher in California once encountered a man at his office sporting long hair, a long beard, a robe belted with rope, and sandals.

"I am Jesus, and I have a message for you," the visitor said.

The preacher replied, "You're not Jesus, but I can try to help you."

"What do you mean? I just told you I was Jesus," the visitor declared, his voice rising slightly.

The preacher's response was simple: "Show me your hands then. I want to see the nail prints, please."

The resurrected Jesus, even today, can show you the signs of His crucifixion.

Indeed, the resurrection proves Jesus' claim to be the Savior of all the world. Other "messiahs" and religious leaders are long dead and buried—in some cases, their tombs are with us to this day. But Jesus is alive in heaven, and He's returning for those who've trusted in Him and to judge the world.

This was also demonstrated by the lives—and martyrdom—of the original disciples, all of whom met gruesome deaths, except for John. That these men would travel to the ends of the known world, at that time, to fearlessly share their faith and accept their own end as the cost of planting the seeds of the church speaks volumes. No rational person would willingly sacrifice their life for something they know is a fraud.

The reality of the resurrection is not only the essential proof of Christian faith, it is also the force that motivates us to share that faith with others. You can confidently tell others of the hope that is within your heart, because we know that Jesus conquered death and is alive today.

Apply It:

Think of ways to share the good news that the God you worship is alive, and that by Jesus' resurrection, those who believe in Him can have hope of life eternal as well.

Dig Deeper:

Mark 5:35–42; Luke 7:11–17; Rev. 1:17, 18

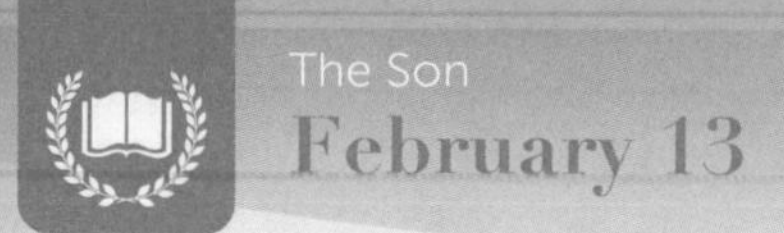

The Ultimate Historian

"He is before all things, and in Him all things consist" (Colossians 1:17).

When we see the light from the "front" star of the Big Dipper constellation, we are actually seeing what it looked like before we were born. This is because that star, Dubhe, is between 60 and 125 lightyears away. That means that it took the light more than 60 years to arrive in our eyes. It is fascinating to consider what is currently happening out there in the Big Dipper that we will not know about until we have entered into eternal life.

Paul explained that Jesus' divine life did not have a beginning. However, unlike the light that we see in the night sky, we have instant access to Christ's companionship and wisdom. We do not have to wait hundreds of years to receive a response to prayer. At the same time, we can trust that Jesus' wisdom far surpasses that of any human because He knows our history better than we do.

Sometimes we have a hard time understanding ourselves, and we ask our parents what we were like as children. God, however, understands our past perfectly. He was there when our great grandparents were making decisions that would affect who we are today. As a result of His exhaustive knowledge of the decisions of every generation that has preceded us, we can trust that Christ knows and will "supply" our "need" (Philippians 4:19).

This also means He is the final authority on our history. Sometimes family members or friends may look down on us because they think they understand our past. However, Christ, who existed before there was a Big Dipper, knows our past and still loves us. "God demonstrates His own love toward us, in that while we were still sinners, Christ died for us" (Romans 5:8). Now that's a piece of history that is life changing!

Apply It:

Tell someone who is younger than you something positive about their history.

Dig Deeper:

John 8:58; John 1:1, 2; Revelation 2:8

The Exact Image

"God ... has in these last days spoken to us by His Son ... who being the brightness of His glory and the express image of His person ..." (Hebrews 1:1–3).

Have you ever heard someone say, "He's the spitting image of his dad"? Where did that phrase originate? There are a couple of theories. Some believe the phrase was originally "splitting image" and derived from the two matching pieces of a split plank of wood. The mirror image of the matching grain has often been used in furniture and musical instruments. And so "splitting image" came to mean "exact likeness."

Others suggest that if someone (or something) is so similar to another, it appears as if that person (or thing) had been spat out of his mouth. A play from 1689, says, "Poor child! He's as like his own daddy as if he were spit out of his mouth." The more exact usage was first quoted in A. H. Rice's *Mrs. Wiggs* in 1901. She wrote: "He's jes' like his pa—the very spittin' image of him!"

The phrase in Hebrews that describes Jesus as "the express image" of God goes far beyond the expression "spitting image." Even the idiom "splitting image" doesn't capture the divine nature of Jesus, for He is not "partly" God but is equal with God. All the attributes of God are in Jesus; He stated, "I and My Father are one" (John 10:30).

Jesus doesn't just look like God on the surface. His divinity goes all the way to the core of His being. He told Philip, "He who has seen Me has seen the Father" (John 14:9). Jesus claimed equality with God when He identified Himself as the "I AM" (John 8:58) of the Old Testament.

Christ not only points us to the Father but is God Himself. People worshiped Jesus after the resurrection (Matthew 28:17). The Bible says, "Let all the angels of God worship Him" (Hebrews 1:6). Someday every knee will bow and "confess that Jesus Christ is Lord" (Philippians 2:10, 11).

Apply It:

Think of two close relatives you know who look very similar. Reflect on how they are different. Even identical twins are not exact in every way.

Dig Deeper:

Matthew 1:23; John 1:1, 14; Romans 9:5

Love Is the Measure

"Every spirit that confesses that Jesus Christ has come in the flesh is of God" (1 John 4:2).

A small study conducted by scientists at the University of California provided insight into how people reason when faced with difficult moral decisions. A group of volunteers were asked to watch videos of people experiencing pain. Some of the people cringed, but others did not. The individuals were then asked to make a difficult hypothetical decision concerning a scenario that could happen during a war. The decision had to do with harming one person in order to save a group of people.

Researchers found that those who cringed during the video were more likely to decide against harming anyone, even if the action would save a larger group. They concluded that when certain people are faced with difficult moral challenges, they are more concerned about the harm others may experience than their own survival.

The selfless reaction of sympathy was intended to be a moral compass for how we view God and make decisions about others. When the apostle John was writing to the churches, he knew that many people would deny that Jesus had actually appeared as a man. Satan would love for people to think that Jesus did not actually become a human because God is too distant and would never come to our dark planet.

But John knew that if he could warn believers about this ploy, they would not miss the main point of the incarnation: that "God is love" (1 John 4:8). Jesus' human nature was the evidence: "In this the love of God was manifested toward us, that God has sent His only begotten Son into the world" (1 John 4:9).

Armed with this truth, believers could know that those who deny this important fact should not be trusted (1 John 4:2). In this way the followers of Christ could navigate through the complicated sea of religious opinions.

Apply It:

Look around as you go through your day and offer to help someone who is hurting.

Dig Deeper:

2 John 1:7; 1 Peter 3:18; Colossians 1:21, 22

Genuine Salvation

"When the fullness of the time had come, God sent forth His Son, born of a woman, born under the law" (Galatians 4:4).

Columbia University-New York Presbyterian Hospital has begun using robot mothers to simulate childbirth. The simulation includes Victoria and her robot baby, who cry and even bleed like humans. This gives nurses and doctors in training the opportunity to practice a live birth without any human risk. In the next room, a real person controls the robot mother and baby in order to make the simulation as realistic as possible.

Although there are certain benefits to simulation, nothing compares to genuine human experience. The Bible assures us that Christ was "born of a woman" (Galatians 4:4) to indicate that the act of salvation was genuine. Jesus had to become fully human in order to save humankind. The law of God did not call for the death of an angel, animal, or robot. It called for the death of a human (Hebrews 2:17).

Despite all of the animal sacrifices that took place before the death of Christ, no human would have been saved if He had not come. The Bible explains this fact when it states, "It is not possible that the blood of bulls and goats could take away sins" (Hebrews 10:4).

Beyond satisfying the demands of the law, Christ's genuine human nature also reconciled the entire human family back to God (2 Corinthians 5:18). This is because as a genuine human, Christ could take the place of Adam as the head of the human family: "The free gift is not like the offense. For if by the one man's offense many died, much more the grace of God and the gift by the grace of the one Man, Jesus Christ, abounded to many" (Romans 5:15).

Although we may rejoice that heavenly angels are working as God's servants in the plan of salvation, the human nature that Christ received remains the essential element.

Apply It:

Have a face-to-face conversation with someone you would normally contact using technology.

Dig Deeper:

Hebrews 10:5–7; 1 Corinthians 15:45, 47; Hebrews 2:9

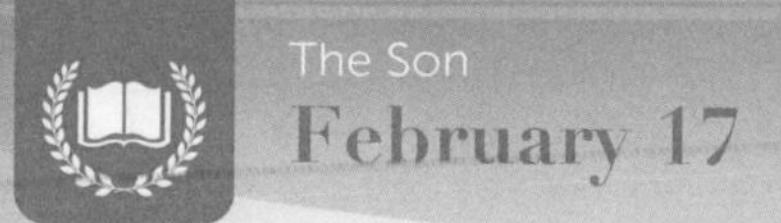

Priceless Research

"Seeing then that we have a great High Priest who has passed through the heavens, Jesus the Son of God, let us hold fast our confession" (Hebrews 4:14).

One of the most expensive research projects in the world has a price tag that continues to rise. So far, the International Nuclear Fusion Project has cost $20 billion, which has come from 35 countries. In order to achieve their goal, scientists need to heat material to a temperature that is ten times hotter than the sun. The research is risky and uncertain, but the hope is that it will lead to the production of an unlimited energy source.

The cost of Christ's incarnation is much higher than all of the research projects of the world combined. However, the guaranteed result is an unlimited energy source called eternal life. By coming into the world, Christ would become our acting representative before the Father in heaven. Like any good representative would do, He became an expert in our experience. His "research" went beyond that of any advocate in history, because He took on the very nature of those whom He would represent.

The Bible says that there was no other way that He could redeem us from our sins: "In all things He had to be made like His brethren, that He might be a merciful and faithful High Priest in things pertaining to God, to make propitiation for the sins of the people" (Hebrews 2:17).

We can know by His experience that Christ really understood what it meant to be tired: "Jesus therefore, being wearied from His journey, sat thus by the well" (John 4:6). We can know He experienced what it meant to feel a sorrow so deep that He longed for companionship: "He said to them, 'My soul is exceedingly sorrowful, even to death. Stay here and watch with Me' " (Matthew 26:38). With all of these experiences in mind, we can trust that He is before the Father presenting our case with the deepest sympathy.

Apply It:

Learn something new about God today by going for a walk out into nature.

Dig Deeper:

Hebrews 4:15, 16; Hebrews 2:18; 1 John 2:1

His Caring Touch

"We do not have a High Priest who cannot sympathize with our weaknesses, but was in all points tempted as we are, yet without sin" (Hebrews 4:15).

Can holding the hand of a loved one actually ease pain? That's what Pavel Goldstein, a researcher at the University of Colorado, wondered when he held his wife's hand during the birth of their daughter. He conducted experiments that show holding the hand of a loved one who is in pain not only brings breathing and heart rate into synchronization, but that brain wave patterns will come into harmony as well.

Goldstein found that being in the same room wasn't nearly as effective at easing the pain of someone you love as actually holding their hand. The brain wave synchronization especially goes up when that person expresses empathy. The more their brains sync, the more the pain goes away. There is healing power in empathetic touch!

Some people argue that God is so transcendent that He is completely out of touch with the human experience. But when Christ came to our earth "in the likeness of sinful flesh" (Romans 8:3), God showed that He is indeed able to "sympathize with our weakness" (Hebrews 4:15). The Greek word for sympathize literally means "to be touched" and "to experience together with."

It's wonderful to study the healings of Jesus in the Gospels. Often the Bible says that Christ touched people. For a man plagued with leprosy, it says, "Jesus put out His hand and touched him" (Matthew 8:3) Of Peter's mother-in-law, who was sick with a fever, Jesus "touched her hand, and the fever left her" (Matthew 8:15).

The touch of Jesus was not merely mechanical in nature, but expressed His concern and love. When two blind men asked Christ to heal them, the Bible says, "So Jesus had compassion and touched their eyes" (Matthew 20:34). Jesus became human and, though He was sinless, we are assured that Christ feels for our sufferings and stands ready to reach out His healing hand and to touch us in our "time of need" (Hebrews 4:16).

Apply It:

Find someone you love who is suffering and sit with them, express empathy for their pain, and then reach out and hold their hand.

Dig Deeper:

Matthew 4:1–11; Romans 12:15; Hebrews 2:18

Jesus as Our Example

"In all things He had to be made like His brethren, that He might be a merciful and faithful High Priest in things pertaining to God, to make propitiation for the sins of the people. For in that He Himself has suffered, being tempted, He is able to aid those who are tempted" (Hebrews 2:17, 18).

Growing up, it's likely you had someone in your life whom you admired—perhaps a teacher, an athlete, or even a political figure. You might have wanted to pattern part of your life after the way he or she lived: "I want to be just like ..."

But even the best of human role models have their flaws. They are, after all, flesh-and-blood beings who are susceptible to human failings and human sins. The "bad" side may not have been evident during their lifetimes, but it's often exposed after their passing, usually via a "tell-all" book or documentary.

There is, as you might imagine (or hope for!), a wonderful exception to the rule. His name is Jesus, and He was fully human and fully divine. He was also sinless. Jesus, we read in Hebrews 4:15, "was in all points tempted as we are, yet without sin."

This is good news for everyone, but especially for those who follow Jesus. We have a role model whom we can emulate without fear. Indeed, acting as much like Jesus as we can is an admirable activity. We should think about what He thought about, love what He loved, and shun what He avoided.

How much happier would our lives be—how much better the whole world would be—if we took Peter's advice: "To this you were called, because Christ also suffered for us, leaving us an example, that you should follow His steps" (1 Peter 2:21).

Apply It:

This week study a Bible passage on Jesus and spend a "thoughtful hour" contemplating the life of Christ. Then, go out and do as He did, wherever you are!

Dig Deeper:

Matthew 8:17; Isaiah 53:4; Hebrews 2:10

A Prophet You Can Trust

"I will raise up for them a Prophet like you from among their brethren, and will put My words in His mouth, and He shall speak to them all that I command Him" (Deuteronomy 18:18).

By the early 2000s, Harold Camping's Christian radio network blanketed the United States, his nightly "Open Forum" question-and-answer program a staple for many listeners.

But Camping, a civil engineer by training who'd owned and sold a construction business in Oakland, California, started to dwell on one theme: Having done the calculations, he was convinced— there was no room for doubt—that Jesus would return on May 21, 2011, to "rapture" the church. When that didn't happen, he reset the date for five months later.

If you're reading this on Earth, you can figure out what happened: The second "prophecy" also failed. Some of Camping's followers, who'd sold their homes and businesses to finance a final witness before the world ended, were disillusioned. His radio network collapsed, and Camping died in 2013, a footnote in Christian history.

Jesus, as a prophet raised up by God, is, of course, far different from the false, date-setting prophets of human history. After Jesus fed the five thousand and the disciples gathered twelve baskets of leftovers, "those men, when they had seen the sign that Jesus did, said, 'This is truly the Prophet who is to come into the world' " (John 6:14).

Many of Jesus' prophecies about the future have been fulfilled—as in the case of the destruction of Jerusalem. Some of them have yet to be fulfilled, such as the final destruction of the wicked. He gave His followers "the testimony of Jesus," which "is the spirit of prophecy," as we read in Revelation 19:10.

There have been—and sadly there still are—people who claim the prophetic mantle but whose predictions fail, sometimes spectacularly. However, that's not the case with Jesus. He is a prophet you can trust, and He is a prophet who loves you and wants to save you.

■ Apply It:

Study Jesus' prophecies—especially the "Olivet Discourse" found in Matthew 24—to gain an insight into what our future holds.

■ Dig Deeper:

Matthew 24:1–51; Matthew 22:36–40; Luke 13:33

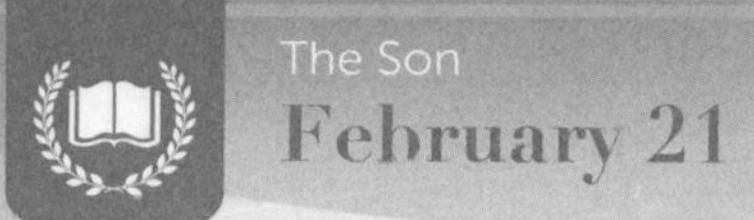

February 21

A Divine Oath

"The Lord has sworn and will not relent, 'You are a priest forever according to the order of Melchizedek' " (Psalm 110:4).

It's the most famous and unforgettable photograph of President Lyndon B. Johnson ever shot: He's taking the oath of office as the 36th president of the United States. John F. Kennedy was dead, recently killed by an assassin's bullet. Johnson is standing in a tiny stateroom aboard Air Force One for the proceeding. He's flanked by his wife, Lady Bird, and Jacqueline Kennedy.

This was the first inauguration of a U.S. President to take place aboard an aircraft, the first to be conducted by a female federal district judge (Sarah T. Hughes), and the first to use a Catholic missal that was found on a side table in Kennedy's Air Force One bedroom. In part, the presidential oath swears that he "will to the best of his ability, preserve, protect, and defend the Constitution of the United States."

As today's Scripture points out, the most solemn oath ever sworn in history was by God Himself when the priesthood of Jesus, the Messiah, was established. The verb "to swear" means to make a solemn vow. Christ's priesthood was not a result of being a descendant of Aaron. God divinely appointed Jesus. Just as Melchizedek was both priest and king, so Christ is our eternal King and Priest.

In the earthly priesthood, the blood of animals was offered, but Christ offered Himself as an atonement for our sins. The earthly priesthood of Jesus was carried out by the Lamb of God. "He made Him who knew no sin to be sin for us, that we might become the righteousness of God in Him" (2 Corinthians 5:21).

Assassin's bullets sometimes change the course of history, but the plans of God will be carried out in the end. Jesus was not a temporary priest, but "a priest forever"—and His sacrifice will forever stand. "For the death that He died, He died to sin once for all" (Romans 6:10).

Apply It:

How many presidential inaugurations have you observed? Have you ever heard the oath end with the words, "So help me God"?

Dig Deeper:

Leviticus 1:4; Psalm 40:6–8; Hebrews 5:1–11

A Perfect Record

"Thanks be to God, who gives us the victory through our Lord Jesus Christ" (1 Corinthians 15:57).

Which NBA team has the best regular-season record of all time at 73–9? Which NBA team has had the most wins (regular-season and postseason combined) of 88–18? Which NBA team has had the most road wins in a regular season at 34? The best start (24–0)? The best road start (14–0)? Longest home winning streak (54)? The list could go on and on for the 2015–16 Golden State Warriors.

The Warriors' 70th season of the franchise in the NBA (54th in the San Francisco Bay Area) was phenomenal. Golden State broke more than 25 NBA records and more than 10 franchise records that season—including most wins ever recorded in a season. The team's regular season is considered to be one of the greatest in professional sports history.

Jesus played the riskiest game in history in a match against the devil, all in order to win the right to save humanity from eternal loss. Christ came to this Earth and lived a perfect life. He never once sinned, and his perfect record qualified Him to serve as our High Priest in heaven. By suffering humiliation, torture, and death, Jesus is now "seated at the right hand of the throne of the Majesty in the heavens, a Minister of the sanctuary" (Hebrews 8:1, 2).

The winning streak of Jesus—perfectly following His Father's will (John 8:29)—allows Him to intercede for us, for "He is also able to save to the uttermost those who come to God through Him, since He always lives to make intercession for them" (Hebrews 7:25). Satan is still trying to point an accusing finger at God's people, but the apostle Paul rightly responds, "Who is he who condemns? It is Christ who died, and furthermore is also risen, who is even at the right hand of God, who also makes intercession for us" (Romans 8:34).

■ Apply It:

Have you ever suffered a loss that later turned out to be a victory?

■ Dig Deeper:

John 16:23; Hebrews 2:17, 18; 1 John 2:1

A Kingdom Forever

"The Lord has established His throne in heaven, and His kingdom rules over all" (Psalm 103:19).

Historical evidence suggests that the reign of Sobhuza II was the longest of any monarch in history. He was the Paramount Chief (and later king) of Swaziland in Southern Africa for 82 years and 254 days. Sobhuza was born on July 22, 1899, and when he was only four months old, his father died. He was chosen as king, but his grandmother and an uncle led the Swazi nation until Sobhuza reached the age of maturity at 21. He ruled until August 1982.

Actually, the longest reign of any monarch in history—as recorded in Scripture—is that of Jesus Christ. "To the Son He says: 'Your throne, O God, is forever and ever; a scepter of righteousness is the scepter of Your kingdom' " (Hebrews 1:8).

Just as earthly rulers who have fought to be crowned king, Christ's kingdom was established through strife. The Bible explains, "The kings of the earth set themselves, and the rulers take counsel together, against the Lord and against His Anointed [Messiah]" (Psalm 2:2). Their efforts failed, and God established Christ on an eternal throne.

The angel Gabriel announced to Mary, "He will reign over the house of Jacob forever, and of His kingdom there will be no end" (Luke 1:33). Earthly kings have come and gone, earthly kingdoms have risen and fallen, but Christ is King forever and His reign is eternal!

Clearly, the Son of God is a full member of the Godhead and shares in the divine rulership of the entire universe. Jesus does not hold a lower position than God the Father or the Holy Spirit but is co-equal in authority and power (1 Corinthians 15:28). Someday we will gather around the throne and sing, "Blessing and honor and glory and power be to Him who sits on the throne, and to the Lamb, forever and ever!" (Revelation 5:13).

Apply It:

Have you ever watched a sovereign being crowned?

Dig Deeper:

Daniel 7:13, 14; John 12:15; Revelation 14:14

Grace and Glory

"They will see the Son of Man coming on the clouds of heaven with power and great glory" (Matthew 24:30).

David, a shepherd boy, was anointed as the future king of Israel. But it would be several years before he would sit on the throne. The arduous journey from pasture to palace was marked with much tribulation.

Eventually, all the elders came to Hebron and "they anointed David king over Israel" (2 Samuel 5:3). This was the third time David was anointed. The first was by Samuel in Bethlehem (1 Samuel 16:13), and the second was by the men of Judah (2 Samuel 2:4).

At this point in David's reign, a capital for the kingdom had not yet been secured. It was after David's third anointing that Jerusalem was conquered and the ark of the covenant was brought to the city with much rejoicing. There are parallels we see between David's reign as king and Jesus' own kingdom.

When Christ was anointed by the heavenly Father and the Holy Spirit at His baptism (Matthew 3:13–17), He entered a period of tribulation in the wilderness. After defeating Satan's temptations, Christ announced, "Repent, for the kingdom of heaven is at hand" (Matthew 4:17). This was speaking of the kingdom of grace that was first offered to humans after Adam and Eve sinned. It would be established by Christ's death, and people could become citizens through regeneration. "Unless one is born of water and the Spirit, he cannot enter the kingdom of God" (John 3:5).

The kingdom of glory will be established at the Second Coming. Following the judgment, after the work of our High Priest is completed, God the Father will give Jesus "dominion and glory and a kingdom" (Daniel 7:14). Soon the kingdom of glory will be established on this Earth at the end of the millennium when the New Jerusalem comes down from heaven (Revelation 21:10, 11). Will you be a part of that kingdom?

Apply It:

Have you ever visited—or do you live in—a country with a monarch?

Dig Deeper:

Mark 1:15; Luke 17:20, 21; John 18:37

The Holy Spirit

5

More than Human

"It seemed good to the Holy Spirit, and to us, to lay upon you no greater burden than these necessary things" (Acts 15:28).

The term "speciesism" was first used by animal rights activist Richard Ryder. He sought to emphasize the misguided stance humans take toward animals in order to justify animal abuse. The idea is that sometimes people working, for instance, in slaughterhouses treat animals like objects. People who believe speciesism is a problem argue that a similar mentality is seen in racism. Historically, some people groups have justified their mistreatment of other groups by labelling them sub-human. While the Bible clarifies what our relationship to animals and people should be, some have missed what it says about the Holy Spirit being a person.

In the Bible, the Holy Spirit is often spoken of as not only doing many of the same things that people do, but also acting in ways that are far beyond human ability. When people treat the Holy Spirit like mindless electricity or an impersonal cosmic force, they are mislabeling Him.

Jesus trusted the wisdom of the Holy Spirit to act as a kind of church administrator: "As they ministered to the Lord and fasted, the Holy Spirit said, 'Now separate to Me Barnabas and Saul for the work to which I have called them' "(Acts 13:2). At the very least, these actions should reveal that the Holy Spirit has the same individual qualities as humans do.

However, the Bible goes further to explain how the wisdom of the Holy Spirit far surpasses that of any created being: "The angel answered and said to her, 'The Holy Spirit will come upon you, and the power of the Highest will overshadow you; therefore, also, that Holy One who is to be born will be called the Son of God' " (Luke 1:35). The Spirit's involvement in the birth of Jesus shows His complete understanding of what it means to be human.

Apply It:

Take the initiative to talk with someone that you normally don't.

Dig Deeper:

John 16:14; Luke 12:12; Romans 8:26

Genuinely God

"Peter said, 'Ananias, why has Satan filled your heart to lie to the Holy Spirit and keep back part of the price of the land for yourself? ... You have not lied to men but to God' " (Acts 5:3, 4).

Art forgery is big business, and the tools for catching peddlers of fake paintings are becoming more sophisticated. Sotheby's, one of the world's largest and most esteemed brokers of fine art, now has its own forensic art analysis department. In order to spot a forgery, the first step is researching its place of origin. You need to determine if a work of art is truly from the time period in which the author lived. But tracing the work's ownership history becomes more difficult the older the art.

Scientific methods of investigation are often used to catch fake works. Ultraviolet fluorescent light can pick up the age of paint and reveal with clearer light the original work. Optical microscopes allow one to see fine details in brushstrokes or ink patterns. Even X-rays and infrared reflectography can reveal what's under the surface.

When it comes to determining whether the Holy Spirit is truly God, we can discover through the best tool available—the Bible—that the Holy Spirit is fully divine. The history of the Holy Spirit can be traced all the way back to Creation. The Scriptures tell us, "The earth was without form, and void; and darkness was on the face of the deep. And *the Spirit of God* was hovering over the face of the waters" (Genesis 1:2, emphasis added).

Not only is the Spirit called "truth" (John 16:13), but the Holy Spirit is omnipotent and delivers spiritual gifts to all believers (1 Corinthians 12:11). The Spirit is omnipresent and will abide with believers "forever" (John 14:16). The Holy Spirit is also omniscient, for "no one knows the things of God except the Spirit of God" (1 Corinthians 2:11).

Ananias tried to lie to the Holy Spirit and discovered that he was lying to God. He learned just how skilled the Divine Spirit is in spotting a fake.

Apply It:

Think of a time when you confused a counterfeit for the real thing. What does this teach you about discovering Bible truth?

Dig Deeper:

Job 33:4; Acts 5:1–11; Romans 8:11

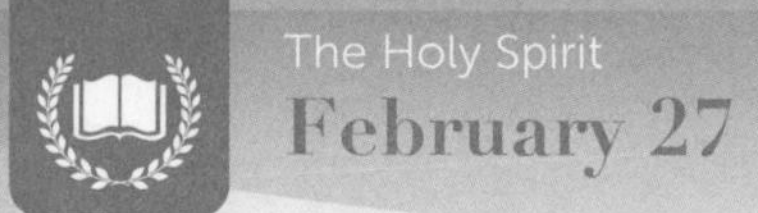

The Promised Helper

"I will pray the Father, and He will give you another Helper, that He may abide with you forever—the Spirit of truth" (John 14:16, 17).

In history, we often learn of those who played a significant role helping others: Tisquantum, a Native American also known as Squanto, was a Patuxet tribe member who was an interpreter and guide for the early Pilgrim settlers at Plymouth, Massachusetts. Thomas Watson assisted Alexander Graham Bell, inventor of the telephone. Bill Gates teamed up with his high school classmate Paul Allen to start the Microsoft Corporation.

In each case, the assistant's help enabled the main person—or group of people—to do far more than the individual could do on his or her own. For the Pilgrims, Squanto's help enabled them to survive a harsh first year in the New World. For Bell, Watson was a partner in experimentation. And for Gates, Allen was a fellow programmer and colleague in the development of computer operation systems and other software.

Those who believe in Christ have access to a Person and a power greater than any human assistant or mentor. God the Holy Spirit—the third member of the Godhead—was intended to live within humanity from the beginning, but Adam and Eve chose against that arrangement.

But Jesus had a promise for His followers: After returning to heaven following the resurrection, Jesus would ask the Father to provide "another Helper, that He may abide with you forever." And forever means exactly that: The Holy Spirit will live within us once we follow Christ all the way.

Jesus personally knew the Spirit's power, for the Holy Spirit conceived Him in Mary's womb. Christ was also baptized by the Spirit, led by the Spirit, and performed miracles through the Spirit's power. Indeed, the Holy Spirit was with Jesus throughout His life and even in the resurrection. It's an example of how the Holy Spirit wants to live and work with us now.

Apply It:

Read about how the Holy Spirit worked in Jesus' life and ask the Spirit to help you in the joys and sorrows of your life.

Dig Deeper:

Matthew 1:8–21; Luke 24:49; Acts 2:2–4

Guided to Safety

"There is therefore now no condemnation to those who are in Christ Jesus, who do not walk according to the flesh, but according to the Spirit. For the law of the Spirit of life in Christ Jesus has made me free from the law of sin and death" (Romans 8:1, 2).

Clutching his briefcase in one hand and his white walking stick in the other, Mike Wyatt ambled toward the train tracks at the Peoria Station in Aurora, Colorado. The station was noisy as usual, and the blind man didn't hear the fast-approaching train. But just as he was about to step onto the tracks, strong arms grasped his own and pulled him backward and out of the danger zone. The grandfather of seven is grateful to the one who saved his life by reaching out to move him to safety.

In the same way, before we come to Jesus, we are spiritually blind and headed toward certain disaster. But the Holy Spirit reaches out to save us by drawing us to Jesus.

Christ told His followers, "I will pray the Father, and He will give you another Helper, that He may abide with you forever" (John 14:16). The Greek word that is translated as "Helper" in this verse is *Parakletos,* which is translated in other versions as "Comforter" and "Counselor." It can also be translated as "Mediator."

In the Bible, only Jesus and the Holy Spirit are referred to by this word. Similarly to the way Jesus is our Helper and Mediator, the Holy Spirit brings us to the safety of our Redeemer and reveals our Savior's love and grace. "The love of God has been poured out in our hearts by the Holy Spirit who was given to us" (Romans 5:5). Indeed, the Scriptures refer to the Holy Spirit as "the Spirit of grace" (Hebrews 10:29). This is a critical function, because it is grace that melts our hearts and begins to transform us into true children of God.

Apply It:

Think back to your conversion experience. How did the Holy Spirit first reveal Jesus' love and grace to your heart?

Dig Deeper:

James 4:5, 6; 1 Corinthians 15:10; 2 Corinthians 9:14

Always on Duty

"I will pray the Father, and He will give you another Helper, that He may abide with you forever" (John 14:16).

How would you like it if someone was always following you around? That's not only what the current president of the United States experiences, but also all former presidents through Secret Service protection. In 2013, President Barack Obama signed the Former Presidents Protection Act that entitles all presidents and their spouses with a lifetime of protection.

Most Secret Service agents are involved in the investigation of crimes, and very few are assigned to protection work. That rigorous job is not for anyone who wants to have a family life. At the drop of a dime, a Secret Service agent has to be ready to go anywhere in the world—sometimes being on the clock for sixty days before taking a break.

God has you covered 24/7 and not with just a host of secret service angels. The very presence of Christ is promised through the divine agent of the Holy Spirit. When the disciples feared the departure of Jesus, Christ said to them, "It is to your advantage that I go away; for if I do not go away, the Helper will not come to you; but if I depart, I will send Him to you" (John 16:7).

The Holy Spirit is not only Christ's representative but brings us the very presence of Jesus. The Lord promised, "I will never leave you nor forsake you" (Hebrews 13:5) and "I am with you always, even to the end of the age" (Matthew 28:20). Since Jesus has chosen to be cloaked with humanity as our High Priest in the heavenly sanctuary, the Spirit—not held to time and place—is able to be with all God's children at any moment, wherever they are on the planet.

How grateful we can be that the Holy Spirit doesn't need a vacation. The Spirit is never worn down by being on duty for long periods of time but is full of energizing power to sustain us when we call for help. Through the presence of the Holy Spirit, we may know that we are fully covered.

Apply It:

Can you think of a time in your life when you especially felt the need for the presence of Jesus?

Dig Deeper:

Isaiah 11:2; John 14:17, 18; 1 Corinthians 3:16

A Different Tour

"I know that this will turn out for my deliverance through your prayer and the supply of the Spirit of Jesus Christ" (Philippians 1:19).

Holograms used to be a science fiction theme, but now they are being used to project celebrities. There are a variety of ways to make a virtual artist "appear" to take a stage. One method involves projecting from a tilted mirror onto a thin screen. A variety of technology has been used to simulate the performances of musicians who have died, with the idea that eventually these musician replicas could even go on tour.

When the living, resurrected Christ returned to heaven, He sent the Holy Spirit to continue His mission on earth. This action brought the presence of Jesus to us in a way that goes beyond any hologram. On a basic level, the Holy Spirit would do many of the things that Christ did while on earth. For example, the Holy Spirit has been spreading the teachings of Jesus as He predicted: "He will glorify Me, for He will take of what is Mine and declare it to you" (John 16:14).

In addition to furthering Christ's work, the Holy Spirit also plays a special role in the new birth conversion of every Christian. Christ relied on the Spirit for this role when He was on earth witnessing to people: "Jesus answered, 'Most assuredly, I say to you, unless one is born of water and the Spirit, he cannot enter the kingdom of God' " (John 3:5).

Beyond the initial conversion, the Holy Spirit is also the essential source of character growth, for we are "strengthened with might through His Spirit in the inner man" (Ephesians 3:16). Like a father raising his children, the Holy Spirit brings the parenting presence of Jesus into your life. This is what Christ meant when speaking of sending the Holy Spirit: "I will not leave you orphans; I will come to you" (John 14:18). As a result of this growth, believers can cooperate directly with the Spirit—not an artificial hologram—to continue spreading the teachings of Christ.

Apply It:

Practice giving good advice to someone younger than yourself who is interested in growing.

Dig Deeper:

1 Corinthians 12:3; 1 Peter 1:2; James 4:5, 6

Leading God's Church

"It seemed good to the Holy Spirit, and to us" (Acts 15:28).

A wise leader once said, "Success without a successor is failure." You might disagree at first—but think about it: Any successful enterprise that doesn't have a plan to continue beyond the working life of its founders may not be successful for very long.

In the business world, companies often take out a "key person" insurance policy to provide cash—and a lot of it—if a top executive dies suddenly. Without that leader, a firm, especially a new one, might falter or even collapse.

The church differs from a business in that we have an Advisor with divine attributes. Throughout the story of the early church, we see again and again the leading and counsel of the Holy Spirit—sometimes telling the church what to do (Acts 13:4) or what not to do (Acts 16:6). The Spirit shepherded and molded the band of Jesus' disciples into a leadership team able to manage a growing community, one that would turn the world "upside down" (Acts 17:6).

Such heavenly direction was not based on nebulous impressions or fickle feelings. The Spirit specifically guided the church. Simeon was told "by the Holy Spirit that he would not see death before he had seen the Lord's Christ" (Luke 2:26). After receiving a vision, Peter was told by the Spirit, "Three men are seeking you" (Acts 10:19). Some disciples "told Paul through the Spirit not to go up to Jerusalem" (Acts 21:4).

Instead of looking to fallible human beings, prudent leaders of God's church will seek the help and guidance of the Holy Spirit in their deliberations. They will pray for help, and listen for the "still, small voice" of direction, which Jesus promised would be given.

Apply It:

When your congregation is trying to decide on a course of action, encourage those making the decision to seek the Holy Sprit's wisdom.

Dig Deeper:

Acts 13:1–4; Acts 16:6, 7; Acts 20:28

Equipper of Gifts

"There are diversities of gifts, but the same Spirit" (1 Corinthians 12:4).

How many different colors are there? Well, let's start with the primary colors—red, blue, and yellow. Then there are the secondary colors—orange, green, and violet. If you purchased a box with 16 Crayola crayons, you'd add carnation pink, blue green, blue violet, red orange, red violet, white, yellow green, yellow orange, brown, and black. Of course, you could purchase the exclusive edition of 152 crayons, which include neon carrot, laser lemon, and bluetiful.

How many different gifts are there in the body of Christ? If you study Romans 12, you'll find seven. In 1 Corinthians 12, Paul lists thirteen gifts. In Ephesians 4, there are five. None of the lists exactly match, which leads Bible scholars to believe that Paul never intended to give us a definitive list, but rather samples of gifts.

What is clear to all who study spiritual gifts is that these special abilities come to believers through the agency of the Holy Spirit. Paul explains, "The manifestation of the Spirit is given to each one for the profit of all: for to one is given the word of wisdom through the Spirit, to another the word of knowledge through the same Spirit" (1 Corinthians 12:7, 8).

The special gifts of the Spirit were not just given in New Testament times. The Old Testament regularly speaks of individuals who were given divine abilities to serve God. "The Spirit of the Lord came upon him [Othniel], and he judged Israel" (Judges 3:10). The Spirit even came upon King Saul, though he later turned from God. (See 1 Samuel 10:1–13.)

Like the various colors in a box of crayons, the Spirit gives diverse gifts to members so that many forms of ministry can take place in the church and the community to build up God's kingdom. No person has all the gifts (1 Corinthians 12:21), yet each believer has at least one gift (v. 15), for "You are the body of Christ, and members individually" (v. 27).

■ Apply It:

Read through the three primary passages on spiritual gifts (Romans 12, 1 Corinthians 12, and Ephesians 4) and prayerfully ask yourself, "What are my gifts?"

■ Dig Deeper:

Exodus 28:3; 31:3; 1 Chronicles 25:1; 1 Peter 4:9–11

An Essential Lifeline

"When they had prayed, the place where they were assembled together was shaken; and they were all filled with the Holy Spirit, and they spoke the word of God with boldness" (Acts 4:31).

A human umbilical cord—a baby's lifeline before its birth—can measure close to 24 inches in length. This ingenious apparatus contains three blood vessels—two to carry waste products out and one that delivers to the baby about a pint of fresh blood, containing oxygen and nutrients, every minute during the final trimester. Due to the activity of embryos, many babies are born with the umbilical cord wrapped around their neck, and about one percent are born with an actual knot in the cord. Thankfully, due to the cord's built-in safety features, this rarely causes problems.

For Christians, the Holy Spirit is just as essential a lifeline. We cannot survive without Him, "for without Me you can do nothing" (John 15:5). Jesus taught that "unless one is born of water and the Spirit, he cannot enter the kingdom of God" (John 3:5). Yet as believers, we need to go beyond justification and receive the fullness of God's Spirit into our lives so we can grow as Christians.

Titus 3:5 says that we need "the washing of regeneration and renewing of the Holy Spirit" (and then explains the reason) "that having been justified by His grace we should become heirs according to the hope of eternal life" (v. 7). Over time, the Spirit works out the necessary progress in our spiritual lives; this is the work of sanctification.

Everything that Jesus wants to do in our lives is done by the Holy Spirit. The Scriptures even refer to Him as the Spirit of Christ (Romans 8:9). Once we have chosen to give our lives to Jesus, we must rely on His Spirit to transform us to be more Christ-like and empower us to reach others for Him. These are things we simply can't accomplish on our own but the Spirit can do through us. If we don't resist the Holy Spirit, He will work continuously in our lives to bring us salvation and maturity.

Apply It:

Ask God each morning to fill you with His Holy Spirit.

Dig Deeper:

Ephesians 5:18; Acts 9:17; Acts 19:1–6

International Broadcasting

"These signs will follow those who believe: In My name they will cast out demons; they will speak with new tongues" (Mark 16:17).

During the 2018 winter Olympics, a broadcaster in Europe gained the rights to broadcast to almost fifty countries. Their task was to produce commentary that was not only translated into the language of every viewing country, but also culturally sensitive. The need for culturally sensitive content became even clearer when a commentator made a comparison between two East Asian countries during the opening ceremonies, leading to an angry outcry from many viewers.

God knows the importance of building relationships for the spread of the gospel. People will have a hard time believing the goodness of God and His plan to save them if the Christian cannot speak a distinct version of their native language. Usually, God sends people to live in the nation they are trying to reach so that they can learn the culture along with the language.

Occasionally, however, the Holy Spirit gives people a supernatural gift for the purpose of quickly spreading the gospel. This first took place when the disciples faced a crowed of foreigners. With the intervention of the Holy Spirit, the people heard the good news in their native language and wondered aloud: "How is it that we hear, each in our own language in which we were born?" (Acts 2:8).

This was a fulfillment of the promise Jesus had made soon after giving the disciples their mission. Empowered by this unusual capacity to suddenly speak numerous foreign languages, the disciples were able to use this diverse gathering to jump start the spread of the gospel. This first reception of the gift became the pattern that the Spirit would duplicate. Looking back at subsequent miracles Peter could say: "As I began to speak, the Holy Spirit fell upon them, as upon us at the beginning" (Acts 11:15).

Apply It:

Learn a phrase in a foreign language. For instance, using an online translation program, practice saying "Jesus loves you" in a different language.

Dig Deeper:

Mark 16:15–17; Acts 2:9–17; Acts 10:1, 44–46

Celebrating Too Early

"In the church I would rather speak five words with my understanding, that I may teach others also, than ten thousand words in a tongue" (1 Corinthians 14:19).

In a major cycling race in 2017, Luka Pibernik celebrated too early and, as a result, lost his lead spot and his shot at victory. Before he finished the final lap, he slowed down and spread his hands out as if he had already won. Soon the main group of cyclists rushed by him, and by that time it was too late for him to regain his lead. Unfortunately, this phenomenon is so common in the athletic world that video compilations of disappointing early celebrations have been produced that last hours.

Paul was concerned that the believers in Corinth, who had received the ability to speak new foreign languages, would celebrate too early. Many of them seemed to be boasting as if the miracle they had received from the Holy Spirit was to be used for showing off. In his first letter, Paul tried to correct their confusion by explaining that the spiritual gift was intended for teaching people the gospel.

Some have misunderstood Paul's admonition in one particular verse to mean that he was speaking of a mysterious heavenly language: "If I pray in a tongue, my spirit prays, but my understanding is unfruitful" (1 Corinthians 14:14). The target audience in which the fruit should be produced is not the speaker. Instead, it is the listening church members for whom the fruitful lesson is intended. In other words, Paul is saying that if he does not speak to people who understand the foreign language he is using to communicate, they will not grow in their understanding.

This is made clear two verses later: "Otherwise, if you bless with the spirit, how will he who occupies the place of the uninformed say 'Amen' at your giving of thanks, since he does not understand what you say?" (1 Corinthians 14:16).

Apply It:

Ask your friends to help you identify a talent you do not realize you have.

Dig Deeper:

1 Corinthians 14:6–9; 1 Timothy 6:20; 2 Timothy 2:16

Creation

6

March 8

The Dynamic Word

"By the word of the Lord the heavens were made, and all the host of them by the breath of His mouth" (Psalm 33:6).

It's been a long road to voice recognition devices like Amazon's Alexa and Apple's Siri. Thomas Edison and Alexander Graham Bell took some of the first steps with the phonograph (1877) and the Dictaphone (1885), but these machines were passive—until Audrey came along in 1952 as the first documented speech recognizer.

Audrey (short for "Automatic Digit Recognition") was a huge machine with a six-foot relay rack, loads of energy-consuming amplifiers, integrators, filters, vacuum tubes, and cables. The room-sized computer, invented by Bell Labs, could distinguish between ten numbers ("0" through "9"). With some fine-tuning, the gargantuan electronic marvel could reach an accuracy level of 97 percent.

Imagine the very elements of the earth recognizing your voice and obeying your commands. That's what happened at Creation when God spoke the earth into existence. "He spoke, and it was done; He commanded, and it stood fast" (Psalm 33:9).

What's even more incredible is that most of what God created (the exceptions being Adam and Eve) did not come from preexisting matter. "By faith we understand that the worlds were framed by the word of God, so that the things which are seen were not made of things which are visible" (Hebrews 11:3).

The Bible says that seven times during the Creation week, God spoke. Don't stumble over the dynamic divine commands of the Lord in Genesis 1. "God said, 'Let there be light'; and there was light" (v. 3). "Then God said, 'Let there be a firmament' ... and it was so" (vv. 6, 7).

The creative energy of God's Word is still active through the "Word of God" in the Bible. Let the powerful Word speak into your heart and watch a new creation spring forth.

Apply It:

Find a meaningful Bible promise (such as Ezekiel 36:26), write it down on a card, then practice memorizing it aloud. Let God's Word change your heart.

Dig Deeper:

Psalm 29:1–11; Psalm 148:5, 6; 2 Peter 3:5

Same Story, Different Style

"This is the history of the heavens and the earth when they were created ..." (Genesis 2:4).

Forty-four men have become president of the United States (as of 2018), and 43 of them were married at one time or another. (James Buchanan, elected in 1857, was the only unmarried president to stay single his whole life.) One of the most interesting insights into these men are the letters they wrote to their wives. Thousands of personal letters, telegrams, cards, and even teletype messages have been saved in collections at the Library of Congress, in public institutions, private family collections, and published works.

Letters expressing fondness are common among the presidents and their wives. Some are flirtatious; others are formal. A few are silly; others express sadness and loneliness. While separated, James Madison wrote to his wife Dolley, "Everything around and within reminds me that you are absent." Lyndon Johnson wrote to his wife, Lady Bird, "I am very madly in love with you."

Obviously, the gushing letters of couples like the Reagans and the Wilsons were completely different in style than when they wrote to senators or ambassadors. And that's true within the Scriptures. Some critics have stated that there are two different accounts of Creation in Genesis 1 and 2 because the style of each differs; one writer could not have written both chapters.

The large overview of Creation in Genesis 1 is complimentary to the narrower view of Genesis 2, which focuses more on the creation of mankind and describes his environment in the garden. The first is more chronological, while the second is more topical and focuses on the nature of humanity and the divine government. Genesis 2 explains, "This is the history (literally "generations") of the heavens and the earth when they were created ..." (v. 4).

Christ had no difficulty harmonizing Genesis 1 and 2 when He quoted them both within the same sentence: "Have you not read that He who made them at the beginning 'made them male and female', and said, 'For this reason a man shall leave his father and mother and be joined to his wife, and the two shall become one flesh'?" (Matthew 19:4, 5). If Jesus accepted both accounts as divine Scripture, connected and harmonious, so should we.

■ Apply It:

See if you can dig up two different styles of letters from your (or your family's) personal collections.

■ Dig Deeper:

Genesis 1:1–31; Genesis 2:1–25

When to Start the Day

"God called the light Day, and the darkness He called Night. So the evening and the morning were the first day" (Genesis 1:5).

To determine how the habits of executives differ from other company workers, two authors assessed more than 35,000 leaders. They found that the more seniority a worker had, the more hours they slept per night. This was not because the executives had more people working under them. Rather, it was because they knew how much more efficient they would be with a few more hours of sleep—and they had the discipline to get to bed early.

This principle is so important that it can be said the day begins during the previous evening. In other words, if we go to bed early, we will be ready to face the following day. This coincides with God's original design for the day. The Bible records that each day of Creation began with the evening and then includes the morning. Those who assume that these days represent thousands of years have to explain why the Bible records that Adam lived less than a thousand years (Genesis 5:5).

When God gave the Israelites instructions concerning festivals, He continued to refer to days using the same formula used in Creation: "It shall be to you a sabbath of solemn rest, and you shall afflict your souls; on the ninth day of the month at evening, from evening to evening, you shall celebrate your sabbath" (Leviticus 23:32).

In addition, God included the exact parallel between the Creation days and the weekly observance of the Sabbath in the fourth commandment: "In six days the Lord made the heavens and the earth, the sea, and all that is in them, and rested the seventh day. Therefore the Lord blessed the Sabbath day and hallowed it" (Exodus 20:11). From this it can be deduced that the days of Creation could not have been longer than 24-hour periods.

Apply It:

Go to bed early tonight.

Dig Deeper:

Deuteronomy 16:6; Genesis 7:11; Exodus 16:1

Heaven and the Heavens

"The sons of God came to present themselves before the Lord, and Satan also came among them" (Job 1:6).

Is there life on other planets? Many research organizations are dedicated to finding extraterrestrial life—beings that do not originate on earth. Search for Extra-Terrestrial Intelligence—SETI, for short—is a collective name for several groups who use the latest technology to monitor the skies for transmissions from civilizations on other worlds. So far, the results have been dismal.

However, the Bible seems to hint about life on other worlds. In fact, Hebrews 11:3 tells us that "the worlds were framed by the word of God."

Some people find the passage "In the beginning God created the heavens and the earth" (Genesis 1:1) to be confusing. What does it mean by "the heavens"? It could possibly be our own solar system, but notice that the verse doesn't include a timeline, so it's also possible that verse 1 is an opening statement broadly identifying God as the Creator of all things—the entire universe. It isn't necessarily saying that the whole universe was created during the six days of Creation.

We see another clue in the book of Job when we read how "the sons of God came to present themselves before the Lord" (1:6). Just as Adam was a "son of God" who represented our world—and eventually gave up that position to Satan—so there are other "sons of God," representatives from other planets, who apparently gathered for the divinely called assembly described in Scripture.

It appears that for a time, Satan had some access to a place in the heavens. Even the devil's own evil spirits appear to have been able to approach God. (See 1 Kings 22:19–21.) But when Christ secured the salvation of the world, "the accuser of our brethren, who accused them before our God day and night" was "cast down" (Revelation 12:10).

Someday there will be a "new heaven and a new earth" (Revelation 21:1) and our enemy will no longer have dominion over this world, for "the ruler of this world is judged" (John 16:11).

Apply It:

Imagine visiting other worlds in the universe. What would you expect to find?

Dig Deeper:

Hebrews 1:2; Exodus 20:11; Revelation 14:7

A Hint from Space

"What is man that You are mindful of him, and the son of man that You visit him?" (Psalm 8:4).

From 3.7 billion miles away, it shows up smaller than the size of a pixel. The famous photograph *Pale Blue Dot* was taken by the Voyager 1 space probe on February 14, 1990. It's a picture of the earth set against the vastness of space. Voyager 1 had finished its primary mission and, as it was leaving the solar system, turned its camera around and took one last picture.

Carl Sagan, the famous American astronomer, cosmologist, astrophysicist, astrobiologist, author, and agnostic, shared his reflections on that dot. He stated in a speech at Cornell University, "Our planet is a lonely speck in the great enveloping cosmic dark. In our obscurity—in all this vastness—there is no hint that help will come from elsewhere to save us from ourselves. It is up to us."

On the contrary, the Bible describes a God who is not distant or indifferent. He is not only a careful planner, but He has deep concern for His creation. God created people to freely choose to be in relationship to Himself or to reject it. (See Joshua 24:15.)

Each member of the Godhead was personally involved in Creation. "In the beginning God created the heavens and the earth. The earth was without form, and void; and darkness was on the face of the deep. And the Spirit of God was hovering over the face of the waters" (Genesis 1:1, 2).

The New Testament describes both the Father and the Son involved in Creation. "God ... has in these last days spoken to us by His Son, whom He has appointed heir of all things, through whom also He made the worlds" (Hebrews 1:1, 2).

Many have perceived God as an uninvolved cosmic force, either as the laws that govern the universe or somehow the essence of all things. But the Bible reveals to us One who is intimately connected to those inhabiting this speck of dust in the vastness of space. "The Word became flesh and dwelt among us, and we beheld His glory, the glory as of the only begotten of the Father, full of grace and truth" (v. 14).

Apply It:

Find a picture of the *Pale Blue Dot*. As you study the photo, repeat the words from today's Scripture text.

Dig Deeper:

Psalm 8:1–9; Ephesians 3:9; Revelation 13:8

Reflecting His Glory

"Let your light so shine before men, that they may see your good works and glorify your Father in heaven" (Matthew 5:16).

Who doesn't relish looking up at the bright moon on a clear night? You might be surprised to know, however, that our rough-surfaced moon, which basically consists of dark, light-absorbing rocks, has the anemic reflecting ability of old asphalt. Yet because of the incredible intensity of the sun and relative nearness of the moon, it appears bright to us against the night sky, especially during a full moon. When the moon is at its fullest and also at its perigee—its closest approach to Earth—it is known as a supermoon. But even the biggest supermoon reflects a mere fraction of the sunlight that hits it.

The Scriptures tell us that "God is love" (1 John 4:16). The reciprocal love of the Godhead extended throughout all Creation. We were created to love and to be loved. But more than that, we were made to reflect God's glory—which is an extension of His love observed through His creativity and His goodness.

God's glory is seen in the natural world, whether on the earth or throughout the cosmos. Psalm 19:1–4 spotlights this truth in splendid poetic form: "The heavens declare the glory of God; and the firmament shows His handiwork. Day unto day utters speech, and night unto night reveals knowledge. There is no speech nor language where their voice is not heard. Their line has gone out through all the earth, and their words to the end of the world."

Everything the Lord made emphatically points us to Him as the Creator. The apostle Paul wrote, "Since the creation of the world His invisible attributes are clearly seen, being understood by the things that are made" (Romans 1:20). As we discover these facets of His beautiful character through the things of nature, we can become more like Him and more brightly reflect His love to others, fulfilling the purpose of our existence and multiplying the blessing for everyone.

Apply It:

When you have a chance, step into your backyard for a few minutes and count the evidences of God's love for you in the things of nature.

Dig Deeper:

2 Corinthians 3:18; 1 Corinthians 6:20; Psalm 86:9

A Weekly Memorial Day

"Oh come, let us worship and bow down; let us kneel before the LORD our Maker" (Psalm 95:6).

To many people, it's just another fun holiday. But to people like Carol Resh, 61, whose son, Army Captain Mark Resh, was killed in Iraq, Memorial Day means a whole lot more. Regarding the day's treatment as just another day off, she said, "It's not that they're doing it out of malice. [The war] just hasn't affected them."

During World War II, more than 12 percent of the U.S. population served in the armed forces. Today, that number is down to less than one-half of a percent. Most Americans don't even personally know a soldier, sailor, or airman. Brian Duffy, commander-in-chief of the Veterans of Foreign Wars, says, "It hurts that, as a society, we don't truly understand and appreciate what the true meaning of Memorial Day is."

That's also true when it comes to Creation. In six days the Lord made the heavens and the earth, but most of the world has forgotten Genesis 1, or worse, ridicules the notion that God made our world. Some say, "Who cares how God created the earth?" Yet our beliefs about beginnings lay a foundation for many areas of our life.

For instance, when we understand that God's creatorship sets Him apart from all other "gods," we realize that the Lord should be the supreme focus of our worship. "All the gods of the peoples are idols, but the LORD made the heavens" (Psalm 96:5).

God as Creator is the basis for our worship because we are His creatures. This is seen in the last call for all the inhabitants of the world to "worship Him who made heaven and earth, the sea and springs of water" (Revelation 14:7).

So also the Sabbath was given as a weekly reminder of Creation—a memorial day. We are told to "remember the Sabbath day. ... For in six days the LORD made the heavens and the earth" (Exodus 20:8, 11). When you understand the true meaning of the Sabbath, God's creation means a whole lot more.

Apply It:

This week welcome the Sabbath by reading passages about God as your Maker.

Dig Deeper:

Genesis 2:2, 3; 1 Chronicles 16:24–27; Isaiah 40:18–26

A Touch of Eden

"Then God saw everything that He had made, and indeed it was very good" (Genesis 1:31).

It's been called the world's largest natural flower garden. The Dubai Miracle Garden not only provides a stunning display of over 60 million flowers, it's a miracle in itself because it sits in the hot, arid desert. The garden opened in 2013 and attracts up to 1.5 million visitors each year.

Over 80,000 square yards of displays greet visitors who are tired of malls, concrete, and steel. Floral structures—including a life-size replica of the Emirates Airbus A380—are covered in beautiful flowers seven months of the year. The 104-degree temperatures make it too challenging to grow flowers in the summer.

When the Lord presented the Garden of Eden to our first parents within the perfect environment of our world, untarnished by sin, it must have been a jaw-dropping sight. God created our planet to communicate His love for humanity. "The LORD God planted a garden eastward in Eden, and there He put the man whom He had formed" (Genesis 2:8).

The Lord's creatorship shows that He is Father of all people. "Have we not all one Father? Has not one God created us?" (Malachi 2:10). It makes all humans brothers and sisters and eliminates any room for racism, bigotry, and other forms of discrimination.

Creation also establishes our responsibility to care for the earth. "God blessed them, and God said to them, 'Be fruitful and multiply; fill the earth and subdue it; have dominion over the fish of the sea, over the birds of the air, and over every living thing that moves on the earth' " (Genesis 1:28). Even the dignity of manual labor is seen from the beginning, for the Lord asked Adam to "tend and keep" the Garden of Eden (Genesis 2:15).

Though our world is filled with evil and sin has marred the creation, it was not that way in the beginning. The Bible says, "His work is perfect" (Deuteronomy 32:4). Everything God made was pronounced "good" (Genesis 1:10, 12, 17, 21, 25). When you visit a flower garden, look closely and you will see glimpses of our first home.

Apply It:

Visit a flower garden or purchase a bouquet of flowers for someone you love. As you enjoy them, think of the very first garden-home given to us by God.

Dig Deeper:

Job 12:7–10; Psalm 24:1; Colossians 1:16, 17

Sacred Relationship

"You formed my inward parts; You covered me in my mother's womb. I will praise You, for I am fearfully and wonderfully made" (Psalm 139:13, 14).

Most visitors to Italy are shocked to discover that he stands seventeen feet tall. Michelangelo's "David," a statue of a muscular young man with a sling over his shoulder, also weighs six tons. The famous sculptor was only 23 when he was commissioned to create the gleaming white statue for the city of Florence. He was the third artist to attempt the project, and he took three years to complete it.

What you see in the Piazza della Signoria is actually a copy. David has suffered damage at least twice over the centuries. His arm was broken—just 23 years after it was completed—when a political activist threw a chair out the window and struck the statue. It was another 400 years before a hammer-wielding vandal broke off a toe in 1991. The original is now protected in the Accademia Gallery Museum in Florence.

When God formed Adam from "the dust of the ground" (Genesis 2:7), He was not creating a piece of inanimate art to be put on display. The Lord "breathed into his nostrils the breath of life; and man became a living being." No artist has the sacred power to create life.

God is still intimately involved in the act of creation. Describing the Lord's hand in forming his body while in his mother's womb, David wrote, "My frame was not hidden from You, when I was made in secret. ... Your eyes saw my substance, being yet unformed" (Psalm 139:15, 16). His language has the echo of a Master Sculptor.

The final product in the creation of the first human was not a lifeless chunk of clay or even a robotic machine. God created a human being intended for real interaction, intelligent thinking, and genuine connection. The story of Creation speaks against the cold, distant theory of evolution and presents to us a personal, meaningful God who cares for us. Creation is the antidote for loneliness in our world when we understand the heart of God.

Apply It:

Pray the prayer of David today: "I will praise You, for I am fearfully and wonderfully made."

Dig Deeper:

Job 10:8, 9; Ecclesiastes 11:5; Isaiah 44:24

No Artistic Block

"We are His workmanship, created in Christ Jesus for good works, which God prepared beforehand that we should walk in them" (Ephesians 2:10).

Take a vacation, go to a conference, read, talk to leaders, and get a hobby. These are some of the recommendations made by successful entrepreneurs for cultivating creativity. The idea is that even the most creative people run into phases when they are stuck. If they have trouble finding ways to innovate in an ever-changing market, these methods are supposed to get their creativity flowing again.

God has no problem being creative. He does not need any of the suggestions these experts provide. The Bible tells us that God is still creating our new identities as Christians and preparing us for the new earth. When the Lord says, "Behold, I make all things new" (Revelation 21:5), remember, that new creation includes you!

The prophet Isaiah and other Bible writers recognized that God's salvation is similar to the work of a potter: "Now, O LORD, You are our Father; we are the clay, and You our potter; and all we are the work of Your hand" (Isaiah 64:8). This imagery of the potter reminds us that as God forms us to reflect His moral image, He is producing new creative masterpieces. It is comforting to think that the Master Artist, who brought this universe into existence, is still at work in our lives.

Furthermore, God does not want to form us back into His image without also providing us with a perfect world. This is why we can look forward to His creative activity in the future when our planet will be remade: "Behold, I create new heavens and a new earth; and the former shall not be remembered or come to mind" (Isaiah 65:17). From this perspective we can be grateful that the source of all creativity will continue to amaze us. While we wait for that day, we can watch His re-creative work in us.

Apply It:

Watch the evening sky for a few minutes.

Dig Deeper:

Matthew 8:8; 2 Corinthians 5:17; Revelation 21:5

No Genesis, No Gospel?

"As in Adam all die, even so in Christ all shall be made alive" (1 Corinthians 15:22).

Sitting before a reporter in Edmond, Oklahoma, Ken Ham—a "young earth creationist" whose Ark Museum attempts to duplicate Noah's Ark to its original scale—was as serious as a heart attack.

Asked why he believed Genesis was so important, Ham replied, "Genesis is the foundation for the whole rest of the Bible. So if Christians don't believe in a literal Genesis, they have no foundation for their doctrine." In other words: No Genesis, no gospel!

As far as we know, Ham does not observe the Bible Sabbath—even though he has said in lectures that the Creation week points to a seventh-day Sabbath. But he is unshakable in his belief that without a "literal" Genesis, there's no basis for Christian doctrine. None.

Part of that "literal" record is the length of Creation: Six 24-hour days. Why? One suggestion is that Jesus, the Creator who speaks in Genesis 1, "took delight in unfolding" the creation. It might relate to the value of each created thing—as the Creator saw each item and pronounced it "very good."

Another explanation is that the six 24-hour days prepare us for the most special day of the week, the Sabbath. After creating everything, including the first man and the first woman, God set apart that final 24-hour period. He rested as an example for us. He sanctified the day, signaling that we should regard it as holy time.

If "a literal Genesis" means so much to someone who doesn't observe the Sabbath as outlined in the Bible, how much more important should it be to those who know this vital truth? God spoke the world into existence in six days, He rested on the seventh, and because of this, we too can rest!

Apply It:

Next Sabbath, remember that God's creative power not only gave us the world in six days, but that He endowed the seventh as a holy, blessed day of rest—for you!

Dig Deeper:

Genesis 1:1–2:3; Exodus 20:8; Mark 2:27

Master of Creation

"All things were made through Him, and without Him nothing was made that was made" (John 1:3).

Famous painters have often worked their likenesses into their creations. Italian Renaissance painters, for instance, often painted themselves into a scene—sometimes off to the side looking out toward the viewer. Michelangelo, in *The Last Judgement,* embedded a self-portrait within the skin of one of the painting's subjects. In *The School of Athens,* Raphael painted himself and other artists of his time—such as Leonardo da Vinci and Michelangelo—into the work. And Caravaggio, in *David with the Head of Goliath,* painted his own features onto the gruesome head of the giant.

When Jesus chose to come to our planet to redeem His fallen children—those made "in His own image" (Genesis 1:27)—the all-powerful Creator of life literally became a part of His own creation. Leaving His omnipresent existence, He entered our dark, sin-ravaged world and gave Himself to save us. As the Scripture says, "The Word became flesh and dwelt among us" (John 1:14).

In His ministry on earth, Jesus' creative power was seen daily in the healing of the blind, the deaf, the lame, the lepers, and those possessed by demons. His life-giving ability was repeatedly demonstrated as He raised the dead (Mark 5:35–42; John 11:38–44). By joining with us, bringing His creative and restorative power to the human race, Jesus brought us hope.

But His sacrifice went even further, as "He humbled Himself and became obedient to the point of death, even the death of the cross" (Philippians 2:8). In this ultimate gift, the same Divine hands that created mankind from the dust of the earth were willingly nailed and scarred to create everlasting life for those He loves.

Jesus is the Master of creation. But His creative power is not limited to the Creation week at the beginning of our existence, or even to His time on this earth. It is ongoing, as Christ continuously recreates, within those hearts who are willing, His transforming and invincible image of love.

Apply It:

List three ways your life has been impacted and transformed by the creative power of Christ.

Dig Deeper:

Matthew 11:5; Ephesians 2:10; 2 Corinthians 5:17

The Nature of Humanity

7

Like Father

"Beloved, now we are children of God; and it has not yet been revealed what we shall be, but we know that when He is revealed, we shall be like Him, for we shall see Him as He is" (1 John 3:2).

Do newborns typically look more like their mothers or their fathers? It depends on whom you ask. In-laws invariably see in their grandchild the facial features of their son or daughter. New mothers often see the features of their husband in their baby. But looks obviously can change. That shock of black hair on your newborn might totally disappear and you may eventually have a blond-haired child.

In a 1995 study at the University of California, people were supposedly much better at matching photos of one-year-old children with their fathers than with photos of their mothers. But many follow-up studies that tried to duplicate this study found that most infants resemble both parents equally. What appears to hold more truth is that dads who tend to resemble their babies on average spend more time with them. And the more attention babies get from their dads, the healthier they are by the age of one (*Journal of Health Economics,* January 2018).

The Bible tells us that people were created in the likeness of God. "Let Us make man in Our image, according to Our likeness" (Genesis 1:26). When the Lord created animals—like birds, fish, reptiles, insects, and mammals—they were made "according to their kind" (v. 21). But humans were made after the divine type, not after some stripe in the animal kingdom.

In an age when many scientists claim that humans have evolved from animals, the Scriptures place a clear line of division between humanity and animals. In fact, Luke goes so far as to plainly call Adam "the son of God" (Luke 3:38). All people may trace their lineage back to Adam and Eve, for God "has made from one blood every nation of men to dwell on all the face of the earth" (Acts 17:26). That means in some way we all share the likeness of our heavenly Father.

Apply It:

Do you look more like your mother or your father? Did that change over time? You can grow to look more like your heavenly Father.

Dig Deeper:

Psalm 8:4–9; Romans 5:12, 19; 1 Corinthians 15:21, 22

Impersonal Power

"The LORD God formed man of the dust of the ground, and breathed into his nostrils the breath of life; and man became a living soul" (Genesis 2:7 KJV).

Wind, water, and sun are not the only forces that can produce clean energy. A British company has begun to install special tiles in areas of high foot traffic. When people step on these tiles they produce energy. According to one calculation, enough people tread the boardwalk in Venice Beach, California, per year to power the appliances of a small restaurant for 320 days.

While people are the source of this power, the energy itself is only a small part of every person. In a similar way, the Hebrew and Greek words in the Bible that are often translated "soul" are used for either the whole person or parts of people. Psalm 105:22 states, "To bind his princes at his pleasure, and teach his elders wisdom." The word translated "pleasure" is the same Hebrew word that is usually translated as "soul." In other places, the same word is translated as "desire" or "life."

The variety of definitions for this word suggests that the Bible is attempting to give a comprehensive view of what people are. In other words, people are not just living things or just appetites. Instead, they have an assortment of characteristics that are always a part of a complete human package. The Bible never speaks of a floating appetite or a disembodied set of emotions.

When a single passage refers to people using a comprehensive meaning, it never speaks of their immortality. Both Old and New Testaments describe how the soul can be killed: "Do not fear those who kill the body but cannot kill the soul. But rather fear Him who is able to destroy both soul and body in hell" (Matthew 10:28). When taken as a whole, the Bible does not isolate parts of humans and reveals that even the most essential aspects are mortal, for the "soul who sins shall die" (Ezekiel 18:4).

Apply It:

Care for a part of your nature that you usually ignore.

Dig Deeper:

Deuteronomy 23:24; Genesis 9:4; Numbers 31:19

The Whole Picture

"My friends, do not be afraid of those who kill the body, and after that have no more that they can do. But I will show you whom you should fear: Fear Him who, after He has killed, has power to cast into hell; yes, I say to you, fear Him!" (Luke 12:4, 5).

John Spilsbury was a British engraver and cartographer who wanted to create an educational tool to teach geography. So he took a world map, affixed it to wood, then carved out each country to create a puzzle—the first puzzle of this sort ever made. The year was 1766, and people loved what he called "Dissected Maps." Eventually these puzzles were created using a jigsaw; thus, they became known as jigsaw puzzles.

When a jigsaw puzzle is taken apart and put back in the box, the picture is gone. That's somewhat like the nature of humanity. Though made up of different entities, people are an organic unity. "The Lord God formed man of the dust of the ground, and breathed into his nostrils the breath of life; and man became a living being" (Genesis 2:7).

The words for "living being" are often translated as "living soul" and come from the Hebrew word *nephesh.* Used in this way, *nephesh* is not a part of a person—like an individual piece in a jigsaw puzzle—but is the whole person (Genesis 14:21).

Sometimes the expression "my soul" or "your soul" is simply referring to the pronoun "I" or "you." For example, "Many are they who say of me [*nephesh*], 'There is no help for him in God' " (Psalm 3:2). Other times *nephesh* refers to the desires or appetites of a person (Proverbs 23:2).

The Greek word *psuche* in the New Testament is similar to the word *nephesh* and is often translated as "life." It even refers to animal life (Revelation 16:3). It also can refer to the emotions, the mind, or the heart—and it can be destroyed (Matthew 10:28).

Like a jigsaw puzzle, when the breath of life separates from the body at death, the person is no longer. But thank God for the resurrection, when we will be restored to wholeness in Christ.

Apply It:

Assemble a jigsaw puzzle this week and remember how God has created you as a whole being.

Dig Deeper:

1 Samuel 19:5; Job 33:4; Luke 12:4

There's Something About You

"Let your light so shine before men, that they may see your good works and glorify your Father in heaven" (Matthew 5:16).

It's happened to all of us at least once, and perhaps more than once. We meet a person and say to ourselves, "You know—they're different. There's just *something* about them."

Obviously, a person whose life has been transformed by a saving encounter with Jesus will be different from what they were before. That's part of what salvation is all about. But what is it that makes us notice a personality in the first place? If, as the evolutionists claim, we're just the result of millions of years of gradual change, what makes a person different than an ocelot or a sloth?

Well, we know the answer: God created man from the dust of the earth and breathed into him the breath of life. That's how man "became a living soul" (Genesis 2:7), and the Hebrew word for that "soul" is *nephesh*, which can also be interpreted to mean personality.

However, a personality wasn't the only thing God gave to Adam, the first man—and to each one of us. God also gave us a *ruach*, as the Hebrew puts it, or a spirit, the "spark of life." *Ruach* is a word with many meanings: Its most common use in the Bible is for "breath" or "wind" or "spirit." But it also has been translated as "courage" (Joshua 2:11) or "strength" (Judges 15:19 NASB). It's a component of that special something that makes us unique and which can impress others for good or for bad.

Yes, there is *something* about you. "Having your conduct honorable among the Gentiles, that when they speak against you as evildoers, they may, by your good works which they observe, glorify God in the day of visitation" (1 Peter 2:12). Let that *something* shine before others so that they may also know they have a loving heavenly Father who has created them with unique characteristics to be used for His glory.

Apply It:

Keep your life in harmony with Jesus and His teachings, so that others will not only see "something" in you, but will also be drawn to the One who put it there!

Dig Deeper:

Genesis 8:1; Ecclesiastes 12:7; Ezekiel 11:19

Rejoicing for Health

"Mary said: 'My soul magnifies the Lord, and my spirit has rejoiced in God my Savior' " (Luke 1:46, 47).

Researchers have begun to use the word "cyberchondria" to refer to an unhealthy obsession with self-diagnosis on the Internet. Self-induced health problems caused by anxiety about sicknesses have been around long before the Internet. However, chronic worriers now have 24-hour access to myriads of health problem descriptions. While the disorder remains controversial, it is clear that the mind can affect the body—and vice versa.

The Bible's description of the unity of humans can be seen by the way that words such as "spirit" and "soul" are used interchangeably. Paul associates the spirit as the part of the human mind that connects with God: "The Spirit Himself bears witness with our spirit that we are children of God" (Romans 8:16). When Mary sang after she was told she would give birth to Jesus, she used the terms "spirit" and "soul" interchangeably—suggesting their close unity.

The body, likewise, plays an integral part in the description of humans: "May the God of peace Himself sanctify you completely; and may your whole spirit, soul, and body be preserved blameless at the coming of our Lord Jesus Christ" (1 Thessalonians 5:23). Although this is the only three-part description of a human in the whole Bible, it reveals that even though there is a part of us that primarily connects with God, our entire being was designed to be made holy by His presence.

With this unity in mind, people have the opportunity to seek for an enriched intellectual life in order to have healthier bodies and a cultivated connection with God in order to find wisdom for life. The reverse is also true: Attention to bodily health can improve our connection with God and our ability to learn. John puts both of them beautifully together in a greeting to the church: "Beloved, I pray that you may prosper in all things and be in health, just as your soul prospers" (3 John 2).

Apply It:

List ten things for which you are thankful.

Dig Deeper:

1 Corinthians 7:34; Romans 12:1, 2; Proverbs 17:22

In His Image

"As we have borne the image of the man of dust, we shall also bear the image of the heavenly Man" (1 Corinthians 15:49).

The oldest known camera photograph was taken by Joseph Nicéphore Niépce, a French inventor. *View from the Window at Le Gras,* a somewhat blurry image, was taken in 1826. But as early as 1816, he was making negative photographs of camera images on paper coated with silver chloride. But Niépce couldn't figure out how to adequately "fix" them to keep them from darkening completely when exposed to light.

The first surviving photograph of a human was taken by Louis Daguerre in 1838. His *Boulevard du Temple* was a candid shot of a busy street in Paris, but the long exposure time made the moving traffic invisible. What can be seen is a distant figure standing on a sidewalk having his boots polished. The man stood motionless long enough to have his image captured.

Wouldn't it be amazing to capture the image of God in a photograph? After all, if humans are made in God's image, doesn't the Lord have physical features? Of course, if God is a spirit, then wouldn't this be impossible? Moses, Aaron, Nadab, Abihu, and seventy elders saw God's feet (Exodus 24:9–11). Moses also saw God's back (Exodus 33:20–23), and Daniel saw a vision of a judgment scene with the Ancient of Days seated on a throne (Daniel 7:9, 10).

The apostle Paul describes Christ as "the image of the invisible God" (Colossians 1:15). Though the Lord is above all that we can picture, the Bible tells us that God is a personal being. We may know this because humans were created in the image of God.

But even more important, people were created "upright" (Ecclesiastes 7:29) and in the *moral* image of God. Humans were given the freedom to love and obey the Lord, or to disobey and distrust God. Adam chose to turn from the Creator and so lost the beautiful image of God in his character. By looking to Jesus, people may regain the quality of being like God (2 Corinthians 3:18)—a quality that cannot be captured on photographic paper, but only in the heart.

Apply It:

Study some paintings of Jesus. What *character* qualities do you see revealed in these images?

Dig Deeper:

Genesis 1:27; Romans 8:29; Hebrews 1:3

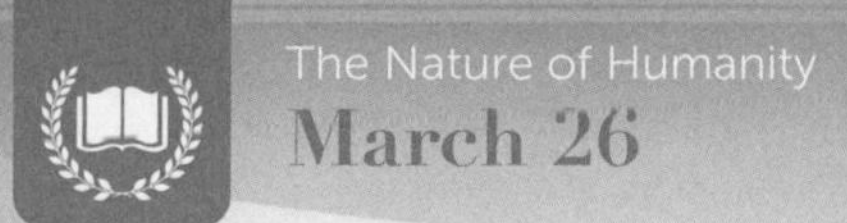

Created for Fellowship

"It is not good that man should be alone" (Genesis 2:18).

Being alone too much can cause physical and psychological harm. It can warp our minds—giving us a distorted view of reality. The late Italian sociologist Maurizio Montalbini proved this when, beginning in December of 1992, he conducted his lengthiest isolation experiment in an underground cave in Pesaro, Italy. During this time, he would double the length on his cycles of sleeping and waking. When he finally emerged from the cave, he fully believed only six months had passed and was startled to discover it had been a year. But the isolation affected more than just his mind. His immune system dropped to the lowest possible level, and he faced a difficult recovery.

While sometimes we need a little "alone time," God created us to interact with each other on a regular basis through friendship, marriage, and families. Our relationships with others, when based on genuine caring, will strengthen our minds and bodies and ward off discouragement.

King Solomon described some of the benefits of true friendship: "Two are better than one. ... For if they fall, one will lift up his companion. But woe to him who is alone when he falls, for he has no one to help him up. Though one may be overpowered by another, two can withstand him. And a threefold cord is not quickly broken" (Ecclesiastes 4:9–12).

We all need support, not only from God, but also from our fellow humans. The Scriptures wisely advise us to "encourage one another and build each other up" (1 Thessalonians 5:11 NIV).

God is a social Being; there is loving interaction between the members of the Godhead and loving interaction with His creatures. Likewise, Jesus asks us to "love one another" (John 13:34). To truly reflect God's character, unselfish love from above must be the driving force in every relationship of our lives. Then we will be fulfilling our purpose and glorifying our Creator who made us to be social beings in His image.

Apply It:

Is God included in your relationships? Have you asked Him to be at the center of your marriage and every friendship?

Dig Deeper:

Philippians 2:4; Proverbs 17:17; Romans 13:8

The Origin of Blindness

"Whose minds the god of this age has blinded, who do not believe, lest the light of the gospel of the glory of Christ, who is the image of God, should shine on them" (2 Corinthians 4:4).

You can't always trust your eyes. If you don't believe it, just study "White's illusion." This brightness illusion happens when horizontal stripes of black and white are partially replaced with gray rectangles. When the gray blocks are bordered by black, they appear darker than the gray blocks bordered by white—even though both sets of gray bars are the same color and opacity. The "Munker's-White illusion" is similar, except it uses color for the same effect.

Eve was deceived by her senses. When Satan appeared to her in the Tree of Knowledge of Good and Evil—a tree God told her to not eat from—she was drawn into a conversation with the devil who was disguised as a serpent. When she repeated God's word, "You shall not eat it, nor shall you touch it, lest you die" (Genesis 3:3), the devil lied to her by saying, "You will not surely die" (v. 4).

Satan then painted an illusion for Eve, claiming that "God knows that in the day you eat of it your eyes will be opened, and you will be like God, knowing good and evil" (v. 5). Eve began to doubt God's word and she became blind. Notice, "When the woman *saw* that the tree was good for food, that it was pleasant to the *eyes*, and a tree desirable to make one wise, she took of its fruit and ate. She also gave to her husband with her, and he ate" (v. 6, emphasis added).

The Bible describes what happened next: "The eyes of both of them were opened, and they knew that they were naked; and they sewed fig leaves together and made themselves coverings" (v. 7). In one sense, sin *closed* their eyes and made them less perceptive of truth. Yes, they now knew sin, but at the expense of having their senses dulled. It was all part of Satan's illusion.

Apply It:

Look up "White's illusion" on the Internet and see how your eyes can deceive you.

Dig Deeper:

Matthew 15:14; John 9:39; 1 John 2:10

Shame Stopper

"If we say that we have no sin, we deceive ourselves, and the truth is not in us" (1 John 1:8).

Although psychologists have found links between shame and eating disorders, addiction, violence, bullying, aggression, and depression, they also offer hope. It turns out that speaking about our shame and differentiating it from our guilt are powerful ways to reduce its destructive power.

The Bible says something similar, but it provides a much more definite and permanent solution to shame. First, the Bible shows that our tendency to sin is the result of sin: "Just as through one man sin entered the world, and death through sin, and thus death spread to all men, because all sinned" (Romans 5:12).

While we may sometimes feel shame even though we didn't do anything wrong, the usual source of our shame, or the feeling that we are flawed, is the breaking of God's law. But we know that God's plan to permanently remove all sin from our lives will also eradicate all of our shame. (See Philippians 3:19.)

Furthermore, even if we have committed sin and feel guilty because of it, we can rejoice that we are not alone in this struggle. Jesus assures us, "I am the vine, you are the branches. He who abides in Me, and I in him, bears much fruit; for without Me you can do nothing" (John 15:5). Sin in our lives can be defeated only when we seek to obey God by being in union with Him and not by our own power.

Abiding in Jesus includes the privilege to pray to Him, verbalizing our discouragement with who we think we are. In these moments, we can also remember that He does not condemn us. Additionally, even when we have wronged Him through our actions, we can run to Him for help in resisting the next temptation. The fact that sin has infected all humans means that everyone we know is facing the same challenge and has the same offer of hope from God.

Apply It:

Tell God about your struggle with shame.

Dig Deeper:

Genesis 3:14; Jeremiah 17:9; Ephesians 2:3

Your Mission Control Center

"A good man out of the good treasure of his heart brings forth good; and an evil man out of the evil treasure of his heart brings forth evil. For out of the abundance of the heart his mouth speaks" (Luke 6:45).

When Neil Armstrong spoke those famous words on July 20, 1969, "Houston, Tranquility Base here. The Eagle has landed," the world was watching the outcome of Apollo 11, the first lunar landing in history. But one group was especially focused on every detail of this historic event—the employees in NASA's Mission Control Center. Charlie Duke, the capsule commentator responded, "Roger, Tranquility. We copy you on the ground. You've got a bunch of guys about to turn blue. We're breathing again. Thanks a lot."

The Mission Control Center, located in Houston, monitored nine Gemini and all Apollo lunar missions, including the Apollo 11 trip to the moon and the last Apollo 17 voyage. The center is housed in Building 30 of the Johnson Space Center. From this room, the NASA team exercised full control of Apollo 11 from liftoff to splashdown.

Just as the Mission Control Center directed all the lunar mission operations, so the human mind and heart are the control center for each person. Solomon states, "Keep your heart with all diligence, for out of it spring the issues of life" (Proverbs 4:23). Sadly, since "all have sinned and fall short of the glory of God" (Romans 3:23), the heart has become the control center for sin in the life.

Jesus explained, "Not what goes into the mouth defiles a man; but what comes out of the mouth, this defiles a man. ... For out of the heart proceed evil thoughts, murders, adulteries, fornications, thefts, false witness, blasphemies" (Matthew 15:11, 19).

The operations of the whole person—the intellect, will, affections, emotions, body—are influenced by the mind and heart. And when we have given control over to Satan, then sin rules the life. That is why we need to follow God's call: "Cast away from you all the transgressions which you have committed, and get yourselves a new heart and a new spirit" (Ezekiel 18:31).

Apply It:

Invite Jesus to take command of your mind and heart today.

Dig Deeper:

Jeremiah 17:9, 10; Psalm 51:10; Ezekiel 36:26

It Only Takes a Spark

"The tongue is a little member and boasts great things. See how great a forest a little fire kindles!" (James 3:5).

It's a legend, but the story seems to be just too good to fade away: A cow in the barn of a Mrs. O'Leary kicked over a lantern, and the spark from that flame started the Great Chicago Fire of 1871. As many as 300 people died, more than 100,000 were left homeless, and approximately 3.3 square miles of the city were reduced to rubble.

Whether it was a barn in the alley behind what was then DeKoven Street or not, we know that *something* sparked that fire in Chicago, and we know that a combination of drought, wood-based construction, high winds, and a fire department skeletal crew—only 17 horse-drawn steam engines for a whole city—helped to propel the destruction.

How does that incident relate to the effects of sin? In the same way that a spark set Chicago ablaze, the very first sin—eating the "forbidden fruit" by our first parents—echoed down the millennia, from one generation to the next, multiplying even more quickly and permanently than did that fire.

The Puritan writer Benjamin Harris, in his 1690 *New England Primer*, summarized it well: "In Adam's fall, we sinned all." That taught a basic theological concept to generations of youngsters, and it's true today: Because of Adam's sin, we have a propensity, a leaning, to commit sin ourselves. The little "spark" of Adam's sin ignited a fire that still consumes today. And even for committed Christians, repeated practice of sin can ignite an inferno of consequences.

The remedy is not to walk around with a fire extinguisher. Instead, we must internalize the truth. "Let this mind be in you which was also in Christ Jesus" (Philippians 2:5). By staying close to Jesus in prayer and in practice, we can call on His help when tempted to play with fire!

Apply It:

Remember that our disposition toward sin isn't only our fault—we inherited it from Adam. But remember, too, that God will supply "the way of escape" from every temptation if we call on Him!

Dig Deeper:

Genesis 4:8, 23; 6:1–5, 11–13; 1 Corinthians 10:13

The Myth Maker

"The word of the LORD is right, and all His work is done in truth" (Psalm 33:4).

He is lauded as an American hero and a great symbol for immigrants escaping the restrictive land of despots. But historians recognize that Christopher Columbus became an icon not by lifting himself up, but by being elevated in the eyes of those who needed a discoverer who faced the unknown sea and triumphed over the dangers of a wilderness.

Washington Irving popularized Columbus through a biography written in 1829, which was more romance than fact. Columbus wasn't interested in establishing the land of the free and the home of the brave as much as moving forward European imperialism and advancing the economy of Spain. Many now believe he spearheaded a massive slave trade and brought disease and warfare that decimated thousands of natives.

The Creation narratives in Genesis are viewed by many as mythology or allegory. Evolutionists claim that science reveals that the idea of our world being created in six days is impossible. Even some Christians try to wed evolution with Creation, claiming that God started some forms of life and then let them evolve.

But these popular views do not square with Scripture. As much as some scientists want to make Darwin an icon of how our world was created, the Bible strips away these views and gives us the truth. "In six days the LORD made the heavens and the earth, the sea, and all that is in them" (Exodus 20:11).

The Word of God rejects a mythical interpretation of Genesis. Job speaks of the transgressions of a real person named Adam (Job 31:33). Solomon affirms that man was created "upright" in the beginning (Ecclesiastes 7:29), not bent over as some lower form of life. Jesus plainly speaks of the creation of mankind (Matthew 19:4, 5).

Ever since Creation, Satan has sought to create a myth over the work of God and has confused many about the origins of humanity. But the student of the Bible knows that the devil "was a murderer from the beginning, and does not stand in the truth ... for he is a liar" (John 8:44).

■ Apply It:

Think of a childhood fairytale you once believed and later discovered was a myth.

■ Dig Deeper:

Isaiah 42:5; 2 Corinthians 11:3; Revelation 12:9

Transformed by Grace

"We all ... beholding as in a mirror the glory of the Lord, are being transformed into the same image" (2 Corinthians 3:18).

Justus von Liebig, a German chemist, invented the first silvered mirrors in 1835. And humans have gotten a clearer picture of themselves ever since. Typical mirrors provide a reversed and flat image, giving a somewhat distorted impression. But a new form of reflection called True Mirror—made with two mirrors joined at a 90-degree angle—gives people a three-dimensional image of themselves as they appear to others. Some people find it intimidating to discover that much detail about their appearance, while others find it entertaining.

Mirrors serve important roles in our culture, but the most useful mirror in the universe is the spiritual mirror that focuses our eyes on Jesus and transforms us into His likeness through the power of His Spirit. He invites us to "be transformed by the renewing of your mind" (Romans 12:2). This is only possible through the New Covenant.

Did you know that God established the covenant to save us even before we were created? (See 1 Corinthians 2:7; 2 Timothy 1:9; and Titus 1:2.) At that time, the Godhead agreed that Jesus would step in and bear our punishment, allowing us to freely receive forgiveness and eternal life. After humanity fell, this plan was revealed to Adam and Eve but, sadly, God's chosen people eventually distorted the covenant of grace into a miserable, futile covenant of works.

The New Covenant, sometimes referred to as "a better covenant," is really God's perfect original covenant without the distortions humans placed on it. Jesus has already confirmed the covenant of grace by His death, resurrection, and intercession for us. "Jesus has become a surety of a better covenant" (Hebrews 7:22).

Through the New Covenant, we may choose to be forgiven and adopted. "Behold what manner of love the Father has bestowed on us, that we should be called children of God!" (1 John 3:1). And after receiving His grace, we can have victorious new lives by keeping our eyes focused on the transforming image of Christ.

Apply It:

Look at yourself in a mirror and remind yourself aloud that you are a child of God.

Dig Deeper:

1 Peter 1:20, 21; Luke 22:20; Hebrews 8:6–13

The Great Controversy

8

The First Rebellion

"War broke out in heaven: Michael and his angels fought with the dragon; and the dragon and his angels fought, but they did not prevail" (Revelation 12:7, 8).

A rebellion is open resistance against the orders of an established authority. The word "rebellion" comes from the Latin verb *re* ("again") and *bellō* ("I wage war"). A rebel is an individual who takes part in a rebellion, usually motivated by feelings of indignation over a situation. While rebellions can sometimes try to evade a power, a revolt seeks to overthrow it.

Sometimes rebellions succeed; sometimes they don't. In 1838, the Cherokees refused to be moved by the U.S. government and stood their ground. Federal troops destroyed their homes and forced them to move west. Over four thousand Cherokees died from the journey of disease and starvation. Their pathway away from home is known as the Trail of Tears.

But the greatest rebellion in the universe took place when Lucifer, an angel who served next to God, decided that he wanted to take the place of God. The Bible explains, "How you are fallen from heaven, O Lucifer, son of the morning! How you are cut down to the ground, you who weakened the nations!" (Isaiah 14:12).

This fallen angel was originally created perfect: "You were the seal of perfection, full of wisdom and perfect in beauty" (Ezekiel 28:12). But something changed within his mind. "Your heart was lifted up because of your beauty; you corrupted your wisdom for the sake of your splendor" (v. 17).

Lucifer didn't want to be *like* God; he wanted to take the place of God. "You have said in your heart: 'I will ascend into heaven, I will exalt my throne above the stars of God" (Isaiah 14:13). Lucifer rebelled against the government of heaven. It was his first step in becoming Satan, the adversary.

The devil's rebellion turned into a revolt. His discontent and disloyalty grew until "war broke out in heaven" (Revelation 12:7). Sadly, a third of the angels joined him and he was cast out of heaven (v. 4). As we'll see, this rebellion appeared to succeed on the earth, but in the end it will end up as a trail of tears for those who join him.

Apply It:

Can you think of a time in your life when you rebelled against an authority?

Dig Deeper:

Isaiah 14:12–17; Ezekiel 28:1–19; Revelation 12:7–12

They Were Conned!

"The serpent was more cunning than any beast of the field which the Lord God had made. And he said to the woman, 'Has God indeed said, "You shall not eat of every tree of the garden"?' " (Genesis 3:1).

Today, Frank Abagnale is a security consultant who lives in South Carolina. But nearly sixty years ago, as a young adult, he pulled off one "con" after another, convincing people he was an airline pilot, a teaching assistant, a physician, even an attorney—when he was, actually, none of these.

He once said, "When people write about me, they usually start off with the headline 'World's Greatest Con Man.' " But after doing time in prisons in three countries, including the United States, Abagnale realized that a life of honesty was better.

While Abagnale pulled off some amazing cons, another figure in history deserves the title of "World's Greatest Con Artist." Satan, in the guise of a talking serpent, convinced Eve that she could partake of something God prohibited and still be okay (Genesis 3:4). She then persuaded Adam (v. 6), and it was in this act that all of humanity lost not only their innocence, but also eternal life (v. 22).

Convincing humans to disobey God required a con far greater than anything Abagnale ever attempted. In describing Satan through the image of the King of Tyre, the Bible says, "By the abundance of your trading you became filled with violence within" (Ezekiel 28:16). The word "trading" is best understood as one who goes about trading evil words. The devil was a slanderer who accused God of injustice.

Eve believed Satan's ploy and disobeyed God's restriction. After that, the downward spiral was assured, culminating in an expulsion from paradise and the introduction of death into the world.

This con gave Satan the audacity to claim to be "ruler of this world" (John 14:30), the world God had wanted Adam and Eve to have dominion over. It changed the course of human history and necessitated the sacrifice of Jesus to redeem a fallen humanity.

Apply It:

Con artists generally succeed because people *want* to trust others. When someone offers something too good to be true, consider the offer and ask God to guide your steps!

Dig Deeper:

Genesis 3:1–7; Proverbs 12:22; Galatians 6:7, 8

Recovery Prediction

"The waters prevailed and greatly increased on the earth, and the ark moved about on the surface of the waters" (Genesis 7:18).

David Abramson, a researcher at the University of New York, has been conducting a long-term study on the survivors of Hurricane Katrina. Abramson's team have surveyed families ever since the storm hit in 2005. They have been looking for ways to predict resiliency among survivors. They have identified that those who are religious believe that they could withstand stressors—and those who had a household income of at least $20,000 were more likely to recover from the storm.

The greatest storm that ever hit the earth took place as a result of human wickedness. When the battle between Christ and Satan moved to our world and humans chose to listen to Satan rather than God, our tendency for evil ignited. The Flood was a response to a pinnacle of moral deterioration and misery: "Then the Lord saw that the wickedness of man was great in the earth, and that every intent of the thoughts of his heart was only evil continually" (Genesis 6:5).

This was only one of many instances in the Bible where God had to intervene to stop the complete corruption of humans as a result of the entrance of sin, through Satan, and the continued activity of God's spiritual enemies upon this planet (vv. 6–8). Eventually, one part of the world would reach another pinnacle of corruption in their crucifixion of Jesus.

Despite these results, God kept His covenant prediction with Abraham, which stated: "I will bless those who bless you, and I will curse him who curses you; and in you all the families of the earth shall be blessed" (Genesis 12:3). Abraham's descendent, Jesus, became the hope of recovery for the planet. It was by His death that the blessing of salvation from sin and Satan began to work. Although the effects of the battle have taken a toll, the recovery has begun.

Apply It:

Talk to someone who has survived a major trauma.

Dig Deeper:

Genesis 3:15; Genesis 4:8; Genesis 22:15–18

A Cosmic Theater

"God has displayed us ... for we have been made a spectacle to the world, both to angels and to men" (1 Corinthians 4:9).

Modern theater can be traced back to the 6th century in Greece; it grew out of a religious ceremony where fifty men chanted a choral song to the god Dionysus. In 534 BC, Thespis of Attica was the first person to speak individual lines to this song. He soon added narration and acted out dramatic episodes. He was so influential that we still call actors Thespians.

Ancient Greek audiences stamped their feet to show appreciation to actors. Greek actors used large masks so that people farthest away could identify each character and what that character was feeling. The masks were built with a megaphone-style mouth piece to help amplify the actors' voices.

The largest acting stage in the universe is earth, and the cast is made up of all humanity. We have been "made a spectacle [literally 'theater'] to the world." The book of Job gives us a glimpse into this cosmic play when the sons of God came before the Lord and Satan joined them. When the Lord asked Satan, "From where do you come?" (Job 1:7), he answered, "From going to and fro on the earth, and from walking back and forth on it."

This heavenly convocation reveals insight into a great battle taking place between good and evil. (See Ephesians 6:12.) Our planet is the stage on which a great struggle is occurring between Christ and Satan for the hearts of people. The life of Job dramatically displays this drama over humanity, which is observed by the beings of other worlds.

When sin broke the relationship between God and humanity (Isaiah 59:2), Jesus came to earth to win back the hearts of His Creation. At center stage between the life and resurrection of Jesus is the death of Christ on Calvary—the main act that will bring an end to this universal conflict.

Apply It:

What part do you play in this great conflict between good and evil?

Dig Deeper:

Job 1:6–12; 2:1–10; Hebrews 10:32, 33; 1 Peter 5:8

The Lawless Planet

"The works of His hands are verity and justice; all His precepts are sure. They stand fast forever and ever, and are done in truth and uprightness" (Psalm 111:7, 8).

It's been called the meanest town in the west. Canyon Diablo was a lawless and violent railroad community in Arizona that sprang up in 1880, when workers laying tracks for a railroad came to the edge of a canyon. Materials for a bridge were the wrong length and shipment delays led to the growth of a community of about two thousand people. Most were railroad workers, but it soon collected outlaws, gamblers, and prostitutes.

At first Canyon Diablo had no lawmen, so gun duels, shootouts, and robberies were common. Main Street was called "Hell Street"—and with fourteen saloons, ten gambling houses, four brothels, and two dance halls, it lived up to its name. Boot Hill cemetery on the edge of town quickly filled with 35 residents, all who were killed in violence. When the railroad bridge was finally completed, the town quickly disappeared.

Earth could be called the meanest planet in the universe. This one rebellious world has turned away from God's moral law. When sin entered—"sin is lawlessness" (1 John 3:4)—people disobeyed the law and brought moral ruin and death.

Satan has not only blamed God for the lawlessness in our world, but he also tempted Christ to break God's law. In the three wilderness temptations, Jesus refused to disobey the commandments of heaven and used Scripture as a powerful weapon. Jesus said, "Man shall not live by bread alone, but by every word that proceeds from the mouth of God" (Matthew 4:4).

In the great duel between good and evil, Satan claims that God's law cannot be kept and that it restricts freedom. But Christ perfectly obeyed God's law (John 15:10) and died on the cross to save law-breakers. His violent death built a bridge from heaven to earth (Genesis 28:12; John 1:51) so that if we accept His atonement for our sins, we can walk away from this mean and broken world.

Apply It:

For which laws in your local community are you most grateful?

Dig Deeper:

Matthew 24:12; Romans 6:19; 2 Thessalonians 2: 7–10

Showdown at Calvary

"Now is the judgment of this world; now the ruler of this world will be cast out" (John 12:31).

Just as he had with Adam and Eve, Satan believed he had Jesus where he wanted Him. After Christ's three years of miracles, preaching, and teaching throughout Israel, religious leaders and the public had largely turned against the Nazarene. The crowds who days earlier welcomed Jesus into Jerusalem with palm fronds and shouts of "Hosanna!" had called out for His blood to be shed (Matthew 27:25).

The Romans weren't all that concerned with Jesus until the people had been stirred up. Provincial officials, worried about keeping order to placate Caesar, heeded the calls of the mob and ordered Jesus' execution. It would be by one of the most agonizing deaths known to that world: death by crucifixion.

What no one knew—not the disciples, not the Pharisees, not the Romans, and certainly not the baying crowd—was that this had all been anticipated in the courts of heaven millennia before. Jesus may have been captured by Roman guards and sentenced by a Roman official, but in actuality, He was prepared to lay down His life to save those willing to trust in His sacrifice (John 10:15)—even those who beat Him, mocked Him, and drove the nails into His hands and feet (Luke 23:34).

Satan thought he'd figured it all out. Stir up the masses, sway corrupt officials more concerned about self-preservation than honest justice, and create a horrific execution. But at the cross, at Calvary, Jesus had the final say: The "ruler of this world" would be "cast out" by a sacrifice that, when accepted, would erase the devil's charges against any human, anywhere, any time.

Jesus' obedience and sacrifice obliterated Satan's scheming. His death can equally wipe away your sins, too, if you're willing to trust Him.

■ Apply It:

No matter how challenging a situation is, remember that Jesus conquered the absolute worst and that His victory is available to you today.

■ Dig Deeper:

John 11:45–54; Matthew 26:63, 64; John 12:27–36

April 8

Who Is Jesus?

"Jesus said to him, 'I am the way, the truth, and the life. No one comes to the Father except through Me' " (John 14:6).

Recently the American Bible Society came under criticism for placing restrictions on the .bible domain for Internet addresses. After purchasing the rights to all websites that would have .bible as their ending, the Society created guidelines that would prevent secular and non-Christian religions from expressing disrespect for the Bible using the .bible domain.

What is clear from this debate is that those who have faith in the Bible as the Word of God have felt the threat of those who would ridicule the Bible as being just a book of fiction. This tension is another reflection of the battle over the identity of Jesus. After all, when the Bible is doubted, the identity of Jesus also comes under question.

This is because the Bible is primarily about who Jesus is. In speaking of the Old Testament, Jesus said: "You search the Scriptures, for in them you think you have eternal life; and these are they which testify of Me" (John 5:39). The New Testament, on the other hand, is obviously about Jesus. Therefore, the battle over the reliability of the Bible is also an extension of the battle over the identity of Jesus.

The identity of Jesus is not only crucial for salvation, but it's also necessary for understanding all truth. When Christ claimed that He is the truth, He was saying that we cannot truly understand anything apart from Him. The apostle Paul, who wrote a large part of the New Testament, affirms how "the truth is in Jesus" (Ephesians 4:21). Therefore, the battle between Christ and Satan has repercussions in every area of knowledge insofar as we cannot truly know something without it being true.

Apply It:

Where it is legally and socially acceptable, post a Bible verse in a conspicuous place.

Dig Deeper:

Matthew 16:13–17; Romans 1:20; Colossians 1:17

The True Center

"Nor is there salvation in any other, for there is no other name under heaven given among men by which we must be saved" (Acts 4:12).

It was a step in the right direction. When Renaissance mathematician and astronomer Nicolaus Copernicus suggested that the planets in our solar system do not revolve around the earth, but around the sun, it was revolutionary. Actually, the concept that the sun is the center of the universe (heliocentrism) can be traced back to Aristarchus of Samos, a Hellenistic writer from the third century BC.

Copernicus's system had several shortcomings, and it would take many later astronomers to fine-tune his model—including Tycho Brahe, Johannes Kepler, Galileo Galilei, and Isaac Newton. Kepler introduced the concept of elliptical orbits, and Galilei gave supporting evidence through the use of the telescope. Galilei was also summoned to Rome in 1633 and put on trial for his beliefs.

Later astronomers, like William Herschel and Friedrich Bessel, demonstrated that the sun is not at the center of the universe. To be even more precise, the Bible teaches that Christ is the center of all things. "In the beginning was the Word, and the Word was with God, and the Word was God. He was in the beginning with God. All things were made through Him, and without Him nothing was made that was made. In Him was life, and the life was the light of men" (John 1:1–4).

The great controversy between Christ and Satan can be understood as a desire by the devil to push Jesus from the center and to make himself the focal point of the universe. The wilderness temptations of Christ bring this out when Satan suggested, "All these things I will give You if You will fall down and worship me" (Matthew 4:9).

While the devil would love for us to see the earth, humans, or even the church as the center of all things, only in Christ do we find the true focus of the universe.

Apply It:

Look up the word heliocentrism in an encyclopedia. Learn how this view shook some church leaders.

Dig Deeper:

Luke 24:25–27; Ephesians 4:21; Revelation 1:8

Stay on Your Toes

"Be watchful, and strengthen the things which remain" (Revelation 3:2).

Today's Bible passage was written and read some two thousand years ago, since Christ first spoke this warning to the church at Sardis. Since we are near the close of history and the return of Jesus—the blessed hope which believers pray to see fulfilled—how much more these words do apply!

Until that great day arrives, the followers of Jesus need to be watchful and vigilant against evil. Just as a railroad train can be derailed by tracks that have been damaged through neglect or vandalism, our journey toward heaven can be thrown off when we succumb to evil.

The Bible often reminds us to keep watch: "Watch therefore, for you do not know what hour your Lord is coming" (Matthew 24:42). A Christian must keep an eye out for potential pitfalls and stumbling blocks along the way. Even though he was defeated at Calvary, Satan still wants to ensnare those who lose sight of the heavenly prize. This is why the Bible tells us, "Keep your heart with all diligence, for out of it spring the issues of life" (Proverbs 4:23).

Peter warns us, "Be sober, be vigilant; because your adversary the devil walks about like a roaring lion, seeking whom he may devour" (1 Peter 5:8). Today, we might use the phrase, "Stay on your toes." Those who are alert are less likely to be deceived than a person who assumes all is well and no dangers are lurking.

Of course, this isn't to suggest we should walk around in a state of paranoia, thinking everyone or everything is going to come against us. God loves the believer; His angels are there to help. But it's important to recognize the potential for evil to intrude and to take steps to guard against this. "Be watchful," Jesus said, and that command is as valid for us today as it was in Sardis those many years ago.

Apply It:

By believing in Jesus and following His commands, you've received an eternal future of happiness and joy. Protect that relationship as diligently as you would anything of great value.

Dig Deeper:

Psalm 24:8; Ephesians 6:13–15; Revelation 14:2

Hope in Suffering

"You have loved righteousness and hated lawlessness; therefore God, Your God, has anointed You with the oil of gladness more than Your companions" (Hebrews 1:9).

When civil war broke out in Syria and claimed the lives of hundreds of thousands of people, many organizations offered to help. But every volunteer can only work within the constraints of their supplies and physical energy. The need is often so great that volunteers express despair when they realize that they have reached their limit.

Amidst all of this suffering, it can be easy to forget that God is also appalled and pained by what His children are experiencing. At the tomb of a friend who died, the Bible says, "Jesus wept" (John 11:35). The Scriptures also state how Christ hates "lawlessness" (Hebrews 1:9), which is the cause of all suffering. Without a knowledge of the battle between Christ and Satan, we might think that God is responsible for suffering.

However, the Bible tells us that it is Satan who is responsible for sin and its resulting misery (Matthew 13:28). Jesus taught this truth through the parable of the wheat and the tares. He explained that those who follow Satan's ways are like the weeds that an enemy has planted in a wheat field. In the process of sharing this parable, Jesus explained, "The enemy who sowed them is the devil, the harvest is the end of the age, and the reapers are the angels" (v. 39).

Although it may be easy to blame the devil for the evil in the world, it is not as easy to suffer with those who are experiencing pain. Yet this is precisely why Jesus' death was a clear demonstration of genuine suffering. While many call for justice now, Christ asks them to wait for the harvest: "He said, 'No, lest while you gather up the tares you also uproot the wheat with them' " (Matthew 13:29). The harvest is the hope of justice from a God who showed His love through suffering.

Apply It:

Pray for someone who is suffering today.

Dig Deeper:

Revelation 21:4; Philippians 2:5–11; Luke 18:7

Where are You?

"This You have seen, O LORD; do not keep silence. O LORD, do not be far from me" (Psalm 35:22).

One of the most damaging communication styles in a marriage is "stonewalling." This happens when your spouse withdraws from the conversation and ignores you. When your husband or wife shuts you down by closing himself or herself off from you, it puts your relationship in a deep freeze. Even if you argue loudly, it's better than completely avoiding your spouse because when your interaction drops to zero, there's no way to move forward.

The next time you're having a challenging conversation with your spouse or significant other, reflect on how you respond or don't respond. Do you attack and then withdraw? Do you lean forward and respond? Do you criticize and then ignore their point of view? By God's grace, don't fall into the habit of walking away—unless you need a little time to cool off. Push yourself to eliminate unkind words or blame and learn to listen with empathy.

Even though God commanded Adam and Eve to stay away from the Tree of Knowledge of Good and Evil, they chose to disobey. The Lord could have thrown up His hands and said, "Fine. Have it your way," and then walked away. But love for the human race—a race that had now stepped into a great battle between good and evil—drove God forward. "The LORD God called to Adam and said to him, 'Where are you?' " (Genesis 3:9).

God's involvement in the mess created by Adam and Eve displays His loving concern for our world. "God so loved the world that He gave His only begotten Son, that whoever believes in Him should not perish but have everlasting life" (John 3:16). The Holy Spirit was sent after Christ returned to heaven so that we would not be left alone as orphans (John 14:16). Even angels from heaven "minister for those who will inherit salvation" (Hebrews 1:14).

In the end, God will not stonewall the sin problem and will ultimately bring it to an end. It is written, "Death is swallowed up in victory" (1 Corinthians 15:54).

Apply It:

If you heard the voice of God ask you, "Where are you?" how would you respond?

Dig Deeper:

Genesis 3:6–19; John 15:13; Romans 5:8

The Life, Death, and Resurrection of Christ

9

April 13

A Unique Blend

"Mercy and truth have met together; righteousness and peace have kissed" (Psalm 85:10).

It's the name of a construction company. One article uses this phrase to describe the combination of elements on earth that make life possible. A vintage antiques store has this name—as does a wedding shop, a coffee company, a bed and breakfast, a software package, and a lecture on the leadership skills of Winston Churchill. People seem to like the expression *a unique blend.*

When it comes to describing the divine attributes of the Godhead, Jesus has blended seemingly divergent elements into a view of God that powerfully brings salvation to our world. We know the Bible verse well: "God is love" (1 John 4:8). But we sometimes struggle to connect love and justice, mercy and truth, peace and righteousness. It can appear like trying to stir together water and wax.

From a human perspective, when a person does wrong, the proper response is to carry out the law and make things right. If a criminal is let off the hook, they'll go back and commit more evil acts. The best approach is to carry out natural consequences and bring down the law ... hard. But God took a different tactic that uniquely blended the fulfillment of the law with compassion.

In the life, death, and resurrection of Christ, the combination of God's love and justice is perfectly offered to our fallen planet. "God so loved the world that He gave His only begotten Son, that whoever believes in Him should not perish but have everlasting life" (John 3:16). Because "the wages of sin is death" (Romans 6:23), we are all in a hopeless state since "all have sinned" (Romans 3:23). But the Lord gave the world an immeasurable present: "The gift of God is eternal life in Christ Jesus our Lord" (Romans 6:23).

God's character is a unique blend of grace and justice. Heaven has enacted a plan to bring salvation to sinful humanity whereby "the righteous requirements of the law" (Romans 2:26) have been satisfied in Christ. For "in Him we have redemption through His blood, the forgiveness of sins, according to the riches of His grace" (Ephesians 1:7).

Apply It:

Think of an illustration in the natural world where two opposites create a whole, such as opposing poles in a magnet.

Dig Deeper:

Exodus 34:6, 7; Isaiah 32:17; Romans 5:18, 19

God Hates Sin

"You, who once were alienated and enemies in your mind by wicked works, yet now He has reconciled" (Colossians 1:21).

Throughout North America, and in many other parts of the world, you might have heard of a so-called "church" that holds protests at funerals of military members killed in battle or victims of AIDS. These demonstrators carry profane signs declaring that God is opposed to this or that person or thing: "God Hates America" is one of the few declarations that has been seen printed.

The group's antics have been widely condemned by Christians and non-believers alike—although the Supreme Court of the United States, in an 8-to-1 vote, upheld their right to protest, no matter how obnoxious and offensive their message.

What God *really* hates, however, is not America. (He has His concerns about the nation, for sure.) Nor does He hate soldiers or people who have contracted a dreaded disease. God doesn't even "hate" sinners!

It's true: God hates *sin*, but He loves those humans who have rebelled against His way, and He desperately wants them to return to Him.

But sin? God's opposition to sin is clear: "You are of purer eyes than to behold evil, and cannot look on wickedness" (Habakkuk 1:13).

Rejecting God provokes Him to wrath, yes, but against the *rejection* and not against the person, whom He loves and wishes to bring to repentance. By embracing Jesus' sacrifice and following God's way, we can be reconciled to Him and escape the wrath designed for sin.

Apply It:

If you know someone who believes God doesn't like them, share the good news: God hates sin, not sinners!

Dig Deeper:

Hebrews 12:29; Romans 3:23; Ephesians 2:3

Responses Available

"That in the ages to come He might show the exceeding riches of His grace in His kindness toward us in Christ Jesus" (Ephesians 2:7).

Educators are concerned about the amount of time children spend in front of screens, from televisions to smartphones and tablets. This is because researchers have found that screen time elicits a biological response that is similar to encountering a danger in the real world. This response includes a faster heartbeat, unusual focus, and higher levels of blood sugar.

The life of Christ is the source of our response of faith and love to God. But unlike the negative effects of too much screen time, reflection on the life of Christ can give us both peace and incredible joy.

There may be times when we feel that we have to manufacture our religious feelings and decisions, but the Bible explains that even our reactions to God are initiated by Him. Although we can reject God's attempts to elicit positive responses from us, we all have the opportunity to let God's goodness lead us to Him. For the apostle Paul, this removes the opportunity for boasting or a sense of religious superiority: "I say, through the grace given to me, to everyone who is among you, not to think of himself more highly than he ought to think, but to think soberly, as God has dealt to each one a measure of faith" (Romans 12:3).

God uses the life of Christ to inspire faith in us because the gift of Jesus is the clearest revelation of God and His love: "The Word became flesh and dwelt among us, and we beheld His glory, the glory as of the only begotten of the Father, full of grace and truth" (John 1:14). Along with inspiring faith in God, the gift of Christ produces in our hearts a love and repentance from sin. When Christ died for us, we saw the culmination of a life of love and goodness.

Apply It:

Play an outdoor game with a child.

Dig Deeper:

Romans 2:4; 1 John 4:19; 1 Corinthians 1:30, 31

At One with God

"God was in Christ reconciling the world to Himself" (2 Corinthians 5:19).

"Hang him." That's the pressure General Douglas MacArthur faced from Washington over what to do with Japan's Emperor Hirohito for war crimes committed during World War II. But when MacArthur saw the total collapse of a nation that revered its divine leader, he concluded that revenge was not justice. Instead, he used his power of influence to walk down the path of reconciliation. History affirms that the rebuilding of this war-torn nation was a triumph.

When Adam and Eve sinned, God had every right to let them die, but instead He took the initiative to reconcile the world to Himself. The Lord did not walk away from Adam and Eve, but actually pursued them in the garden (Genesis 3:9). Sinners are reconciled to God, not God to sinners.

The plan to lead people back to God came through Jesus Christ. "If when we were enemies we were reconciled to God through the death of His Son, much more, having been reconciled, we shall be saved by His life" (Romans 5:10). The word "atonement" captures this coming together and means to be "at one" in a relationship that has been estranged.

Christ's gift to us goes beyond paying the penalty for our sins. Jesus certainly died as the "Lamb of God who takes away the sin of the world!" (John 1:29). The sanctuary service affirms the necessity of killing a sacrificial lamb. But it also reveals the intercessory ministry of Jesus in the heavenly sanctuary, where the benefits of His perfect sacrifice deepen our reconciliation with God.

Jesus' atonement was not only carried out for us, but transforms us from within to make us new in Christ. Reconciliation is not just a way to escape punishment, but to rebuild our lives into the image of our Creator. "Therefore, if anyone is in Christ, he is a new creation; old things have passed away; behold, all things have become new" (2 Corinthians 5:17).

■ Apply It:

Are you estranged from someone to whom you need to be reconciled? Pray for God's power to lead the way to peace.

■ Dig Deeper:

Leviticus 4:26; Ephesians 1:19–23; Hebrews 9:22

Justice at Calvary

"It is a joy for the just to do justice, but destruction will come to the workers of iniquity" (Proverbs 21:15).

He is known to have authored the worst single decision in the history of the U.S. Supreme Court—the pro-slavery *Dred Scott v. Sandford.* Chief Justice Roger Taney was at one time more moderate on the issue of slavery. As a young man, he called slavery a "blot on our national character." But in his old age, his views hardened; he believed men and women of African descent were inferior and had no rights. In truth, the *Dred Scott* decision was a blot on the nation's character.

Satan has attempted to leave a blot on God's character, claiming that the holy law cannot be kept and should be discarded. But Calvary proved otherwise. Christ's death affirmed the necessity of the law. The Bible teaches that God's commandments are heaven's eternal code of conduct. "The works of His hands are verity and justice; all His precepts are sure. They stand fast forever and ever, and are done in truth and uprightness" (Psalm 111:7, 8).

If humanity would be saved, the death of Christ was necessary in order for God to maintain His justice and righteousness. Through Jesus' perfect sacrifice, the Lord could be both just and merciful. Christ's death satisfied divine justice, and God was willing to accept it in the place of our death.

People may choose to reject the atoning blood of Jesus and not receive the forgiveness of their sins. In so doing, they become subjects of God's wrath against unrighteousness. "He who believes in the Son has everlasting life; and he who does not believe the Son shall not see life, but the wrath of God abides on him" (John 3:36).

Christ's atoning sacrifice for you was the single best decision in the history of the universe. Have you accepted Jesus as your Savior?

Apply It:

Can you think of one of the best judges in the history of the Bible?

Dig Deeper:

Deuteronomy 16:19; 1 Kings 10:9; Psalm 89:14

Twice Mine!

"Whom God set forth as a propitiation by His blood, through faith, to demonstrate His righteousness, because in His forbearance God had passed over the sins that were previously committed" (Romans 3:25).

The story is told of a boy who built a toy sailboat and lost it on a large lake in the heart of the big city. Weeks later, he saw the boat—his boat—in a shop window, but, despite his pleas to the owner, was required to scrape together every penny he had to purchase that which his own hands had made.

"Now you're twice mine," the boy said to the boat as he walked out of the store. "First, I made you, and then I paid to get you back!"

You can see the analogy, right? God made us, but sin put us in Satan's shop window. In order to reclaim fallen humanity, a price had to be paid for sin—the ultimate price, in fact, being the death of Jesus, God's only begotten Son, on a cross of shame.

God's righteousness had to be satisfied, but if God simply destroyed every sinner, there would be no one left. "There is none righteous, no, not one" (Romans 3:10).

The cost of redemption is beyond anything the human mind can imagine. Not only did Jesus have to come to earth as a human, He bore our sins and the required separation from God during an agonizing crucifixion. Think about it: Jesus, who spoke the world into existence—"by Him all things were created that are in heaven and that are on earth, visible and invisible" (Colossians 1:16)—had to die in order to redeem the humans He made.

Like that little boy, Jesus can say of those who follow Him, "First I made you, and then I paid to redeem you!" When a sinner receives Christ as their Savior, their sins are wiped out, their debt is paid. And the reward is far better than being back on a young boy's shelf!

Apply It:

Today, tell someone you know—or someone you've just met—that God loves them so much that He wants to call them "twice Mine."

Dig Deeper:

Exodus 29:18; Leviticus 1:9; Ephesians 5:2

April 19

Core Change

"All we like sheep have gone astray; we have turned, every one, to his own way; and the LORD has laid on Him the iniquity of us all" (Isaiah 53:6).

Going from blond to brunette has been called a health hazard due to the toxic chemicals involved in the process. Recently, however, scientists have been experimenting with a new material: graphene. This safer substance is processed into a gel and sprayed onto hair in order to provide a color change that lasts for 30 washes.

Unlike the superficial changes made by beauticians, Christ came to transform our sinful state by taking our sins upon Himself. Naturally, we could not change, and the sins we had already committed should have killed us. "Can the Ethiopian change his skin or the leopard its spots? Then may you also do good who are accustomed to do evil" (Jeremiah 13:23).

The Bible teaches that our sins—indeed, the sins of the "whole world" (1 John 2:2)—were transferred to Jesus. Isaiah expressed how God the Father would honor Jesus for taking the punishment for our law-breaking: "I will divide Him a portion with the great, and He shall divide the spoil with the strong, because He poured out His soul unto death, and He was numbered with the transgressors, and He bore the sin of many, and made intercession for the transgressors" (Isaiah 53:12).

Jesus never sinned in order to take our sins upon Himself. This is why Isaiah points out that He was being treated *like* a sinner, even though He committed no sin. As a result of His true innocence, He could take our sins and give us His innocence instead.

David realized this when he repented of his sins of adultery and murder; he prayed, "Create in me a clean heart, O God, and renew a steadfast spirit within me" (Psalm 51:10). In effect, he was believing that because of the right relation to God that the coming Messiah would have, David could receive forgiveness. By starting afresh, he could begin to live the beautiful way of life that the Messiah would live.

Apply It:

Respond with kindness to an unkind act directed toward you.

Dig Deeper:

Isaiah 53:10; Galatians 1:4; 1 Corinthians 15:3

Power in the Blood

"The life of the flesh is in the blood, and I have given it to you upon the altar to make atonement for your souls; for it is the blood that makes atonement for the soul" (Leviticus 17:11).

In 1628, the English physician William Harvey discovered the circulation of blood in the human body. Soon after this, the first-known blood transfusion was attempted. The first successful transfusion was accomplished by Richard Lower, who kept dogs alive by transfusing blood from other dogs.

An American physician, Philip Physick, performed the first human blood transfusion in 1795 but did not publish his work. James Blundell, a British obstetrician, successfully transfused human blood in 1818 to treat a postpartum hemorrhage. He used the patient's husband as a donor and saved the woman's life. Blood transfusions have come a long way since then, with the identification of blood types, the use of antibiotics to control infections during transfusions, the preservation of blood, and the creation of blood banks.

Blood played a central role in the sanctuary services established by God to atone for sin through the sacrifice of animals. In fact, Israel was instructed to no longer make blood sacrifices apart from the temple to other gods, otherwise "that man shall be cut off from among his people" (Leviticus 17:9). Blood represented life and was not even to be eaten (verse 10); if game was killed in the field, the blood was to be poured out on the ground and covered (verse 13).

The blood of the Old Testament ceremonies pointed forward to the sacrificial blood spilled by Christ on the cross. The Bible explains, "How much more shall the blood of Christ, who through the eternal Spirit offered Himself without spot to God, cleanse your conscience from dead works to serve the living God?" (Hebrews 9:14).

We are saved by the blood of Christ "whom God set forth as a propitiation by His blood, through faith, to demonstrate His righteousness" (Romans 3:25). Jesus blood satisfied the demands of the law so that we can live eternally.

Apply It:

Have you ever donated blood? Do you know someone whose life was saved by a blood transfusion?

Dig Deeper:

Matthew 26:28; John 6:53–58; 1 John 4:10

A Ransom for Many

"The Son of Man did not come to be served, but to serve, and to give His life a ransom for many" (Mark 10:45).

In July of 1941, Franciszek Gajowniczek, a Polish soldier who was imprisoned at the Auschwitz concentration camp, knew he was a dead man. In punishment for the escape of ten prisoners, the Nazi commandant picked out ten other prisoners who would be starved to death.

"My wife! My children!" was Gajowniczek's anguished cry. Then another prisoner, a Roman Catholic cleric named Maximillian Kolbe, stepped forward: "He has a family; let me take his place."

The commandant agreed and Kolbe, not Gajowniczek, eventually died. It's fascinating to know that Kolbe had never met Gajowniczek. His offer was truly selfless, and it was gratefully received.

After four more years of captivity, Gajowniczek was liberated. He was reunited with his wife, but his sons had been killed in a Soviet bombardment. For the rest of his life—another 50 years—the onetime soldier told everyone about the man who became his ransom.

But Gajowniczek is not the first person in human history to be spared a death sentence because someone else stepped up to take their place. The fact is, every person who has ever lived, and every person alive today, is under a death penalty, since "the wages of sin is death" (Romans 6:23).

Franciszek Gajowniczek did not deserve to die in a Nazi concentration camp. Neither did Maximillian Kolbe. Their confinement and Kolbe's death were due to cruel, inhuman, and criminal actions by a government determined to enforce its will.

By contrast, because everyone has sinned, and because death is the price that must be paid for sin, then Jesus' substitution for us is a truly grand, world-changing gesture. His once-for-all sacrifice guarantees us more than a few more decades of existence. It guarantees those who accept His sacrifice a life throughout eternity!

Apply It:

Let someone know today that, if they choose to believe, they've been redeemed because Jesus has taken their place.

Dig Deeper:

Galatians 3:10–13; Hosea 13:14; Titus 2:14

The Final Revolution

"You were not redeemed with corruptible things, like silver or gold, from your aimless conduct received by tradition from your fathers" (1 Peter 1:18).

Like many former Communist cities, Prague is a mixture of architecture and culture that retains some of the scars of the past. Travelers can see bland apartment buildings that have often been associated with Soviet-era politics. With the fall of Communism in the Czech Republic in 1989, the cultural icons of the past have moved into the Communism museum and antique shops.

Christ's death is accomplishing a transformation in this world on a much greater scale than any political shift. Jesus bought us back from the slavery of sin through His death. This means we can respond in loving service. In other words, by freeing us from another master we can choose to become servants in His kingdom.

The apostle Paul described it by warning against a casual attitude toward our new duty: "You were bought at a price; therefore glorify God in your body and in your spirit, which are God's" (1 Corinthians 6:20). Without the proper context, we might be tempted to think that having to serve a new master is not much better than having been in slavery to sin in the first place. However, it is important to remember that our new service is not burdensome.

In the writings of John, we find that even the heavenly songs involve rejoicing in the salvation we have received: "You are worthy to take the scroll, and to open its seals; for You were slain, and have redeemed us to God by Your blood out of every tribe and tongue and people and nation, and have made us kings and priests to our God; and we shall reign on the earth" (Revelation 5:9, 10). This song is a praise sung specifically for Jesus, in whose service we can find the greatest pleasure. Among other things, that service involves ruling this earth!

Apply It:

Volunteer to do a task you know you will enjoy.

Dig Deeper:

1 Corinthians 7:23; Romans 6:22; 1 Corinthians 6:19

From Death to Life

"As in Adam all die, even so in Christ all shall be made alive" (1 Corinthians 15:22).

Carl Ruse of the U.S. Air Force arrived at the Yokkaichi-Ishihara Sangyo labor camp in Nagoya, Japan, in September 1944. Captured by the Japanese over two years earlier, Ruse had been starved down to 80 pounds and had lost hope of surviving much longer. But then a fourteen-year-old Japanese boy who worked at the factory where Ruse was laboring began—at the risk of his own life—to smuggle food to the emaciated prisoner of war. It saved Ruse's life. A year later, the newly freed Ruse took food rations to the boy's family as a gift, and the boy gave him a small photo of himself. The memory of this boy's kindness made Ruse a better person throughout his life; he was devoid of the bitterness that gnawed at the hearts of so many POWs.

In a sense, we humans are all prisoners of war in the great conflict between good and evil. Due to the sad choice of our ancestor Adam, our enemy is able to enslave us, starve us spiritually, and destroy us. "Your adversary the devil walks about like a roaring lion, seeking whom he may devour" (1 Peter 5:8). Left to ourselves, we would have no hope.

But Jesus stepped in as the representative of all humanity and was willing to risk His life, and even to die, "that whoever believes in him should not perish" (John 3:16). Through His death and resurrection, we can receive spiritual food, forgiveness, and healing. Through His provision, we are rescued, reconciled to God, and given life that never ends.

Because of Adam's sin, we've inherited the rebellious tendency to turn away from God—the only One who can help us—and are headed for certain disaster. As the prophet Isaiah wrote, "All we like sheep have gone astray; we have turned, every one, to his own way" (Isaiah 53:6). But Jesus has the power to help us—if we choose—reverse our self-destructive path, point us in the right direction, and save us.

Apply It:

List three reasons you are thankful that Jesus is your representative.

Dig Deeper:

1 John 2:1, 2; Romans 5:18, 19; 1 Peter 3:18

Covered in Righteousness

"That He might present her to Himself a glorious church, not having spot or wrinkle or any such thing, but that she should be holy and without blemish" (Ephesians 5:27).

What's the most expensive piece of clothing you have ever purchased? Imagine buying your loved one an evening gown that costs $30 million. The Nightingale of Kuala Lumpur dress was designed by Faisol Abdullah in 2009. Studded with 750 diamonds, the red burgundy taffeta, chiffon, silk, and satin dress literally sparkles.

There's a far more expensive wedding garment that cost all of heaven, but it's being offered to you at no charge. This free gift came through the shed blood of Christ on Calvary. The robe of Jesus' perfect righteousness is necessary for you to enter the gates of heaven and join in the great wedding supper (Revelation 19:9).

The perfect life that Christ offers is portrayed in a parable where guests were invited to a wedding. Each guest was offered a wedding garment. "But when the king came in to see the guests, he saw a man there who did not have on a wedding garment. So he said to him, 'Friend, how did you come in here without a wedding garment?' And he was speechless" (Matthew 22:11, 12). Coming to the wedding was not enough; he needed a wedding garment.

The same imagery is portrayed in the parable of the lost son. When the prodigal son returned home, broken and repentant, the father quickly told the servants to cover this son who was in filthy clothing. "Bring out the best robe and put it on him" (Luke 15:22).

Sinners need more than their ragged garments removed, they need new clothing. That is, they need a new life in Christ. When Jesus rose from the dead, His perfect life empowered us to live like Christ and "follow His steps" (1 Peter 2:21). When we depend on the life and death of Jesus, we are promised that His righteous life will be ours. As Paul stated, "I can do all things through Christ who strengthens me" (Philippians 4:13).

Apply It:

What's the most expensive piece of clothing you have ever purchased?

Dig Deeper:

Genesis 3:21; Zechariah 3:3, 4; Revelation 7:14

April 25

Empty No More

"If Christ is not risen, then our preaching is empty and your faith is also empty" (1 Corinthians 15:14).

What is the essential difference between Jesus and every other supposed "messiah" in human history? With enough searching, you can likely find the remains of every one of these claimants, except one: Jesus. There are sites purporting to be His tomb, but each of them is empty. No body, no bones, no dust, no trace of the Son of God's remains.

Without the resurrection, Jesus is just another poseur, another claimant to a messianic title, of which there have been many—both religious and political—over the centuries. But we know, from history and from their gravesites, that all of these claimants are dead. All, that is, except for Jesus, who arose on the third day and later ascended into heaven, where He "sat down at the right hand of the throne of God" (Hebrews 12:2).

We know this because there were dozens of witnesses to the resurrection and ascension. We know it because those witnesses boldly proclaimed these facts in the face of fierce opposition. And we know it because many of those would be martyred for their beliefs. No one willingly surrenders their life for something they know is a lie.

Perhaps the most important argument for the resurrection of Jesus is the difference it has made in the lives of tens of millions of people through the years—and even today. Men and women have shed addictions, lost their anger, and have become productive citizens and loving family members because of the change that faith in Jesus has brought. That's a living witness to an ever-living Savior.

Apply It:

Study the Gospel accounts of Jesus' life, death, and resurrection to see how many doubted Him—but also how others believed and the change it made in their lives.

Dig Deeper:

1 Corinthians 15:1–17; Luke 24:36–43; Hebrews 8:1, 2

Long Lost Relatives

"To the intent that now the manifold wisdom of God might be made known by the church to the principalities and powers in the heavenly places" (Ephesians 3:10).

The war between North and South Korea separated some people for 67 years. At one point, 39,000 South Koreans had registered with a Red Cross program that arranges family reunions.

Although we are different from the angels, we have one major thing in common with them: We were both created by the same God. Yet sin has separated us from them, and direct interaction between humans and angels is rare. This is largely due to the problem of sin.

Through the death of Christ, however, the sin problem has been conquered. His death began the removal of the final obstacle between us and the holy angels. The apostle Paul records that God will "reconcile all things to Himself, by Him, whether things on earth or things in heaven, having made peace through the blood of His cross" (Colossians 1:20).

Today we have angels all around us, all the time. However, the removal of sin—explained later in the teaching about the sanctuary—prepares the way for us to see and talk to the angels when Christ comes. This means that Jesus' death has an impact on every creature in the universe!

By the central sacrifice in the plan of salvation, the angels were able to see God's wisdom. They were moved to worship Jesus when His death revealed His great love and wisdom. This resulted in a reunion of worship toward our common Creator. The Bible records that moment when "at the name of Jesus every knee should bow, of those in heaven, and of those on earth, and of those under the earth, and that every tongue should confess that Jesus Christ is Lord, to the glory of God the Father" (Philippians 2:10, 11).

Apply It:

Try to re-connect with a distant relative.

Dig Deeper:

1 Peter 1:12; Luke 15:7; Hebrews 2:7

April 27

Futility

"By grace you have been saved through faith, and that not of yourselves; it is the gift of God" (Ephesians 2:8).

It's a beautiful spring day and you decide to wash and wax your new SUV. After grabbing soap, a bucket, a brush, and hose, you carefully rinse down your precious vehicle and began cleaning every square inch of paint, chrome, and glass. After it dries, you apply a layer of car wax and then begin to tediously polish it until your SUV glows.

When the job is complete and your eyes shine with pride, you jump inside, rev up the engine, and head to the nearest off-road vehicle park. Plunging down a dirt road, you spy a giant mud puddle up ahead. With glee, you step on the gas and plow into the gooey mess. Gobs of dirt and mud now cover your gleaming vehicle. A few hours later, as you pull into the driveway, your spouse looks out the window and mutters, "Futility."

There is another activity that serves no useful purpose in the spiritual life—the effort to try and gain salvation by our own works. The apostle Paul addressed the futility of trying to keep the law in our own power. It is akin to trying to wash your car with a bucket of mud. He explains that "a man is not justified by the works of the law but by faith in Jesus Christ" (Galatians 2:16).

Christ's death on the cross affirms the uselessness of salvation by works, for if we could be saved by our own acts of righteousness then the atonement would be unnecessary. For "by the deeds of the law no flesh will be justified" (Romans 3:20), yet we may be "justified freely by His grace through the redemption that is in Christ Jesus" (verse 24).

When we accept God's gift through faith, "we have peace with God through our Lord Jesus Christ" (Romans 5:1). Such peace can never come from our futile efforts; it is the result of true faith that brings Christ into the heart (Galatians 2:20).

Apply It:

Think of a time in your life when your efforts have been fruitless. What needed to change?

Dig Deeper:

Job 15:31; Psalm 94:11; 1 Corinthians 15:17

A Deeper Connection

"Most assuredly, I say to you, hereafter you shall see heaven open, and the angels of God ascending and descending upon the Son of Man" (John 1:51).

In May 1844, Samuel F. B. Morse inaugurated the world's first commercial telegraph line. Within ten years, more than 20,000 miles of telegraph cable crisscrossed the United States. By 1854, Cyrus West Field, a businessman and financier from New York City, set about to string a cable that would stretch across the Atlantic Ocean to Britain.

Field's first attempt was made in 1857, but the cable broke twice and had to be pulled off the sea floor and repaired. Another unsuccessful effort was made the next year. Finally, in August 1858, a complete cable was laid and Queen Victoria sent a message to President James Buchanan praising "this additional link between the nations." Buchanan replied, "May the Atlantic telegraph, under the blessing of heaven, prove to be a bond of perpetual peace and friendship between kindred nations."

When Christ came to our world to live and die and rise again, He restored a link between heaven and earth that would never be broken. Jesus explained this divine connection to Nathanael when He said that angel messengers would ascend and descend "upon the Son of Man" (John 1:51).

Christ's reference went back to a dream God gave Jacob of a ladder that "was set up on the earth, and its top reached to heaven; and there the angels of God were ascending and descending on it" (Genesis 28:12). God assured the deceptive young man that He was reaching down to restore a broken connection. He desires to do the same with you.

When we receive Christ into our hearts, it creates a bond of peace and friendship with God. Our relationship becomes deeper and stronger as we grow in grace. Paul describes the power of this connection: "Now may the God of peace Himself sanctify you completely; and may your whole spirit, soul, and body be preserved blameless at the coming of our Lord Jesus Christ" (1 Thessalonians 5:23).

Apply It:

What is the furthest long-distance telephone call you have ever made?

Dig Deeper:

John 1:14; 2 Corinthians 5:20, 21; Colossians 1:20

The Experience of Salvation

10

Turning Around

"Turn to Me with all your heart, with fasting, with weeping, and with mourning" (Joel 2:12).

If you're moving to another state and are concerned that you'll have to learn to recognize a whole new set of road signs, you have nothing to worry about. Traffic and road signs are consistent nationwide. From Florida to Washington, all highway traffic signs are green with white lettering. All parking signs are white with green lettering. And all warning signs are yellow with black lettering.

But it wasn't always this way. The first stop sign appeared in Detroit in 1915. It was originally yellow and stayed that way for about thirty years before it was changed to red. One reason the color was changed was to make it consistent with red traffic signals. Another reason is that durable fade-resistant red paint was finally made available.

One of the most important road signs in the Christian life is the U-turn. In the experience of salvation, turning around is called repentance. The Greek word for repent means "to change one's mind." Jesus promised that the Holy Spirit would come and "convict the world of sin, and of righteousness, and of judgment" (John 16:8). Conviction is like a stop sign that makes us quit moving in a certain direction and change course.

When the heart is convicted of sin, it is prepared to make an important choice. When the Holy Spirit, through the preaching of Peter, convicted people at Pentecost of their need of a Savior, they wanted to know what to do. The Bible says, "When they heard this, they were cut to the heart, and said to Peter and the rest of the apostles, 'Men and brethren, what shall we do?' " (Acts 2:37). Peter's response was simple and clear: "Repent" (verse 38).

Repentance comes before forgiveness, yet we do not have the ability to produce a repentant heart in our own power. It is "the goodness of God [that] leads you to repentance" (Romans 2:4). Nothing so moves the heart to repent than beholding Christ. "And I, if I am lifted up from the earth, will draw all peoples to Myself" (John 12:32).

Are you ready to stop and make a U-turn?

Apply It:

The next time you see a U-turn sign, thank God for the opportunity to turn toward Him.

Dig Deeper:

Psalm 51:1–19; Proverbs 28:13; Acts 5:31

A New Wash

"He made Him who knew no sin to be sin for us, that we might become the righteousness of God in Him" (2 Corinthians 5:21).

Something as simple and common as laundry is changing. People used to wash certain clothes using the hot or warm water setting on their laundry machines. As a result of newly developed detergents, however, all laundry can now be thoroughly washed using the cold-water setting. This is because most detergents can dissolve just as well in cold water as they do in hot water.

Many people struggle with the stains of their past mistakes. They try to make themselves feel better by volunteering or doing community service. While some of these strategies may be innocent, God's plan is to give them a more powerful experience.

The experience of justification is illustrated in a striking matter in the story of Joshua the high priest. This man had a checkered past. The metaphor of dirt on his garments was used to represent the guilt and condemnation that Joshua deserved. When Joshua's faults were pointed out by Satan, God stepped in: "He answered and spoke to those who stood before Him, saying, 'Take away the filthy garments from him.' And to him He said, 'See, I have removed your iniquity from you, and I will clothe you with rich robes' " (Zechariah 3:4).

The new clothing that Joshua received represented the new way of life that he began to live. On the one hand, Joshua's faith in the removal of his past sins was the reception of his new right standing with God. On the other hand, his reception of that right standing was also shown in his new way of life: "Thus also faith by itself, if it does not have works, is dead" (James 2:17).

Joshua wasn't trying to cover up his sinful past by doing good; rather, he was doing good now that the guilt of his past life no longer burdened him.

Apply It:

Encourage someone who is discouraged by their past.

Dig Deeper:

Romans 5:19; Philippians 3:9; Zechariah 3:2

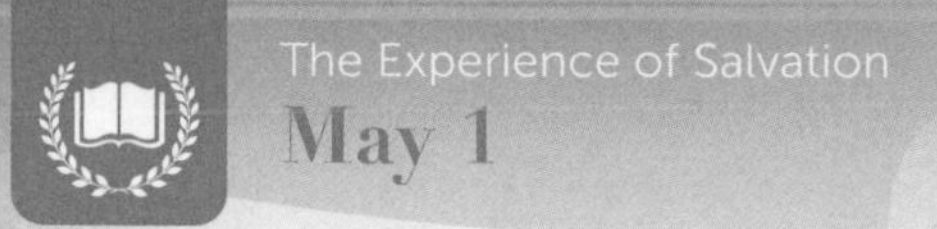

Genuine Faith

"In Christ Jesus neither circumcision nor uncircumcision avails anything, but faith working through love" (Galatians 5:6).

"The proof is in the pudding." What does this old British proverb mean? The original version stated, "The proof of the pudding is in the eating." It meant that you had to try out food to really know whether or not it tasted good. Centuries ago, pudding was not a sweet dessert but a type of sausage filled with minced meat and other animal tidbits that could be treacherous to the tongue.

When it comes to the experience of salvation, faith is a central factor. "By grace you have been saved through faith, and that not of yourselves; it is the gift of God" (Ephesians 2:8). But how do you know if you have genuine faith? Paul encourages us: "Examine yourselves as to whether you are in the faith" (2 Corinthians 13:5). What convincing proof reveals true faith? After all, Jesus said, "Not everyone who says to Me, 'Lord, Lord,' shall enter the kingdom of heaven" (Matthew 7:21).

A clue comes at the end of one verse that clarifies who will enter heaven: "He who does the will of My Father in heaven." How can that be when we know "that a man is not justified by the works of the law but by faith in Jesus Christ" (Galatians 2:16)? Our standing before God does not depend on our good or bad deeds. "Abraham believed God, and it was accounted to him for righteousness" (Romans 4:3).

When we look carefully at the type of faith Abraham had, we discover that "by faith Abraham obeyed" (Hebrews 11:8). His genuine faith was not passive or merely intellectual, but was revealed in a life of obedience to God. James explained the evidence of true faith: "Faith by itself, if it does not have works, is dead" (James 2:17).

Paul dealt with the fallacy of obtaining justification through our works. James dealt with the fallacy of claiming justification without corresponding works. Neither works nor a dead faith lead to salvation. The proof of true faith is in the pudding.

Apply It:

What types of evidence do you expect to see in a person who truly loves another person?

Dig Deeper:

Romans 4:9, 10; Hebrews 11:8–12; James 2:14–26

A Reputation Restored

"He made Him who knew no sin to be sin for us, that we might become the righteousness of God in Him" (2 Corinthians 5:21).

Two years after he stepped down as the U.S. Secretary of Labor, Raymond J. Donovan was acquitted of state charges of grand larceny and fraud related to a large New York City construction business, of which he owned half. Standing outside of the courtroom where he'd been on trial for nine months, Donovan said to reporters, "To which office do I go to get my reputation back?"

Those who come to Jesus in faith, repenting of their sins, may have lost their reputations on earth. If those sins were not overly public, they might still appear "respectable" in the community, although if others knew their past, that could crumble.

But in the divine exchange that is the salvation process, where Christ's righteousness replaces your unrighteousness, your *heavenly* reputation is restored at once: " 'Come now, and let us reason together,' says the Lord, 'though your sins are like scarlet, they shall be as white as snow; though they are red like crimson, they shall be as wool' " (Isaiah 1:18).

It's not merely your reputation that's restored; so is your right-standing with God. A holy God could not allow unholy, sinning people in His heaven. When you genuinely repent and confess your transgressions, your sin is removed and you are "white as snow" in God's sight.

Raymond J. Donovan returned to his business and eventually sold his share of the company to an overseas buyer to live a presumably happy and comfortable life. For those who believe Jesus' promise of salvation, the future is even brighter: "See, I have removed your iniquity from you, and I will clothe you with rich robes" (Zechariah 3:4). The result? An eternity of happiness in the presence of the One who redeemed us!

Apply It:

After we receive by faith the "divine exchange," think of how God now wants to work a "divine change" in our lives.

Dig Deeper:

Zechariah 3:1–5; 2 Corinthians 5:17–20; 1 Peter 2:24

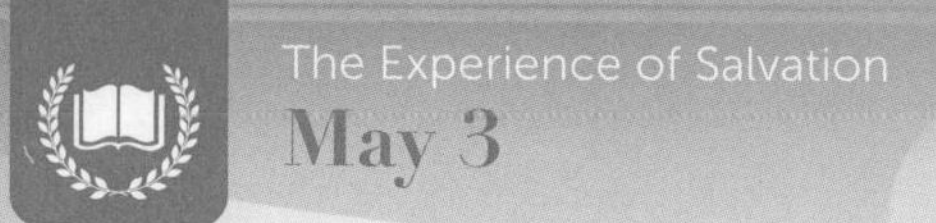

Set Apart

"To all who are in Rome, beloved of God, called to be saints ..." (Romans 1:7).

It's considered a mark of recognition for over 800 individuals and companies. British Royal Warrants of Appointment are given to tradesmen who supply goods or services to households of Her Majesty The Queen, His Royal Highness The Duke of Edinburgh, or His Royal Highness The Prince of Wales. These coveted warrants enable suppliers to advertise the fact that they supply the royal family with their goods and services.

God has called His people to be saints, which literally means "holy ones." It's a mark of recognition found throughout the New Testament, but not in a way the world honors individuals. The word "saint" comes from the Greek word *hagios* and means "separated from a common to a sacred use." Saints are set apart by God for a holy purpose. "We are His workmanship, created in Christ Jesus for good works, which God prepared beforehand that we should walk in them" (Ephesians 2:10).

From the same root word for saints comes the word sanctification (*hagiasmos*), which means "to make holy." Paul explains that true repentance and justification leads to sanctification, "not by works of righteousness which we have done, but according to His mercy He saved us, through the washing of regeneration and renewing of the Holy Spirit" (Titus 3:5). Justification and sanctification are two phases in salvation. Justification is what God does *for* us, while sanctification is what God does *in* us.

One Christian writer summarized sanctification like this: "The righteousness by which we are justified is imputed; the righteousness by which we are sanctified is imparted. The first is our title to heaven, the second is our fitness for heaven" (*Messages to Young People,* p. 35). Both come by faith in what God does, never from our own works.

Apply It:

Do you have any special items (like dishes) that are set apart in your home only for special occasions?

Dig Deeper:

John 17:17; 1 Thessalonians 5:23; 2 Timothy 2:21

A New Beginning

"When the fullness of the time had come, God sent forth His Son, born of a woman, born under the law, to redeem those who were under the law, that we might receive the adoption" (Galatians 4:4, 5).

It started when Li Lijuan took time to help a small orphan girl who was begging by the side of the road and ended up adopting her. Since then, the once-successful businesswoman has adopted over seventy children—many of them abandoned or orphaned. A number of the children have serious medical problems requiring expensive treatments and surgeries. Once a millionaire, Li sacrificed every cent of her accumulated wealth to help her adopted children and provide them with a safe, loving home where many of them found acceptance for the first time in their lives.

The Bible says that when we come to Jesus and give our lives to Him, we are adopted into God's family. We become His sons and daughters, and the King of the universe becomes our Father. "You did not receive the spirit of bondage again to fear, but you received the Spirit of adoption" (Romans 8:15).

We can be sure that we are accepted by God because He has promised to wash away all the sins from our past—regardless of how terrible—and cover us with the righteousness of Christ. After making a long list of horrific sins, the apostle Paul wrote, "Such were some of you. But you were washed, but you were sanctified, but you were justified in the name of the Lord Jesus and by the Spirit of our God" (1 Corinthians 6:11). Salvation is for *every* person who will accept it.

When we stand justified by Christ's grace and mercy, the absence of guilt is healing. As we receive His grace each day and are filled with His love and gradually transformed into His image, we will be living victorious lives that are no longer controlled by sin. Best of all, God promises that if we stay in this relationship with Him, we have eternal life (1 John 5:12).

Apply It:

Say a prayer of thanks to God that He has arranged for your adoption into His wonderful family.

Dig Deeper:

1 John 1:9; Ephesians 1:7; Romans 6:4

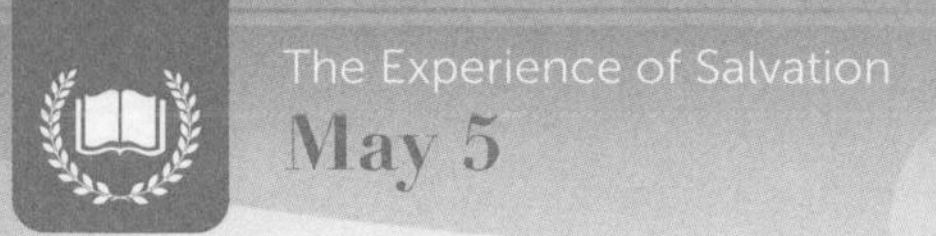

Called to Holiness

"If anyone cleanses himself from the latter, he will be a vessel for honor, sanctified and useful for the Master, prepared for every good work" (2 Timothy 2:21).

Would you be proud to be called a wild pig? That's what happened in 1909, after the University of Arkansas' football team, known then as the Cardinals, beat Louisiana State University (LSU). Coach Hugo Bezdek called his players "a wild band of Razorback hogs." Within a year, the student body voted to change the official mascot to a Razorback.

Razorbacks are not gentle barnyard pigs. They are known to be tough and at times ill-tempered. But their fearlessness and doggedness gave inspiration to the football team's nickname. Since the 1960s, a live Razorback (today it is a Russian boar) has made its debut at university games.

Christians are called to a life of fearlessness and doggedness, not after the manner of a wild boar, but after the character of Christ. "God did not call us to uncleanness, but in holiness" (1 Thessalonians 4:7). In order to live this sanctified life, God has given every believer "power according to the Spirit of holiness" (Romans 1:4).

Such a changed life does not begin with outward performance but an inward change. The apostle Paul prayed that God "would grant you, according to the riches of His glory, to be strengthened with might through His Spirit in the inner man, that Christ may dwell in your hearts through faith; that you, being rooted and grounded in love" (Ephesians 3:16, 17).

When you surrender your life to Jesus, He works in your life and transforms you into a new creation. "Just as you presented your members as slaves of uncleanness, and of lawlessness leading to more lawlessness, so now present your members as slaves of righteousness for holiness" (Romans 6:19). We can then proudly be called "children of God" (1 John 3:2).

Apply It:

Try to think of the different terms God uses to describe His people (church, beloved, bride, son/daughter, etc.).

Dig Deeper:

Romans 8:12–17; Galatians 2:20; 2 Corinthians 5:17

Fresh From Old

"Do not be conformed to this world, but be transformed by the renewing of your mind, that you may prove what is that good and acceptable and perfect will of God" (Romans 12:2).

Researchers from Columbia University recently looked at the brains of healthy people who had died suddenly. They found that the brains of older people were able to produce new brain cells like those of younger people. Although there are other factors to consider, this discovery undermines previous beliefs about healthy older people.

God can work miracles in the brain of any person. When the Holy Spirit dwells in people, He brings the presence of Christ to them. This is why the apostle Paul could say, "I have been crucified with Christ; it is no longer I who live, but Christ lives in me; and the life which I now live in the flesh I live by faith in the Son of God, who loved me and gave Himself for me" (Galatians 2:20).

Knowing that Christ is dwelling in us should fill us with hope that we are becoming new people through His presence (Ephesians 3:17). When He comes to dwell with us, He desires to engage our decision-making abilities in the process of transformation. In other words, God does not want us to fear that He will take over our identity without our permission. Instead, He encourages us to commune with Him and to make decisions that put His words into action.

When He was on earth, Jesus described the experience of transformation by using the metaphor of eating and drinking: "He who eats My flesh and drinks My blood abides in Me, and I in him" (John 6:56). This process may begin with an intellectual understanding of the plan of salvation, but our interactions with God are most effective when they also involve our emotions and decisions. Meditating on the Word of God is the first step.

Apply It:

Make a conscious effort to make at least one decision today that is based on the Bible.

Dig Deeper:

2 Corinthians 4:16; 1 Thessalonians 5:23; Titus 3:5

Unbelievable Power

"You shall receive power when the Holy Spirit has come upon you" (Acts 1:8).

You probably wouldn't be impressed by its name—the Wärtsilä RT-flex96C—but you might be stunned by the size of this monster engine. This jaw-dropping diesel motor is the largest and most powerful in the world today. Built in Finland, the RT-flex96C's fourteen cylinders can deliver over 80,000 KW of power—enough to run a small city.

The engine stands 44 feet tall, is 90 feet long, and weighs a whopping 2,300 tons. Each of the giant 14 cylinders consumes 6.5 ounces of diesel in just one cycle, which is actually quite efficient considering the size of motor. The Wärtsilä RT-flex96C was made for a cargo ship that carries 11,000 20-foot shipping containers between the United States and China at a breakneck speed of 31 knots.

There is a greater power at your disposal, enough to perform the most difficult task on the planet: changing the human heart. Jesus' "divine power has given to us all things that pertain to life and godliness, through the knowledge of Him who called us by glory and virtue, by which have been given to us exceedingly great and precious promises, that through these you may be partakers of the divine nature, having escaped the corruption that is in the world through lust" (2 Peter 1:3, 4).

We may be transformed into the image of our Creator when we partake of Christ. "Put on the Lord Jesus Christ, and make no provision for the flesh, to fulfill its lusts" (Romans 13:14). This sanctifying process is progressive and continues as we abide in Jesus. Just as we grow daily through the food we consume, so may we continuously grow in the Lord. The fuel for the Christian is the Word of God. "Man shall not live by bread alone, but by every word that proceeds from the mouth of God" (Matthew 4:4).

Jesus explained the power of the Word: "The words that I speak to you are spirit, and they are life" (John 6:63). Are you ready to tap into an unbelievable source of power that can transform your character?

Apply It:

What is the largest engine you have ever seen? How does it compare to the power heaven offers to every believer?

Dig Deeper:

Zechariah 4:6; Philippians 4:13; 2 Timothy 1:7

Two Transformations

"The fruit of the Spirit is love, joy, peace, longsuffering, kindness, goodness, faithfulness, gentleness, self-control. Against such there is no law" (Galatians 5:22, 23).

At the end of World War II, Louis Zamperini finally came home. An Olympic runner for the United States in 1936, he was a bombardier during the war. After his plane crashed in the Pacific, he survived 46 days on a life raft only to become a Japanese prisoner-of-war.

Zamperini suffered brutal treatment at the hands of his captors, but he survived. Following his return, he married and had two children. But the memories of his captivity haunted him, and he turned to alcohol to numb the pain. His home life became desperate, and Zamperini's wife Cynthia finally begged him to attend a Billy Graham crusade in Los Angeles in 1949.

There, facing a crisis that could have cost him his marriage and children, Zamperini accepted Graham's invitation to trust in Jesus. After that, Zamperini's life dramatically changed.

His story of triumphing over tragedy became history, the subject of several motion pictures and the bestselling book *Unbroken*. Less noted from some accounts is the change in Zamperini's life after he accepted Christ: The nightmares stopped, the drinking ended, and Zamperini was able to forgive the Japanese who tortured him.

What happened to Louis Zamperini after his conversion is a miraculous transformation that can happen to each believer after receiving Jesus as Savior. When we surrender to God's will, we can exchange our old behaviors for "kindness, goodness, faithfulness, gentleness, [and] self-control." Don't you believe this world could use a lot more kindness and goodness, not to mention gentleness?

If the only thing salvation gave us was the opportunity to have eternal life in heaven, that would be far more than enough, and far more than we would deserve. But eternity is not the only part of the package: By having our very natures renewed, receiving the positive attributes we may not have always shown before, we can start living in our own "heaven on earth" starting today!

Apply It:

As you thank God for His goodness and for the gifts of the Spirit that come with salvation, remember to exercise those gifts, especially when things get tough!

Dig Deeper:

Mark 9:2–29; Jude 24; 2 Corinthians 10:5

Mature in Christ

"You shall be perfect, just as your Father in heaven is perfect" (Matthew 5:48).

He started out as a bean farmer. Axel Erlandson was born in Sweden, emigrated to Minnesota as a young boy, and then moved once more to California where he married and worked his fields. One day, in 1925, he noticed how some branches in his hedgerow had grown together and it sparked an idea to shape trees as a hobby. He created designs on paper and then pruned, grafted, and bent small trees to train them into unique shapes.

Today, you can observe Erlandson's astounding work at Gilroy Gardens in California. It features 24 trees that were grown and shaped with multiple trunks, basket-weave patterns, and hearts. Alex kept his methods a secret; when children asked how he got his trees to grow like this, he would reply, "I talk to them."

Erlandson was called a tree shaper, but there is a spiritual arborist who bends, prunes, grafts, and shapes lives to perfection. Through the work of the Holy Spirit, God is perfecting a people into His image (Ephesians 3:16, 19). The Bible word for perfect in Hebrew is *tam* or *tamim* and means "complete," "wholesome," and "blameless." The Greek word for perfect is *teleios* and means "full-grown," "mature," and "having attained its purpose."

Noah, Abraham, and Job were described as perfect and blameless (Genesis 6:9; 17:1; Job 1:1, 8), though each had imperfections. In the New Testament, perfect describes mature people who have lived up to the best available light and reached the potential of their spiritual, mental, and physical powers. Paul explains, "Brethren, do not be children in understanding; however, in malice be babes, but in understanding be mature [*teleioi*]" (1 Corinthians 14:20).

We can never claim perfection in our own power, for it is through the Holy Spirit that we become like Christ in character. In horticultural words, Jesus captured it well: "I am the vine, you are the branches. He who abides in Me, and I in him, bears much fruit; for without Me you can do nothing" (John 15:5).

Apply It:

The next time you plant a seed, remember Christ's plan and power to grow you into His mature likeness.

Dig Deeper:

Ephesians 4:13, 14; Philippians 3:15; Hebrews 5:14

Growing into Perfection

"Everyone who partakes only of milk is unskilled in the word of righteousness, for he is a babe. But solid food belongs to those who are of full age" (Hebrews 5:13, 14).

Artificially manufactured baby food has been around as long as humans. In the 17th to 19th centuries, "pap" was made by soaking bread in milk or water and then poured or blown into the baby's mouth from a "pap boat." In the mid-1800s, several European companies manufactured baby food, including the Swiss merchant Henri Nestle, who sold Nestle's Milk Food in the United States and other countries. In America, meat, fruit, and vegetable-based commercial baby food began to be marketed in the 1920s, with Clapp's, Gerber, and Beech-Nut becoming popular. One of the more interesting early flavors marketed by Gerber was liver soup.

In our Christian experience, we need to move beyond the soft spiritual food of babyhood. Part of perfecting our characters as God's children and preparing for our future in heaven is to grow past the basic truths, grasp the deep lessons our heavenly Father wants us to understand, and develop holy characters. It's His purpose "that we should no longer be children, tossed to and fro and carried about with every wind of doctrine ... but, speaking the truth in love, may grow up in all things into Him who is the head—Christ" (Ephesians 4:14, 15).

God wants us to "be filled with the knowledge of His will in all wisdom and spiritual understanding" and to be "fruitful in every good work" (Colossians 1:9, 10). Of course, none of us can produce this kind of spiritual maturity within ourselves; it can only be realized when we have Christ living daily within our hearts.

The process of sanctification is often a struggle as we learn to yield our will to Him and resist temptations. But He has promised to strengthen us. Today, He assures you that He is "able to keep you from stumbling, and to present you faultless before the presence of His glory with exceeding joy" (Jude 1:24).

Apply It:

What solid spiritual food are you consuming today?

Dig Deeper:

Hebrews 6:1; Philippians 1:9–11; Philippians 2:12, 13

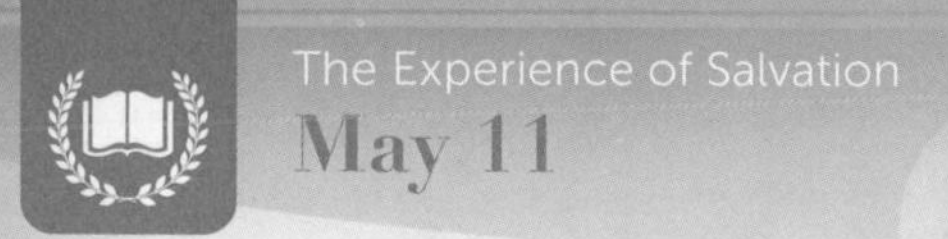

Our Full Stature in Christ

"Till we all come to the unity of the faith and of the knowledge of the Son of God, to a perfect man, to the measure of the stature of the fullness of Christ" (Ephesians 4:13).

Can you predict how tall a child will end up being as an adult? Some people would say, "Sure, just take a look at the parents." But it's more complex than that. Several factors are at play, including the growth of other family members, when the child reaches puberty, chronic illnesses that he or she may have had, and nutrition intake.

Pediatricians track a child's height and weight with every checkup so they can plot their growth on a chart and compare it with what is typical for healthy boys and girls. Genes play a large role in determining how tall you will be. Girls start their growth spurt around age 9 to 10, with their fastest growth peaking around age 12. Boys start their growth spurt around age 11 and hit their peak at 13.

The Bible describes a transformation that will take place in our bodies at the Second Coming. We are not only justified in Christ and sanctified by the Holy Spirit, but we will be glorified when Jesus returns. Paul describes this: "If the Spirit of Him who raised Jesus from the dead dwells in you, He who raised Christ from the dead will also give life to your mortal bodies through His Spirit who dwells in you" (Romans 8:11).

This final redemption is something we can look forward to when Jesus returns. Paul explains, "The earnest expectation of the creation eagerly waits for the revealing of the sons of God" (v. 19). Then he adds, "Not only that, but we also who have the firstfruits of the Spirit, even we ourselves groan within ourselves, eagerly waiting for the adoption, the redemption of our body" (v. 23).

While God desires that we keep growing each day, we may be completely perfect now in Christ. Yet our ultimate transformation will take place when Jesus comes again. Until then, we should be careful about our "height," as Paul warned, "Let him who thinks he stands take heed lest he fall" (1 Corinthians 10:12).

Apply It:

How tall are you? How tall do you think you will be in the kingdom of heaven?

Dig Deeper:

Mark 4:28; 1 Corinthians 15:35–58; Ephesians 4:13

Enjoy the Time

"There is none righteous, no, not one" (Romans 3:10).

Some parents feel silly reading to or playing with their children. In order to show them how important these interactions are to children, researchers from New York University School of Medicine videotaped parents playing with their children. After the interactions, the researchers would play back the video and point out how much their children enjoyed the interaction. Children who received this type of attention improved in their behavior.

God cares about our behavior, but it is not the basis for our salvation. Even if we put a lifetime of grueling effort into performing righteously, we would still need to rely on Christ's death and His perfect life. The prophet Isaiah has one of the most memorable expressions of this point: "We are all like an unclean thing, and all our righteousnesses are like filthy rags; we all fade as a leaf, and our iniquities, like the wind, have taken us away" (Isaiah 64:6).

Isaiah understood that even our best behavior cannot accomplish our salvation. To God it is not pretty. It means that we must rely on God to make us into truly beautiful people. It also means that we can see how much God loved us in sending Jesus to take our place in life and death: "But of Him you are in Christ Jesus, who became for us wisdom from God—and righteousness and sanctification and redemption" (1 Corinthians 1:30).

Led by this knowledge, we can enjoy our interactions with God, knowing that we are not striving to be pleasing enough to Him, but rather are being transformed because we know how much He loves us. It is when we rely on Jesus' faith, righteousness, and relationship with God that we can enjoy our own interactions with God.

Apply It:

Take time to read a book to a child this week.

Dig Deeper:

Daniel 9:7; Romans 3:23; Isaiah 53:6

Growing in Christ

11

May 13

Life Begins with Death

"We were buried with Him through baptism into death, that just as Christ was raised from the dead by the glory of the Father, even so we also should walk in newness of life" (Romans 6:4).

A Russian team of scientists stumbled across a cache of seeds that were hidden by squirrels. What's amazing is that the seeds had been buried by squirrels *thousands* of years ago near the banks of the Kolyma River in Siberia. The seeds were encased in ice 124 feet below the permafrost and surrounded by layers of mammoth, bison, and woolly rhinoceros' bones.

What was even more stunning about these ancient seeds was that the Russian team was able to take viable plant material from them, place them in vials, and successfully germinate plants. The plants were identical to the modern *S. stenophylla*—except the flowers were shaped a little differently. The plants grew well, flowered, and then, after a year, created seeds of their own.

It's an odd idea to many people to say that life begins at death, but it's an encouraging truth for the Christian. We know well that "the wages of sin is death" (Romans 6:23). But how does life come from death? Christ illustrates this through a seed. "Most assuredly, I say to you, unless a grain of wheat falls into the ground and dies, it remains alone; but if it dies, it produces much grain" (John 12:24).

Paul the apostle explained that "just as through one man sin entered the world, and death through sin" so also "through one Man's righteous act the free gift came to all men" (Romans 5:12, 18). This righteous act was the death of Christ on Calvary, and the free gift is eternal life (Romans 6:23).

But there is another death that must take place to receive this gift—death to self. Paul told us, "I have been crucified with Christ; it is no longer I who live, but Christ lives in me; and the life which I now live in the flesh I live by faith in the Son of God, who loved me and gave Himself for me" (Galatians 2:20). It adds new meaning to the idea that we are dying to live!

Apply It:

Plant a seed this week and remember that it is through dying that we might live.

Dig Deeper:

Deuteronomy 30:19; John 5:24; Romans 5:10

Death to Self

"I have been crucified with Christ; it is no longer I who live, but Christ lives in me; and the life which I now live in the flesh I live by faith in the Son of God, who loved me and gave Himself for me" (Galatians 2:20).

When Kenneth Smith, a 72-year-old retiree in Riverside, California, was killed in a tragic accident, the world, at first, didn't pay much attention. But when it surfaced that Smith in his childhood was known as Darwood Kaye, and had portrayed "Waldo" in the *Little Rascals* series of short films, news agencies took notice.

Once Smith's acting career ended, the young man became more interested in spiritual matters and attended a religious college; he was later ordained a minister, serving at six different churches in California. In 1957, the Smith family began a fourteen-year stay in Thailand, doing missionary work before returning to America where he finished his career in several congregations.

But unlike many other former "child stars," Smith never dwelled on the past. He didn't go to fan club meetings or nostalgia conventions. He wasn't ashamed of his past; rather, it was just that—his past. To borrow from the apostle Paul, Darwood had been crucified with Christ. Paul lived the life of Jesus, who said, "Whoever exalts himself will be humbled, and he who humbles himself will be exalted" (Matthew 23:12).

For believers, finding a new life in Christ doesn't mean you have to ignore your past and any accomplishments of your earlier years. After briefly describing his own life, the apostle Paul quickly added, "I also count all things loss for the excellence of the knowledge of Christ Jesus my Lord, for whom I have suffered the loss of all things, and count them as rubbish, that I may gain Christ" (Philippians 3:8).

Kenneth Smith built something more lasting than a "highlight reel" of acting appearances and so may you, "for we do not preach ourselves, but Christ Jesus the Lord" (2 Corinthians 4:5).

Apply It:

Think of someone you know (or perhaps a Bible character) who was transformed by a powerful encounter with Jesus. Ask God to help you put Jesus and His will ahead of your desires and see where He leads!

Dig Deeper:

Romans 6:6–11; John 12:24; 2 Corinthians 5:17

Living a New Life

"If anyone is in Christ, he is a new creation; old things have passed away; behold, all things have become new" (2 Corinthians 5:17).

Recidivism is a huge problem. The tendency of a convicted criminal to reoffend, according to the U.S. Bureau of Justice Statistics, is high. In a study of 405,000 released prisoners in 30 states, 68 percent were arrested for a new crime within three years of their release from prison. Three-quarters (77 percent) were arrested within five years. (The study tracked arrests, not reimprisonments.)

In another study by the Pew Center on the States, about 43 percent of prisoners released in 2004 were sent back to prison in 2007. Only marginal improvements have been made to rehabilitate ex-cons in the last ten years, even though spending on programs has increased from $30 billion to $50 billion annually.

Imagine a church that teaches that if anyone is in Christ, that person is forgiven, but he is still the same old person. His old life has not changed, and he ends up right back where he started. Yet millions buy into this cheap form of grace and fall back into the prison house of sin. The apostle Paul explains, "Do we then make void the law through faith? Certainly not! On the contrary, we establish the law" (Romans 3:31). God wants to write His life-giving law on our hearts—not remove it (see Jeremiah 31:33).

There is no question that "by grace you have been saved through faith, and that not of yourselves; it is the gift of God" (Ephesians 2:8), but Paul continues that "we are His workmanship, created in Christ Jesus for good works" (v. 10). God has not only saved us from the results of sin but has empowered us to live free from the bondage of sin. "Stand fast therefore in the liberty by which Christ has made us free, and do not be entangled again with a yoke of bondage" (Galatians 5:1).

Do you really want to go back to prison?

Apply It:

Have you ever visited a prison or jail (or perhaps been put there)? How did it feel when the gates and doors closed behind you?

Dig Deeper:

Jeremiah 29:11; Ezekiel 11:19; Ephesians 4:22–24

Free From Expectations

"Most assuredly, I say to you, unless one is born of water and the Spirit, he cannot enter the kingdom of God" (John 3:5).

While there are a number of serious disadvantages to the high expectations that women feel concerning their appearance, criticism of these expectations appears to be backfiring. One of the latest responses to these expectations has been called "beauty-standard denialism." This is roughly defined as speaking as though there are no expectations for beauty, when in fact they are as prevalent as ever.

The transformation that the Holy Spirit brings is both beautiful and, in some respects, a call for renouncing an unhealthy obsession with outward beauty. Peter encourages, "Do not let your adornment be merely outward ... rather let it be the hidden person of the heart" (1 Peter 3:3, 4). Paul described the transformation that the Spirit brings: "To be carnally minded is death, but to be spiritually minded is life and peace" (Romans 8:6).

To be carnally minded is to allow unhealthy obsessions to take control. The reverse of this is to allow the Holy Spirit to guide us into a life of freedom, for "where the Spirit of the Lord is, there is liberty" (2 Corinthians 3:17). This means that when our desires seem out of control, or our culture is trying to constrain us, we receive the power to redirect our attention. What becomes central to us is pleasing God.

This does not mean that God wants us to be disengaged from the world around us. Otherwise, Jesus would not have said to the Father: "I do not pray that You should take them out of the world, but that You should keep them from the evil one" (John 17:15). Most Christians will face situations where discerning the right thing to do is not easy. However, part of the promised growth is the guidance of the Holy Spirit: "When He has come, He will convict the world of sin, and of righteousness, and of judgment" (John 16:8). When we rely on the Holy Spirit for moral guidance, He will teach us how to draw people to Jesus without becoming trapped.

Apply It:

Redirect the attention of someone who is unnecessarily worried.

Dig Deeper:

John 14:17; Galatians 5:22, 23; 2 Corinthians 3:17, 18

Unified by His Love

"Love your enemies, bless those who curse you, do good to those who hate you, and pray for those who spitefully use you and persecute you, that you may be sons of your Father in heaven" (Matthew 5:44, 45).

Chris was only ten years old when he was abducted by a male nurse who had cared for his elderly uncle. The kidnapper burned him with cigarettes, stabbed him with an ice pick, and shot him, leaving him for dead in the Everglades. Chris survived, but the bullet, which entered one temple and exited the other, left him blind in one eye.

Yet years later, when the kidnapper—by then a blind, elderly nursing home resident—confessed to the crime, Chris reacted in an unusual way. He went to see the man who had tried to kill him and offered friendship. He began to visit the man daily and read to him from the Bible, even taking his young daughter along. Chris stated that it was his faith that enabled him to release his bitterness and forgive.

As Christians, we are asked to live lives that reflect the love of Christ. He instructed us to love God with all our heart, soul, and mind (Matthew 22:37). But that vertical relationship is just one part of the equation. He included the horizontal—our relationships with others—when He said, "You shall love your neighbor as yourself" (Matthew 22:39). And we must love everyone regardless of social position, age, gender, race, or nationality, recognizing their dignity as children of God.

Perhaps the most difficult part of loving others is forgiving them, but it's not optional. Jesus said we must "forgive our debtors" (Matthew 6:12) in order to receive God's forgiveness. Most of us aren't victims of horrendous crimes, but sometimes we may have trouble forgiving even small infractions.

How can we forgive more easily? The key is love. It was love that fueled the forgiveness Jesus showed to those who persecuted, tortured, and killed Him. And it is only through His supernatural love within us that we can truly forgive others and live in the unity God desires for us.

Apply It:

Ask Jesus to fill you with His love so you can be ready to forgive.

Dig Deeper:

Luke 23:34; John 17:20, 21; Luke 10:25–37

Eternal Bread

"It is written, 'Man shall not live by bread alone, but by every word that proceeds from the mouth of God' " (Matthew 4:4).

It took eighteen bakers working through the night to create the longest loaf of bread in history. Using 2,500 pounds of flour, the bakers made a loaf that was 3,600 feet long—that's over two-thirds of a mile! The world record breakers from Umberto, Italy, had no problem figuring out what to do with the bread when they finished. The bakers cut it up and served it as a snack to the hundreds of helpers and spectators.

Every human body demands nutrition to grow and function. The most essential spiritual food in the world to human life is the Word of God. Jesus, who is identified as the Word in John 1:1, referred to Himself as the "bread of life" (John 6:35). He explained, "He who comes to Me shall never hunger." Christ demonstrated the value of the Word of God when battling the enemy in the wilderness temptations. He quoted Scripture three times to drive away the devil (Matthew 4:1–11).

How do we become spiritually strong and resistant to Satan? Through a personal, prayerful, and daily study of the Bible, we are able to push back the forces of darkness. "Your word I have hidden in my heart, that I might not sin against You" (Psalm 119:11). Just as our bodies need daily nourishment to maintain our health, so must we daily feed on the Scriptures to build our faith.

Jesus so identified His words with spiritual life that He once explained, "He who eats this bread will live forever" (John 6:58). People misunderstood Him to mean that people must literally eat His body, but He explained, "The words that I speak to you are spirit, and they are life" (v. 63). The words of Christ make up the most important bread in history.

Apply It:

The next time you eat a meal, thank God for the food found in the Bible—nourishment that leads to eternal life.

Dig Deeper:

Exodus 16:1–36; Deuteronomy 8:3; John 6:22–71

God Answers Prayer

"I am the Lord *your God, who brought you out of the land of Egypt; open your mouth wide, and I will fill it"* (Psalm 81:10).

Let's say you woke up one morning burdened to start an orphanage. What would you consider a top priority? Fundraising might be a good choice, since it's tough to do much of anything in this world without money.

But more than 180 years ago, a German-born preacher living in Bristol, England, decided to do things differently. A cholera outbreak had orphaned hundreds of children in the British city, and George Mueller wanted to help.

His principal concern, though, was that people would see God's hand in meeting the project's needs, so Mueller never asked for money. He would discover a need, pray, and it would be met in what some would call a miraculous fashion. During his life, his orphanages cared for more than 10,000 children— supported by over $120 million in today's dollars that came through prayer.

George Mueller's story reminds us to not only "pray without ceasing" (1 Thessalonians 5:17) but to have a deeper trust in God. "Now this is the confidence that we have in Him, that if we ask anything according to His will, He hears us" (1 John 5:14).

Citing it here is not to suggest readers try to "pray up" a few million dollars. Rather, it is to demonstrate a life of faith and believe that "my God shall supply all your need according to His riches in glory by Christ Jesus" (Philippians 4:19). Having a fruitful prayer life can mean serving and growing a local church, enjoying a career of service to others, or being a successful spouse and parent.

But the key to receiving from God is to ask. Jesus told a parable about a persistent widow to illustrate "that men always ought to pray and not lose heart," as we read in Luke 18:1. The life of prayer really is a life of *always* praying, and always acknowledging that we are dependent upon our heavenly Father's care.

Apply It:

How important is prayer in your life? Talk with God as you would to a loving father, because He truly does love you and your needs are safe in His hands.

Dig Deeper:

Luke 18:1–6; Ephesians 6:18; 1 Thessalonians 5:16–18

The Ever-bearing Christian

"By their fruits you will know them" (Matthew 7:20).

Sweet ripe strawberries are a favorite fruit around the world. But did you know it is the only fruit that wear its seeds on the outside? The average strawberry is speckled with over 200 seeds, which technically *doesn't* make them a berry, like grapes, which have seeds on the inside. Actually, strawberries are a member of the rose family, which is why they smell as sweet as they taste.

The average American eats about three-and-a-half pounds of fresh strawberries each year. Most strawberry plants fall into two groups—June-bearing and ever-bearing. The June-bearing produces berries in June and the ever-bearing typically produces a crop in June and another in the fall. But a new type, called "day-neutral," produces strawberries throughout the growing season—flowering regardless of the length of the period of light it is exposed to.

Followers of Jesus should not be seasonal Christians. They should be like ever-bearing plants that produce the fruits of the Spirit (Galatians 5:22, 23) regardless of outward circumstances. Some believe that salvation by grace means fruit bearing is unnecessary. Though we are not saved by works, our salvation leads us to seek to obey God's will.

Jesus explained, "Abide in Me, and I in you. As the branch cannot bear fruit of itself, unless it abides in the vine, neither can you, unless you abide in Me" (John 15:4). What is the purpose of staying united with Christ? "By this My Father is glorified, that you bear much fruit" (v. 8).

No matter our surroundings, when we are connected to Christ, our lives will reveal the fruits of His character. "I am the vine, you are the branches. He who abides in Me, and I in him, bears much fruit; for without Me you can do nothing" (v. 5). Ever-bearing fruit in the life of a Christian reveals a sign of spiritual growth and indicates that we are truly abiding in Jesus.

Apply It:

What fruit would you choose to represent your Christian life? Why do you choose that fruit?

Dig Deeper:

Ezekiel 17:23; Matthew 7:15–20; Colossians 1:9–11

Anticipating Victories

"Thanks be to God, who gives us the victory through our Lord Jesus Christ" (1 Corinthians 15:57).

Scientists have found that composite metal foam provides great advantages to armored vehicles, such as tanks. The material is made of metal but resembles a sponge, or Swiss cheese, because of its holes. This texture not only makes the armored vehicles much lighter, but also absorbs more of the shock from explosions.

God knew that we would fare much better if we were made aware that we are in the middle of a war (see Revelation 12:17). For this reason, we find examples in Scripture of the battles that take place in the lives of believers. Job suffered greatly because of this controversy, as did the apostles who, after being beaten, rejoiced "that they were counted worthy to suffer shame for His name" (Acts 5:41).

The Bible helps us to take the necessary precautions that He has prepared for us. In the first place, He assured us that Christ has not only won the victory for us, but also provided us with the means for victory.

One greatest assurance is the protection of the holy angels: "The angel of the Lord encamps all around those who fear Him, and delivers them" (Psalm 34:7). When we have confidence that we are protected, we can focus on protecting ourselves with the armor of God.

The apostle Paul described the armor using words that describe the character of Jesus: "Stand therefore, having girded your waist with truth, having put on the breastplate of righteousness" (Ephesians 6:14). However, the same passage also tells us that the armor is a belief in God's work to bring about this character transformation. Such a change comes about by "the renewing of your mind" (Romans 12:2) in the Word of God.

An understanding of God's work on our behalf begins with the Bible but then moves into our daily lives. In our day-to-day experience, we can exercise faith by speaking of the good things that God will do for us and by reading affirming Scripture truths that tell us, "This is the victory that has overcome the world—our faith" (1 John 5:4). In this way, we will be *wearing* our beliefs.

Apply It:

Tell a friend about the fulfillment of a Bible promise that you are anticipating.

Dig Deeper:

Psalm 91:11; Ephesians 6:12, 13, 15–18; Revelation 12:17

A Sacred Gathering

"Let us consider one another in order to stir up love and good works, not forsaking the assembling of ourselves together, as is the manner of some, but exhorting one another, and so much the more as you see the Day approaching" (Hebrews 10:24, 25).

Rallies and protest marches in Washington, D.C. have been taking place since 1893, when Fry's Army organized a protest march by unemployed American workers. Events held at the National Mall take place between the U.S. Capitol and the Lincoln Memorial. In 1995, the National Park Service quit releasing crowd size estimates for Mall rallies after a controversy concerning the Million Man March.

Over the years, there have been marches against nuclear weapons, marches to commemorate Martin Luther King Jr., repeated protests against the Vietnam War, pro-life marches, pro-choice marches, and, more recently, the March for Our Lives student-led demonstration. Turnout was estimated to be between 1.2 and 2 million people, making it the largest protest in American history.

The Bible encourages the "assembling of ourselves together," not for the purpose of protest, but to worship God and fellowship with one another. The early church understood and practiced coming together. "When the Day of Pentecost had fully come, they were all with one accord in one place" (Acts 2:1). When the Holy Spirit was poured out, the results were astounding. "Those who gladly received his word were baptized; and that day about three thousand souls were added to them" (v. 41).

Another reason Christians come together is for corporate worship. It affirms our identity as believers in God who "are a chosen generation, a royal priesthood, a holy nation, His own special people, that you may proclaim the praises of Him who called you out of darkness into His marvelous light" (1 Peter 2:9).

Such gatherings not only provide encouraging opportunities for interpersonal relationships and spiritual growth, but they become a witness to the world. "Believers were increasingly added to the Lord, multitudes of both men and women" (Acts 5:14).

Apply It:

What is the biggest crowd you have ever been in? Was it a sports event, a concert, a rally, or a church gathering?

Dig Deeper:

Deuteronomy 31:12, 13; Matthew 18:20; Colossians 3:16

The Church

12

A Heavenly Call

"There is one body and one Spirit, just as you were called in one hope of your calling" (Ephesians 4:4).

It's no surprise that he made the first long-distance call. On February 12, 1877, Alexander Graham Bell demonstrated his new invention, the telephone, to an audience in Salem, Massachusetts, by calling his assistant, Thomas Watson, who was eighteen miles away in Boston. *The Rutland Daily Globe* reported, "It was a very noteworthy occasion, certainly; and the complete success attained led to the discussion of many plans for the further practical utilization of the telephone."

You have received a long-distance call all the way from heaven. This was no ordinary call. "You are a chosen generation, a royal priesthood, a holy nation, His own special people, that you may proclaim the praises of Him who called you out of darkness into His marvelous light" (1 Peter 2:9). God has called a people out of every nation on earth to be one great family.

The Bible speaks of these called people as the church—which is the Greek word *ekklesia* and means "a calling out." In secular Greek society, this term simply referred to a general gathering. In the Old Testament, the Hebrew equivalent, *qahal,* referred to an assembly or congregation. "The king turned around and blessed the whole assembly of Israel, while all the assembly of Israel was standing" (1 Kings 8:14).

In the New Testament, the word "church" was applied to those who believed in Jesus as the Messiah, who accepted Him and His teachings, and who were joined to the organization set up by Him. The church was also spoken of as "one body in Christ" (Romans 12:5). As Ephesians 4:4 states, there is "one body" because "you were called in one hope." It's a call you should always answer.

Apply It:

Who is your favorite person to call long distance?

Dig Deeper:

1 Samuel 17:47; 1 Corinthians 11:18; Ephesians 4:11–16

From Wilderness to World Changers

"These who have turned the world upside down have come here too" (Acts 17:6).

Did you know that God had a church for thousands of years before Jesus' birth in Bethlehem?

You can read it in your Bible; in Acts 7:38, referring to the One whom Moses called "that Prophet," Stephen identified Him as Jesus: "This is he who was in the congregation in the wilderness."

From the beginning of the Bible, the idea of God having a people separate from the world is a key theme. Abram, later Abraham, was told to leave Ur: "Get out of your country, from your family, and from your father's house, to a land that I will show you. I will make you a great nation; I will bless you, and make your name great; and you shall be a blessing" (Genesis 12:1, 2).

Abraham was "called out" from his homeland to follow God. Moses and the children of Israel were "called out" of bondage to be God's people. From the time of Joshua, the Israelites were the congregation of God in the world—called to be separate from the pagan practices of their neighbors. The Bible says they actually had "the gospel ... preached ... to them" (Hebrews 4:2).

And in the New Testament, there are 117 instances of the church named using the Greek word *ekklesia*, which means "the called-out ones." But unlike that ancient "congregation in the wilderness," the ranks of the New Testament church were and remain open to Jew and Gentile alike, following Jesus' command to "make disciples of all the nations" (Matthew 28:19).

If you are following Jesus, you also are one of those "called out" to make a difference for God in this world. You can share the good news with others, express God's love for humanity in acts of service, and pray that one day, soon, His kingdom will indeed come!

Apply It:

Reflect on the long history of God calling out those He loves. Let this motivate you to share God's Word with others around you.

Dig Deeper:

Exodus 19:6; Deuteronomy 28:9; Galatians 3:26–29

Body Talk

"You are the body of Christ, and members individually" (1 Corinthians 12:27).

Imagine waking up one morning and hearing your kidneys talking to you. "You know, we've been doing a lot of cleaning up around here and don't receive much appreciation for all our hard work. So, we're taking the day off!" What would happen if your kidneys took a vacation? Your whole body would suffer.

Using the analogy of a human form, the apostle Paul describes the nature of the church as a physical body: "As the body is one and has many members, but all the members of that one body, being many, are one body, so also is Christ" (1 Corinthians 12:12). The head of the church is not a pastor or some officer in a building somewhere, but Christ (Ephesians 4:15).

The metaphor of a body teaches us that the church is to be a unified whole and that all the different members of the body depend upon one another. "If the foot should say, 'Because I am not a hand, I am not of the body,' is it therefore not of the body?" (1 Corinthians 12:15). Many different types of gifted members make up the body of Christ. All are essential to the whole as they are dependent upon one another.

Some members of the body may feel so essential that they elevate their gifts above others. Paul warned, "If the whole body were an eye, where would be the hearing? If the whole were hearing, where would be the smelling?" (v. 17). In other words, God intentionally created diversity in the body, not only that many things would be accomplished for His work, but that members would feel their need of one another.

You are an important part of the body of Christ. The Lord has uniquely created you to unselfishly contribute to the well-being of the whole church. So if you wake up some morning and contemplate taking a long vacation away from church, remember, you make a difference!

Apply It:

Which body parts do you think are most essential to the life of your body? Could that part exist for very long separated from the rest of the body?

Dig Deeper:

1 Corinthians 12:1–31; Colossians 1:18; Ephesians 5:23

Temple of Love

"Do you not know that you are the temple of God and that the Spirit of God dwells in you?" (1 Corinthians 3:16).

The lowest social class in India is the Dalit class, known as "untouchables." Members of the bottom level of the caste are not allowed to enter temples, attend schools where members of higher caste levels attend, or drink from the same wells from which members of higher caste levels drink. Recently, however, a priest carried a Dalit man into a temple in an effort to break the tradition.

The Bible uses the metaphor of the temple to describe the church of God. Unlike the customs in some cultures, however, the Bible speaks of all people being welcomed into the church. At the same time, the use of the temple metaphor suggests that being a member of God's church leads to a closer walk with God and calls for a particular level of reverence toward church membership.

To better understand this analogy, it is helpful to consider that it is people who make up the temple of God on earth regardless of the buildings in which they worship: "You also, as living stones, are being built up a spiritual house, a holy priesthood, to offer up spiritual sacrifices acceptable to God through Jesus Christ" (1 Peter 2:5).

Church membership should reflect people who reflect the character of Christ. Though we are always growing in Jesus, there should be a commitment to follow the teachings of Scripture and strive for holiness through the power of the Spirit.

A similar metaphor shows that the character of each member of a church is what creates the temple of God, regardless of the appearance of the building: "If anyone's work which he has built on it endures, he will receive a reward" (1 Corinthians 3:14). This can mean that while we minister to all people, we should be selective when choosing a marriage or business partner (2 Corinthians 6:14, 16). This is just one of the many ways that we can make God's temple attractive to others.

Apply It:

Plan a social gathering with someone you consider spiritual.

Dig Deeper:

Ephesians 2:20; 1 Corinthians 3:9–15; 1 Peter 2:4, 6

A Holy Bride

" 'The marriage of the Lamb has come, and His wife has made herself ready.' And to her it was granted to be arrayed in fine linen, clean and bright" (Revelation 19:7, 8).

It was the happiest day of her life—February 10, 1840—when Queen Victoria entered Chapel Royal at St. James' Palace behind Albert of Saxe-Coburg, her beloved husband-to-be. As she glided gracefully down the aisle, a dozen blushing bridesmaids carried her long and elegant bridal train. Victoria's exquisite lace-trimmed satin dress and lace veil were stunningly crafted in pure white—which popularized a trend that continues to this day.

The Scriptures portray the church, the bride of Christ, as attired in pure, clean garments, "not having spot or wrinkle or any such thing, but that she should be holy and without blemish" (Ephesians 5:27). But how does the church, filled with faulty people, become so clean and lovely? The church is made up of individuals who certainly cannot generate goodness through their own efforts. In fact, the Word of God assures us that "all our righteousnesses are like filthy rags" (Isaiah 64:6).

We can be thankful that Jesus gave Himself for the church and that He invites each of us personally to be covered by His spotless righteousness. "Come now, and let us reason together ... though your sins are like scarlet, they shall be as white as snow; though they are red like crimson, they shall be as wool" (Isaiah 1:18).

Jesus is the only One who can cut away our filthy rags, wash us clean, and give us new hearts and victorious lives. He's the only One who can keep us on the right track and purify our lives, and He longs to do these things for each one of us. Have you accepted His incredible invitation?

Apply It:

Search for a painting or photograph of Queen Victoria's wedding dress. Ask God to cover you with the pure white robe of Christ's righteousness.

Dig Deeper:

Hosea 2:19; 2 Corinthians 11:2; Ephesians 5:25, 26

A Heavenly City

"You have come to Mount Zion and to the city of the living God, the heavenly Jerusalem, to an innumerable company of angels, to the general assembly and church of the firstborn who are registered in heaven" (Hebrews 12:22, 23).

Jerusalem is one of the most well-known cities in the world. But did you know that it has 1,578 public gardens and parks, 2,000 archaeological sites, 70 cultural centers, 60 museums, 3.4 million annual tourists, and 90,000 hotel rooms? The city has grown significantly since the time of King David.

Since three major religions consider Jerusalem to be a sacred city, it has also become one of the most controversial pieces of real estate on the planet. According to Wikipedia, "During its long history, Jerusalem has been attacked 52 times, captured and recaptured 44 times, besieged 23 times, and destroyed twice." The name *Jerusalem* means "city of peace," but it has been anything but peaceful.

While the eyes of many Christians are focused on the current city in the present-day Middle East, the Bible speaks of the city as a symbol for God's church, the New Jerusalem. The apostle lifts our sights to "Mount Zion and to the city of the living God, the heavenly Jerusalem" (Hebrews 12:22). This spiritual counterpart identifies God's people as having their "citizenship ... in heaven" (Philippians 3:20).

Paul uses the earthly Jerusalem as a symbol for those who have attempted to be "justified by law" (Galatians 5:4) and are in "bondage" (4:25). The true children of God have been "born according to the Spirit" (4:29) and are now part of "the Jerusalem above," which "is free" and "is the mother of us all" (4:26).

It is a fascinating experience to walk the old streets of Jerusalem and learn about biblical history. But that can never compare with walking "the street of the city" that is "pure gold, like transparent glass" (Revelation 21:21). Don't settle for being only a tourist to a restless city. You can be a citizen of a heavenly city of peace that will last for eternity.

Apply It:

What famous cities have you visited in your lifetime? How do you think they compare to the heavenly Jerusalem?

Dig Deeper:

Psalm 48:2; Galatians 4:21–31; Revelation 21:9–27

Safe in the Family

"From whom the whole family in heaven and earth is named" (Ephesians 3:15).

During the 92nd birthday party of Queen Elizabeth, police shut down roads and armed guards were conspicuously stationed all around Royal Albert Hall. The security concern was due not only to the presence of the queen, but also to the many other members of the royal family in attendance.

In contrast to the security needed by the royal family, the church of God is designed to be a place that calls all people into God's family. This does not mean that all people are already a part of God's family, for then no one would be free to reject that status. Instead, they have the opportunity to become children of God.

The Bible describes this process as an adoption or a new birth. In both instances, it appears as though the decision is a personal one, between the individual and God. However, once the decision is made, the individual gains caring siblings who take responsibility for their family.

The apostle Paul showed that this was a commonly understood status on two different occasions: "I commend to you Phoebe our sister, who is a servant of the church in Cenchrea, that you may receive her in the Lord in a manner worthy of the saints, and assist her in whatever business she has need of you; for indeed she has been a helper of many and of myself also" (Romans 16:1, 2).

There was a standard of conduct in the church that went beyond superficial kindness. The mutual support extended to encouragement and approval in God-given missions: "When James, Cephas, and John, who seemed to be pillars, perceived the grace that had been given to me, they gave me and Barnabas the right hand of fellowship, that we should go to the Gentiles and they to the circumcised" (Galatians 2:9).

Apply It:

Ask a member of your church about their biggest dream in serving God.

Dig Deeper:

Romans 8:14–16; 1 John 1:3, 7; Ephesians 1:4–6

"I'm no volunteer! I'm a regular!"

"Take up the whole armor of God, that you may be able to withstand in the evil day, and having done all, to stand" (Ephesians 6:13).

In the parlor of his home in 1878, William Booth was dictating the words of an annual report for his East London evangelistic outreach. His eldest son, Bramwell, stood nearby while an aide, George Scott Railton, wrote down Booth's words.

"The Christian mission," William Booth began, "is a volunteer army ..."

Bramwell interrupted. You see, in Victorian-era Britain, military volunteers were not looked upon favorably. "Volunteer? I'm no volunteer; I'm a regular!" was Bramwell's retort. The elder Booth told Railton to strike out "volunteer" and replace it with the word "salvation"—which is why the organization has been known for most of the past 150 years as The Salvation Army, with William Booth as its first General.

Today, Booth's movement operates in 128 nations, and its military-style uniforms, marching bands, and titles may make it the most visible representation of the Christian church as an army.

But the notion of the church as God's army is indeed an old one. God's followers have long been engaged in a battle against Satan and his fallen angels, and while the struggle has been long—and remains today—we know what the ultimate outcome will be: God and His people triumph!

Between now and that day of victory, however, the struggle is real. As Paul wrote to the believers at Corinth, "The weapons of our warfare are not carnal but mighty in God for pulling down strongholds, casting down arguments and every high thing that exalts itself against the knowledge of God, bringing every thought into captivity to the obedience of Christ" (2 Corinthians 10:4, 5).

Just as Bramwell remonstrated all those decades ago, let us commit ourselves to being "regular" soldiers in the battle against sin, and for the hearts and minds of those held in the enemy's grip!

Apply It:

As you go about your daily routine, remember you are in enemy territory. Satan wants to distract believers from reaching their heavenly goal and from bringing others to Jesus. By God's grace, fight the good fight of faith.

Dig Deeper:

Acts 20:29, 30; 1 Timothy 4:1; Revelation 12:12, 17

Identifying the Church

"Other sheep I have which are not of this fold; them also I must bring, and they will hear My voice; and there will be one flock and one shepherd" (John 10:16).

How good are you at picking out a criminal? One way suspects might be identified is by a police lineup, where a suspect, along with several "fillers"—people with a similar look—stand side-by-side before witnesses who are often sitting behind a one-way mirror to remain anonymous. Police are not allowed to say or do anything to persuade witnesses to choose someone in the lineup. Some research indicates that sequential lineups (suspects presented one after another) have a higher rate of correct identification than simultaneous lineups (suspects presented all at once).

How good are you at picking out a member of God's church? Well, it depends on whether you mean the visible or invisible church! You might be fairly accurate pointing out a person who is a member of a local church, but a true follower of God might be more difficult to identify. Some people may not look like Christians to you, but "when Gentiles, who do not have the law, by nature do the things in the law, these, although not having the law, are a law to themselves, who show the work of the law written in their hearts, their conscience also bearing witness ... in the day when God will judge the secrets of men" (Romans 2:14–16).

The visible church is organized for fulfilling Christ's great commission to carry the gospel to the entire world (Matthew 28:18–20). The invisible church includes all believers everywhere in the world who may or may not be part of the visible church. Jesus explained, "Other sheep I have which are not of this fold; them also I must bring, and they will hear My voice; and there will be one flock and one shepherd" (John 10:16).

God is leading His people, through the Holy Spirit, from the invisible church to the visible church. By uniting with the visible church, followers of Jesus may fully experience true fellowship and unite in full service to finish God's mission on earth.

Apply It:

Are you a member of God's invisible church? What keeps you from joining His visible church?

Dig Deeper:

John 4:23; Ephesians 1:15–23; Revelation 14:12

Dual Citizenship

"[Jesus] said to them, 'Render therefore to Caesar the things that are Caesar's, and to God the things that are God's' " (Matthew 22:21).

The Pharisees were on a rampage to entrap Jesus in an argument that could lead to His execution. In one instance, they sent their own disciples with the Herodians (Jews who supported Roman rule) to entangle Christ in a discussion that would either make Jesus an enemy of the Jews or a rebel in the eyes of Rome. They asked Him, "Is it lawful to pay taxes to Caesar?" (Matthew 22:17).

Christ didn't hesitate to call their bluff. "Why do you test Me, you hypocrites? Show Me the tax money" (v. 18, 19). They handed him a silver denarius, and He asked them, "Whose image and inscription is this?" (v. 20). They told Him, "Caesar's." Then Jesus said to them, "Render therefore to Caesar the things that are Caesar's, and to God the things that are God's" (v. 21). The Bible says that when they heard His response, "they marveled, and left Him and went their way" (v. 22).

Some have wondered, "If I become a Christian and seek to follow after God, how does that impact my relationship with the governments of this world?" Jesus' answer reveals a balance that recognizes the need for earthly authorities, but not in a way that compromises one's citizenship in heaven. If the two are ever in conflict, "we ought to obey God rather than men" (Acts 5:29)

Membership in the church does not necessarily put us in conflict with being under the authority of a local government. The apostle Paul spoke of such governing leaders: "He is God's minister to you for good. But if you do evil, be afraid; for he does not bear the sword in vain; for he is God's minister, an avenger to execute wrath on him who practices evil" (Romans 13:4). In almost the same language as Jesus, Paul said, "Render therefore to all their due" (v. 7).

Being a good citizen on earth prepares us to be citizens in heaven.

Apply It:

Of which country are you a citizen? What are some earthly authorities you submit to?

Dig Deeper:

Mark 12:13–17; 1 Corinthians 14:33; 1 Peter 2:13–15

God's 'Cloning' System

"Man shall not live by bread alone, but by every word that proceeds from the mouth of God" (Matthew 4:4).

Anyone who has served in the military knows the purpose of basic training. The goal is to take a collection of individuals from varied backgrounds and mold them into a unit that works as one. By the end of this basic training, they march in step, perform assigned tasks in the same manner, and support one another. Personalities aren't erased; rather, they are redirected for the common goal of the team.

That's not a precise analogy to how the church functions, but it might give you an idea. The church's chief function is to make disciples who, through the Holy Spirit, reflect the life and mind of Christ. This happens when we "live ... by every word that proceeds from the mouth of God."

C.S. Lewis, a Christian writer in the 20th century, put it this way in his book *Mere Christianity*: "The Church exists for nothing else but to draw men into Christ, to make them little Christs. If they are not doing that, all the cathedrals, clergy, missions, sermons, even the Bible itself, are simply a waste of time. God became Man for no other purpose."

That's why the church gathers weekly for worship. That's why Christian fellowship is supposed to be different than fellowship found at the corner bar. It's why the church offers ordinances such as baptism and foot washing. And it's why the church's emphasis is on instructing believers in what the Bible says.

There are any number of social clubs in the world in which folks can escape the burdens of daily life—centered around sports, hobbies, or other pursuits. But the church was not established to be a social club. It's God's hospital for healing wounded souls and His academy for producing saints who'll uplift the world.

Apply It:

Whenever you attend a worship service—or a church committee or board meeting—remember to build others up and share with them the good news!

Dig Deeper:

Hebrews 10:25; 1 John 1:3, 6, 7; Matthew 28:20

Spiritual Order

"Let all things be done decently and in order" (1 Corinthians 14:40).

The first edition was titled *Pocket Manual of Rules of Order for Deliberative Assemblies.* It grew out of an experience in 1863, when U.S. Army Major Henry Martyn Robert was asked to preside over a church meeting. In his study of parliamentary procedure, Robert felt there was a need for a manual to bring consistency and order to many types of organizations.

His much-needed book was based on the rules and practice of Congress. It was retitled *Robert's Rules of Order* and has guided church groups, county commissions, homeowner associations, nonprofit associations, school boards, and more. As of this writing, the book has sold more than 5.5 million copies and has undergone eleven revisions.

After Jesus' ascension, there was an immediate need for order in the new church. The disciples' first act of organization was to replace Judas (Acts 1:15–26). As the church grew, the apostles realized that it was impossible for them to preach the gospel while carrying out the everyday needs of a growing church. So they chose seven men to "serve tables" so that they could continue to focus on prayer and "the ministry of the word" (Acts 6:2, 4).

As the church continued to grow into Asia and Europe, new churches needed leaders, so elders were ordained "in every church" (Acts 14:23). When the church faced a crisis, representatives from the churches, along with the apostles, met to discuss and make decisions to guide the church (Acts 15:6–29). This meeting reveals the need for a general council when issues arise that impact the entire church.

While *Robert's Rules of Order* can play a helpful part in establishing guidelines for conducting church business, the essential guide for the early church was the Holy Spirit—as it remains for the church today. The first order of every gathering for church work should include prayer so that all will be "filled with the Holy Spirit" (Acts 4:31).

Apply It:

What different types of church meetings have you attended?

Dig Deeper:

Exodus 18:13–27; Proverbs 15:22; Acts 13:1–3

More Than a Jack of All Trades

"All authority has been given to Me in heaven and on earth" (Matthew 28:18).

In a strategy called "authority positioning," corporate leaders recommend that businesses present themselves as possessing expertise on one or two particular topics. The idea is that a business does not attempt to be knowledgeable about all things, but rather shows focus and depth on a few topics. In this way, the public comes to consider them the authority on that particular topic and seeks out their business.

In contrast to this strategy is the authority expressed by Jesus. Because of His death and resurrection, He received authority over all things—including the leadership of His church on earth. This means that regardless of the position one holds in the church, all authority flows from Jesus.

The work of salvation that He began led to His authority to establish different positions in the first place: "He Himself gave some to be apostles, some prophets, some evangelists, and some pastors and teachers" (Ephesians 4:11).

In order to maintain this authority appropriately, Christ gave the Scriptures to prevent any one person in the church from abusing power. The authority received by Timothy in the early church was based on and guided by his knowledge of salvation through Jesus. This was recognized by the apostle Paul: "From childhood you have known the Holy Scriptures, which are able to make you wise for salvation through faith which is in Christ Jesus. All Scripture is given by inspiration of God, and is profitable for doctrine, for reproof, for correction, for instruction in righteousness, that the man of God may be complete, thoroughly equipped for every good work" (2 Timothy 3:15–17).

This meant that for Timothy, and any other member, the Scriptures were enough to empower and guide any particular work in the church. While not everyone is called to the same kind of work, every person is to rely on the Scriptures.

Apply It:

Ask church leaders and fellow members what type of work in the church fits you best.

Dig Deeper:

Ephesians 4:7–10, 12, 13; John 16:13–15; 1 Corinthians 11:23–29

Tell It to the Church

"Whatever you bind on earth will be bound in heaven, and whatever you loose on earth will be loosed in heaven" (Matthew 18:18).

Can one bad apple really spoil the whole bunch? That's the conclusion in an article titled, "How One Bad Employee Can Corrupt a Whole Team" (*Harvard Business Review,* March 5, 2018). Apparently, even the most honest employees "become more likely to commit misconduct if they work alongside a dishonest individual." Also, honest employees rarely influence dishonest employees to make better choices. In other words, "Among co-workers, it appears easier to learn bad behavior than good."

The Bible gives guidelines on redemptive church discipline. God calls on the church to impress upon erring members the need to change their ways. The church of Ephesus was commended because it "cannot bear those who are evil" (Revelation 2:2). When private offenses happen between members, Jesus encourages you to "go and tell him his fault between you and him alone" (Matthew 18:15). If this person listens to you, "you have gained your brother."

But what if the sinning brother doesn't listen? Jesus recommends involving the fewest people possible in seeking resolution by teaching "take with you one or two more" (v. 16), and then finally, "if he refuses to hear them, tell it to the church" (v. 17). Under the guidance of the Holy Spirit, if these Bible guidelines are followed, there may come a time when the church will need to disfellowship a member.

Some apples are so bad that the apostle Paul suggests prompt action. Regarding a member who was flagrantly living immorally, he said, "Do you not know that a little leaven leavens the whole lump? Therefore purge out the old leaven" (1 Corinthians 5:6, 7). He even says "not to keep company with anyone named a brother, who is sexually immoral, or covetous, or an idolater, or a reviler, or a drunkard, or an extortioner—not even to eat with such a person" (v. 11).

Bad apples really can corrupt the whole bunch!

Apply It:

Can you think of a time when you observed how one person's misconduct influenced others to follow suit?

Dig Deeper:

2 Thessalonians 3:6–14; Titus 3:10, 11; Revelation 2:14, 15, 20

The Remnant and Its Mission

13

The Great Apostasy

"Beloved, do not believe every spirit, but test the spirits, whether they are of God; because many false prophets have gone out into the world" (1 John 4:1).

He has been called the most successful double agent of World War II. Juan Pujol Garcia, known by the British codename Garbo and the German codename Alaric Arabel, was initially turned away by the Allies when offering his services. Originally from Spain, Juan became a successful agent for the Germans, who asked him to travel to Britain. He agreed—but instead he went to Lisbon and created bogus reports for the Nazis.

Eventually, the Allies accepted Pujol. He moved with his family to Britain where he created a network of nearly thirty fictional agents for the Germans. Garbo played a key role in misleading the Germans on the timing and location of the invasion of Normandy in 1944. His fictional spy network was so convincing that his German handlers did not try to recruit additional spies in the United Kingdom.

The devil is like a double agent, for what better way could he bring down God's church than by corrupting it from within? Jesus warned His disciples of a coming deception: "Beware of false prophets, who come to you in sheep's clothing, but inwardly they are ravenous wolves" (Matthew 7:15).

The apostle Paul was equally direct about a coming apostasy. "I know this, that after my departure savage wolves will come in among you, not sparing the flock. Also from among yourselves men will rise up, speaking perverse things, to draw away the disciples" (Acts 20:29, 30). The devil used deceived church leaders who looked like genuine believers, but they led many away from Bible truth.

Garbo successfully mixed truth with error and led the Germans astray. Satan has done this and more—and the Bible predicts that before the end of time Satan will work "with all power, signs, and lying wonders, and with all unrighteous deception among those who perish, because they did not receive the love of the truth, that they might be saved" (2 Thessalonians 2:9, 10). But we can spot fictitious reports from Satan if we stand on the Word of God (Matthew 7:24–27).

Apply It:

Have you ever been tricked into believing something that was not true?

Dig Deeper:

Matthew 24:4–35; 2 Thessalonians 2:1–12; 1 John 4:1–3

Falling Into Deception

"I have this against you, that you have left your first love" (Revelation 2:4).

The online sale of products has been artificially controlled by fake reviews. Journalists have found that some sellers offer money in exchange for positive reviews. These sellers solicit this service using social media in hopes that they will not be tracked down. Online sales platforms have started eliminating dishonest sellers because customer trust is so crucial to business success.

God knew that His church would be negatively transformed as a result of deception. For this reason, he used multiple prophets to let His people know that the church would not always remain pure. He wanted to warn His true followers that He does not approve of everything done by those who merely claim to follow Him.

The apostle Paul provides one of the clearest explanations concerning what would happen in the church in the last days. In one of his letters, he stated, "Let no one deceive you by any means; for that Day will not come unless the falling away comes first, and the man of sin is revealed, the son of perdition" (2 Thessalonians 2:3). In other words, Jesus would not return until after corruption would enter the church.

As a result of corruption, a demonic power would arise in the church. Although the power is named as though it were a single person, Paul goes on to explain that it would arise through deception and gain a following: "With all unrighteous deception among those who perish, because they did not receive the love of the truth, that they might be saved" (2 Thessalonians 2:10). It seems as though the primary antidote to this crisis within the church is a solid commitment to the truth of God. At the same time, we know that we have assurance of God's help in this process of resisting Satan's lies.

■ Apply It:

Leave an honest review for a product you've recently purchased.

■ Dig Deeper:

2 Thessalonians 2:4–9, 11–17; 1 John 2:22; Revelation 2:5

The Suffering Church

"The woman was given two wings of a great eagle, that she might fly into the wilderness to her place, where she is nourished for a time and times and half a time, from the presence of the serpent" (Revelation 12:14).

The fairytale wedding of the century quickly turned into a nightmare marriage. When Prince Charles married Lady Diana Spencer, the relationship disintegrated rapidly. She described her wedding day as "the worst day of my life." She fought against the strict protocols of royal life; he found romance with a mistress. Soon their dirty laundry was aired to the public. The royal couple separated and eventually divorced. Some of the biggest story-book weddings don't always live happily ever after.

Augustine dreamed of a union that he believed would bring peace and unity to the world. In his famed *The City of God,* the influential church father outlined the idea of a universal church in control of a universal state. But the marriage of church and state was an unholy alliance that led to the persecution of God's people.

When Emperor Justinian made the bishop of Rome head over all the churches, and when Justinian's general Belisarius liberated Rome in AD 538, the pope could exercise authority to enforce the teachings of the church and eliminate heretics. Thus began a 1,260-year period of suffering for the church as foretold in Bible prophecy. "He shall speak pompous words against the Most High, shall persecute the saints of the Most High, and shall intend to change times and law. Then the saints shall be given into his hand for a time and times and half a time" (Daniel 7:25).

The world became a literal battlefield for Christians, whose spilled blood stained the church. But the Lord protected a remnant. "Then the woman [the true church] fled into the wilderness, where she has a place prepared by God, that they should feed her there one thousand two hundred and sixty days" (Revelation 12:6). At the end of this prophetic period, in 1798, the apostate church received a deadly blow (Revelation 13:3).

Apply It:

Have you ever suffered persecution for your faith? How did you find comfort and strength?

Dig Deeper:

Daniel 12:7; 2 Timothy 3:12; Revelation 12:13–17; 13:5–7; 17:6

Deadly Beliefs

"Babylon was a golden cup in the LORD's hand, that made all the earth drunk. The nations drank her wine; therefore the nations are deranged" (Jeremiah 51:7).

The three friends never intended that their prank would turn deadly. But when they removed a Florida stop sign in February 1996, three teenagers drove through the intersection and into the path of an eight-ton truck and were killed. The pranksters, all in their early twenties, were sentenced to fifteen years in prison. The stop sign was found on the side of the road near the accident.

Like changing traffic signs, Bible truth was hidden by the established church centuries ago, and it has caused untold confusion and led many into fatal beliefs. The church of Rome based these unscriptural doctrines on tradition, and the outcome was a relentless persecution of dissenters, corruption, and spiritual decline. The Word of God describes her false teachings: "Babylon ... has made all nations drink of the wine of the wrath of her fornication" (Revelation 14:8).

The Roman church defined the head of the church on earth as the vicar [substitute] of Christ. Yet the Bible teaches "Christ is the head of the church; and He is the Savior of the body" (Ephesians 5:23). The apostate church also shifted the eyes of church members from the heavenly priesthood of Christ to an earthly priesthood. But the Scriptures state, "We have a great High Priest who has passed through the heavens, Jesus the Son of God" (Hebrews 4:14).

The fallen church also taught that good works are meritorious and give a person a just claim to salvation. In fact, they asserted that extra good works could be used to benefit others and a shortage of good works could be atoned for in purgatory. Yet God "has saved us ... not according to our works, but according to His own purpose and grace" (2 Timothy 1:9).

When we turn away from the signs of truth in the Bible, we put our spiritual lives at risk and will eventually be led down a fatal road.

Apply It:

Have you ever believed something that was false? How did you learn the truth?

Dig Deeper:

Proverbs 14:12; Hebrews 4:14–16; Revelation 18:3

Buried Treasure

"I rejoice at Your word as one who finds great treasure" (Psalm 119:162).

Back in 1992, Eric Lawes was doing a favor for a friend in the town of Hoxne in England, using a metal detector to sweep a field for a lost hammer. Before long, he had dug up silver spoons, gold and silver coins, and a piece of gold jewelry. Archaeologists were called in, and soon they had unearthed a chest filled with ancient treasures. The Hoxne Hoard was the biggest single cache of Roman gold and silver ever found in Britain; it was valued at $1.75 million at the time.

The great men of the Reformation rediscovered priceless biblical treasures that had been lost for centuries. Many of the truths of Scripture that had been buried by the Roman church and hidden from the common people were brought back into the light—including the crucial gospel teaching that justification is achieved only through faith in Jesus Christ: "By grace you have been saved through faith, and that not of yourselves; it is the gift of God" (Ephesians 2:8).

The Reformers were careful to point out that salvation cannot—as the Roman church taught—be earned by works of penance or any good works on the part of the believer. Grace is a gift from God. "If by grace, then it is no longer of works; otherwise grace is no longer grace" (Romans 11:6).

While rejecting many unbiblical, man-made traditions of the Roman church, the Reformers affirmed the Bible's higher authority as the infallible Word of God. They embraced the words of the apostle Paul, who wrote, "All Scripture is given by inspiration of God, and is profitable for doctrine, for reproof, for correction, for instruction in righteousness" (2 Timothy 3:16).

Many don't realize how the work of the Reformers has benefitted them in a tangible way. Their passionate defense of conscience influenced the eventual proclamation of religious liberty in many parts of the world, including America. Freedoms we enjoy today in speech, politics, worship, and even the arts, are linked to the Reformation.

Apply It:

Think of one treasure you have recently discovered in the Word of God.

Dig Deeper:

2 Peter 1:20, 21; 2 Timothy 3:15; Psalm 119:105

Stagnated Reformation

"So we have the prophetic word confirmed, which you do well to heed as a light that shines in a dark place, until the day dawns and the morning star rises in your hearts" (2 Peter 1:19).

Have you ever bitten into a piece of fruit expecting it to taste deliciously sweet only to discover it was unripe, bitter, and perhaps woody? Fruits that are ripe generally become sweeter, less green, and softer. Some fruits—such as apples, bananas, and pears—are purposely picked green in advance of shipping and will still ripen if they are not picked too early. Other fruits must be picked ripe and will not ripen more after being picked, such as blackberries, cherries, and grapes.

The Protestant Reformation should not have ended in the sixteenth century. Though the great Reformers uncovered many truths lost during the apostasy of the church, they had not discovered all the light God wants revealed. The sun had risen, but there was still progress to be made "until the day dawns and the morning star rises in your hearts" (2 Peter 1:19).

More fruit needed to be picked. More precious Bible teachings needed to be uncovered—such as baptism by immersion, a true understanding of what happens at death, and the biblical Sabbath. Instead of advancing the Reformation, their successors held onto the achievements of the Reformers. In the process, the Reformation stagnated.

When Israel was unfaithful to God and did not advance in spiritual growth, they became "like rotten figs that cannot be eaten" (Jeremiah 29:17). By focusing on the Reformers' words and opinions instead of the words of the Bible, the Protestant churches lost their footing and momentum. Jesus said, "A good tree cannot bear bad fruit, nor can a bad tree bear good fruit" (Matthew 7:18). Cold and formal dogmatism crept into these churches.

When Scripture no longer speaks to your heart and the Bible is studied as a merely intellectual pursuit, the fruit of life could be spoiled.

Apply It:

What have you found to most help your Bible study to be fruitful?

Dig Deeper:

Amos 8:1, 2; Matthew 12:33; Philippians 1:6

He Wouldn't Surrender

"The dragon was enraged with the woman, and he went to make war with the rest of her offspring, who keep the commandments of God and have the testimony of Jesus Christ" (Revelation 12:17).

No one anticipated disaster down the tracks. It was September 1, 1894, and by three o'clock in the afternoon, the Minnesota sky was black as night. Passengers on the train traveling toward Hinckley soon saw burning trees on both sides of the tracks. They were headed toward one of the most devastating firestorms in U.S. history.

The smoke and flames became so thick that the train finally stopped and began to back away from town. The fire was so close that parts of the train ignited. Passengers inside the coaches panicked. The heat was unbearable. But through it all, a faithful porter named John Blair patiently passed out wet towels for women to cover their hair. He quietly walked up and down the aisles, talking calmly until the train finally backed away from the fire. He is credited for saving lives.

In Revelation, we read of a fiery dragon [Satan] who "was enraged with the woman [the church], and he went to make war with the rest [remnant] of her offspring, who keep the commandments of God and have the testimony of Jesus Christ" (Revelation 12:17). Like John Blair, this faithful group persists in their loyal service in the midst of a firestorm. They are called "the remnant" because, though multitudes desert their faith, they are "faithful until death" and will receive "the crown of life" (Revelation 2:10).

The dedication found in this remnant surpasses even people like Blair, for God's faithful will stand strong against persecution. Though the enemy breathes fire of destruction, angels of heaven stand guard over these loyal believers who cannot see through the flames. (See Daniel 3:16–27.)

An angel from heaven told the apostle John that God's followers must have "the testimony of Jesus," which "is the spirit of prophecy" (Revelation 19:10). If you would be among the remnant, you must cling to Jesus and His Word. Then you will be delivered from earth's most devastating firestorm!

Apply It:

Read about John Huss (Jan Hus), a faithful Protestant Reformer who was burned at the stake for his faith. He demonstrated the persistence of a loyal servant of God.

Dig Deeper:

2 Chronicles 30:6; Ezra 9:14, 15; Isaiah 10:20–22

Genuine Faith

"Here is the patience of the saints; here are those who keep the commandments of God and the faith of Jesus" (Revelation 14:12).

You are shocked by your good fortune and think it might even be an answer to your prayers. You discover an incredible deal on a Rolex watch, a timepiece you've coveted for years. The online seller promises it is authentic—and for just $150, the luxurious watch can be yours. But there's a catch: The watch is a counterfeit.

If you're interested in a genuine Rolex watch, you can spot a fake by following some basic rules. First, look at the price. Most of these valuable timepieces start at $2,000. Next, consider the seller. Like purchasing a home, you should look at "location, location, location." A swap meet or a side alley is not a good place to purchase an authentic Rolex. There are other, finer details you can spot on the watch itself if you know what you're looking for.

When identifying God's people at the end of time, the Bible says that they have "the faith of Jesus." The Lord's remnant people are characterized by a faith that is similar to that of Jesus. The Bible shows us that Christ had an unshakeable faith in "every word that proceeds from the mouth of God" (Matthew 4:4).

The faith of Jesus was not a passive belief in God. It compelled Him to obey His Father's will from a heart of love. "If you love Me, keep My commandments" (John 14:15). God's remnant people will "keep the commandments" (Revelation 14:12) because of their faith in Jesus.

God's last-day people will also have faith that Jesus came from heaven as the Savior of the world. Like the Samaritans who were moved by the testimony of the woman at the well, we too may say, "Now we believe, not because of what you said, for we ourselves have heard Him and we know that this is indeed the Christ, the Savior of the world" (John 4:42).

Jesus is the true and authentic Messiah from heaven. You can test Him and see for yourself!

Apply It:

Have you ever purchased something that claimed to be authentic but ended up being a fake?

Dig Deeper:

Isaiah 29:13; Matthew 7:21–23; James 1:26

Quality Imitation

"He who says he abides in Him ought himself also to walk just as He walked" (1 John 2:6).

Some insects use imitation to survive. For instance, the walking leaf looks like the leaves in its surrounding environment. Other insects, like the Atlas moth, imitate other dangerous creatures; the markings on its wings look like snake heads. These designs are intended to scare off predators.

For the people of God living in the last days, imitation is not a survival strategy, except in a qualified sense. The remnant people of God know that they are saved by the righteousness and grace of Jesus. However, they also know that the law of God was intended to be kept in order to experience the highest quality of life. This is one of the reasons why Jesus asked His disciples to follow in His footsteps in keeping them.

Jesus described the keeping of the commandments as directly related to dwelling in His love: "If you keep My commandments, you will abide in My love, just as I have kept My Father's commandments and abide in His love" (John 15:10). This must be what it means to truly have life.

Although it is true that our commandment-keeping is evidence of our faith, it is also true that we can only keep them by the power of God. Part of keeping the commandments is learning how to rejoice in God even during difficult times. The apostle Paul seemed to have learned this important lesson when he stated, "I can do all things through Christ who strengthens me" (Philippians 4:13). He was not just learning how to live the best life; he was imitating Jesus.

Even while facing unjust treatment, Christ consistently followed His Father's will. In the last days, the people of God will do the same: "For to this you were called, because Christ also suffered for us, leaving us an example, that you should follow His steps" (1 Peter 2:21).

Apply It:

Spend time with a friend who inspires you to be your best.

Dig Deeper:

Matthew 7:21; Exodus 20:1–17; Matthew 19:17

Eyewitness Report

"The testimony of Jesus is the spirit of prophecy" (Revelation 19:10).

In a courtroom of law, an "eyewitness testimony" is an account of a bystander who directly observed a specific incident under investigation. What the person remembers is critical evidence to reveal what took place. A testimony, usually given under oath, is a solemn declaration of fact and may be oral or written.

The book of Revelation begins with interesting statements that give evidence to the credibility of the contents presented by the apostle John. "The Revelation of Jesus Christ, which God gave Him to *show* His servants—things which must shortly take place" (Revelation 1:1, emphasis added). John "saw" this revelation, which came from Jesus. "He sent and *signified* it by His angel to His servant John" (Ibid., emphasis added). His eyewitness report affirms the authenticity of this message.

Notice that John "*bore witness* to the word of God, and to the *testimony* of Jesus Christ, to all things that he saw" (verse 2, emphasis added). The language almost has the feel of a courtroom statement, which declares that what follows is trustworthy. John gave us an eyewitness account of the revelations given by Jesus about things that *will* take place at the end of time. Thus, the messages of Revelation are prophetic.

When identifying God's end-time people, an angel tells John—who tried to worship this angel—"See that you do not do that! I am your fellow servant, and *of your brethren who have the testimony of Jesus*" (Revelation 19:10, emphasis added). What is this testimony? The angel defines it as "the spirit of prophecy."

Jesus gives prophecy to the church—as we see in the book of Revelation—to guide His people in the closing days of earth's history. This prophetic guidance makes the remnant a prophetic people who proclaim a prophetic message. This underlies the importance of studying prophecy and preparing the world for Jesus' soon return.

Apply It:

What is your favorite chapter in the book of Revelation?

Dig Deeper:

Ephesians 4:11–13; 2 Peter 1:19–21; Revelation 12:17

June 16

Persisting without Bitterness

"The woman was given two wings of a great eagle, that she might fly into the wilderness to her place, where she is nourished for a time and times and half a time" (Revelation 12:14).

During his years of imprisonment on the infamous Robben Island and in other South African prisons, Nelson Mandela never gave up on his vision of abolishing apartheid, the system of racial oppression in that country. That struggle sent Mandela to jail, separated him from his family, and sparked a global network of support for his movement.

Yet even though Mandela suffered greatly, he refused to be bitter: "Resentment is like drinking poison and then hoping it will kill your enemies," he famously said. He faced disappointments along the way but emerged from prison not only a free man, but also as the eventual president of South Africa.

Nelson Mandela persevered even when things seemed to be at their worst.

The emergence of the remnant church at the close of a long period of persecution (Daniel 7:25) came as people around the globe were studying ancient Bible prophecies and seeing where those prophecies led. There was unmistakable evidence that God's hand was moving in world events and that the devil was working fast "because he knows that he has a short time" (Revelation 12:12).

But why a remnant church? Clearly, the Reformation begun by Martin Luther and his peers centuries earlier had stagnated. There was no longer that same spirit of reformation. Even as the 1798 captivity of the pope—precisely at the end of the 1,260 years prophesied in Daniel 7:25—came to pass, there were only a few stirrings among those in the churches founded by Luther and other Reformers.

God saw the need for action by His people to share the end-time message with others. In many places around the world, Christians studied the Word and recognized that "the time of the end" (Daniel 12:4) had come. God led those Bible students (like Joseph Wolff and William Miller) to proclaim the message of the Second Advent and the freedom it will finally bring from this bitter prison house of sin.

Apply It:

Remembering the faithfulness of the pioneering Reformers and of the believers in the Second Advent, resolve to stay committed to your faith and the message you've received.

Dig Deeper:

Revelation 12:14–17; Daniel 7:25; Daniel 12:4

Truth Travels

"I saw another angel flying in the midst of heaven, having the everlasting gospel to preach to those who dwell on the earth—to every nation, tribe, tongue, and people" (Revelation 14:6).

While plants do not have legs to walk, their seed can travel. Some seeds have parachutes or wings that allow them to glide as they fall to the ground. The wind can carry some seeds hundreds of miles away. Some are like hitchhikers and can stick to you or animal fur and travel to new places. There are seeds that float in water, like the coconut, and are able to take an ocean voyage to a faraway beach.

How do the seeds of the gospel travel? God has chosen messengers, like you, to carry the everlasting hope of salvation "to every nation, tribe, tongue, and people" (Revelation 14:6). God's remnant people are symbolized by an angel sharing the gospel with the world.

Notice the urgency of how this gospel seed is spread: "Saying with a loud voice, 'Fear God and give glory to Him, for the hour of His judgment has come' " (verse 7). It is a sober call to repentance and reverence that impacts our entire lives. The Bible explains how we are to glorify God: "Whether you eat or drink, or whatever you do, do all to the glory of God" (1 Corinthians 10:31).

This "hour of His judgment" message also tells us that we are living in the final moments before Christ's return. The high priest ministry of Jesus in the heavenly sanctuary (Hebrews 9:11, 12) is near completion and judgment in favor of God's people and against sin and apostasy is about to be carried out (Daniel 7:22).

In the first angel's message, we are told to "worship Him who made heaven and earth, the sea and springs of water" (Revelation 14:7). The final choice everyone will need to make is whether to worship the true God of heaven or to worship the beast and his image (Revelation 13:3, 8, 15). This clear reference to the fourth commandment, God's holy Sabbath on the seventh day of the week, divides the faithful from the false.

Are you carrying God's end-time truths to your corner of the globe?

Apply It:

Go outside and look for natural seeds. How do they travel? How can you carry the gospel seed to others?

Dig Deeper:

Matthew 28:19, 20; John 15:8; 1 Corinthians 6:19, 20

Almost Universal

"Another angel followed, saying, 'Babylon is fallen, is fallen, that great city, because she has made all nations drink of the wine of the wrath of her fornication' " (Revelation 14:8).

Universal basic income is the idea that every person should receive an income even in the absence of employment. This idea has drawn more attention in recent years because of the effectiveness of robots in the work force. Presidents of giant corporations have said that traditional employment is changing and, as a result, universal income may be a good option. Regardless of whether such a program would be beneficial, it is clear that it would have an impact on culture.

Any program that has a far-reaching influence should be carefully scrutinized. In one sense, the second angel's message of Revelation 14 is saying that just because something is popular in most of the Christian world does not mean that it is true or safe.

The nation of Babylon represents the beast of Revelation and was symbolic for a corrupt religion. The second angel's warning predicts that "she has made all nations drink of the wine of the wrath of her fornication" (Revelation 14:8). In other words, the church would reach out to government leaders in an effort to gain political power. By using the metaphor of adultery, John expressed that the union of religion and politics is unholy and repulsive to God.

John states that Babylon is the one "with whom the kings of the earth committed fornication, and the inhabitants of the earth were made drunk with the wine of her fornication" (Revelation 17:2). Most Protestants in the Reformation era believed that the name "Babylon" was a reference to the church of Rome because of its corruption.

Their interpretation is still relevant because the church of Rome continues to seek political influence. Yet there is hope for every member of any corrupt religion because they have the power to leave: "I heard another voice from heaven saying, 'Come out of her, my people, lest you share in her sins, and lest you receive of her plagues' " (Revelation 18:4).

Apply It:

Use your vote to prevent your government from favoring a single religion.

Dig Deeper:

Genesis 11:1–9; Isaiah 14:4, 12–14; Revelation 13:15–17

A Drink of Wrath

"A third angel followed them, saying with a loud voice, 'If anyone worships the beast and his image, and receives his mark on his forehead or on his hand, he himself shall also drink of the wine of the wrath of God' " (Revelation 14:9, 10).

What is the worst drink for your body?

Sodas and diet sodas rank near the top because they have zero nutritional value, high sugar content, and are linked to a myriad of diseases. Energy drinks are also causing health problems, especially for children and teens. The extraordinarily high caffeine content has contributed to large numbers of caffeine overdoses, and half of these occurred in those younger than nineteen years old.

We could add to this list alcoholic drinks, energy shots, fancy coffee drinks, slushies, sports drinks, milk shakes, colas, powdered fruit drinks, and more!

But there is one drink you'll never want to taste: "the wine of the wrath of God, which is poured out full strength into the cup of His indignation" (Revelation 14:10). The third angel's message is the most solemn warning in all of the Bible and describes the fearful results of worshiping the beast and his image. The beast is the church-state union that dominated the Christian world for centuries and is the "man of sin" (2 Thessalonians 2:2–4) and the "little horn" (Daniel 8:9). (See also Daniel 7:8, 20–25.)

During earth's final crisis, only two classes of people exist: those who worship God on the seventh-day Sabbath according to the fourth commandment (Exodus 20:8–11) or those who worship the beast according to manmade laws (Revelation 13:16). Both groups will suffer. Those who are obedient to God will suffer the wrath of the dragon (12:17) and be threatened with death (13:15). Those who worship the beast and his image will experience the seven last plagues (Revelation 15, 16).

If you do not want to "drink of the wine of the wrath of God," then you'll want to be among those who will drink "of the water of life freely to him who thirsts" (Revelation 21:6).

Apply It:

What is the worst drink you've ever tasted? What is the best drink you've ever had?

Dig Deeper:

Jeremiah 25:15–17; Daniel 8:9–12; Revelation 18:1–9

Unity in the Body of Christ

14

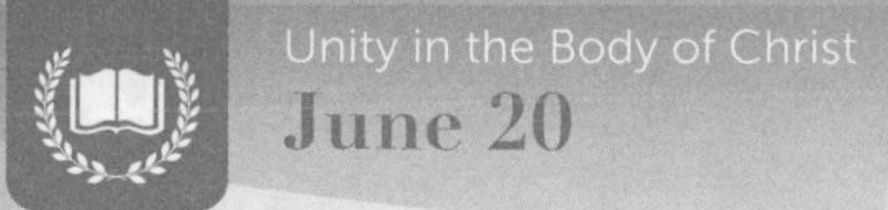

The Best Tool

"The glory which You gave Me I have given them, that they may be one just as We are one" (John 17:22).

There's nothing quite like owning a Swiss Army knife. This multi-tool pocketknife, first manufactured in 1891, generally includes the main spear point blade with a variety of other tools, such as a screwdriver, can opener, nail file, and more. You can always recognize the knife by the red handle with the cross logo, which is Switzerland's coat of arms.

If you're interested in having more tools on your knife, you can always opt for the Swisschamp, which has 8 layers of tools with 33 functions. And if you really want to go all out, then you can get the Wenger Giant, which packs 141 functions into 87 implements. It's nine inches wide and weighs two pounds—and costs $1,400.

What is the church's most powerful witnessing tool? You won't find it at your local Christian bookstore. Nothing gives evidence for the gospel of Christ more than Christians who live in loving harmony. Jesus said, "I in them, and You in Me; that they may be made perfect in one, and that the world may know that You have sent Me, and have loved them as You have loved Me" (John 17:23).

The Savior taught His disciples about the essence of His kingdom the evening before His death, but they were too busy thinking about who would hold the highest position in heaven. Even while humbly washing their feet, Jesus knew they would "not understand" (John 13:7).

So on the way to Gethsemane, Jesus prayed "that they all may be one, as You, Father, are in Me, and I in You; that they also may be one in Us, that the world may believe that You sent Me" (John 17:21). This unity is the church's most powerful tool for sharing the gospel, because it gives evidence of Christ's supreme love for lost people.

Apply It:

Picture your church as a toolbox filled with loving members who work in harmony to build God's kingdom. What kind of tool represents you best?

Dig Deeper:

John 13:34, 35; 17:20–26; Romans 12:5; Ephesians 4:4, 6

The Hidden Force

"I, therefore, the prisoner of the Lord, beseech you to walk worthy of the calling with which you were called, with all lowliness and gentleness, with longsuffering, bearing with one another in love, endeavoring to keep the unity of the Spirit in the bond of peace" (Ephesians 4:1–3).

Isaac Newton has been called the man who put science in motion. He summarized in three simple laws how things in our universe move. The first law states that things that are still stay still and things that are moving keep moving—unless a force of some kind pushes or pulls on them. For instance, picture yourself standing on a skateboard. Unless you push off against something, you'll go nowhere.

Newton explained that motion is caused by forces. If you kick (a force) a ball, the ball goes flying through the air (motion). But some forces don't always make things move. A skyscraper has a lot of forces acting on it, but it doesn't go anywhere. Forces are the hidden power behind everything that happens in our world, including the church.

Unity in the church happens through the moving force of the Holy Spirit. The power of the Spirit doesn't pull people apart—it pushes members closer together. "By one Spirit we were all baptized into one body" (1 Corinthians 12:13). It doesn't matter if a person is rich or poor, male or female, "whether Jews or Greeks, whether slaves or free" for all have "been made to drink into one Spirit" (v. 13).

The result is a "unity of the Spirit in the bond of peace" (Ephesians 4:3). Everything done on every level of the church takes place through the foundation of our triune God. "There are diversities of gifts, but the same Spirit. There are differences of ministries, but the same Lord. And there are diversities of activities, but it is the same God who works all in all" (1 Corinthians 12:4–6).

The force of the Holy Spirit will draw God's people together in a bond of unity that cannot be broken, for it is the hidden power of the Spirit that puts the church into motion.

Apply It:

What one thing is preventing your church from becoming more unified?

Dig Deeper:

Romans 15:5, 6; 1 Corinthians 1:10; 2 Corinthians 13:11

Out of Many, One Body

"He has made from one blood every nation of men to dwell on all the face of the earth" (Acts 17:26).

One blogger noted that while American currency is inscribed with the words "E Pluribus Unum," or, "out of many, one," it's easier said than done when it comes to achieving unity in the church.

It was, after all, quite a thing when non-Jewish believers in Jesus were accepted into the early church in the months after the resurrection. Traditionally, observant Jews had little to do with "gentiles," particularly when it came to worship. The apostle Peter's vision changed all that: Speaking of new believers coming into the faith, a "voice spoke to him again the second time, 'What God has cleansed you must not call common [unclean]' " (Acts 10:15).

Spurred on by the heavenly directive to accept all who believed, the apostles soon took the gospel message to the farthest reaches of the known world, making their faith a global movement.

The church as it exists today is a wonderful mosaic of people and practices. Some congregations sit on cushioned pews in air-conditioned buildings, while others rest on hard benches under thatched roofs supported by poles. Worship music can range from trained professionals to enthusiastic amateurs.

But it's not the construction of the church building, or the composition of the music team that constitutes a congregation. It's the hearts of love, compassion, and service that come together, week after week, to worship God and learn more about Him and His ways.

In 1 Corinthians 2:12, we learn about how so diverse a group of believers can find that unity: "Now we have received, not the spirit of the world, but the Spirit who is from God, that we might know the things that have been freely given to us by God." It's the presence of the Holy Spirit that enables us to be united in faith and in doctrine. Thank God for that!

Apply It:

The next time you worship in church, look around at the great diversity of people.

Dig Deeper:

1 Corinthians 12:11; John 15:1–6; Acts 13:1–5

A Heavenly Union

"How good and how pleasant it is for brethren to dwell together in unity!" (Psalm 133:1).

The European Union (EU) has been considered by some a failed experiment. While it has set high goals—the convenience of one currency, the enhancement of mutual prosperity, and a reduction of political tensions after centuries of hostility—many blame the EU for the unemployment of tens of millions of Europeans.

Some economists believe the EU must be more fully integrated to prosper, but the chances of that happening are close to impossible. To set up a government like the United States would be too big of a leap. Most Europeans shudder at the thought of a "United States of Europe." Perhaps it would be better to go back to helping the nations of Europe function independently.

Some Christians think the same way about the church. The different temperaments, cultures, ideologies, and theological viewpoints—even within the same denomination—make members wonder if independent congregations would prosper more on their own. Yet the Bible says, "As we have many members in one body, but all the members do not have the same function, so we, being many, are one body in Christ, and individually members of one another" (Romans 12:4, 5).

The unity of the church is a powerful witness to the world. Not only is it "good and pleasant" for Christians to "dwell together in unity," but it is shockingly unusual—especially in the eyes of the world where the enforcement of laws is often the means of creating unity.

When Christians live in unity, the church's work is enhanced and prospers. Members become "God's fellow workers" (1 Corinthians 3:9), "all speak the same thing," and there are "no divisions among" members since each is "perfectly joined together in the same mind" (1 Corinthians 1:10).

Though the church struggles to reflect the character of Christ, in the end it will not be a failed experiment, but a divine success made possible by the Holy Spirit.

Apply It:

Think of a time when you worked closely with a team in a unified way. What helped you achieve this unity?

Dig Deeper:

Acts 2:1; 1 Corinthians 3:3; Philippians 2:1–3

Unified by His Spirit

"As many of you as were baptized into Christ have put on Christ. There is neither Jew nor Greek, there is neither slave nor free, there is neither male nor female; for you are all one in Christ Jesus" (Galatians 3:27, 28).

Despite the fact that identical twins are genetic clones who generally grow up in the same environment—participating in similar activities and eating the same foods—their lives and health often turn out very differently. For instance, if one identical twin develops rheumatoid arthritis, there's only a 15 percent chance that the other will also. Of course, there are many thousands of differences of all kinds among identical twins, for they each have their own unique personalities and temperaments and often strongly disagree with each other.

If identical twins with the same genes and environment can clash, how can a church filled with diverse individuals from all backgrounds ever achieve unity? The answer, of course, is only through the power and miraculous intervention of God. In Jesus' prayer for all believers, His petition was that we "all may be one, as You, Father, are in Me, and I in You; that they also may be one in Us" (John 17:21).

Each believer can become a successful part of the body of Christ, the church, only when Jesus abides within the heart. And the only way this can happen is through the indwelling of His Spirit, "the Spirit of Christ" (Romans 8:9).

The Holy Spirit is the essential glue that binds us together as believers. Through the Spirit, we set our differences aside and focus on bringing honor to the name of Jesus. Furthermore, the Spirit of Christ leads us into all truth, bestows spiritual gifts with which to benefit others, and helps us to "grow up in all things into Him who is the head—Christ" (Ephesians 4:15). Through God alone, we are empowered to bear good fruit to honor Him and reflect His love.

Apply It:

Have you ever been acquainted with a set of identical twins? How were they similar? In what ways were they different?

Dig Deeper:

John 16:13; Ephesians 4:1–6; Philippians 2:4

Drawing Power

"I, if I am lifted up from the earth, will draw all peoples to Myself" (John 12:32).

What weighs 35 tons, uses 4,000 gallons of water per minute to keep cool, cost $14.4 million to build, and operates at minus 456 degrees Fahrenheit? Meet the record-breaking 45 tesla hybrid magnet—located in Tallahassee, Florida, at the National High Magnetic Field Laboratory.

This whopper of a magnet is way more than you'd need to hang your children's artwork on your refrigerator. It's used by more than 1,600 scientists each year from around the world for research. With enough copper wiring to supply 80 homes—that's four miles of wire stretched out—it costs about $1,452 an hour to run. The magnetic power of the tesla hybrid magnet equals well over 4,000 fridge magnets.

However, the greatest magnetic pull in the universe cannot be manufactured by humans. It is a force that does not pull on magnetic materials, such as iron, but rather on human hearts. Jesus said that His crucifixion would "draw all peoples" (John 12:32) to Himself. No person is excluded from the captivating power of the cross of Calvary.

Christ has called us to "love your neighbor as yourself" (Matthew 22:39). But is this really possible? We can only love others through the power that comes from Jesus, who said "without Me you can do nothing" (John 15:5). The love of the Savior for our world led Him to give up His life. When we are drawn to Christ, we will be drawn to follow His example of self-sacrificing love.

Unity among God's people comes when we are drawn by the magnetic love of Jesus displayed on the cross. Christ did not die only for a certain race or gender. His death was for all—every nationality, class, and color—all are wanted. Such love cannot be built in a laboratory, for it is divine and has the power to unite heaven and earth.

Apply It:

Find a magnet in your home and hold it close to magnetic material. As you feel the pull of the magnetic force, think of the draw that the cross of Calvary has on the human heart.

Dig Deeper:

John 13:34; Galatians 6:2; 1 John 3:16

Continuous Learning

"He sent them to preach the kingdom of God and to heal the sick" (Luke 9:2).

A leader of a top technology corporation has stated that the company's ideal job candidate is someone who is willing to keep learning. This trait is especially valuable for an industry that changes rapidly all the time. Although it may seem like tech companies would want a specialist, sometimes those specialists come with inflexible biases.

The Bible tells us that unity in the church does not come automatically. Instead, people should be willing to work for it. Sometimes this means seeing a different perspective.

One of the most important factors that brings unity is a shared common goal. This is why Jesus spoke about the importance of following in His footsteps of preaching and healing. He explained that His people were to go to many cities to "heal the sick there, and say to them, 'The kingdom of God has come near to you' " (Luke 10:9).

There are many ways we can be a healing presence. This could mean praying for the sick, encouraging them to practice healthy habits, or helping them heal emotionally through our friendship and love. Additionally, we are to speak about the kingdom of God. This means we should be finding ways to explain how relevant the Bible is to people's lives today. The task is not easy because people change and so do their cultures.

Jesus likely anticipated that we might grow weary of adapting to changing circumstances. Perhaps this is one of the reasons behind team work: "After these things the Lord appointed seventy others also and sent them two by two before His face into every city and place where He Himself was about to go" (Luke 10:1). By going out in groups of two, His followers would naturally see more than one way to achieve the mission.

Apply It:

Team up with at least one church member who is witnessing.

Dig Deeper:

Ephesians 4:1–3; 1 Timothy 5:1, 2; 1 Corinthians 1:2

Bridging the Gap

"I urge you, brethren, note those who cause divisions and offenses, contrary to the doctrine which you learned, and avoid them" (Romans 16:17).

The Royal Gorge bridge, the brainchild of Lon P. Piper, stretches 1,260 feet across the Arkansas River—which plunges 955 feet below. Located near Cañon City, Colorado, it remains the highest bridge in the United States. Construction on the bridge started in June 1929 and was completed in six months.

The bridge spans a canyon of the Arkansas River—one of the deepest in Colorado. The gorge is known as the Grand Canyon of the Arkansas River, with a maximum depth of 1,250 feet. The bottom of the canyon, carved through granite by the river, is only 50 feet wide, while the top is 300 feet wide. On June 11, 2013, a wildfire broke out in the area and destroyed 48 buildings at the park on both sides of the gorge but only lightly damaged some bridge planks.

Some of the deepest gorges in the world have divided church members and created disunity in the church. Attitudes of selfishness, pride, superiority, prejudice, and faultfinding have caused separation among members, damaging the cause of Christ. The apostle Paul warned against such division: "I plead with you, brethren, by the name of our Lord Jesus Christ, that you all speak the same thing, and that there be no divisions among you, but that you be perfectly joined together in the same mind and in the same judgment" (1 Corinthians 1:10).

When the church in Galatia was being torn by division, Paul counseled believers to "walk in the Spirit, and you shall not fulfill the lust of the flesh" (Galatians 5:16). When members walk in the Spirit, they will produce the fruits of the Spirit and draw people together. "The fruit of the Spirit is love, joy, peace, longsuffering, kindness, goodness, faithfulness, gentleness, self-control" (vv. 22, 23).

The deep gorge left by sin, which separates us from God and from one another, was bridged by Christ on the cross. His love reaches across and cares for even "the least of these My brethren" (Matthew 25:40).

■ Apply It:

What is the highest or the longest bridge you have ever crossed?

■ Dig Deeper:

Amos 3:3; 1 Corinthians 1:10–13; Titus 3:10

Deadly Division

*"There is a way that seems right to a man,
but its end is the way of death"* (Proverbs 14:12).

Florida, the Sunshine State, is known for more than beaches and oranges. It also has some of the deadliest highways in America. Six out of ten of the most dangerous roadways are found there, with US-1 as the worst. According to the National Highway Traffic Safety Administration, this 544-mile stretch of asphalt has seen 1,011 deadly crashes in the last decade and accounts for 1,079 fatalities.

But don't blame senior drivers for car accidents in Florida. Research points to distracted driving as the primary cause. There's no law against talking or texting while driving in the alligator state. On the other hand, the safest stretch of highway in the nation is I-95 in Rhode Island, with only 0.1 fatal crashes per million vehicles on the road—that's compared to 2.78 on Florida's US-1.

It is the Lord's plan for His people to travel on the right path to the kingdom. That road is based on Bible truth that sanctifies the heart (John 17:17). When believers receive Christ, they are less inclined to experience head-on spiritual collisions with others. "The glory which You gave Me I have given them, that they may be one just as We are one: I in them, and You in Me; that they may be made perfect in one, and that the world may know that You have sent Me, and have loved them as You have loved Me" (vv. 22, 23).

Following the Scriptures leads to safety and freedom. When we stop pursuing the way of truth, people are led down pathways that lead to death. But, as Jesus said, "If you abide in My word, you are My disciples indeed. And you shall know the truth, and the truth shall make you free" (John 8:31, 32).

Stay on the Bible highway. It's the safest road you can travel.

Apply It:

What's the most difficult road you've ever traveled?

Dig Deeper:

Job 23:11; Matthew 7:13; John 14:6

Baptism

15

The Supreme Example

"Jesus came from Galilee to John at the Jordan to be baptized by him. And John tried to prevent Him, saying, 'I need to be baptized by You, and are You coming to me?' " (Matthew 3:13, 14).

King Christian X of Denmark noticed a Nazi flag flying over a Danish public building during World War II at the time of the Nazi occupation of his country. He immediately called the German commandant and demanded that the flag be taken down. The commandant refused. "Then a soldier will go and take it down," insisted the king. "He will be shot," threatened the commandant. "I do not think so," replied the king, "for I shall be the soldier." Within minutes, the flag was taken down.

When Jesus asked John to baptize Him, the wilderness preacher refused. But Christ insisted and set an example by giving divine sanction to the ordinance of baptism. "Permit it to be so now, for thus it is fitting for us to fulfill all righteousness" (Matthew 3:15), explained the Savior. We are all invited to partake in baptism, for it symbolizes receiving the righteousness of Christ. Since Jesus, who was sinless, was baptized, we, who are sinners, should follow in His steps (1 Peter 2:21).

At the end of Christ's ministry on earth, He commanded His disciples: "Go therefore and make disciples of all the nations, baptizing them in the name of the Father and of the Son and of the Holy Spirit, teaching them to observe all things that I have commanded you" (Matthew 28:19, 20). Jesus' commission makes it clear that baptism is a requirement for becoming part of His church. It demonstrates that the ruling power in one's life has changed from Satan to Jesus.

Some have been threatened with death for taking the step of baptism. But in a spiritual sense, we all lay down our lives in the watery grave of baptism. "Do you not know that as many of us as were baptized into Christ Jesus were baptized into His death?" (Romans 6:3).

Apply It:

Have you taken the important step of baptism?

Dig Deeper:

Matthew 3:13–17; Mark 16:14–18; Romans 6:1–11

Is Baptism Essential?

"As they went down the road, they came to some water. And the eunuch said, 'See, here is water. What hinders me from being baptized?' " (Acts 8:36).

Is baptism essential? Does a new believer *have* to get all wet?

These might seem like odd questions to those who've been baptized, but some still do question the necessity. After all, they assert that the thief on the cross was promised salvation and didn't have a chance to be baptized. (See Luke 23:43.)

So, is baptism optional? Probably not, and we can find the reasons for this in the Bible.

First, of course, is the example Jesus gave: "Jesus came from Galilee to John at the Jordan to be baptized by him. And John tried to prevent Him, saying, 'I need to be baptized by You, and are You coming to me?' But Jesus answered and said to him, 'Permit it to be so now, for thus it is fitting for us to fulfill all righteousness.' Then he allowed Him" (Matthew 3:13–15).

Then comes the instruction Jesus gave the disciples following the resurrection: "Go therefore and make disciples of all the nations, baptizing them in the name of the Father and of the Son and of the Holy Spirit" (Matthew 28:19, 20). Does that sound optional?

Finally, there are repeated instances of believers in the New Testament who were baptized: the three thousand on Pentecost, the Ethiopian eunuch, Lydia of Thyatira, the Philippian jailer, and so on.

The lesson seems clear: if it is possible for a new believer to be baptized, it should be done. Will God understand if a person cannot be baptized? God knows the heart of all people. But if it's possible to fulfill the command, we should obey. If you have been baptized, remember the significance of it. If not, resolve to accomplish this as soon as possible.

Paul said it well in his defense before the Pharisees in Jerusalem: "Why are you waiting? Arise and be baptized, and wash away your sins, calling on the name of the Lord" (Acts 22:16).

Apply It:

If you know someone who is confused about baptism, encourage them to step out in faith and obey Jesus' instruction.

Dig Deeper:

Luke 3:16; Acts 10:48; 1 Peter 3:21

One Baptism

"When all the people were baptized, it came to pass that Jesus also was baptized" (Luke 3:21).

When eating Italian food, do you dip your warm sourdough bread into olive oil that has a splash of balsamic vinegar? People do this all the time—in America, but not in Italy. If you ever happen to visit the famous Ristorante La Sponda in Positano, Italy, you might get a strange look from the waiter if you ask for a little bowl of olive oil in which to plunge your Ciabatta bread.

The Bible actually has a story about bread being dipped into a dish. When Christ celebrated the Passover meal with His disciples in the upper room the night before His crucifixion, He said, "He who *dipped* his hand with Me in the dish will betray Me" (Matthew 26:23, emphasis added). The dish was a sauce used with the unleavened bread and bitter herbs eaten with the Passover meal.

The Greek word used for "dipped" has the root word *baptizō,* which was often used in New Testament times to describe the immersing of a cloth in dye or in filling a vessel with water by submerging it. This same word described John's baptism of Jesus in the Jordan River. "Jesus came from Galilee to John at the Jordan to be baptized [*baptize*] by him" (Matthew 3:13).

There are many different forms of baptism used in the Christian world. Some churches use immersion (dipping); others use aspersion (sprinkling); and still others use affusion (pouring). Yet the apostle Paul described just "one Lord, one faith, *one baptism*" (Ephesians 4:5, emphasis added). The Bible clarifies Christian baptism as immersion—or dipping under water. Jesus "was baptized by John *in the Jordan*" (Mark 1:9, emphasis added).

Whether you enjoy dipping your bread in olive oil, sprinkling herbs on top, or smearing it with peanut butter, the Bible describes only one way to be baptized—to be fully immersed in water. The word baptize itself is one of many ways we know this is the practice approved by God.

■ Apply It:

How many different forms of baptism have you witnessed?

■ Dig Deeper:

John 3:23; Acts 8:38, 39; Colossians 2:12

Baptized by Immersion

"Jerusalem, all Judea, and all the region around the Jordan went out to him and were baptized by him in the Jordan, confessing their sins" (Matthew 3:5, 6).

The Jordan River, once robust and healthy, has today become compromised by pollution. Its flow has been greatly diminished through the diversion of about 90 percent of its water for crops and cities. Indeed, the Dead Sea, which depends on water from the Jordan, has been losing over three feet of water per year. Some environmentalists are hoping that the desalination of ocean water to provide a fresh drinking supply will eventually take some of the strain—and drain—off the Jordan. Despite the river's struggles, each year about half a million Christians visit the site of thousands of years of vibrant history, and many of these pilgrims choose to be baptized there.

The New Testament says that John the Baptist baptized people in the Jordan. Mark 1:5 tells us, "Then all the land of Judea, and those from Jerusalem, went out to him and were all baptized by him in the Jordan River, confessing their sins."

Scripture confirms that these repentant believers were baptized by immersion. "Now John also was baptizing in Aenon near Salim, because there was much water there" (John 3:23). The fact that he needed "much water" indicates that he wasn't simply sprinkling people.

Jesus' baptism in the Jordan also shows that immersion was performed. Matthew wrote that after Jesus had been baptized by John, He "came up immediately from the water" (Matthew 3:16) and Mark described Christ as "coming up from the water" (Mark 1:10).

This practice continued in the early church after Jesus ascended to heaven. One of the best examples is that of Philip the evangelist when he baptized the Ethiopian. "He commanded the chariot to stand still. And both Philip and the eunuch went down into the water, and he baptized him" (Acts 8:38). Verse 39 adds that afterward they "came up out of the water."

Scripture makes it clear that those who choose baptism by immersion are following the example of Jesus.

Apply It:

What do you think it would be like to be baptized in the Jordan River?

Dig Deeper:

Matthew 3:6, 16; Colossians 2:12; Ephesians 4:5

Dead and Alive

"Reckon yourselves to be dead indeed to sin, but alive to God in Christ Jesus our Lord" (Romans 6:11).

How would you like to have the ability to survive being frozen and then thawed out and live normally? That happens every year to the wood frog. This little amphibian can withstand up to 70 percent of its body being frozen, including its brain. Not only that, when temperatures plunge, the wood frog's heart stops and it quits breathing.

But when spring rolls around with warmer weather, the frog thaws out and reverts back to normal. That's because wood frogs have special proteins that remove most of the water out of the frog's cells and replace it with a type of glucose that keeps them from freezing solid. When their bodies warm back up, water returns to the frog's cells. It kind of gives new meaning to the word "croak."

The Christian also experiences a spiritual state of death and life as represented by the ordinance of baptism. Jesus connected His own death to baptism when He told His disciples, "Are you able to drink the cup that I drink, and be baptized with the baptism that I am baptized with?" (Mark 10:38). In addition, His emergence from the waters of baptism foretold His resurrection (Romans 6:4, 5). These spiritual truths are meaningful only through baptism by immersion.

When believers are baptized, it symbolizes death to sin—for we are "crucified with Christ" (Galatians 2:20). The apostle Paul explains that "our old man was crucified with Him, that the body of sin might be done away with, that we should no longer be slaves of sin" (Romans 6:6). Death to self is essential, for "he who has died has been freed from sin" (v. 7). What's even more miraculous is that "if we died with Christ, we believe that we shall also live with Him" (v. 8).

Apply It:

Can you think of other creatures that appear to "die" on the outside but then come back to life?

Dig Deeper:

Luke 12:50; 2 Corinthians 5:17; Galatians 3:27

Continuous Learning

"As many of you as were baptized into Christ have put on Christ" (Galatians 3:27).

In the days leading up to the royal wedding between Prince Harry of the United Kingdom and his American fiancé, the news media began asking readers to give marriage advice to the happy couple. Historically speaking, it is uncommon for citizens to give advice on personal matters to their sovereigns.

Baptism is similar to marriage in that it is a symbol of a covenant relationship with God. All who are baptized into Christ become royalty and share in some of the responsibilities of caring for this world.

In the Old Testament, the people of God had two primary symbols of their agreement with God: circumcision and purification rituals. Some of these purification rituals developed into the practice of baptism by the time that Christ was about to begin His ministry. However, it was not until the Jerusalem council that a decision was made on whether circumcision would continue as a symbol.

The leaders of the church, under the guidance of the Holy Spirit, decided that circumcision would no longer be necessary: "Since we have heard that some who went out from us have troubled you with words, unsettling your souls, saying, 'You must be circumcised and keep the law'—to whom we gave no such commandment" (Acts 15:24). This meant that baptism would be the only symbol of entering into a covenant relationship with Jesus.

Paul wrote about this: "In Him you were also circumcised with the circumcision made without hands, by putting off the body of the sins of the flesh, by the circumcision of Christ, buried with Him in baptism, in which you also were raised with Him through faith in the working of God, who raised Him from the dead" (Colossians 2:11, 12). In some ways, the symbol of baptism is even more powerful than a wedding ceremony, because it shows the death of the old way of life.

Apply It:

Tell someone who has not yet been baptized about your baptismal experience.

Dig Deeper:

Jeremiah 31:33; Galatians 3:28, 29; Romans 2:28, 29

Purified for Service

"I indeed baptize you with water unto repentance, but He who is coming after me is mightier than I, whose sandals I am not worthy to carry. He will baptize you with the Holy Spirit and fire" (Matthew 3:11).

Gold is not naturally found in the pure state in which you see it used commercially. It contains impurities like copper, zinc, iron, or silver and must be purified to become 24-karat gold (99.95 percent pure). Different methods can be used to purify gold, which include the use of acid, fire, or electricity (or a combination of these). The most ancient method, one mentioned in the Bible, uses high levels of heat. "The refining pot is for silver and the furnace for gold, but the LORD tests the hearts" (Proverbs 17:3).

When Jesus was baptized, He received a special outpouring of the Holy Spirit, anointing Him for service. "When He had been baptized, Jesus came up immediately from the water; and behold, the heavens were opened to Him, and He saw the Spirit of God descending like a dove and alighting upon Him" (Matthew 3:16). This reveals that water baptism and Spirit baptism belong together.

John the Baptist told us that Christ would "baptize you with the Holy Spirit and fire" (verse 11). This purifying process was spoken of by Isaiah, who wrote that the Lord would wash away the sin of His people "by the spirit of judgment and by the spirit of burning" (Isaiah 4:4) and "thoroughly purge away your dross, and take away all your alloy" (1:25).

Because "God is a consuming fire" (Hebrews 12:29), we know that when we give ourselves completely to Christ and symbolize our commitment in baptism, the Holy Spirit comes into the life and begins the process of removing all unrighteousness. Being baptized with the Spirit is compared to fire, for through our daily trials we become more like Jesus. "He knows the way that I take; when He has tested me, I shall come forth as gold" (Job 23:10).

Apply It:

Watch a video or read an article that explains the process of refining gold. Reflect on how this describes the process of the Holy Spirit purifying your heart.

Dig Deeper:

Numbers 31:23; 1 Peter 1:7; Revelation 3:18

A Heavenly Society

"Repent, and let every one of you be baptized in the name of Jesus Christ for the remission of sins; and you shall receive the gift of the Holy Spirit" (Acts 2:38).

Have you ever wanted to join an exclusive club? Get ready to dish out a bucket of cash. Vail Resorts Signature Clubs in Colorado offer some of the best ski resorts in the world. The costs vary, but if you choose the Vail Mountain Club, get ready to plunk down a $275,000 deposit and pay annual dues of $6,932. But you can save a lot by joining the Augusta National Golf Club in Augusta, Georgia. This exclusive club has around 300 members and initiation fees run between $25,000 and $50,000. You might run into Warren Buffett while putting on the practice green.

Did you know that there are qualifications for joining the best organization in the universe—the kingdom of heaven? It doesn't take a bank account, but it does require a broken heart. When a multitude heard Peter preach on the day of Pentecost, "they were cut to the heart" and asked, "What shall we do?" (Acts 2:37). Peter told them, "Repent, and ... be baptized" (verse 38).

Hearing and believing the Word of God preached produced faith in the hearts of these hearers, for "faith comes by hearing, and hearing by the word of God" (Romans 10:17). Unless people see their lost condition, confess their sinfulness, submit themselves to God, and repent, they are not prepared for baptism. Dying to sin and living for Christ is what baptism symbolizes.

Repentance means more than saying, "I'm sorry." True repentance is an experience shown in the life and will "bear fruits worthy of repentance" (Matthew 3:8). Becoming part of the body of Christ isn't like paying money to join an earthly club. It requires a relationship with Jesus that is based on a recognition of sin in our lives and a daily need to abide in Him (John 6:56). Unless we have faith in Christ and repent, we are not ready to join a society that will someday permit us to stand on streets of gold.

Apply It:

Have you ever joined any type of club or association? What were the qualifications for joining?

Dig Deeper:

Mark 16:16; John 15:1–8; Acts 18:8

Too Young

"When they believed Philip as he preached the things concerning the kingdom of God and the name of Jesus Christ, both men and women were baptized" (Acts 8:12).

A French perfume designer produced a fragrance for children. In Europe, the brand quickly became a common gift among people who follow fashion trends. However, the trend has not caught on in the United States, where parents are concerned about the danger of the ingredients in perfumes.

Baptism is much more important than a fashion statement. For this reason, the Bible makes it clear that infants are not ready for this important step. This is clear not only because of the many examples of adult baptisms in the Bible, but also because of the steps leading up to that important decision.

In the case of the Ethiopian, Phillip began to lead him to the important decision by asking him about his level of understanding: "Philip ran to him, and heard him reading the prophet Isaiah, and said, 'Do you understand what you are reading?' " (Acts 8:30). It was not until after Philip had explained how salvation comes through Jesus that he offered to baptize the man.

The occasion where small children were brought to Jesus provides a contrast to Philip's story. When a group of mothers decided that they wanted Jesus' blessing upon their children, they brought them to Him: "Jesus said, 'Let the little children come to Me, and do not forbid them; for of such is the kingdom of heaven.' And He laid His hands on them and departed from there" (Matthew 19:14, 15).

Other parts of the Bible record that Jesus' disciples were baptizing people. However, by merely laying His hands on the children in order to bless them, Jesus showed that they were not ready for baptism. If He felt that they were ready, He would have asked His disciples to baptize them.

Apply It:

If you or a family member has a child that has not been dedicated, consider having them presented to the Lord in a special service.

Dig Deeper:

John 3:22; Acts 9:17, 18; John 4:2

A Burial With Benefits

"Seek those things which are above, where Christ is, sitting at the right hand of God. Set your mind on things above, not on things on the earth" (Colossians 3:1, 2).

Even though most Christian churches practice baptism, a few denominations do not follow the practice. Two members of such a church once asked their pastor whether it would be okay to go around the corner and be baptized. They didn't want to join the other church, they said; they merely wished to be immersed in water as the Bible commands.

"Well," the preacher replied, "I don't mind if you do that, but be sure you come back as better members of our church than when you left!" That pastor knew something: If someone goes through the ritual of baptism, it's supposed to result in more than the need for a towel. Life changes should be evident in the one who's been baptized.

Your focus should be different. Instead of thinking about the world and how to achieve success, the new believer's thoughts, after baptism, should be directed toward "things above," and how to please God.

Your fellowship should be different. Rather than hanging out with the "old crowd"—especially if former associates led you into sin—your life will center around a local congregation and your part in serving there. The church needs the participation of every believer.

Your faith should be different. Now that you know the importance of having a relationship with Jesus, your faith will be active and will motivate you to share the good news. An old saying suggests that individual Christians "may be the only Bible some folks ever read," which means that a believer's actions will preach the gospel as effectively, if not more so, than a thousand pamphlets.

In baptism, the believer's old life is symbolically "buried." Rising from that burial, the new believer has the opportunity to show that faith in Jesus is something that transforms lives (Acts 8:39). Be sure to remember it—and live it!

Apply It:

Whether you've just been baptized or your baptism took place years ago, remember to rejoice in what God has done for you!

Dig Deeper:

2 Peter 1:2; 1 Peter 2:2–5; Ephesians 4:12

The Lord's Supper

16

Bowing in Greatness

"Let nothing be done through selfish ambition or conceit, but in lowliness of mind let each esteem others better than himself" (Philippians 2:3).

Hudson Taylor, one of the greatest missionaries to China, was scheduled to speak at a large church in Australia. The moderator of the service introduced the missionary in eloquent and glowing terms. He told the large congregation all that Taylor had accomplished in China and then presented him as "our illustrious guest." Taylor stood quietly for a moment and then opened his message by saying, "Dear friends, I am a little servant of an illustrious Master."

That's not the attitude you would have found among Jesus' disciples in the upper room the night before He was crucified. The future leaders of the church had instead been arguing about who would hold the top positions in the kingdom of heaven. It broke Christ's heart, for this was to be a special occasion. "He said to them, 'With fervent desire I have desired to eat this Passover with you before I suffer; for I say to you, I will no longer eat of it until it is fulfilled in the kingdom of God' " (Luke 22:15, 16).

Traditionally, a servant would wash the feet of guests before the evening meal, but the disciples sat down with dirty feet and would not humble themselves to perform such a menial task. To impress the men with an unforgettable lesson, the Master "rose from supper and laid aside His garments, took a towel and girded Himself" (John 13:4). Jesus, who laid aside His kingly garments, came down from heaven to be a Servant among servants. He knelt down, washed the feet of each disciple, and redefined the meaning of greatness in the eyes of the world.

Both the ordinance of foot washing and the Lord's Supper make up the Communion service and are given by Jesus to help us not only draw closer to Him, but to become like Him. We stand tallest when we are able to say, "I am a little servant of an illustrious Master."

Apply It:

Have you ever participated in the Lord's Supper? If so, what part of the service is most meaningful to you?

Dig Deeper:

Matthew 26:26–28; Luke 22:24; John 13:14–17

A Perfect Example

"If I then, your Lord and Teacher, have washed your feet, you also ought to wash one another's feet. For I have given you an example, that you should do as I have done to you" (John 13:14, 15).

Did you know that the human ankle and foot contain more than 100 muscles, tendons, and ligaments, 26 different bones, and 33 separate joints? No wonder our feet are so versatile. For some people, feet even take the place of hands. Jessica Cox, a motivational speaker from Arizona, was born without arms and uses her feet not only to ambulate but also to drive a car, ride a bicycle, and propel herself while scuba diving. She's the first armless person to earn a black belt in taekwondo and also the first to earn a pilot license. She can even insert and remove her contact lenses with her feet.

When Jesus knelt before His disciples with a basin of water and began to wash away the dust and dirt, He was focused on their soiled hearts rather than their soiled feet. Indeed, His symbolic act overflowed with a deeper meaning.

The disciples had been focused on themselves and on achieving positions of honor in His kingdom. They had forgotten what Jesus had earlier revealed as the secret of being truly great: "Whoever desires to be first among you, let him be your slave—just as the Son of Man did not come to be served, but to serve" (Matthew 20:27, 28).

In order to receive the close communion with Christ that we so desperately need, our hearts need to be humble—washed clean of selfish ambition, resentfulness, pride, and jealousy. Only Jesus can accomplish this in us. In washing His disciples' feet, the King of all creation took "the form of a bondservant" (Philippians 2:7) and gave us the perfect example of humble service to others.

The ordinance of foot washing commemorates Christ's condescension from heaven's glory, fulfills His instruction to "do as I have done to you" (John 13:15), and puts our hearts in the right spirit to honor Him by serving others.

■ Apply It:

Imagine being a disciple in the upper room and having Jesus wash your feet. How would you feel?

■ Dig Deeper:

1 Corinthians 11:27–29; John 13:16, 17; Galatians 5:13

A Higher Cleansing

"When He had washed their feet, taken His garments, and sat down again, He said to them, 'Do you know what I have done to you?' " (John 13:12).

If you are looking to take a luxurious bath, you might consider purchasing one of the most expensive bathtubs in the world. This $845,000 tub is literally a gem because it was cut from a single Amazonian crystal stone. It's six feet, six inches long, weighs two tons, and can be purchased from Harrods store in London. The bath was sculpted with diamond cuts and left partially rough to expose the natural beauty of the crystal.

If you are looking to have your heart washed clean from sin, there is no bathtub in the world that will remove the filth of unrighteousness. When David sinned, he prayed, "Wash me thoroughly from my iniquity, and cleanse me from my sin" (Psalm 51:2). The repentant king wasn't looking to have a relaxing soak in a hot tub. He cried out, "Create in me a clean heart, O God, and renew a steadfast spirit within me" (verse 10).

When Jesus instituted the ordinance of foot washing as a preparation to partake of the Lord's Supper, it was meant to do much more than clean one's feet. It represented a higher cleansing of the heart. Though baptism symbolizes the beginning of our walk with God, foot washing is a reminder of our ongoing need for heart renewal. Peter asked Jesus to bathe him all over; Christ said, "He who is bathed needs only to wash his feet" (John 13:10).

Just as the disciples—who wore open sandals on their feet—needed to regularly wash the dust and dirt from their feet, so the Christian needs regular heart cleansing. In our daily walk with God, we make mistakes and must humble ourselves like Peter before Christ who "loved the church and gave Himself for her, that He might sanctify and cleanse her with the washing of water by the word" (Ephesians 5:25, 26).

Apply It:

Do you need to take a bath or just have your feet washed?

Dig Deeper:

Jeremiah 33:8; Hebrews 9:14; 1 John 1:7–9

A Ritual Unlike Any Other

"If I then, your Lord and Teacher, have washed your feet, you also ought to wash one another's feet" (John 13:14).

Students of the world's many and various religions will be hard pressed to find a ritual of humility quite like that demonstrated by Jesus in John's Gospel account and replicated by many of His followers today.

After all, both in Jesus' day and in our own, feet are often viewed as one of the body's more challenging features. They're often dirty (think of the sandals in Jesus' day and in ours), sometimes calloused or otherwise unattractive, and generally not the thing we first consider when meeting another person.

Next consider the context of Jesus' time: For centuries, the washing of a traveler's feet was considered to be the task of a servant or the traveler himself (Genesis 18:4). When David's servants came to fetch Abigail to be his wife, her first offer was to "wash the feet of the servants of my lord" (1 Samuel 25:41). Foot-washing was not generally the task of the master of the house, certainly not that of Jesus, *right?*, whom His disciples knew as "the Christ, the Son of the living God" (Matthew 16:16).

Yet here is Jesus washing His disciples' feet. He explained that this was an example for each of His followers, that "a servant is not greater than his master" (John 13:16), and that "if you know these things, blessed are you if you do them" (v. 17).

The Christian practice of washing each other's feet is distinct. It is an ordinance of humility, yes, but it's one where each serves another and is served in return. This creates a "fellowship of forgiveness," as writer C. Mervyn Maxwell once explained, where we are all encouraged to seek God's grace both in serving another and in praying with and for them—acknowledging our need for the other person's spiritual help.

It's a wonderful thing, and it's only found among the followers of Christ!

Apply It:

Whenever you have the opportunity to participate in this ordinance, remember Who initiated it and why it is so important for each of us today.

Dig Deeper:

Judges 19:21; Luke 7:44; Matthew 6:14, 15

Kneeling in Service

"You, brethren, have been called to liberty; only do not use liberty as an opportunity for the flesh, but through love serve one another" (Galatians 5:13).

The U.S. government provides a military funeral for members of the Armed Forces upon request of the family. It often features guards of honor, the firing of volley shots as a salute, the playing of "Taps" by a lone bugler, and a flag-draped coffin. There are several types of military funerals, including standard honor, full honor, and armed forces.

One of the most moving parts of the ceremony is the presentation of the flag to the next of kin by an honor guard. After the flag is meticulously folded, the presenter will usually kneel while presenting the flag and then state: "On behalf of the President of the United States, the United States [Army, Marine Corps, Navy, Air Force, or Coast Guard], and a grateful nation, please accept this flag as a symbol of our appreciation for your loved one's honorable and faithful service."

When Christ knelt to wash the feet of His disciples, He demonstrated that He "loved them to the end" (John 13:1). Kneeling before these followers, who would later abandon Him, He showed them that the highest form of love is self-sacrificing service. Paul also affirmed, "Through love serve one another" (Galatians 5:13).

The very act of kneeling down is a reminder to not lift oneself up in feelings of supremacy. It is showing love without jealousy or prejudice. It is a call to love all people—regardless of culture, race, gender, or nationality. "Let nothing be done through selfish ambition or conceit, but in lowliness of mind let each esteem others better than himself" (Philippians 2:3).

There is no greater form of faithful service than to kneel and perform the honorable duty of washing the feet of a fellow-member of the body of Christ. In following the example of Jesus, you will demonstrate honorable and faithful service for the government of heaven.

■ Apply It:

Watch a military funeral and specifically observe the flag presentation where the officer kneels before the family member.

■ Dig Deeper:

Matthew 20:28; 1 Corinthians 9:19; Philippians 2:5–11

Everyday Unity

"When He had given thanks, He broke [the bread] and said, 'Take, eat; this is My body which is broken for you; do this in remembrance of Me' " (1 Corinthians 11:24).

The Putka Bakery in Poland is trying to unite people through the baking of bread. They have been running an advertisement in which bakers from minority groups bake bread. The message is that although these groups have been the target of hate speech, the bread they bake tastes the same as bread baked by anyone else.

Part of the reason Jesus may have chosen the symbols of foot washing, eating, and drinking was because these were common, everyday practices. Through these symbols people would be able to commune with Him and with each other, knowing that God was the provider of their common positive experiences.

More than this, the communion, or sense of unity, is mostly created by the powerful way in which the breaking of the bread and the pouring of the grape juice is reminiscent of Christ's loving sacrifice. That these were the intended meanings can be seen in the apostle Paul's explanation: "The cup of blessing which we bless, is it not the communion of the blood of Christ? The bread which we break, is it not the communion of the body of Christ?" (1 Corinthians 10:16).

It is likely that Jesus chose the Passover season to institute the Communion service because His sacrifice would free us from sin and death—just as the Israelites commemorated their freedom from literal slavery in Egypt. In describing this freedom, Jesus said: "Whoever eats My flesh and drinks My blood has eternal life, and I will raise him up at the last day" (John 6:54).

When He spoke these words, Jesus was using a metaphor that would later become a ritual. In both cases, He wanted people to grasp that we can unite with Him through experiences like the reading of His Word and remembering that He sustains every moment of our lives.

Apply It:

Before a Communion service, list some experiences for which you are thankful.

Dig Deeper:

1 Corinthians 11:20; 1 Corinthians 10:21; Acts 20:7

Pure Bread and Grape Juice

"Unless you eat the flesh of the Son of Man and drink His blood, you have no life in you" (John 6:53).

Wine is big business in California and has exploded in growth in the last twenty years, increasing by 2,000 percent. In the 1990s, there were thirty wine producers in the Golden State; today, there are 700. Yet with only one million acres dedicated to wine making, the United States ranks sixth in the world. Even so, there are more wine sellers in America than there are people in Iceland. About 550,000 merchants sell wine in the states, while Iceland's population is only 330,000.

Some people wrongly assume that Jesus served fermented wine at the Last Supper. The Bible speaks against alcoholic beverages and supports the use of unfermented grape juice. "Thus says the Lord: 'As the new wine is found in the cluster, and one says, "Do not destroy it, for a blessing is in it" ' " (Isaiah 65:8). This wine that is "in the cluster" is nonalcoholic.

Christ used many metaphors to describe His life and teachings, including, "I am the true vine" (John 15:1) and "I am the bread of life. He who comes to Me shall never hunger, and he who believes in Me shall never thirst" (John 6:35). Such expressions are not meant to be taken literally, but as illustrations of deeper spiritual truths.

Leaven (yeast) symbolizes sin in the Bible. "Purge out the old leaven, that you may be a new lump, since you truly are unleavened. For indeed Christ, our Passover, was sacrificed for us. Therefore let us keep the feast, not with old leaven, nor with the leaven of malice and wickedness, but with the unleavened bread of sincerity and truth" (1 Corinthians 5:7, 8). This was why unleavened (unfermented) bread and unfermented grape juice were used at the Passover meal.

The very symbols for Christ's body and blood should not be confused or tainted with the symbols of sin, for we have been redeemed "with the precious blood of Christ, as of a lamb without blemish and without spot" (1 Peter 1:19).

Apply It:

Do you know someone whose life has been ruined by alcoholic beverages?

Dig Deeper:

Proverbs 23:29–35; Matthew 27:34; John 6:22–58

More Than a Memorial Meal

"Most assuredly, I say to you, unless you eat the flesh of the Son of Man and drink His blood, you have no life in you. Whoever eats My flesh and drinks My blood has eternal life, and I will raise him up at the last day" (John 6:53, 54).

For hundreds of years—continuing to this day—there's been a measure of confusion about the Lord's Supper and what its elements mean. When Jesus said of the bread, "This is My body," (Matthew 26:26) and of the unfermented wine, "This is my blood" (verse 28), did He mean to suggest that these were transformed into actual flesh and blood, or did He point us toward something else?

The Bible answer is far greater than some imagine. Just as the Lord spoke sometimes in parables, using symbolic language to explain essential concepts, so too are the elements of the Lord's Supper—the bread and the wine—symbolic of the ingesting of God's Word.

At the beginning of His ministry, Jesus rejected Satan's suggestion that He, Jesus, call on angels for bread while He hungered: "Man shall not live by bread alone," Jesus replied, "but by every word that proceeds from the mouth of God" (Matthew 4:4). This suggests that God's Word is our true food, essential for our spiritual growth.

The cup, which represents Christ's blood, symbolizes His sacrifice for us. "He was wounded for our transgressions," we read in Isaiah 53:5. In that same verse, we read that by His stripes—the scourging Jesus underwent—"we are healed." The cup also symbolizes God's promise of healing.

Because these elements represent the words and the life of Jesus, it's important that hearing the Word—receiving a biblical sermon—be part of the Communion experience. We not only partake of the Word in the Communion elements, but we do so in hearing the Word expounded.

Far from being a somber ritual, partaking of the Lord's Supper is a tremendous opportunity to not only remember Jesus' sacrifice, but also to receive the Word of God and integrate it into our lives.

Apply It:

As you partake of the elements of the Lord's Supper, remember what they represent and thank God for His provision!

Dig Deeper:

Matthew 26:27; John 6:36; 1 Corinthians 10:16

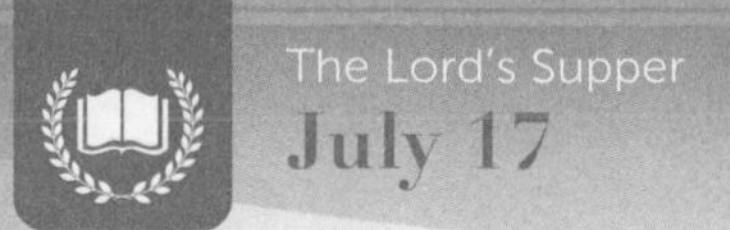

One Bread, One Body

"We, though many, are one bread and one body; for we all partake of that one bread" (1 Corinthians 10:17).

In a survey of 506 pastors conducted by *Christianity Today*, 95 percent can tell you the story of a major conflict in their church and 20 percent could describe one happening at this very moment. Sadly, conflict is pretty common in many churches. According to 85 percent of the pastors surveyed, the issue of control was the leading contributor. Who makes decisions outdistanced matters such as doctrine or cultural issues. Besides the personal pain felt by pastors, most of them reported how conflicts damaged relationships in the church.

Participating in the Communion service can help bring healing to churches filled with strife and divisiveness. The corporate experience of celebrating the Lord's Supper brings unity and stability, for it demonstrates communion with Jesus and one another. Paul explains, "The cup of blessing which we bless, is it not the communion of the blood of Christ? The bread which we break, is it not the communion of the body of Christ? For we, though many, are one bread and one body; for we all partake of that one bread" (1 Corinthians 10:16, 17).

Think of how the Communion bread is broken into many pieces and eaten by all the different members. It symbolizes how all the many parts of the congregation are united in Christ and are a part of His one body. Publicly participating in these ordinances shows how Christians belong to one family, whose head is Christ. "There should be no schism in the body, but that the members should have the same care for one another" (1 Corinthians 12:25).

We stand on common ground at the Lord's table, for we all acknowledge our sinfulness and need of a Savior. Jesus said, "Drink from it, all of you. For this is My blood of the new covenant, which is shed for many for the remission of sins" (Matthew 26:27, 28). Taking part in Communion renews our pledge to God and to loving one another. It's the perfect antidote to conflict.

Apply It:

Have you ever observed a church being torn apart by conflict? How does the Communion service bring people together?

Dig Deeper:

Luke 22:20; Acts 2:41–47; 1 Corinthians 1:10

Invitation to a Banquet

"Blessed are those who are called to the marriage supper of the Lamb!" (Revelation 19:9).

Fine dining was so important to King Charles II that he followed elaborate rituals for his meals. For instance, every week he would eat his dinner "on display" in the Banqueting House or Presence Chamber, with spectators watching in awe as uniformed servants paraded before the king with dozens of dishes for him to choose from. And for banquets, he pulled out all the stops, sitting at an elevated table beneath an ornate canopy. The elegant tableware included a monogrammed linen tablecloth, gold plates, a gilt castle that dispensed salt and spices, and a golden fountain that spouted wine and water. The three men who attended the king at mealtimes—a carver, a server, and a cup bearer—were always required to serve the king on bended knee.

Although our Savior deserves infinitely more honor than all the earthly kings who have ever lived, when we meet at the great heavenly banquet of the redeemed called the "marriage supper of the Lamb," Jesus Himself—the King of kings—will serve *us!*

To those who faithfully serve Him on this earth, and who obey His instruction to "let your waist be girded and your lamps burning" (Luke 12:35) as they diligently wait for His return, Jesus promises, "Blessed are those servants whom the master, when he comes, will find watching. Assuredly, I say to you that he will gird himself and have them sit down to eat, and will come and serve them" (Luke 12:37).

As He celebrated the Passover for the last time, Jesus pointed the minds of His disciples forward to this great future celebration in heaven when He promised, "I will not drink of this fruit of the vine from now on until that day when I drink it new with you in My Father's kingdom" (Matthew 26:29).

One of the greatest aspects of the Lord's Supper is the anticipation of the happiness we will have when we are finally able to see Jesus face to face and fellowship with Him eternally in His everlasting kingdom.

Apply It:

Have you ever attended a banquet? If so, what was its purpose?

Dig Deeper:

1 Corinthians 11:26; John 14:3; Revelation 3:20

In a Worthy Manner

"Whoever eats this bread or drinks this cup of the Lord in an unworthy manner will be guilty of the body and blood of the Lord" (1 Corinthians 11:27).

"One must act in a fashion that conforms to one's position and with the reputation that one has earned." That's the motto of the National Honor Society, a nationwide organization for high school students that emphasizes academic achievement, leadership, service, and character. The eligibility requirements include having a GPA of 3.0, serving in the community, demonstrating leadership qualities (being resourceful, good problem solvers, etc.), and having a good character (honesty, reliability, courtesy, etc.).

Did you know that there are qualifications for participating in the Lord's Supper? Jesus administered the Communion only to His professed followers and so the service is open to all professed Christians. But there's more. Paul instructs that we not partake of the supper "in an unworthy manner" (1 Corinthians 11:27). Apparently, members of the church in Corinth were participating in the Lord's Supper in an unbecoming fashion.

Paul explained, "Let a man examine himself, and so let him eat of the bread and drink of the cup. For he who eats and drinks in an unworthy manner eats and drinks judgment to himself, not discerning the Lord's body" (verses 28, 29). Before taking part in the Lord's Supper, believers should prayerfully reflect on the purpose of the Communion, review their own Christian experience, confess their sins, and seek to restore broken relationships.

You don't need high academic marks to partake of the bread and grape juice that commemorate the Lord's death. What's most important is that each person think about the condition of his heart and not be quick to judge others. After all, Jesus participated in the service with Judas, a thief and traitor. Open sin does disqualify a person from taking part (1 Corinthians 5:11).

When each person earnestly searches their own heart and then makes a recommitment to Christ, the emblems that represent the death of Jesus for our sins become deeply meaningful and bring a blessing that lifts us up to a heavenly society.

Apply It:

Before participating in the Lord's Supper, take time to prayerfully reflect on the condition of your heart.

Dig Deeper:

Psalm 139:23, 24; 1 Corinthians 11:17–34; 2 Corinthians 13:5

Literal Constraint

"Man shall not live by bread alone, but by every word that proceeds from the mouth of God" (Matthew 4:4).

Friends and family members of cancer patients and health professionals have been asking people to stop using the language of war to refer to the suffering that comes from cancer. "Battling" or "fighting" are metaphors that have led some cancer patients to feel guilty for "losing." As a result, some have even avoided preparing for or discussing death with their loved ones.

Some metaphors can be problematic if taken too literally. The words of Jesus during the Last Supper have been taken literally by people for centuries in a number of denominations. They believe that the bread and wine that are blessed by a priest actually become the body and blood of Jesus. The primary issue with this interpretation of the biblical metaphor is that it suggests that salvation and the presence of Jesus can only be accessed through a particular church that has the power to work this miracle.

Jesus promised His presence through His Holy Spirit, rather than through the blessing of a priest: "You are not in the flesh but in the Spirit, if indeed the Spirit of God dwells in you. Now if anyone does not have the Spirit of Christ, he is not His" (Romans 8:9). The presence of Christ can be experienced by faith during a Communion service and also when there are no clergy present.

Furthermore, it is important to note that there were other times when Jesus used the metaphor of eating and drinking to refer to people receiving and following His words: "It is the Spirit who gives life; the flesh profits nothing. The words that I speak to you are spirit, and they are life" (John 6:63). This coincides with the preaching of the Bible during Communion services when the symbols of Jesus are consumed.

Apply It:

Pray for the presence of Jesus at an unconventional time during your day.

Dig Deeper:

Jeremiah 15:16; Revelation 10:9; 1 Peter 2:2

Spiritual Gifts and Ministries

17

July 21

Power to Witness

"Now concerning spiritual gifts, brethren, I do not want you to be ignorant" (1 Corinthians 12:1).

Almost from the very beginning of the internal combustion engine, Gottlieb Daimler and Rudolf Diesel began tinkering with ways to increase the power and reduce the fuel consumption of their engines by compressing the combustion air. Not until 1925 was Swiss engineer Alfred Büchi able to successfully create exhaust gas turbocharging and increase the power of engines by 40 percent.

In the 1970s, after the oil crisis, turbocharging became more common and the word "turbo" was fashionable. Most automobile manufacturers offered at least one turbocharged model, but these vehicles guzzled gas and soon disappeared from the market. Today, turbocharging is seen less from a performance perspective and more as a means of reducing fuel consumption and emissions.

Before returning to heaven, the resurrected Christ promised His disciples that He would provide them with power to advance the work of the church. "You shall receive power when the Holy Spirit has come upon you; and you shall be witnesses to Me ... to the end of the earth" (Acts 1:8). It was like turbocharging the church with divine energy. On the day the Holy Spirit was poured out, three thousand people were baptized (Acts 2:41).

The power that propelled the church came through special gifts bestowed on members by the Holy Spirit. Paul explained, "To each one of us grace was given according to the measure of Christ's gift. Therefore He says: 'When He ascended on high, He led captivity captive, and gave gifts to men' " (Ephesians 4:7, 8). It is these divine abilities that enable the church to accomplish its work.

Just as Christ received a special anointing by the Spirit to prepare Him for ministry (Acts 10:38), so the Lord promises to baptize all believers with the Spirit to add power to their witness. This is revealed in the diverse talents given "each according to his own ability" (Matthew 25:15), which helps the "effective working" of the church. It's heaven's form of turbocharging the body of Christ.

Apply It:

Have you ever observed Spirit-filled believers serving in the church in places that match their God-given gifts? What is it like?

Dig Deeper:

Matthew 25:14–30; Mark 13:34; Acts 1:4–8

Working Together

"I thank my God always concerning you for the grace of God which was given to you by Christ Jesus ... so that you come short in no gift, eagerly waiting for the revelation of our Lord Jesus Christ" (1 Corinthians 1:4, 7).

There are those people in a church—perhaps in your congregation—who seem to be doing the right thing, at the right time, and in the right place. If your congregation has a choir, that's an obvious example. People working together to sing in harmony and give praise to God certainly is the manifestation of a spiritual gift.

But so are the folks who make an effort to ensure that visitors, guests, and newcomers from all walks of life feel welcome. That also is a gift. Let's not forget those who work behind the scenes to make sure the sanctuary is ready for worship service, who prepare and distribute the church bulletin, and who take up, safeguard, and count the offering.

You might not feel "gifted" in finances, but praise God there's a church treasurer who is. That treasurer might be thankful they're not tasked with having to greet folks at the door—a job that requires an outgoing personality.

In short, when we look at those who are filling important roles in a congregation, whether on the platform or "behind the scenes," it's important to remember that in working together, these people are helping the "body"—the church—to function.

Some may prefer one kind of food that another might disdain. Our tastes in clothes might vary from one to another. And not everyone at church drives the same kind of car. While our tastes may develop from various sources, our gifts are the manifestation of God's provision to each of us (1 Corinthians 12:4–6). But it is our love for Jesus and His church that brings us together. Sharing our gifts produces harmony within the congregation, the church at large, and, as we shall soon see, in heaven itself.

Apply It:

Take a few moments this Sabbath to observe how many different types of gifts you see functioning in your church.

Dig Deeper:

Proverbs 27:17; Romans 12:16; Revelation 7:9

July 23

Body Parts Matter

"God composed the body, having given greater honor to that part which lacks it, that there should be no schism in the body, but that the members should have the same care for one another" (1 Corinthians 12:24, 25).

Have you ever wondered if you have useless body parts? Some believe that humans have evolved beyond needing certain parts, such as wisdom teeth, the tailbone, or appendix. But before you begin disposing of your ear lobes, tonsils, or gallbladder, you might discover that these body parts actually serve a purpose.

For instance, who needs fingerprints? They make it easier for police to identify someone who has committed a crime, but what's their purpose? Actually, the ridges on your fingers help you pick up and grip objects. Living without fingerprints would be difficult for people who work with their hands.

Some Christians are tempted to think that there are useless members in the body of Christ. While it is true that certain members living openly in sin may need to be separated from the church, we should be careful to avoid judging the value of each person.

Paul warned the church in Corinth that each member of the body is valuable. "If the foot should say, 'Because I am not a hand, I am not of the body,' is it therefore not of the body? And if the ear should say, 'Because I am not an eye, I am not of the body,' is it therefore not of the body?" (1 Corinthians 12:15, 16).

He went further to explain how "those members of the body which seem to be weaker are necessary. And those members of the body which we think to be less honorable, on these we bestow greater honor" (verses 22, 23). It's tempting to elevate the visible gifts in the body of Christ—like those who serve up front on Sabbath—and think less of those who are less visible—like those who maintain the facility. But every member is important, for "God has set the members, each one of them, in the body just as He pleased" (v. 18).

Apply It:

If you had to lose a part of your body, which one would you choose?

Dig Deeper:

Matthew 18:1–5; 1 Corinthians 12:12–27; Ephesians 4:1–16

The Essential Element

"Follow the way of love and eagerly desire gifts of the Spirit" (1 Corinthians 14:1 NIV).

Although the International Space Station (ISS) holds backup oxygen supplies in tanks, the bulk of the air the astronauts breathe is supplied by electrolysis. In this process, electricity generated by the massive solar panels outside the ISS is routed through water, separating the oxygen and hydrogen atoms to produce oxygen and hydrogen gas. The explosive hydrogen gas is sent outside, while the essential element—oxygen—enters the cabin ventilation system, providing fresh air.

The essential element in our service to God is not skill, intelligence, knowledge, or even spiritual gifts. The indispensable element is love. The apostle Paul expressed it this way: "Though I speak with the tongues of men and of angels, but have not love, I have become sounding brass or a clanging cymbal. And though I have the gift of prophecy, and understand all mysteries and all knowledge, and though I have all faith, so that I could remove mountains, but have not love, I am nothing. And though I bestow all my goods to feed the poor, and though I give my body to be burned, but have not love, it profits me nothing" (1 Corinthians 13:1–3).

In other words, regardless of what spiritual gifts we are given, love must be the motivating force behind those gifts or we are simply wasting our time. This is the "more excellent way" referred to in 1 Corinthians 12:31.

Yet as sinful humans, we can't generate that kind of love on our own. Only the Lord can transform our hearts so that we will reflect His *agape* love—His unconditional love that is so giving and self-sacrificing.

In addition to the gifts of the Spirit, God wants us to have the fruit of the Spirit: "love, joy, peace, longsuffering, kindness, goodness, faithfulness, gentleness, self-control" (Galatians 5:22, 23). When we reflect this unselfishness in our service to others, we possess the essential element and will truly be following "the way of love."

Apply It:

Which fruit of the Spirit do you think needs strengthening in your life?

Dig Deeper:

1 Corinthians 13:4–13; Ephesians 5:9; Ephesians 3:17–19

July 25

Serving to Glorify

"If anyone ministers, let him do it as with the ability which God supplies, that in all things God may be glorified through Jesus Christ, to whom belong the glory and the dominion forever and ever" (1 Peter 4:11).

On May 9, 1864, Union Army General John Sedgwick was probing skirmish lines with his troops at the beginning of the Battle of Spotsylvania Courthouse in Virginia during the American Civil War. Suddenly, shots rang out from Confederate sharpshooters about a thousand yards away. Sedgwick's men ducked for cover.

The general strode around in the open and chided his men, saying, "What? Men dodging this way for single bullets?" The men continued to flinch at every shot. Sedgwick then said, "Why are you dodging like this? They couldn't hit an elephant at this distance." Moments later, the general was struck by a bullet under the left eye and fell dead.

A crucial quality necessary when using one's spiritual gifts is humility. (See 1 Corinthians 4:7.) When God provides unique talents to members, it is not for their self-glorification but is meant to uplift their Creator. Paul introduced the biblical teaching on spiritual gifts by stating, "For I say, through the grace given to me, to everyone who is among you, not to think of himself more highly than he ought to think, but to think soberly, as God has dealt to each one a measure of faith" (Romans 12:3).

In discussing the importance of service in the Christian life, the apostle Peter likewise encouraged members to minister "with the ability which God supplies, that in all things God may be glorified through Jesus Christ" (1 Peter 4:11). There is no room for pride, for the ones who live for God will "have fervent love for one another" (verse 8).

Boasting is no way to die. "By this we know love, because He laid down His life for us. And we also ought to lay down our lives for the brethren" (1 John 3:16). Sacrificial love for God and others is the highest form of service when using our spiritual gifts.

Apply It:

In what ways could you sacrifice yourself for others this coming week?

Dig Deeper:

John 15:13; Ephesians 4:2; Philippians 2:3, 4

Attractive Growth

"From whom the whole body, joined and knit together by what every joint supplies, according to the effective working by which every part does its share, causes growth of the body for the edifying of itself in love" (Ephesians 4:16).

Artificial intelligence appears to be the future of company recruitment. In order to avoid political bias, programmers build software that selects between job candidates by predicting their performance at a particular position. These predictions are not solely based on interviews; they may also draw on behaviors that are recorded on social media.

The Christian church works very differently from most companies. Instead of selecting the best candidates for church membership, churches recruit everyone—and allow the Holy Spirit to empower every member to help every other member become more like Jesus.

Then the church grows in numbers as the members become more attractive in character. The apostle Paul recorded the growth process when he wrote about the talents that Jesus gave after His ascension: "He Himself gave some to be apostles, some prophets, some evangelists, and some pastors and teachers, for the equipping of the saints for the work of ministry, for the edifying of the body of Christ" (Ephesians 4:11, 12).

In this passage, Paul is using the metaphor of Christ's body to refer to the members of the church. When Jesus gives the talent of teaching to some church members, for example, they can teach other members how to live like Jesus.

When people learn about Jesus and become like Him, they attract others and the membership grows. Paul described this growth in character and in numbers when he wrote about how God would continue to give gifts or skills: "Till we all come to the unity of the faith and of the knowledge of the Son of God, to a perfect man, to the measure of the stature of the fullness of Christ" (Ephesians 4:13). In other words, people are drawn to groups that are growing and going places.

Apply It:

Find a way to help another church member this week.

Dig Deeper:

Ephesians 4:1–3; Ephesians 4:7; Ephesians 4:14, 15

Equipped for Teamwork

"He Himself gave some to be apostles, some prophets, some evangelists, and some pastors and teachers, for the equipping of the saints for the work of ministry" (Ephesians 4:11, 12).

Have you ever wondered why geese fly in a "V" formation? One bird leads the flock for a time to minimize wind resistance and then drops back when it tires so a different bird can take the lead. Scientists have discovered that when geese fly in this formation, each bird's flapping wings create an uplift for the bird that follows. Together the entire flock can fly over 70 percent farther than if each goose flew alone.

This example of teamwork has been called synergy, the cooperation of more people or elements working together to produce a result greater than the result achieved individually. The word synergy comes from the Greek word *synergos* and simply means "working together."

Synergy describes God's plan for how the church should function. Paul says that under Christ "the whole body" is "joined and knit together by what every joint supplies, according to the effective working by which *every part does its share,*" which results in the "growth of the body for the edifying of itself in love" (Ephesians 4:15, 16, emphasis added).

The human body is made up of interdependent parts. When members function independently, they are like cancer cells that take from the body but do not give to the body. Just as body parts need each other, so members of the church need one another.

Many assume that the pastor is the primary worker in the church while the members cheer the clergy forward. Yet Scripture identifies some who "equip" members for service. "He Himself gave some to be apostles, some prophets, some evangelists, and some pastors and teachers, *for the equipping of the saints for the work of ministry*" (verses 11, 12, emphasis added).

Together, pastors and members make up the church—and when they work as a team, the church will go much further in growth than it ever could if individuals worked alone.

Apply It:

Do your gifts lend themselves toward equipping others for ministry or for directly doing ministry?

Dig Deeper:

Exodus 18:1–27; Matthew 25:20; 2 Timothy 3:16, 17

Unity in Diversity

"In whom the whole building, being fitted together, grows into a holy temple in the Lord" (Ephesians 2:21).

Before Jesus' resurrection, His followers were almost exclusively Jews. And while some were members of the Sanhedrin, the ruling religious council—such as Nicodemus and Joseph of Arimathea—they were all of the Hebrew tradition.

Suddenly, after the resurrection and powerful advancements in the church described in the book of Acts, things changed. Gentiles, who had never practiced the Jewish laws and customs, were unexpectedly welcomed into the fellowship. This disturbed some, to be sure, but it also raised a question: Was everyone supposed to worship together?

The answer, of course, is yes. God's church today is made up of people from "all nations, tribes, peoples, and tongues" (Revelation 7:9). We come together from different backgrounds, different cultures, and yet we are to be "fitted together" as a gift of the Holy Spirit.

Years ago, a church member boasted that he could go to a different country and, upon finding a member of his denomination, would see someone who wore the same kind of clothing, ate the same food, and had the same thoughts as the visitor did. Today, a Christian visiting a congregation in Nairobi, Kenya, or Pune, India, or Tokyo, Japan, will find differences in worship, attire, and certainly at potluck!

God didn't call all sorts of people into the church in order to produce a series of uniform clones or robots. One reason He brings people from every walk of life into His church is to show the kind of diversity we'll see in heaven.

How should believers react when newcomers arrive, especially if they don't look like us? With gratitude, hospitality, and the realization that God's work isn't finished yet. He's bringing people in to join the most glorious family imaginable, and we're privileged to be a part of that!

■ Apply It:

Thank God for the different people in your congregation—and remember to also personally thank them for being there!

■ Dig Deeper:

1 Corinthians 6:19–20; Ephesians 4:16; Revelation 7:9

Beneficial Gifts

"You shall receive power when the Holy Spirit has come upon you; and you shall be witnesses to Me in Jerusalem, and in all Judea and Samaria, and to the end of the earth" (Acts 1:8).

Some people give clothing subscription boxes as graduation gifts. These boxes come regularly in the mail with a variety of garments that are often chosen based on a quiz concerning the receiver's preferred styling. The clothes that the receivers end up wearing partially reflect the giver. This is because the giver chooses a particular subscription company.

Jesus gives us practical gifts for the purpose of showing and telling others about Him and His plan to save us. Unlike some clothing items, however, these gifts were not intended to be something used strictly for our own pleasure. Instead, they were designed to bring others into a saving relationship with Him. Neither are gifts given when our hearts are not right with God. (See Acts 8:21.)

The author of the letter to the Hebrews explained that the gifts of the Holy Spirit were a way for God to show the importance and authenticity of His plan of salvation: "How shall we escape if we neglect so great a salvation, which at the first began to be spoken by the Lord, and was confirmed to us by those who heard Him, God also bearing witness both with signs and wonders, with various miracles, and gifts of the Holy Spirit, according to His own will?" (Hebrews 2:3, 4).

The first example of the reception of the gifts came on the day of Pentecost after Christ's ascension. On that day, Peter explained that the ability to speak foreign languages was evidence that Jesus had been enthroned in heaven: "Therefore being exalted to the right hand of God, and having received from the Father the promise of the Holy Spirit, He poured out this which you now see and hear" (Acts 2:33). This enthronement meant that Jesus was truly the promised Savior whose life, death, resurrection, and heavenly ministry give Him the authority to save people from their sins and from the suffering of death.

Apply It:

Put a dormant talent to use again.

Dig Deeper:

Luke 24:49; Ephesians 4:11; John 15:26, 27

Using the Gift

"Well done, good and faithful servant; you have been faithful over a few things, I will make you ruler over many things. Enter into the joy of your lord" (Matthew 25:23).

A British crypto investor, James Howells, spent a week in 2009 mining bitcoins—a type of digital currency—and earned over 7,500 of them. He stored the long, complex keys to each coin on a hard drive and put it in his desk. Unfortunately, when he cleaned out the desk a few years later, he accidentally threw away the hard drive. Though the bitcoins weren't worth a great deal when he first accumulated them, their value had skyrocketed. His lost bitcoins may have been worth as much as $9.9 million dollars.

We have all mourned a lost opportunity. But when it comes to using our spiritual gifts, we can't afford to let opportunities slip through our fingers. Unused spiritual gifts tend to wither away, so we have a responsibility to use them wisely.

Jesus told a story to illustrate the importance of using our talents and gifts. "The kingdom of heaven is like a man traveling to a far country, who called his own servants and delivered his goods to them. And to one he gave five talents, to another two, and to another one, to each according to his own ability" (Matthew 25:14, 15).

The servants who diligently used their gifts found that they were multiplied, while the one servant who hid his gift made no profit at all and eventually lost that gift—earning him the title of "wicked and lazy servant" (verse 26).

Our responsibility in utilizing our gifts is not to ourselves but to God. We need to persist in putting our spiritual gifts to good use in bringing others to Jesus. Then, by His grace, we will one day hear the words: "Well done, good and faithful servant; you were faithful over a few things, I will make you ruler over many things. Enter into the joy of your lord" (v. 21).

Apply It:

Are you using all of the spiritual gifts you've been given? Which gifts has God been multiplying in your life?

Dig Deeper:

1 Peter 4:10; Ephesians 2:10; Galatians 6:9

Discovering Your Gifts, Part 1

"The manifestation of the Spirit is given to each one for the profit of all" (1 Corinthians 12:7).

Stephen Covey's *First Things First* is a popular self-help book that presents a time management approach designed to increase effectiveness based on values. Covey describes how some people are driven by the clock instead of the compass, making choices on what is urgent but not necessarily important. By identifying your primary principles, you will be guided to "true north" instead of being distracted by things that don't provide a long-term benefit.

Using a matrix to outline the urgent, not urgent, important, and not important, Covey helps people prioritize their work by seeing how they are often motivated by the urgent but not always important. The area we are most likely to neglect are important areas, such as exercise and planning.

For the Christian, the most important daily work is to spend time with God and seek to be filled with the Spirit. Because the Lord does not pester us, such quiet time can fall into the not urgent category, though it is important. And this was the first work given by Christ to the disciples after returning to heaven. Jesus commanded them to wait for the Promise of the Father "which ... you have heard from Me. ... You shall be baptized with the Holy Spirit not many days from now" (Acts 1:4, 5).

It is through the Holy Spirit that we receive spiritual gifts and the power to do the work of Christ. "The manifestation of the Spirit is given to each one" (1 Corinthians 12:7). After listing gifts, Paul explains how the "Spirit works all these things, distributing to each one individually as He wills" (verse 11).

The first step in discovering your spiritual gifts is to prayerfully seek the outpouring of the Holy Spirit in your life. Though it may not seem to be an urgent step, it is essential—for it is only through the Spirit that we may know and receive the divine abilities to be effective servants for Christ.

Apply It:

Spend specific time this week praying daily for the Holy Spirit to come into your heart and reveal to you the special gifts He has given you.

Dig Deeper:

Jeremiah 29:13; Matthew 7:7, 8; Hebrews 11:6

Discovering Your Gifts, Part 2

"The heart of the prudent acquires knowledge, and the ear of the wise seeks knowledge" (Proverbs 18:15).

Have you ever had trouble finding a book in your local library? You'll probably have more luck if you head over to the British Library—the world's largest. The national library contains over 170 million items from countries all over the world. If you need to find a book, manuscript, journal, newspaper, magazine, sound recording, video, play-script, patent, database, map, stamp, print, or drawing, saunter over to the British Library.

If you are trying to find your spiritual gifts, the best place to begin—after asking for the Holy Spirit's guidance—is to study the Bible. We are encouraged to "search the Scriptures" (John 5:39), to rightly divide "the word of truth" (2 Timothy 2:15), to study "the Scriptures daily" (Acts 17:11), and to "grow in the grace and knowledge of our Lord and Savior Jesus Christ" (2 Peter 3:18).

There are four major passages in the New Testament that provide examples of spiritual gifts: 1 Corinthians 12:8–10, 28 (wisdom, knowledge, faith, healings, miracles, prophecy, discernment, tongues, interpretation, apostleship, teaching, helps, administration); Romans 12:6–8 (not repeating previously listed gifts: encouragement, giving, leadership, mercy); Ephesians 4:11, 12 (evangelism, shepherding). Some also include craftsmanship (Exodus 31:3), artistic communication (Psalm 45:1; 1 Chronicles 25:1), intercessory prayer (Exodus 17:9–12), and hospitality (1 Peter 4:9).

None of the lists of spiritual gifts in the Bible is identical to another, which suggests that there might be other gifts not mentioned in the Scriptures that the Holy Spirit gives to the church to accomplish certain goals. Christians who have dedicated their entire lives to Jesus will use all their gifts—natural or spiritual—to build up the kingdom.

Some Christians do not think they have a spiritual gift, but the Bible says, "The Spirit is given to each one" (1 Corinthians 12:7) and gifts are distributed by the Spirit "to each one individually as He wills" (verse 11). You are gifted—and if you are unsure just how, go to God's library, the Bible, and pray for divine insight.

Apply It:

Which gifts listed in Scripture do you most identify with?

Dig Deeper:

Matthew 25:19–23; Galatians 5:13; Ephesians 2:10

Discovering Your Gifts, Part 3

"Test all things; hold fast what is good" (1 Thessalonians 5:21).

If you think you've run into a few too many problems in a day, then you haven't tackled The Beast, the world's largest inflatable obstacle course. In 2018, a Belgian company connected several of these courses together to create a 1,625-foot long world record mega-obstacle course. It features 60 challenges and takes about 10 minutes to run, climb, and crawl through toward the finish line.

You might think discovering your spiritual gifts is a bit like running through an obstacle course. Actually, finding your fit in ministry might take a little trial and error. But there's nothing wrong with experimenting. When Paul wrote about spiritual gifts, he began by encouraging us not to "be conformed to this world, but be transformed by the renewing of your mind, that you may prove what is that good and acceptable and perfect will of God" (Romans 12:2). Some translations use the word "test" to discern God's will.

After praying for guidance from the Holy Spirit and studying the Scriptures, try out an area of ministry. Talk with a ministry leader in the church and watch how members serve in that area. When you step into a new role, even for a short period of time, do not confuse being nervous with lacking a particular gift. Everyone feels apprehensive the first time they try something new.

While there are many spiritual gift assessments you can find online, think of these as a starting place, not an ending point. Be open to areas of service that are providential. The Lord may want you to do a "new thing" (Isaiah 43:19) that may stretch you beyond your comfort zone. When God called Gideon, he replied, "How can I save Israel? Indeed my clan is the weakest in Manasseh, and I am the least in my father's house" (Judges 6:15). When faced with this impossible obstacle, God told Gideon, "Surely I will be with you" (verse 16).

As you seek to serve the Lord, pray fervently, step forward humbly, and believe that God will open a way.

Apply It:

Find a spiritual gift assessment and consider where God might lead you to serve.

Dig Deeper:

2 Timothy 1:9; 2 Peter 1:10, 11; James 2:5

Discovering Your Gifts, Part 4

"As they ministered to the Lord and fasted, the Holy Spirit said, 'Now separate to Me Barnabas and Saul for the work to which I have called them.' Then, having fasted and prayed, and laid hands on them, they sent them away" (Acts 13:2, 3).

For 900 years, coronations of British kings and queens have taken place at Westminster Abbey. The last one took place June 2, 1953, when Princess Elizabeth became Queen Elizabeth II—the 39th Sovereign to be crowned. The event was the first to be televised and was watched by 27 million people in the UK alone.

Coronations are often elaborate, marking the investiture of a monarch with regal power. In the New Testament, another simple ceremony marked the beginning work of Paul and Barnabas as missionaries. After the church fasted and prayed, the Holy Spirit said to separate the two for the work to which He had called them (Acts 13:2).

It was not to invest power in these two men that they were confirmed by the church, but a recognition of what the Holy Spirit was already doing in their lives. The ceremony took place after the missionary gift was given to Paul and Barnabas. So also, the gifts of the Spirit are not given by the body of Christ, but they are to be acknowledged by God's people as coming from heaven.

In discovering our spiritual gifts, we should not neglect the input of others. Often it is more difficult to recognize one's own gifts than the gifts of others. Perhaps that is why the Bible tells us that "in the multitude of counselors there is safety" (Proverbs 11:14). Since God gives gifts to build up the church, we should expect the body of Christ to confirm our gifts and not rely on our feelings.

Gifts are not given to lift ourselves up or to be used for our own benefit, but to follow Christ's example: "Even the Son of Man did not come to be served, but to serve" (Mark 10:45).

Apply It:

Ask a few godly people who know you well what they perceive are your primary spiritual gifts. Listen carefully and look for patterns in what you hear.

Dig Deeper:

Matthew 20:27, 28; Acts 6:1–7; 2 Timothy 1:6

Status Symbol

"I wish you all spoke with tongues, but even more that you prophesied; for he who prophesies is greater than he who speaks with tongues, unless indeed he interprets, that the church may receive edification" (1 Corinthians 14:5).

Water bottles with crystals at the bottom have become a status symbol. At first, proponents of a kind of religious belief, which includes reverence toward crystals, promoted them enthusiastically. However, it soon became less of a religious fad when people simply wanted to have a pretty water bottle with a special crystal compartment at the bottom.

The Bible records that the people living in Corinth had a problem with spiritual status symbols. However, one status symbol was built on an authentic spiritual gift: the miraculous ability to speak a foreign language.

Paul records how important boasting was to the Corinthians when he stated: "When one says, 'I am of Paul,' and another, 'I am of Apollos,' are you not carnal?" (1 Corinthians 3:4). It appears that people were boasting about which teacher had taught them, as if this showed some kind of superiority. Paul labeled this attitude as carnal—a selfish way of thinking.

He tried to prevent this attitude when he explained that the gift of tongues was meant to be a sign for unbelievers: "Tongues are for a sign, not to those who believe but to unbelievers; but prophesying is not for unbelievers but for those who believe" (1 Corinthians 14:22). This does not mean that prophesying should be used as a status symbol, but rather that it could be used to bring those in the church closer to God.

The wrong attitude, however, could result in neglect. Using the metaphor of the human body, Paul explained that those with one gift should not disrespect those with another: "The eye cannot say to the hand, 'I have no need of you' " (1 Corinthians 12:21).

Apply It:

Encourage someone who has a different gift than you.

Dig Deeper:

1 Corinthians 12:8–10; 1 Corinthians 13:1; 1 Corinthians 14:23–25

Not So Mysterious

"We speak the wisdom of God in a mystery, the hidden wisdom which God ordained before the ages for our glory" (1 Corinthians 2:7).

Malaysian Airlines Flight 370 has been missing since March 8, 2014. The Malaysian government eventually gave up on the expensive search to find the wreckage. This disappearance is one of the most well-known modern mysteries.

The word "mystery," however, has not always been used to refer to something that cannot be solved. Just as a future discovery of the missing airplane would bring resolution, the New Testament uses the word "mystery" to describe something that was hidden in the past but is now revealed.

Paul's explanation of this point is one of the clearest. In speaking of the glory of God's reward for His followers, Paul stated, "God has revealed them to us through His Spirit. For the Spirit searches all things, yes, the deep things of God" (1 Corinthians 2:10). This is one example of something that he calls a "mystery" earlier in the chapter but later explains it as a revelation from God.

Unfortunately, many have used the modern definition of the word "mystery" (an unsolvable thing) to interpret what happens when someone has received the gift of tongues. Paul described one instance of this process later in the same letter: "He who speaks in a tongue does not speak to men but to God, for no one understands him; however, in the spirit he speaks mysteries" (1 Corinthians 14:2).

Many Christians believe that these "mysteries" can never be explained. However, for Paul, these mysteries that were spoken were only unknown because the hearers did not know the language of the person who was moved by the Spirit of God. Speaking a foreign language best helps the body of Christ when someone can interpret the speaker's message for the benefit of all.

Apply It:

Restart a spiritual project you have given up on.

Dig Deeper:

Mark 4:11; Ephesians 1:9; Colossians 1:27

The Gift of Prophecy

18

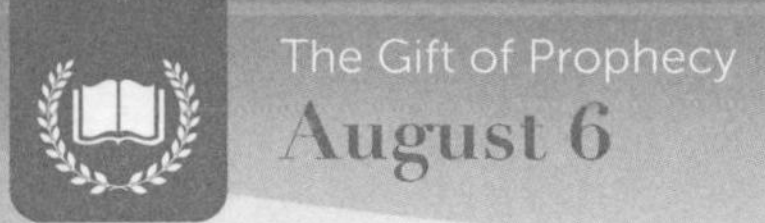

Believe His Prophets

"Surely the Lord GOD does nothing, unless He reveals His secret to His servants the prophets" (Amos 3:7).

Jehoshaphat was in deep trouble. The king of Judah was surrounded by enemies and didn't know what to do. So "Jehoshaphat feared, and set himself to seek the LORD, and proclaimed a fast throughout all Judah" (2 Chronicles 20:3). He prayed, "O our God ... we have no power against this great multitude that is coming against us; nor do we know what to do, but our eyes are upon You" (verse 12).

"Then the Spirit of the LORD came upon Jahaziel ... and he said, 'Listen, all you of Judah ... Do not be afraid nor dismayed because of this great multitude, for the battle is not yours, but God's' " (vv. 14, 15). Then, with boldness, Jahaziel proclaimed, "You will not need to fight in this battle. Position yourselves, stand still and see the salvation of the LORD" (v. 17).

The next day, Jehoshaphat assembled his soldiers to go out. After the inspiring words of Jahaziel, he reminded his men, "Believe in the LORD your God, and you shall be established; believe His prophets, and you shall prosper" (v. 20). Then he arranged a choir "who should sing to the LORD, and who should praise the beauty of holiness, as they went out before the army" (v. 21).

What happened next was nothing short of miraculous, for the enemy armies fought with and destroyed one another—"no one had escaped" (v. 24). After the victory, it took three days to gather all the spoil. Peace came to God's people when they believed in His prophets.

That was not the case with King Ahaz, a ruler who led Judah into idolatry. It was to this stubborn king who refused to listen to the prophetic words of Isaiah that the Lord declared, "If you will not believe, surely you shall not be established" (Isaiah 7:9). Ahaz died and was buried without honor in Jerusalem, unworthy of a burial in the royal tombs (2 Chronicles 28:27). Such is the end of those who will not listen to God's prophets.

Apply It:

Can you think of a time you refused to listen to godly advice and you ended up in trouble?

Dig Deeper:

Numbers 12:6; Isaiah 6:8, 9; Jeremiah 23:22

News in Advance?

*"Give no regard to mediums and familiar spirits;
do not seek after them, to be defiled by them:
I am the LORD your God"* (Leviticus 19:31).

Every day, millions around the world look up a small superstitious feature still found in most newspapers—one that purports to tell them how their lives are going to turn out. Yet horoscopes are so generic that they have been shown to be worthless. An experiment in 1948 gave people with different birth dates the exact same horoscope, and everyone said it was accurate for them!

But the Bible warns, "Give no regard to mediums and familiar spirits; do not seek after them, to be defiled by them" (Leviticus 19:31). Even so, many still *want* to know the future. They'd like to know the news before it happens; who can blame them? Such insights could help a person avoid tragedy, reap a financial windfall, or even change the course of world events.

While the Bible does not offer information on which stock to buy or who's going to win the next election, God has, throughout history, commissioned individuals to go forth and prophesy. Such proclamations were not always forecasts; rather, they contained encouragement and warnings for God's people and for those around them.

The book of Exodus contains an example of God designating a prophet, not for the children of Israel, but for the Pharaoh oppressing them: "The LORD said to Moses: 'See, I have made you as God to Pharaoh, and Aaron your brother shall be your prophet. You shall speak all that I command you. And Aaron your brother shall tell Pharaoh to send the children of Israel out of his land' " (7:1, 2).

Prophets also delivered God's judgment to Israel's leaders: After King David's adultery with Bathsheba and murder of Uriah, the prophet Nathan confronted him: "You are the man!" (2 Samuel 12:7).

In Bible times, prophets didn't always deliver "news in advance," which is called predictive prophecy. But their counsel came from God, and those who obeyed it prospered. The same is true today: Heeding prophetic wisdom brings blessings.

Apply It:

Can you think of some prophetic insights that people who read the Bible have, but that are not understood by the world at large?

Dig Deeper:

2 Peter 1:21; 1 Samuel 9:9; Daniel 2:24–45

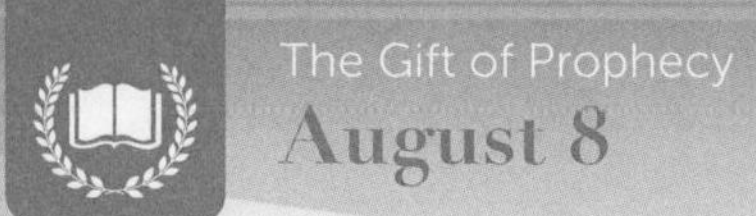

Direct-to-Voter

"You are no longer strangers and foreigners, but fellow citizens with the saints and members of the household of God, having been built on the foundation of the apostles and prophets, Jesus Christ Himself being the chief cornerstone" (Ephesians 2:19, 20).

A recent report revealed that approximately two thirds of Americans receive some of their news through social media, making it a prime outlet where politicians can speak directly to their audiences. A number of senators and representatives have already begun broadcasting their campaigns on social media.

Because of sin, God could no longer communicate face-to-face with humans (Isaiah 59:2). Prophets have provided the most direct form of communication between God and humans ever since. This avenue of contact was foundational in establishing the people of God.

Once the line of communication was opened, some of the prophetic messages were written down and became the Scriptures—e.g., see 2 Peter 3:16. Other prophetic messages were not written down or they were lost—e.g., see Colossians 4:16. All the messages were given "for the equipping of the saints for the work of ministry, for the edifying of the body of Christ" (Ephesians 4:12).

However, this edification, or character growth, was also intended to attract people to join the church. This would require that members accomplish the mission of the church by going out and lovingly telling people the good news. Sometimes even the planning of missionary journeys was made by God through prophets.

This was the case with Paul and his companions: "Now in the church that was at Antioch there were certain prophets and teachers: Barnabas, Simeon who was called Niger, Lucius of Cyrene, Manaen who had been brought up with Herod the tetrarch, and Saul. As they ministered to the Lord and fasted, the Holy Spirit said, 'Now separate to Me Barnabas and Saul for the work to which I have called them' " (Acts 13:1, 2). The prophetic communication of God through prophets initiated some of the first missionary journeys.

Apply It:

Pray for guidance for the missionaries in your church.

Dig Deeper:

Acts 16:6–10; 1 Corinthians 14:3, 4; Acts 11:12

Fighting Fragmentation

"We should no longer be children, tossed to and fro and carried about with every wind of doctrine, by the trickery of men, in the cunning craftiness of deceitful plotting" (Ephesians 4:14).

A law in the European Union protects people in other countries. This is because people are now seen as "data subjects," or targets of data collection. What matters to the European Union is not whether a person resides in Europe, but rather if they are a target of corporations that are located in Europe.

Christ knew that there would be a risk of fragmentation in the church. For this reason, He gave prophecy and other gifts to the church as a way of keeping His people encouraged and united. (See 1 Corinthians 12:4–7.) One source of unity is having a similar set of beliefs. Paul was likely thinking of this when he spoke of the benefits of the spiritual gifts as coming "till we all come to the unity of the faith and of the knowledge of the Son of God, to a perfect man, to the measure of the stature of the fullness of Christ" (Ephesians 4:13).

This "unity of the faith" is produced most of all by the prophetic messages that became Scripture. However, there are also instances where prophets confirmed a church decision in order to prevent divisions. An example of this took place in response to the controversy over whether people should keep the ceremonial laws of the Old Testament. After a church council decided that those laws were no longer binding, a couple of prophets confirmed the decision: "Now Judas and Silas, themselves being prophets also, exhorted and strengthened the brethren with many words" (Acts 15:32).

The prediction of coming challenges also prevented people from leaving the church as a result of discouragement. Prophets in the New Testament predicted Paul's imprisonment and the famine that would require special help for believers in Judea. Doubtless, these prophets prevented many people from leaving the church or giving up their faith in discouragement.

Apply It:

Help a foreign believer feel welcomed in your church.

Dig Deeper:

Acts 11:27–30; Acts 20:23; Acts 21:4, 10–14

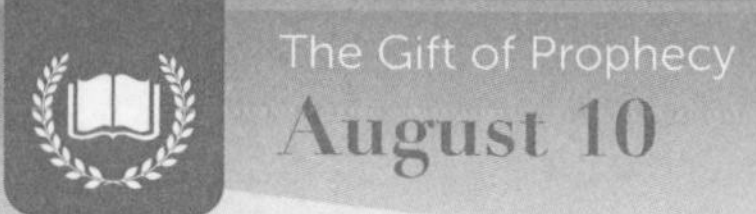

Gifts Increase Stature

"Till we all come to the unity of the faith and of the knowledge of the Son of God, to a perfect man, to the measure of the stature of the fullness of Christ" (Ephesians 4:13).

Puberty can be a chaotic time of change for teens, when growth spurts increase height and muscles change shape. Most girls start this development between the ages of 8 and 13, and their growth spurt takes place between the ages of 10 and 14. Boys begin this change between the ages of 10 and 13, and they continue to grow until they're about 16.

Researchers have narrowed down typical ages for other types of peak performance that goes beyond height and the teen years. For instance, muscle strength tends to hit a high at age 25 and bone mass is at its maximum at age 30. These, of course, are averages.

At what age does the church reach maturity? Paul explains that gifts have been given to the body of Christ until "we all come to the unity of the faith and of the knowledge of the Son of God, to a perfect man, to the measure of the stature of the fullness of Christ" (Ephesians 4:13). It is obvious we have not reached our peak maturity, so we still need the gifts of the Spirit, including the gift of prophecy.

Gifts must still operate in the church to help members complete their God-given work. That's why the apostle warned, "Do not quench the Spirit. Do not despise prophecies" (1 Thessalonians 5:19, 20). He also counseled the church, "Pursue love, and desire spiritual gifts, but especially that you may prophesy" (1 Corinthians 14:1). The gift of prophecy was intended to continue to bring life and strength to God's people.

Though we have seen a marked declension of the prophetic gift throughout church history, the Bible indicates a revival of that gift during the last days when God's people will "keep the commandments of God and have the testimony of Jesus Christ" (Revelation 12:17). An angel explains to John that "the testimony of Jesus is the spirit of prophecy" (19:10).

Apply It:

Have you reached your peak height as a Christian? If so, at what age did this take place?

Dig Deeper:

1 Samuel 2:26; 1 Corinthians 14:39; Ephesians 4:30

Final Warning

"It shall come to pass afterward that I will pour out My Spirit on all flesh" (Joel 2:28).

In the 1950s, during the Cold War when Americans feared a nuclear attack, Chrysler built the loudest siren ever constructed. The Chrysler Air-raid Siren was 12 feet long with six, three-foot-long horns and weighed close to three tons. It produced 138 decibels of sound, which could be heard 25 miles away. The siren's warning wail was so loud that it could deafen anyone within 200 feet and so powerful that it could cause paper in the immediate area to burst into flames.

Before Jesus' first coming, John the Baptist was sent to give a loud warning to prepare the way for the Messiah. Referring to John, Isaiah predicted that he would be the "voice of one crying in the wilderness: 'Prepare the way of the LORD' " (Isaiah 40:3).

Just before Jesus' second coming, the alarm will be sounded again. Speaking of the last days, in part, Joel delivered this message: "It shall come to pass afterward that I will pour out My Spirit on all flesh; your sons and your daughters shall prophesy, your old men shall dream dreams, your young men shall see visions. And also on My menservants and on My maidservants I will pour out My Spirit in those days" (Joel 2:28, 29).

A partial fulfillment came during Pentecost. When the apostles preached to the crowd in a variety of languages, Peter began his explanation by referring to the same prophecy when he said, "This is what was spoken by the prophet Joel" (Acts 2:16).

This is an exciting time to be engaged in God's work. As followers of Jesus, we can expect to be part of the last great warning message, during which "whoever calls on the name of the LORD shall be saved" (Joel 2:32).

Apply It:

How is God leading you to sound the alarm of Jesus' soon return?

Dig Deeper:

Acts 2:2–21; Matthew 13:30, 39; Revelation 6:12–17

Prophetic Gift in the Remnant

"By a prophet the Lord brought Israel out of Egypt, and by a prophet he was preserved" (Hosea 12:13).

A passport is a travel document that confirms the identity and nationality of the holder and is mostly used for international travel. One of the earliest references to a type of paper passport is found in the Bible. When Nehemiah requested permission from the Persian king Artaxerxes to travel back to his homeland, he asked that "letters be given to me for the governors of the region beyond the River, that they must permit me to pass through till I come to Judah" (Nehemiah 2:7). By God's grace, "the king granted them to me" (verse 8).

The Israelites were able to travel because of the prophetic work of Moses. "By a prophet the Lord brought Israel out of Egypt, and by a prophet he was preserved" (Hosea 12:13). So also it was Moses "who was in the congregation in the wilderness with the Angel who spoke to him on Mount Sinai, and with our fathers, the one who received the living oracles to give to us" (Acts 7:38).

Like the Old Testament church in the wilderness that left Egypt, God's last-day people will also be guided by the prophetic gift in preparation for the Second Coming. Revelation describes these loyal believers who comprise the remnant as they "who keep the commandments of God and have the testimony of Jesus" (Revelation 12:17). The "testimony of Jesus is the spirit of prophecy" (19:10).

This gift of prophecy is a distinct characteristic of God's last-day church through which Jesus testifies to His people. It leads the body of Christ toward the Bible and obedience, and without it the church turns toward lawlessness. As Jeremiah explained, "The Law is no more, and her prophets find no vision from the Lord" (Lamentations 2:9).

If you are among those who desire to travel off this sin-polluted world to the heavenly Canaan, you can be assured that you will find the prophetic gift found among His people. It's a heavenly passport that will guide you to the Scriptures, which speak of a "better ... country" (Hebrews 11:16).

Apply It:

Have you ever traveled to a foreign country and needed special travel documents?

Dig Deeper:

Isaiah 11:11; Hebrews 11:15, 16; Revelation 21:27

Comfort in Crisis

"The dragon was enraged with the woman, and he went to make war with the rest of her offspring, who keep the commandments of God and have the testimony of Jesus Christ" (Revelation 12:17).

A showdown is soon coming. Just about every corner of the Bible directs the reader's attention to it, beginning in Genesis 3:15, where we read God's declaration to the serpent: "I will put enmity between you and the woman, and between your seed and her Seed; He shall bruise your head, and you shall bruise His heel."

That verse points toward the Great Controversy between Christ and Satan. It's a theme that recurs throughout Scripture, culminating in the final conflict outlined in the book of Revelation.

But did you notice something essential in Revelation 12:17? The dragon—another designation for Satan—attacks those who have "the testimony of Jesus." They have faith in Jesus, yet those living at the time of this battle have never met the physical Jesus who was crucified, buried, and resurrected some two thousand years earlier. So how do they have this faith?

In Revelation 19:10 we read, "The testimony of Jesus is the spirit of prophecy." There is a body of writing—called the "Spirit of Prophecy"—that offers a testimony of Jesus so strong, so compelling, that it carries believers forward with hope and peace even into the most difficult of times.

In an age where believers worldwide are being asked to tolerate, and even endorse, behaviors that run contrary to God's revelations in Scripture and in Creation, firm resolve will be needed to withstand the attacks of the dragon before and during that final conflict.

In Daniel 12:1, we read a stunning forecast of those last days: "There shall be a time of trouble, such as never was since there was a nation." Praise God that we have a faithful testimony to guide us through that storm!

Apply It:

Read a chapter from the inspiring book *The Great Controversy.* Notice how it points people to the Scriptures and prepares them for the coming of Jesus.

Dig Deeper:

Acts 20:27; Revelation 14:9–12; Revelation 20:4

Other Prophets

"To the law and to the testimony! If they do not speak according to this word, it is because there is no light in them" (Isaiah 8:20).

He was almost never found. For years, Howard Carter, a British archaeologist, had systematically scoured the Valley of the Kings looking for the tomb of a little-known king named Tutankhamun. Then on November 4, 1922, while digging in the Valley of the Kings, Carter found a stairway that led him to the unopened tomb.

Tutankhamun had rested in obscurity for three thousand years. After the excavations of the late 1800s, most archaeologists thought the valley had given up all its secrets, but Carter believed there was a tomb of an obscure king from the 18th dynasty. What he uncovered—priceless treasures, thrones, statues, chariots, and even a solid gold coffin—has since made the boy king Egypt's most famous Pharaoh.

Most people know the famous prophets of the Bible because they have books named after them—Samuel, Isaiah, Jeremiah, Daniel, Ezekiel, etc. Even Moses was a prophet who left us with the first five books of the Old Testament. But sometimes we forget about other prophets and prophetesses who are not well-known, since they didn't leave major testimonies that became part of the Bible—for example, Agabus (Acts 11:28) and Philip's four daughters (Acts 21:9).

The prophet Joel wrote how the Holy Spirit would be poured out at the time of the end: "Your sons and your daughters shall prophesy, your old men shall dream dreams, your young men shall see visions. And also on My menservants and on My maidservants I will pour out My Spirit in those days" (Joel 2:28, 29).

We've already learned that the gift of prophecy would continue after the close of the Bible canon. This gift would continue to uphold the Scriptures, explain its teachings, and edify the church. Postbiblical prophets would help the church carry out its mission, but never contradict previously recorded divine revelation. (See Daniel 9:2.) The same God who inspired the prophets of the Bible gives the prophetic gift to His last-day people with messages that do not supersede Scriptures.

Apply It:

Choose one of the lesser known prophets in the Bible and read about them.

Dig Deeper:

Acts 2:14–39; Ephesians 1:17–19; 1 John 4:1

Testing for Hope

"When the word of the prophet comes to pass, the prophet will be known as one whom the LORD has truly sent" (Jeremiah 28:9).

Researchers have developed a blood test that is able to predict ovarian cancer with 90 percent accuracy and pancreatic cancer with 80 percent accuracy. The test offers hope for early detection, which can help stop cancers before they spread. However, before the test becomes public it has to be tested further.

God knows that communication with Him is important, so He provided a way for us to test those who claimed to have a message from Him. Unlike human-made tests, this test could identify a false prophet, or a true prophet, with perfect accuracy.

The primary criteria that prophets must meet to show that they are speaking the truth is that they deliver messages that are consistent with previous prophetic teachings. Isaiah set forth this test most clearly when he commanded people to go to "the law and to the testimony! If they do not speak according to this word, it is because there is no light in them" (Isaiah 8:20).

Isaiah was speaking of testing those who claimed to be communicating with the dead, which was one form of false prophecy. Previous true prophets had provided "testimony" concerning God, and Moses had written most of the law. Anyone who claims to have supernatural contact should be tested by whether they are giving a consistent picture of the God described by previous prophets, such as Moses.

Even if they pass the first part of the test, they must also predict accurately when they prophesy: "When a prophet speaks in the name of the LORD, if the thing does not happen or come to pass, that is the thing which the LORD has not spoken; the prophet has spoken it presumptuously; you shall not be afraid of him" (Deuteronomy 18:22). Only100-percent accuracy could reveal that God was behind a prophecy.

Apply It:

Compare the last questionable theory you heard with the teaching in the Bible.

Dig Deeper:

James 1:17; 1 Thessalonians 5:20–22; 1 John 4:1

Authentic Products

"You will know them by their fruits. Do men gather grapes from thornbushes or figs from thistles?" (Matthew 7:16).

People buy food and drink from specific areas of the world because of the reputation those regions have for such products. Growers can also benefit from a "geographical indications" label. This label means that only growers who meet certain production requirements can use the name of the region to sell their products.

God is also concerned with ensuring His children receive authentic messages from Him. For this reason, He warned His followers that the difference between true and false prophets could be discerned by the results of their alleged identities.

True prophets were holy people who lived relatively holy lives: "Prophecy never came by the will of man, but holy men of God spoke as they were moved by the Holy Spirit" (2 Peter 1:2). Those who claimed to be messengers sent from God but who lived in sinful abandon were not to be believed.

Additionally, even if they appeared to be living in harmony with God's law, their messages also had to be tested (1 John 4:1) to see if they led to righteous living. This is because the gifts of the Spirit were given to build up God's people. Church growth takes place by attracting others to Jesus through the fruitful lives of members, as can be seen in the life of John the Baptist. (See John 1:6–8.)

One of the most important messages for leading people to a righteous life is that Jesus really came to the earth as a human and lived a sin-free life, which was ended in His sacrifice on our behalf. This message of Jesus' life is so central that it became a bare minimum message for any prophet: "By this you know the Spirit of God: Every spirit that confesses that Jesus Christ has come in the flesh is of God" (1 John 4:2).

A true prophet upholds Christ as the Messiah and lives by the messages spoken. It's an authentic way to know you are receiving truth from heaven.

Apply It:

Use an inviting manner when you share the messages of the Bible prophets.

Dig Deeper:

1 John 4:3; Matthew 7:18–20; James 5:17

A Reproach to the Cause

"A good name is to be chosen rather than great riches" (Proverbs 22:1).

Warren Buffet once said, "It takes twenty years to build a reputation and five minutes to ruin it."

Reputation is made of glass and can easily break. Unfortunately, the Internet provides opportunity for anyone to say anything they like with little or no consequence for falsehoods. "Yellow journalism," a phrase coined in the late nineteenth century, describes the use of misleading sensationalized stories by newspapers to improve circulation. It cares more about making money and less about reputations.

Perhaps that is why Ellen White, a woman who has been recognized by many as having the gift of prophecy, was cautious about assuming the title prophetess. There were many men and women in the late 1800s and early 1900s claiming to have this gift—a gift the Bible indicates will be active in God's end-time churches that "keep the commandments of God and have the testimony of Jesus Christ" (Revelation 12:17). Many people of ill repute gave the biblical work of a prophet a bad name.

Ellen White chose to not use the title prophetess when speaking of her work, but she didn't object to others who called her by that title. She explained that many people asked her at the beginning of her work if she was a prophet. She explained, "I am the Lord's messenger. I know that many have called me a prophet, but I have made no claim to this title. ... Why have I not claimed to be a prophet? Because in these days many who boldly claim that they are prophets are a reproach to the cause of Christ; and because my work includes much more than the word 'prophet' signifies. ... To claim to be a prophetess is something that I have never done." John the Baptist exhibits the same humble spirit in John 3:30.

The apostle Paul encouraged Christians to "test all things; hold fast what is good" (1 Thessalonians 5:21). Read Ellen White's writings for yourself before you decide whether or not her messages are authentic. And be cautious about yellow journalism.

Apply It:

Have you ever fallen for fake news and later discovered the truth?

Dig Deeper:

1 Kings 22:1–28; Ecclesiastes 7:1; 1 Peter 2:12

Citywide Test

"Declaring the end from the beginning, and from ancient times things that are not yet done, saying, 'My counsel shall stand, and I will do all My pleasure' " (Isaiah 46:10).

Singapore has built a small city to test self-driving vehicles. The model city is complete with bus stops, a small hill, and a rain machine. Officials of the country are boasting that they are the first to take a serious approach to testing self-driving vehicles.

Many Christians have taken a serious approach to testing the prophetic status of a nineteenth century American woman: Ellen G. White. Using the biblical tests of a prophet, they have concluded that she was indeed an authentic prophetess.

Her use of the Bible is profuse and reveals her profound esteem for it. Furthermore, her explanation of biblical passages often provides insights that have impressed Bible scholars. However, the test of doctrinal agreement between new and established prophets is the most important consideration.

This harmony was important to the people of Berea: "These were more fair-minded than those in Thessalonica, in that they received the word with all readiness, and searched the Scriptures daily to find out whether these things were so" (Acts 17:11). Like the Bereans, many who have been open to new revelation yet are loyal to the Scriptures believe Ellen White's teachings were in harmony with Scripture.

Another test can be drawn from Jesus' prophetic ministry: "I have told you before it comes, that when it does come to pass, you may believe" (John 14:29). The ministry of prophets should follow Jesus' example and inspire faith using predictions. Ellen White passed this test also. Her prediction concerning the rise of spiritualism, for example, has been confirmed by many. The importance of spiritualism—or communication with spirits—in American history seems like common knowledge to present-day historians. However, in her time this movement was relatively small. Her accurate prediction has inspired faith in God's warnings on this issue.

Apply It:

Compare Ellen White's warnings about tobacco in the late nineteenth century with modern discoveries on the harmfulness of smoking.

Dig Deeper:

1 Thessalonians 5:20, 21; 1 Samuel 3:19; Isaiah 44:24–26

A Living Legacy

"If there is a prophet among you, I, the Lord, make Myself known to him in a vision; I speak to him in a dream" (Numbers 12:6).

Over a seventy-year period, Ellen White had more than two thousand visions. By the end of her life, her written output totaled some 25 million words—an astonishing amount for someone who left school in the third grade. After 125 years in print, her book *Steps to Christ* has been released in more than 165 languages, reaching millions.

Those facts alone would be enough to establish Ellen White as a leading voice of her age, as well as to cement her legacy. But her writings on health, education, temperance, work, and family—to name just a few subjects—are in a class of their own.

What God did working through this small-of-stature, large-of-heart messenger was to deliver precise counsel on so many topics to a world nearing its close. In case after case, Ellen White's writings have been confirmed—not only by the experience of those who've received their guidance, but also by scientific research.

We now know that a plant-based diet, accompanied by exercise, rest, and trust in God, is the best way to ensure a long, healthy life. For example, the *Journal of Geriatric Cardiology* (May 2017) states, "Diet and lifestyle, particularly plant-based diets, are effective tools for type 2 diabetes prevention and management."

Science has recently confirmed that even so-called "moderate" consumption of alcohol has detrimental, lasting health consequences. For example, the *British Medical Journal* (June 2017) writes, "Moderate alcohol consumption is a risk factor for adverse brain outcomes and cognitive decline."

Ellen White's writings are not a substitute for the Bible, and she said her work was a "lesser light" meant to direct people to the "greater light" of Scripture. And it has done so for 175 years: Millions who have read and studied her work have found a deeper faith in Christ and in the Bible and its promises. Truly there was "a prophet among you," and truly her legacy is a living one!

Apply It:

Read *Steps to Christ* and reflect on its message. Then give a copy to someone searching for hope.

Dig Deeper:

Daniel 10:8; Acts 10:11; Acts 22:17, 18

Pointing People Home

"When He, the Spirit of truth, has come, He will guide you into all truth; for He will not speak on His own authority, but whatever He hears He will speak; and He will tell you things to come" (John 16:13).

When a couple of Japanese students got lost at night in the mountains, they found their way out through an unexpected, four-legged furry friend. When their car's navigation system failed to lead them the right way, a forest cat came out of nowhere and began walking and running down the road in front of their car. Eventually, it led them back to the main road and to safety.

Jesus promised that the Spirit would guide His followers into truth. "The Helper, the Holy Spirit, whom the Father will send in My name, He will teach you all things, and bring to your remembrance all things that I said to you" (John 14:26). One way this happens is through the prophetic gift.

The gift of prophecy, as exhibited in the life of Ellen White, is never to be a substitute for the Bible, but rather to serve as a guide to the Scriptures. She believed the Bible is the supreme standard and called the Word of God "an authoritative, infallible revelation of His will. They are the standard of character, the revealer of doctrines, and the test of experience" (*The Great Controversy,* p. 93).

Because so many have turned away from the Bible, she saw her work as leading people back to the Word, to the greater light of the Scriptures. Sometimes even those who claimed to stand on Bible truth would misinterpret the Scriptures and lead people astray. This was nothing new in the days of the apostles. Peter warned, "There were also false prophets among the people, even as there will be false teachers among you, who will secretly bring in destructive heresies" (2 Peter 2:1).

Just as a guide for people who get lost while traveling through unknown territory, the gift of prophecy is a lesser light to lead people to the greater light of the Bible.

Apply It:

Have you ever gotten lost on a trip or a hike? How did you find your way back home?

Dig Deeper:

Romans 15:4; 2 Peter 1:21; 1 John 4:1

The Law of God

19

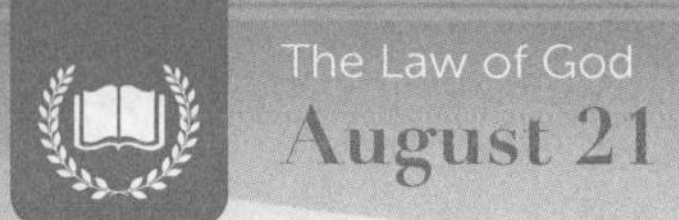

The Eternal Law

"Till heaven and earth pass away, one jot or one tittle will by no means pass from the law till all is fulfilled" (Matthew 5:18).

One of the most famous and well-preserved cuneiform laws used throughout the ancient Middle East is the Code of Hammurabi (now "Hammurapi"). The seven-foot-tall basalt stone shaped like a large finger was discovered in 1901 and provides insights into the Babylonian code of law in ancient Mesopotamia around 1750 BC. Because it preceded the laws of Moses in the Pentateuch and has some similarities, critics have claimed that Moses plagiarized from the Code of Hammurabi and did not receive the law of God from the Lord on Mount Sinai.

Actually, a careful study of the similar instances in the two laws reveals distinct differences between them. God's law reveals that sin is the reason a nation is destroyed—something missing in the Code of Hammurabi. The religious foundation in God's law, "Be holy, for I am holy" (Leviticus 11:45), is nowhere to be found in the ancient cuneiform civil laws.

The Bible reveals a knowledge of God's law that preceded the time of Moses. Adam and Eve were aware of God's law for "whoever commits sin also commits lawlessness, and sin is lawlessness" (1 John 3:4). It was through Adam's sin that death came to our world. "Therefore, just as through one man sin entered the world, and death through sin, and thus death spread to all men, because all sinned" (Romans 5:12).

We can go further back than Adam and know that the law existed in heaven before Lucifer rebelled, for "God did not spare the angels who sinned, but cast them down" (2 Peter 2:4).

After being in bondage in Egypt for hundreds of years, God's people lost their understanding of the law. Upon being freed, the Lord delivered them to a place where "they might observe His statutes and keep His laws" (Psalm 105:45). At Sinai, God gave the people His laws in direct, clear, and simple terms.

Apply It:

Which of the Ten Commandments is most often kept in your community? Which one do you think is broken most often?

Dig Deeper:

Psalm 111:7, 8; Isaiah 40:8; Galatians 3:19

Holy Words

"The Lord came from Sinai, and dawned on them from Seir; He shone forth from Mount Paran, and He came with ten thousands of saints; from His right hand came a fiery law for them" (Deuteronomy 33:2).

Volcán de Fuego (Spanish for "Volcano of Fire") is one of the most active volcanoes in the world. Located just 27 miles from Guatemala City, it has erupted more than 60 times since 1524. In 2012, an explosive eruption forced 33,000 to evacuate.

On June 3, 2018, the volcano erupted, killing over 100 people and injuring 300. It was the deadliest eruption since 1929. Entire villages were covered in ash, and most deaths were caused by pyroclastic flows. Heavy rainfall then created dangerous volcanic mudflows and a nine-mile-high ash column shut down the country's primary airport for a time.

Imagine how the Israelites felt as they stood at the base of Mount Sinai. Moses had instructed the people to wash their clothes and prepare to meet the Lord. Strict guidelines were to be followed, including not touching the mountain lest man or beast die. God was about to meet His people and speak to them His holy law, the Ten Commandments.

Soon the people were led out of the camp to the foot of the mountain. "Now Mount Sinai was completely in smoke, because the Lord descended upon it in fire. Its smoke ascended like the smoke of a furnace, and the whole mountain quaked greatly. And when the blast of the trumpet sounded long and became louder and louder, Moses spoke, and God answered him by voice" (Exodus 19:18, 19).

The scene was somewhat like a volcano about to explode and "all the people who were in the camp trembled" (verse 16). After hearing the Lord speak the Ten Commandments, the people told Moses, "You speak with us, and we will hear; but let not God speak with us, lest we die" (20:19). But Moses understood that they needed to hear God's law—a law to be respected and loved.

Apply It:

Have you ever talked with a law officer about a traffic infraction? How did you feel?

Dig Deeper:

Exodus 20:1–21; Deuteronomy 4:7–14; Hebrews 12:18–24

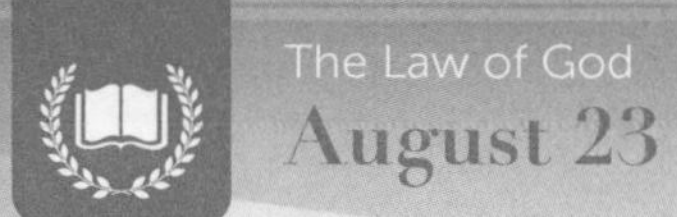

More Than Opinion

"Whoever commits sin also commits lawlessness, and sin is lawlessness" (1 John 3:4).

A recent poll shows that 49 percent of Americans believe that U.S. moral values are in a poor state. While this percentage is not a majority, it marks the most negative view of the moral state of the nation since 2002.

The Ten Commandments are an obvious moral standard and represent one set of moral values. However, God's eternal law was designed to go beyond opinion and perception. Because it deals with motives and thoughts, His law is also called spiritual.

People cannot change their hearts without the transforming power of the Holy Spirit. This is clear when we see the character traits that come only from the Holy Spirit: "The fruit of the Spirit is love, joy, peace, longsuffering, kindness, goodness, faithfulness, gentleness, self-control. Against such there is no law" (Galatians 5:22, 23). While outward behavior may sometimes fool a naive portion of the population, the inner fruit of the Spirit cannot be manufactured without the Spirit of God.

Furthermore, the lack of the fruit of the Spirit also means that a person is not abiding in faith to God and to His law. We know this because of the way Jesus pointed out the spiritual nature of the law: "You have heard that it was said to those of old, 'You shall not murder, and whoever murders will be in danger of the judgment.' But I say to you that whoever is angry with his brother without a cause shall be in danger of the judgment. And whoever says to his brother, 'Raca!' shall be in danger of the council. But whoever says, 'You fool!' shall be in danger of hell fire" (Matthew 5:21, 22).

Jesus used two of the Ten Commandments as examples of how lawbreaking is a spiritual issue. It is more than just an action. It is something that begins in the thoughts. Therefore, it is unavoidable without the help of the Holy Spirit.

Apply It:

Earnestly pray for the Holy Spirit to give you deep victory over a besetting sin in your life.

Dig Deeper:

Romans 7:14; John 15:4; Acts 1:8

Simple Summary

"He who looks into the perfect law of liberty and continues in it, and is not a forgetful hearer but a doer of the work, this one will be blessed in what he does" (James 1:25).

When Google released a list of seven principles by which it will abide in its development of artificial intelligence, many news outlets felt it was mostly a promise to abstain from making weapons or spying. However, the principles also set forth a number of positive plans that stem from the company's attempt to benefit society.

The Ten Commandments are often seen as a list of barriers or bans. However, the Bible makes it clear that people cannot keep the moral law by simply abstaining from certain activities.

This point is especially clear in Jesus' interaction with the rich young ruler. Jesus cited a few of the commandments when He asked the man if he had kept the law. The commandments that Jesus did not mention were all prohibitive as they appeared on Mount Sinai.

However, when the man affirmed his keeping of all of the commandments, Jesus explained the broader positive meaning of the law: "When Jesus heard these things, He said to him, 'You still lack one thing. Sell all that you have and distribute to the poor, and you will have treasure in heaven; and come, follow Me' " (Luke 18:22). This means that the commandments also involve an active expression of love toward people.

Jesus' explanation coincides with His summary of the law: "You shall love the LORD your God with all your heart, with all your soul, with all your mind, and with all your strength. This is the first commandment. And the second, like it, is this: 'You shall love your neighbor as yourself' " (Mark 12:30, 31).

From a simple summary such as this, even a child could understand the law of God. Yet even the barriers in the law—those that keep us from long-term sadness—are simple enough for most people to understand.

Apply It:

This week go out of your way to show love to someone who needs it.

Dig Deeper:

Deuteronomy 6:7; Galatians 6:2; Romans 13:8

Broad Freedom

"Let us hear the conclusion of the whole matter: Fear God and keep His commandments, for this is man's all" (Ecclesiastes 12:13).

Vietnam has passed laws that strictly regulate the Internet. For instance, one such law requires foreign companies to store their data for Vietnamese customers in Vietnam. Internet providers are also required to remove content that the government doesn't want on the Internet within a day of notification.

Laws that have to do with Internet regulation raise questions about property rights and the ability to communicate truth. Both of these areas are dealt with by at least two of the comprehensive principles in the Ten Commandments: the eighth and ninth.

It is impossible to escape the comprehensive nature of God's eternal law on any issue. This is because they were designed by the Creator to help define our relationships with Him and with others. This is illustrated when a lawyer once asked Christ, "Which is the great commandment in the law?" (Matthew 22:36). Jesus' answer shows the broad application of God's law. " 'You shall love the Lord your God with all your heart, with all your soul, and with all your mind.' This is the first and great commandment. And the second is like it: 'You shall love your neighbor as yourself.' On these two commandments hang all the Law and the Prophets" (Matthew 22:37–40).

By writing the Ten Commandments with His own finger, God was also showing that the law involves a relationship with Him. (See John 14:15.) The broad nature of the principles in the Ten Commandments can also be seen by looking at how they begin. Jesus focused on the principle of loving God first because He knew that people would not be able to love one another without loving God first.

The apostle John explained this point when he stated: "If someone says, 'I love God,' and hates his brother, he is a liar; for he who does not love his brother whom he has seen, how can he love God whom he has not seen?" (1 John 4:20). Unlike human laws, God's law always guides us to harmony.

Apply It:

Find a new area of your work where you can apply God's law.

Dig Deeper:

Exodus 34:28; Luke 10:27; Deuteronomy 6:4, 5

The Centerpiece of the Sanctuary

"When He had made an end of speaking with him on Mount Sinai, He gave Moses two tablets of the Testimony, tablets of stone, written with the finger of God" (Exodus 31:18).

For 800 years, the Crown Jewels of the United Kingdom have been used for the sovereign's coronation regalia. The 140 royal ceremonial objects are carefully guarded in the Tower of London and are comprised of crowns, swords, scepters, maces, trumpets, robes, rings, and more. Among the 23,578 precious and semi-precious stones is the Cullinan I—the largest clear-cut diamond in the world.

The centerpiece of the Crown Jewels is St Edward's Crown, one traditionally used for English and British monarchs at their coronations since the thirteenth century. The original crown was lost after Parliament abolished the monarchy in 1649, but the present version was made for Charles II in 1661. It is made of solid gold, weighs 4.9 pounds, and is decorated with 444 precious and semi-precious stones.

The centerpiece of the Old Testament sanctuary is found in the Most Holy Place. Inside this room was the golden ark of the covenant that held the law of God, the Ten Commandments, which was written on stone by the finger of God (Exodus 31:18). Nothing was more precious to the nation of Israel than these two tablets of stone. Unlike the Crown Jewels, which are viewed by over 2.5 million visitors each year, the sacred law was kept protected from curious eyes.

This law was unlike the additional laws written down by Moses on parchment and placed beside the ark (Deuteronomy 31:26). The Ten Commandments are the only words God spoke audibly to the entire nation. Moses explained, "These words the Lord spoke to all your assembly, in the mountain from the midst of the fire, the cloud, and the thick darkness, with a loud voice" (Deuteronomy 5:22).

Civil laws, which focused on the civil affairs of Israel, and ceremonial laws, which regulated the sanctuary services, were not the same as the moral law of Ten Commandments. They were written down by Moses who was instructed to "put it beside the ark of the covenant of the Lord your God" (Deuteronomy 31:26).

Apply It:

Think of a museum you have visited and the most treasured object you have ever viewed.

Dig Deeper:

Exodus 31:18; Deuteronomy 10:2; James 1:25

A Delightful Law

"Oh, how I love Your law! It is my meditation all the day. You, through Your commandments, make me wiser than my enemies; for they are ever with me" (Psalm 119:97, 98).

In Blythe, California, it's against the law to wear cowboy boots if the wearer owns fewer than two cows. In Boston, there's a law on the books requiring folks to take a bath before turning in for the night. And in Minneapolis, a law says you're not allowed to drive a red car down Lake Street.

Contrast all the laws man has created—and there are many—with the law of God. His law is based on love to God and love to one another. "We love Him because He first loved us" (1 John 4:19).

When the basis of our actions is love, keeping the law isn't an inconvenience. "This is the love of God, that we keep His commandments. And His commandments are not burdensome" (1 John 5:3). When we do not murder or commit adultery, and when we honor our parents, we are promised blessings.

God's laws were given to sustain life for humanity. Not a single one of them is intended to bring anyone harm. Each law is created for our true welfare, that we may fare well in this life and be fitted for the life to come.

When we read in Leviticus 19:18, "You shall not take vengeance, nor bear any grudge against the children of your people, but you shall love your neighbor as yourself: I am the Lord," we're seeing a principle that could make the world a better place. If everyone did this—loved their neighbor as themselves—wars would cease, crime would be eliminated, and courtesy would rule the day.

The apostle Paul declared to the young Christian community in Rome that "the law is holy, and the commandment holy and just and good" (Romans 7:12). It's there for us to appreciate and, yes, delight in!

Apply It:

Think about the ways in which God's law has protected and shaped your life—especially in how it's kept you from harming yourself or those for whom you care.

Dig Deeper:

Psalm 119:127, 143; 1 Timothy 1:9; 1 John 5:3

Carried by a Loving Father

"If you keep My commandments, you will abide in My love, just as I have kept My Father's commandments and abide in His love" (John 15:10).

Zy, a boy from Thailand, climbs mountains, but he can't do it alone. Born with one-and-a-half arms, an abnormal leg, no right leg, and dislocated hips, Zy is completely reliant on his father's strength to carry both of them uphill. Together they have conquered some challenging summits—including Mount Kilimanjaro, where Zy became the youngest disabled person to reach the 19,341-foot peak.

When it comes to keeping God's commandments—in letter and in spirit—we are, without God's power, as helpless as a disabled person attempting to climb Everest, for "the carnal mind is enmity against God; for it is not subject to the law of God, nor indeed can be" (Romans 8:7). Yet we have a loving Father who will transform and carry us. "Even to your old age, I am He, ... I will carry you! I have made, and I will bear; even I will carry, and will deliver you" (Isaiah 46:4).

God's will for mankind is that we keep all of His commandments. "Whoever shall keep the whole law, and yet stumble in one point, he is guilty of all" (James 2:10).

We can be sure it is His will that we keep *all* His commandments because Jesus clearly explained, "Till heaven and earth pass away, one jot or one tittle will by no means pass from the law till all is fulfilled. Whoever therefore breaks one of the least of these commandments, and teaches men so, shall be called least in the kingdom of heaven; but whoever does and teaches them, he shall be called great in the kingdom of heaven" (Matthew 5:18, 19).

God's commandments reflect His character of love and are given to bless our lives and to keep us from harm. Cherished in the heart and practiced in the life, they lead us toward salvation through Jesus Christ. Through the power of His Spirit within us, we can joyfully keep His commandments and triumph over sin in our lives to show our love and gratitude to Him.

Apply It:

Have you ever climbed a mountain? What were the factors that made your climb successful?

Dig Deeper:

John 15:10; John 14:21; 1 John 2:3–6

An Accurate Measurement

"Honest weights and scales are the LORD's; all the weights in the bag are His work" (Proverbs 16:11).

"There certainly can't be a greater grievance to a traveler from one colony to another than the different values their paper money bears." So wrote an English visitor to America in 1742. Monetary values before the American Revolution greatly varied—each colony had its own conventions, tender laws, and coin ratings, and each issued its own paper money.

The Coinage Act of 1792 created the U.S. dollar as the country's standard unit of money. It created the U.S. Mint and also regulated coinage in the States. The act established the silver dollar as the unit of money declared to be lawful tender, and it set up a decimal system for U.S. currency.

The standard of righteousness in the universe is the law of God. David wrote of God that "all Your commandments are righteousness" (Psalm 119:172). While the nations of the world may set up their own monetary systems and laws for justice, the Ten Commandments lay the foundation for the principles used in the final judgment of the world.

Solomon admonished, "Fear God and keep His commandments, for this is man's all. For God will bring every work into judgment, including every secret thing, whether good or evil" (Ecclesiastes 12:13, 14). The standard for judgment is not set up by a committee, by popular vote, or by acts of earthly governments.

Even the human conscience is a poor guide for accurately guiding people justly. The apostle Paul describes some consciences as "being weak" (1 Corinthians 8:7). Of those who lie and are hypocritical, he says their consciences are "seared with a hot iron" (1 Timothy 4:2). Just as monetary values in early American history were inconsistent, so the minds of men cannot accurately determine true justice.

Only hearts that have been compared to God's great standard—His holy law—can keep us from wandering into sin.

Apply It:

Do you collect coins as a hobby? What is the most valuable coin you own?

Dig Deeper:

Deuteronomy 4:8; Psalm 119:142; Matthew 23:28

Love Mirror

"By the deeds of the law no flesh will be justified in His sight, for by the law is the knowledge of sin" (Romans 3:20).

In a study on perceptions concerning God's face, researchers found that most of the Christians surveyed chose a kinder picture of a man over its grumpier counterpart. Additionally, the study found that people generally believe God resembles their own facial features. In other words, they could look in a mirror to see their picture of God.

The law of God functions in almost the exact opposite manner. It reveals the ways in which humans differ from God in their character and behavior. Although it also functions like a mirror, it exposes the sins that people commit and their tendency to commit sins.

A passage in the writings of James describes this process: "If anyone is a hearer of the word and not a doer, he is like a man observing his natural face in a mirror; for he observes himself, goes away, and immediately forgets what kind of man he was" (1:23, 24). Here he seems to be saying that people often conveniently forget their sins soon after identifying them by looking at God's law. This suggests that a look into God's law will reveal the areas in one's life where they are separating from God.

Although some sins may seem obviously wrong to people who do not know the law of God, there are others that cannot be truly discerned without it. This is especially true when considering the depths of sin. The apostle Paul explained that he would have had a tough time identifying sin without the law of God: "What shall we say then? Is the law sin? Certainly not! On the contrary, I would not have known sin except through the law. For I would not have known covetousness unless the law had said, 'You shall not covet' " (Romans 7:7).

Apply It:

Ask God to work in you today as you adjust your life according to God's law.

Dig Deeper:

Romans 3:19; 1 John 3:4; James 1:25

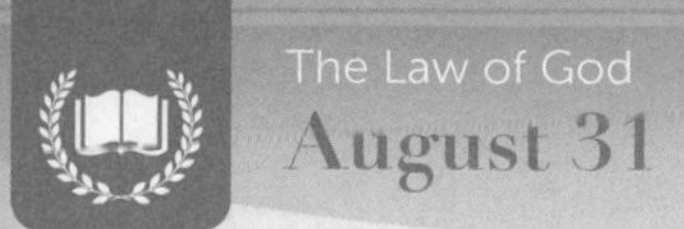

The Stone of Conversion

"Repent therefore and be converted, that your sins may be blotted out, so that times of refreshing may come from the presence of the Lord" (Acts 3:19).

The philosopher's stone is a legendary substance supposedly capable of turning base metals, like mercury, into gold or silver. For hundreds of years, the search for this stone, which was also supposed to help people achieve immortality, was called the Magnum Opus (the "Great Work").

Of course, these early researchers didn't understand that substances like mercury and gold were different atomic elements that couldn't be changed at whim in laboratory reactions—until the dawn of the nuclear age, when physicists have transformed one element to another with nuclear reactors.

In 1980, researchers at the Lawrence Berkeley National Laboratory succeeded in making small amounts of gold from bismuth. But particles created from the atomic collisions were so minute that they were difficult to detect even with a spectrometer. One author said, "It would cost more than one quadrillion dollars per ounce to produce gold by this experiment." The going rate for gold at that time was $560 an ounce.

The Bible speaks of a stone that is necessary to the conversion of the human heart and leads to the Source of eternal life—the Ten Commandments. David wrote, "The law of the Lord is perfect, converting the soul" (Psalm 19:7). When people understand their true character by looking at the commandments, they feel their need of a Savior.

But the law can never save us. While it can reveal sin, it cannot remove sin. Like a mirror that can show us dirt on our face (James 1:23), it cannot take away sin. We must come to Jesus to be purified. (See Zechariah 13:1.)

God's law plays an important role as an agent of conversion and has been compared to a "tutor to bring us to Christ, that we might be justified by faith" (Galatians 3:24). But the transformation can happen only by the "blood of the Lamb" (Revelation 7:14).

Apply It:

Think of a time you looked in the mirror and were surprised to discover a smudge on your face that you knew nothing about.

Dig Deeper:

Ezekiel 36:26; John 3:16; James 1:22–25

Free at Last!

"Most assuredly, I say to you, whoever commits sin is a slave of sin" (John 8:34).

Spend any time with people who've battled an addiction—gambling, alcohol, drugs—and you'll often hear the same thing: "I was always a slave to getting my next *fix*" (meaning their next illicit experience). They were, effectively, slaves to their sin.

Some folks argue that obeying God's law is in itself slavery. We're free from the law, they argue, and are no longer in "bondage" to those musty Old Testament commands. They claim, "There is therefore now no condemnation to those who are in Christ Jesus" (Romans 8:1) and emphasize "what the law could not do in that it was weak through the flesh" (v. 3).

While it is true that the ceremonial law of the ancient Hebrews is no longer binding today—Jesus fulfilled its requirements—it's also true that the moral law, spelled out in the Ten Commandments, is as binding as it ever was. We still need to recognize God as the sole deity. We still should not bow down to idols. We still should observe the Sabbath, honor our parents, and so on.

Why? Why not work seven days a week if we choose? Why not mix in a little idol worship? Because when we abandon God's law, His order for our lives, we open ourselves up to become slaves. (See Hebrews 11:15.). After the French Revolution, the new government created a "week" of ten days, with the final day being the "day of rest." This new system didn't last long, because workers were exhausted by such long stretches of labor.

Within the law of God—whether it's about our work week, our personal lives, or our health—experience has shown, time after time, that following God's law produces great freedom and benefits. As Paul wrote, "Where the Spirit of the Lord is, there is liberty" (2 Corinthians 3:17).

Following God's law brings lasting benefits and a true sense of freedom!

Apply It:

Review the Ten Commandments today (Exodus 20) and think about how each law keeps us free from sin, sickness, and sorrow in life.

Dig Deeper:

Psalm 119:45; James 2:8; James 1:25

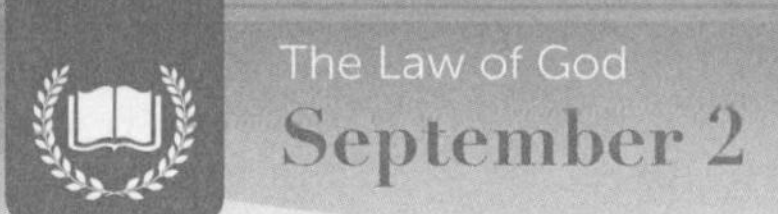

Restraining Violence

"Righteousness exalts a nation, but sin is a reproach to any people" (Proverbs 14:34).

Which are the most peaceful nations? If you follow the Global Peace Index (GPI), the latest (2017) statistics place Iceland, New Zealand, Portugal, and Austria. The least peaceful include Syria, Afghanistan, South Sudan, and Yemen. Three broad areas are measured to determine peacefulness: the level of societal safety and security, the extent of ongoing domestic and international conflict, and the degree of militarization.

The GPI indicates that in the past decade, world peace has deteriorated at a rate of 2.14 percent. Over the past five years, the world has seen historically high numbers of people killed by terrorist incidents. One of the challenges in measuring this index (such as violence against children) is the lack of reliable international data.

The Bible teaches that the law of God restrains evil in our world. When those living before the flood cast off the commandments of the Lord, "The earth also was corrupt before God, and the earth was filled with violence" (Genesis 6:11; see also Matthew 24:12). Jesus predicted the same for the time before the Second Coming: "As it was in the days of Noah, so it will be also in the days of the Son of Man" (Luke 17:26).

Wickedness floods the world when the Decalogue is ignored because God's law restrains sin and promotes right behavior. "It is an abomination for kings to commit wickedness, for a throne is established by righteousness" (Proverbs 16:12). A nation will not prosper when it turns from the law of God. "By the blessing of the upright the city is exalted, but it is overthrown by the mouth of the wicked" (Proverbs 11:11).

Moses outlined the blessings of obedience for Israel. "Now it shall come to pass, if you diligently obey the voice of the Lord your God, to observe carefully all His commandments which I command you today, that the Lord your God will set you high above all nations of the earth" (Deuteronomy 28:1, 2). Such respect for the law of God will put a nation at the top of the list for enjoying peace.

Apply It:

What is the most violent country or city you have visited?

Dig Deeper:

Leviticus 26:1–46; Deuteronomy 28:1–68; Psalm 119:165

Signal Attack

"The dragon was enraged with the woman, and he went to make war with the rest of her offspring, who keep the commandments of God" (Revelation 12:17).

Hurricane Maria's 110 MPH winds severely damaged the Arecibo Observatory, one of the world's largest single-dish radio telescopes. To survey the destruction, a crew of employees paddled kayaks under the telescope, where an eight-foot-deep lake had formed. They concluded that repairs would take two years.

In the time leading up to the Second Coming, another means of communication with the heavens will become subject to attacks. However, this time the attacks will not be from natural disasters. Instead, it will come from a government that will use its influence to attempt to "change times and law" (Daniel 7:25). This is problematic because God's law is a core part of heaven's communication regarding the definition of love. In other words, the law describes the type of character that everyone who is saved will possess.

The prophet Daniel describes the attack on God's law by speaking of the rise of the power carrying it out: "He shall speak pompous words against the Most High, shall persecute the saints of the Most High. ... Then the saints shall be given into his hand for a time and times and half a time" (Daniel 7:25). Although this attack began when this power first arose, it will continue until the return of Christ.

Paul warned of this unholy power, "Let no one deceive you by any means; for that Day will not come unless the falling away comes first, and the man of sin is revealed, the son of perdition" (2 Thessalonians 2:3).

Unlike any human-made product, the law cannot be destroyed. However, humans will play a part in defending it. They will do this by keeping the law and by calling others to worship God, which includes obedience to the law: "Fear God and give glory to Him, for the hour of His judgment has come; and worship Him who made heaven and earth, the sea and springs of water" (Revelation 14:7).

Apply It:

Which of the Ten Commandments do you think is most needed in your community right now?

Dig Deeper:

Revelation 14:12; 1 John 5:3; Revelation 13:3

Reactive Laws

"The temple of God was opened in heaven, and the ark of His covenant was seen in His temple. And there were lightnings, noises, thunderings, an earthquake, and great hail" (Revelation 11:19).

Soon after the European Union met with the head of Facebook, government leaders complained that they had missed an opportunity to hold the company accountable for leaking private data. The failure meant that they would need to make up new laws to police the company.

In contrast to the way human governments work, God bases His judgments on laws that existed before the creation of humans. While governments create new laws to deal with citizens finding new ways to harm others, God will simply carry out His judgments based on His unchanging law—a reflection of His unchanging character.

The seven last plagues are some of the ways that His judgments are carried out. These plagues resemble the painful experiences—such as sores—that the Egyptians went through when they refused to let the Israelites leave.

These judgments take place just before the Second Coming and are a response to the breaking of God's law. This can be seen when the ark of the covenant is made visible just before the angels that deliver the plagues come out of the temple, where the ark is located: "After these things I looked, and behold, the temple of the tabernacle of the testimony in heaven was opened" (Revelation 15:5). James also connects law and judgment when he writes: "Speak and so do as those who will be judged by the law of liberty" (James 2:12).

The phrase that John used to describe the ark would have been reminiscent of the role of the Ten Commandments as a testifying witness for or against a law breaker or a law abider. This description can be seen when God wrote the commandments: "When He had made an end of speaking with him on Mount Sinai, He gave Moses two tablets of the Testimony, tablets of stone, written with the finger of God" (Exodus 31:18). John used the word "testimony" to remind readers that the plagues are a response to the breaking of the law.

Apply It:

Strive to be fair to all.

Dig Deeper:

Revelation 11:18; Exodus 34:27, 28; Numbers 1:50

A Perfect Mix

"The mercy of the Lord is from everlasting to everlasting ... to those who remember His commandments" (Psalm 103:17, 18).

Everyone knows that water and wax do not mix well. But perhaps they have never seen a wax fire, which is made when hot wax is doused in water. Pouring water on burning wax can create a fireball because the water hitting the hot wax almost instantly vaporizes, sending the wax into the air as tiny droplets. With a much bigger surface exposed to oxygen, the wax explodes into flames. This is why you should never put out a liquid fire, such as burning grease, with water; rather, use baking soda.

Some believe God's law and the gospel don't mix. Efforts to combine the two are seen as distorted or even destructive. Since the law condemns, doesn't the gospel simply abolish the law? There's no question that we are not saved "by works of righteousness which we have done, but according to His mercy" (Titus 3:5). Yet throughout Scripture, we see the law and the gospel in perfect harmony.

When Adam and Eve sinned, God did not nullify the law but combined the law and gospel in the life of Christ. The good news is that "He made Him who knew no sin to be sin for us, that we might become the righteousness of God in Him" (2 Corinthians 5:21).

But Jesus' death, while freeing us from the condemnation of the law, also empowered us to keep the law through His indwelling Spirit. God blessed Abraham with grace "in order that he may command his children and his household after him, that they keep the way of the Lord, to do righteousness and justice" (Genesis 18:19).

The gospel does not remove the law but actually brings it closer to home, for God promises, "I will put My law in their minds, and write it on their hearts" (Jeremiah 31:33). Now that's a great mix!

Apply It:

Think of a time when the grace of God made it possible for you to keep His law.

Dig Deeper:

Psalm 40:8; John 8:29; Hebrews 8:10

Where Law and Grace Meet

"Is the law sin? Certainly not! On the contrary, I would not have known sin except through the law" (Romans 7:7).

During the summer of 1954, a tent revival at the corner of Smythe and High in Montgomery, Alabama, drew a thousand people each night. Many came to hear the messages of E.E. Cleveland, an evangelist sharing the three angels' messages.

The outreach got the attention of two Sunday-keeping preachers who had yet to burst upon the national scene: the Rev. Ralph David Abernathy and the Rev. Dr. Martin Luther King, Jr. The two pastors were concerned that Cleveland was "stealing their sheep," so they had interrupted their vacations to hear this visiting minister who'd captured so much attention. On meeting Cleveland, Dr. King said, "I was informed that a 'Black Billy Graham' was preaching the gospel, but all I heard was 'the law, the law, and the law.' "

Cleveland replied, "You must have arrived late, because all I preached was the Lord, the Lord, and the Lord."

From the beginning of the Decalogue (Exodus 20:1), we read of God, who gives the law, as the Redeemer of His people. But He gave the law to instruct us, to show us what sin is, and to point us toward the ultimate salvation He would provide through Jesus Christ. In fact, the very sacrifices specified in Exodus point toward the ultimate sacrifice Jesus would make, one far exceeding the worth of bulls and rams.

Yes—there is a law of God, but it points toward a Savior: "If the blood of bulls and goats and the ashes of a heifer, sprinkling the unclean, sanctifies for the purifying of the flesh, how much more shall the blood of Christ, who through the eternal Spirit offered Himself without spot to God, cleanse your conscience from dead works to serve the living God?" (Hebrews 9:13, 14).

It was at Sinai that law and grace met, the one foreshadowing the other. Praise God that He had a plan!

Apply It:

Review the Ten Commandments in Exodus 20 and the sacrifices described in Leviticus 1; see how the two elements point toward salvation.

Dig Deeper:

Exodus 20:1, 2; Exodus 24:9–18; Deuteronomy 31:26

No Ceremonies Here

"Do not think that I came to destroy the Law or the Prophets. I did not come to destroy but to fulfill" (Matthew 5:17).

Moses ben Maimon, a medieval Jewish scholar, once listed a total of 613 commandments in the Hebrew Bible that an observant believer must follow. Many of these, of course, were moral laws such as those forbidding murder, adultery, lying, and theft. But many were ceremonial.

Keeping up with these 613 commandments isn't an easy task, yet Jesus fulfilled all the requirements of the law during His time on Earth.

And then, at His death, those ceremonial requirements were abolished—an act symbolized by the supernatural tearing of the temple veil in front of the Holy of Holies. There was no longer a barrier between man and God that could be crossed only by a sanctified priest. All believers had access!

His fulfillment of the law didn't just mean completing its requirements for Himself. In this case, Jesus completed the task for all of us. Ritual observances are no longer required for access to God and His blessings. (See Matthew 5:17.)

It's important to remember this does not eliminate the demands of the moral law. You can't kill, cheat on your spouse, or steal—and expect God's approval. (The Bible Sabbath—the seventh day of the week—is part of the moral law. Indeed, it's at the center of the Ten Commandments—a sign of God's love and care for His people in providing a mandated rest from all labor once a week.)

But do we have to keep the rituals of the Old Covenant? Do we have to trek to Jerusalem three times a year to worship? Must we engage in tasks that foreshadowed what Jesus Himself abundantly fulfilled? No.

The rituals, ceremonies, and practices of the former time were completed—fulfilled—in Christ. Today, Gentile and Jewish believers in Jesus can unite without having to examine each other's practice of things no longer demanded. This fulfillment stands at the heart of Christian liberty!

Apply It:

Study some of the rituals found in the Old Testament and see how they foreshadowed what Jesus did at the cross. In doing this, consider how Christ has made us free from these rituals.

Dig Deeper:

Matthew 27:51; Hebrews 10:1; Colossians 2:14–19

Out of Love

"Christ is the end of the law for righteousness to everyone who believes" (Romans 10:4).

Next door to a shopping mall in northern Virginia is the tiny chapel of a Sabbath-keeping church. The location attracts attention, as does the motto on their sign: "Keeping the Sabbath Out of Love."

Christ's death fulfilled the requirements of the ceremonial law, but the Ten Commandments spoken by God—are not temporary. Jesus intends for His followers to keep these even today.

John Calvin, the famous reformer, said the law "is the eternal rule of a devout and holy life." We do not keep the law to earn salvation; we observe the moral law because it provides both a framework for that "devout and holy life," as well as a means to demonstrate our love for the One Who redeemed us from sin's penalty.

When Paul wrote that "Christ is the end of the law for righteousness" (Romans 10:4), he did not mean that we should get rid of the law. "Do we then make void the law through faith? Certainly not! On the contrary, we establish the law" (Romans 3:31). His point is that we should never attempt to keep the law in order to earn salvation.

In the seventh chapter of Luke's Gospel, we get a glimpse of what it means to love Jesus for what He has done. A Pharisee is entertaining the Master when a woman of poor reputation comes to Him. She weeps at Jesus' feet, wipes them with her hair, and anoints them with a costly fragrant oil.

Simon the Pharisee protests, but Jesus points out that Simon offered no water for Him to wash His sandal-clad, dusty feet, but the woman never ceased to minister to Him. Jesus said the woman's actions demonstrated her love for the One who forgave her many sins. However, He added, "to whom little is forgiven, the same loves little" (Luke 7:47).

When we love Jesus, we will want to express it in tangible ways. One of the most tangible is to honor and keep His commandments.

Apply It:

Study each of the Ten Commandments and think about how observing each shows love to God—and to your neighbors.

Dig Deeper:

Romans 6:13, 14; Romans 8:1; Romans 6:1

The True Sign

"Not everyone who says to Me, 'Lord, Lord,' shall enter the kingdom of heaven, but he who does the will of My Father in heaven" (Matthew 7:21).

Perhaps you've seen old military movies showing someone approaching a sentry who calls out, "Friend or foe?" A countersign was then used by the person coming up to the sentry—a word or other signal used to verify his or her security clearance. During World War II, a well-known sign-countersign used by Allied forces on D-Day was the challenge "flash" (given by the sentry) and "thunder" (the response), after which the welcome was given.

Entering the kingdom of heaven requires more than just saying the right password. In fact, even performing certain actions that look good on the surface will not be accepted. Jesus explained, "Many will say to Me in that day, 'Lord, Lord, have we not prophesied in Your name, cast out demons in Your name, and done many wonders in Your name?' And then I will declare to them, 'I never knew you; depart from Me, you who practice lawlessness!' " (Matthew 7:22, 23).

But didn't Jesus teach that His grace removed any requirement to keep the law? Far from it! Christ plainly said, "If you want to enter into life, keep the commandments" (Matthew 19:17). The Savior came not only to redeem humanity, but to vindicate the law of God through His life. "This is My commandment, that you love one another *as I have loved you*" (John 15:12, emphasis added).

We cannot keep the law in our own power, but only by abiding in Christ. Paul explained, "I have been crucified with Christ; it is no longer I who live, but Christ lives in me; and the life which I now live in the flesh I live by faith in the Son of God, who loved me and gave Himself for me" (Galatians 2:20).

The password to heaven is not a secret word, but a life that has been changed by the grace of Christ and shows obedience to God.

Apply It:

Can you think of a secret password you used as a child when playing with others?

Dig Deeper:

John 14:15; John 15:4; 1 John 2:3

September 10

Blessings all Around!

"If you diligently obey the voice of the LORD your God, to observe carefully all His commandments which I command you today ... the LORD your God will set you high above all nations of the earth" (Deuteronomy 28:1).

In 2022, according to researchers, Americans will spend $13 billion a year for self-improvement products and services—up from just under $10 billion in 2016.

That means a lot of people are willing to put down serious money to find out how to live their lives better. They'll pour over books, watch DVDs, and listen to audio recordings as they hunt out the key to success and happiness.

Surprisingly, a lot of that expenditure might be unnecessary. Instead of chasing after a formula, there's an easier path: "Diligently obey" God's law. That's it!

The Lord promises blessings for those who "observe carefully all His commandments." We read, "Blessed shall you be in the city, and blessed shall you be in the country. Blessed shall be the fruit of your body, the produce of your ground and the increase of your herds, the increase of your cattle and the offspring of your flocks. Blessed shall be your basket and your kneading bowl. Blessed shall you be when you come in, and blessed shall you be when you go out" (Deuteronomy 28:3–6).

That sounds like being blessed on every side, in just about every circumstance. And you don't have to read a self-help bestseller or attend a seminar to obtain the benefits!

While these verses do not promise a life devoid of problems and sorrow, the implication is clear: Those who strive to keep God's law will have an advantage over those who do not. In later verses, we read about the curses God places on those who do not listen to His Word.

Those who obey God in this time are, as Peter said, "a chosen generation, a royal priesthood, a holy nation, His own special people" (1 Peter 2:9). What a great blessing that is!

Apply It:

Think about the many blessings God promises to those who obey His laws and share the ones you've found with a friend today.

Dig Deeper:

Psalm 119:1; Isaiah 48:18; Proverbs 7:1–5

The Sabbath

20

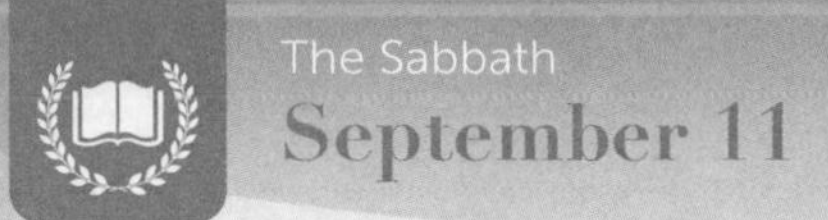

Established from the Beginning

"On the seventh day God ended His work which He had done, and He rested on the seventh day from all His work which He had done. Then God blessed the seventh day and sanctified it, because in it He rested from all His work which God had created and made" (Genesis 2:2, 3).

The H. J. Heinz Company, an American food processing business most known for its ketchup, was established in 1869. Henry J. Heinz started out by selling his mother's famous horseradish, which he manufactured in the basement of his father's home.

The original slogan for the company was "57 varieties" even though Henry had over 60 products. Heinz picked the number randomly after he saw an advertisement of a shoe store in New York City boasting "21 styles." He chose the number 57 because he liked the sound of it, selecting "7" because of, in his words, the "psychological influence of that figure and of its enduring significance to people of all ages."

Actually, there is an enduring significance to the number "7" that goes all the way back to Creation. The Sabbath institution was established at the very beginning of earth's history after God made a perfect world. "In six days the LORD made the heavens and the earth, the sea, and all that is in them, and rested the seventh day. Therefore the LORD blessed the Sabbath day and hallowed it" (Exodus 20:11).

Three divine actions established the seventh-day Sabbath. The first is that God "rested and was refreshed" (Exodus 31:17), not because the Lord was physically tired, but that He ceased from His labor of creating the world. God rested and so He commands us to rest and remember (Exodus 20:8).

God also "blessed the seventh day and sanctified it" (Genesis 2:3), making the Sabbath a day of divine favor and blessing for people. By sanctifying this day, the Lord set it apart for a holy use. It was because of the desire of our Creator to foster the divine-human relationship that the seventh day was set aside. It's a day with enduring significance to people of all ages.

Apply It:

How many 7s can you find in your life (birthdays, anniversaries, house numbers, license numbers, etc.)?

Dig Deeper:

Genesis 2:1–3; Exodus 20:8–11; Deuteronomy 5:12–15

Food Without Labor

"Tomorrow is a Sabbath rest, a holy Sabbath to the Lord. Bake what you will bake today, and boil what you will boil; and lay up for yourselves all that remains, to be kept until morning" (Exodus 16:23).

There are parts of cities in the United States that the government considers "food deserts"—areas that don't have a well-stocked supermarket, where fresh produce is not widely available, and where many of the eating choices are far less than healthy. So-called "junk food" abounds in these places.

There have been efforts to change this picture, in part by offering large chains financial or tax incentives to open stores in these neighborhoods and by sponsoring "farmer's markets" where produce is available. Some of those living in these neighborhoods no longer have to drive or take a series of bus rides to get fresh, wholesome food.

But did you know there was a time when God was directly responsible for feeding not just a community, but an entire nation? We read about this in Exodus, where the Israelites were promised a daily portion of manna.

How did the Israelites gather this manna morning by morning and still keep the Sabbath holy? On the sixth day of the week, which we know as Friday, the Israelites were commanded to gather a double portion. Do that any other day of the week and the leftovers would quickly spoil. Do that every day-before-the-Sabbath, and their food would stay fresh.

For forty years and for more than *two thousand* weekly Sabbaths, the plan worked. Perhaps Jesus was alluding to this level of divine care when He said, "Look at the birds of the air, for they neither sow nor reap nor gather into barns; yet your heavenly Father feeds them. Are you not of more value than they?" (Matthew 6:26).

This miracle of the manna points toward a promise in Psalm 37:25: "I have been young, and now am old; yet I have not seen the righteous forsaken, nor his descendants begging bread."

Apply It:

Approach God in prayer with confidence, knowing that if He took care of the Israelites in the desert, He will look after you too.

Dig Deeper:

Exodus 15:26; Exodus 16:4, 16–19; Exodus 20:8–10

An Official Seal

"I saw another angel ascending from the east, having the seal of the living God" (Revelation 7:2).

It began as "a family journal conducted in the interests of the higher life of the household." Clark W. Bryan first published *Good Housekeeping* magazine in 1885 and soon started a campaign against misrepresentations made by suppliers of food and other products. In 1900, it created the Good Housekeeping Experiment Station to study problems facing homemakers. By 1902, the station tested products and accepted advertising for those that met its approval. Then in December 1909, the first "approved" list of 21 products was featured, along with the now familiar Good Housekeeping Seal of Approval.

God has a seal of approval; it's not a physical stamp placed on products, but rather an invisible sign that is given to identify His people. The apostle John wrote, "I looked, and behold, a Lamb standing on Mount Zion, and with Him one hundred and forty-four thousand, having His Father's name written on their foreheads" (Revelation 14:1). This seal stands in opposition to the mark of the beast discussed in Revelation 13—a sign of loyalty to Satan.

What sign reveals our allegiance to God as our Creator and Redeemer? In the very heart of the Ten Commandments, we discover the Sabbath (Exodus 20:10, 11), which functions as the seal of God's law by stating three elements: the name of the owner of the seal ("the LORD your God"), His title as Creator (who "made"), and jurisdiction ("the heavens and the earth, the sea, and all that is in them").

The final controversy will reveal the loyalties of all humanity to the beast or to the God of heaven and earth. Allegiance to the beast is represented as a "mark on their right hand or on their foreheads" (Revelation 13:16). Loyalty to God is symbolized by a seal—"having His Father's name written on their foreheads" (Revelation 14:1).

Those who receive God's seal of approval are described in the last part of chapter 14 as "those who keep the commandments of God and the faith of Jesus" (verse 12).

Apply It:

Look over some of your household products and see if you can discover some type of seal of approval.

Dig Deeper:

John 6:27; Ephesians 4:30; 2 Timothy 2:19

One Act, Two Results

"Pray that your flight may not be in winter or on the Sabbath" (Matthew 24:20).

After a hive of Africanized bees attacked a woman in Florida, a local bee rescuer moved the hive into isolation. Because the queen bee was replaced with a less aggressive species, the hive will house mild-mannered honeybees in a couple of generations of bees.

This beekeeper was saving people from more attacks while at the same time keeping the bees from extermination. Jesus also has a role that involves creation and redemption. As Creator and Savior, Jesus is the main recipient of Sabbath worship.

Jesus explained that even after His work on earth would be finished, the Sabbath should continue to be observed. When the disciples asked Him about the destruction of the temple, which would take place long after His ascension to heaven, He told them that they would have to run away from the armies that would surround Jerusalem.

That moment of flight could fall on any day of the week, but Jesus asked them to pray that it would not take place on the Sabbath. This was significant because earlier in His ministry He had explained that He had the authority over the Sabbath: "Therefore the Son of Man is also Lord of the Sabbath" (Mark 2:28). He was indicating that He had instituted the Sabbath and could change it if He wished. However, by asking His disciples to pray that they would not have to flee Jerusalem on the Sabbath, He was confirming that it should continue to be observed.

That observance makes sense in light of Christ's ongoing work of salvation in heaven. The entire work of salvation is memorialized in the Ten Commandments: "Remember that you were a slave in the land of Egypt, and the Lord your God brought you out from there by a mighty hand and by an outstretched arm; therefore the Lord your God commanded you to keep the Sabbath day" (Deuteronomy 5:15). In other words, the Exodus was a metaphor for salvation.

Apply It:

Help an evangelist during the next Sabbath.

Dig Deeper:

1 Corinthians 8:6; John 19:30; Luke 23:54

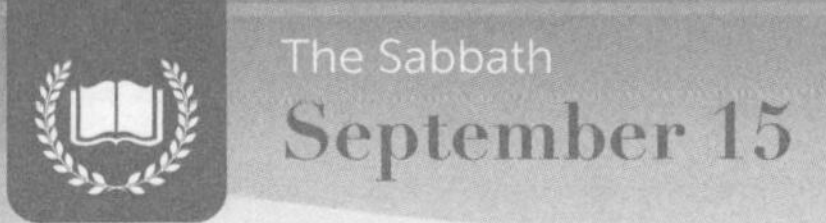

September 15

Which Day Is the Lord's?

"I was in the Spirit on the Lord's Day, and I heard behind me a loud voice, as of a trumpet" (Revelation 1:10).

Did you know that every day, around 15 million people celebrate their birthday? More people have birthdays in August than any other month (about nine percent), followed by July and September. The month with the least birthdays is February. More people are born on Tuesday than any other day, and the day of the week with the least birthdays is Sunday.

Each week, everyone is called to celebrate the birthday of the creation of our world. God said, "Remember the Sabbath day, to keep it holy. Six days you shall labor and do all your work, but the seventh day is the Sabbath of the Lord your God" (Exodus 20:8–10). This is God's day, set apart by Him to remind us that He is our Creator. Yet humans have attempted to change that day.

Many believe that John was speaking of Sunday when he stated that he was "in the Spirit on the Lord's Day" (Revelation 1:10). But the Sabbath commandment clearly designates "the seventh day" as God's day, not the first day of the week. The Lord called the Sabbath "My holy day" (Isaiah 58:13) and Jesus spoke of Himself as "Lord of the Sabbath" (Mark 2:28).

The disciples honored the seventh day at Jesus' death when preparing His body for burial (Luke 23:56). They resumed their work "on the first day of the week" (Luke 24:1).

The apostles worshiped on the seventh day as well. When Paul traveled, he attended the synagogue on Sabbath (Acts 13:14). But what did Paul do if there was no synagogue to attend? "On the Sabbath day we went out of the city to the riverside, where prayer was customarily made; and we sat down and spoke to the women who met there" (Acts 16:13).

There is not even one Bible verse that commands us to worship on any other day of the week than the seventh day. Only Sabbath is called blessed and holy in Scripture. No teaching in the New Testament indicates that it was ever changed.

Apply It:

What was the largest birthday celebration you ever attended?

Dig Deeper:

Isaiah 66:22, 23; Acts 17:1, 2; Acts 18:4

A Perpetual Memorial

"The heavens and the earth, and all the host of them, were finished. And on the seventh day God ended His work which He had done, and He rested on the seventh day from all His work which He had done. Then God blessed the seventh day and sanctified it, because in it He rested from all His work which God had created and made" (Genesis 2:1–3).

Visit the grave of U.S. President John F. Kennedy at Arlington National Cemetery, and you'll see a flame that is always lit. Called "the eternal flame," it continually burns as a reminder of a president who served his nation.

For nearly 50 years, the flame burned without interruption. In early 2013, a temporary flame was installed while several months of work took place to renovate the permanent flame. It cost $350,000 to repair and renew this never-ending tribute.

Every week, those who trust in God have the opportunity to observe a different memorial, one that celebrates creation, not destruction, honoring life instead of remembering death.

That memorial is the Sabbath day (Exodus 20:8–11). God blessed and sanctified this *one* day out of seven, establishing it as a memorial to His creative work. This monument to creation was not made by human hands, has never gone out of operation, and requires no periodic repairs—only weekly observance.

Throughout Scripture, we see calls to remember the link between the Sabbath and Creation: "I saw another angel flying in the midst of heaven, having the everlasting gospel to preach to those who dwell on the earth—to every nation, tribe, tongue, and people—saying with a loud voice, 'Fear God and give glory to Him, for the hour of His judgment has come; and worship Him who made heaven and earth, the sea and springs of water' " (Revelation 14:6, 7).

It would be enough just to be told we should fear and honor God because judgment has arrived. But we are commanded to worship Him because He created the heavens and the earth. It's not a temporary request, but an eternal reminder (Exodus 31:13–17).

Apply It:

Contemplate why the Sabbath-Creation link is so important.

Dig Deeper:

Exodus 20:11, 12; Psalm 33:6; John 5:16, 17

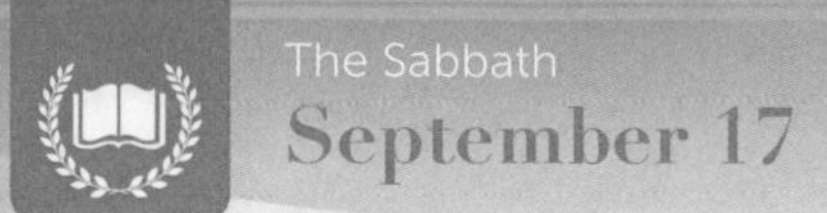

Saved from Bondage

"Remember that you were a slave in the land of Egypt, and the Lord your God brought you out from there by a mighty hand and by an outstretched arm; therefore the Lord your God commanded you to keep the Sabbath day" (Deuteronomy 5:15).

Paul Geidal was granted parole from prison, but he did not want to leave. Having lived for 63 years locked up for a murder he committed in 1911—when he was 17 years old—the 80-year-old inmate didn't think he could make it on the outside after all those years. So he stayed behind bars for another six years and broke a record—becoming the longest-serving prison inmate in the United States (68 years, 245 days). He later died in a nursing home at the age of 93.

After God delivered Israel from bondage in Egypt, He taught them to keep the Sabbath, not only as a memorial of Creation, but also of redemption. People of all ages can be in bondage to the things of this world and need to constantly be reminded that God will set them free. And so, in giving the Sabbath commandment a second time, God was reminding His people to remember the Sabbath as a symbol of how "the Lord your God brought you out from there by a mighty hand and by an outstretched arm; therefore the Lord your God commanded you to keep the Sabbath day" (Deuteronomy 5:15).

Keeping the Sabbath is an invitation for God to transform our lives—a process we call sanctification. The Bible says, "Speak also to the children of Israel, saying: 'Surely My Sabbaths you shall keep, for it is a sign between Me and you throughout your generations, that you may know that *I am the Lord who sanctifies you*' " (Exodus 31:13, emphasis added).

By obeying the fourth commandment, we honor God as the Creator *and* Redeemer, the One to whom we are loyal. When we keep the Sabbath holy, the Spirit works a change in our hearts, and the day that was set aside for a holy purpose becomes a symbol of a people who are set free from sin.

Apply It:

Have you ever visited a prison or jail? What was it like to go behind locked doors?

Dig Deeper:

Ezekiel 20:20; Galatians 5:1; Hebrews 13:12

Loyal Companion

"Here is the patience of the saints; here are those who keep the commandments of God and the faith of Jesus" (Revelation 14:12).

Robots and chatbots are being developed to help fight loneliness and expensive hospital bills among the elderly. Chatbots are computer programs that can carry on a conversation with people. Some robots do this as well, and some have been made to look like fuzzy baby seals that simulate sympathy.

While robots may be able to help the elderly in practical ways, their loyalty is somewhat inauthentic. The Sabbath day was created to provide companionship time with God and to be a sign of authentic loyalty to Him.

Although domestic animals and friends play a crucial role in fulfilling social needs, God also designed humans to enjoy Him as their companion. Unfortunately, there is always the chance that our work and social life will choke out our friendship with God. Jesus spoke of this danger in the parable of the sower. The growth of the seed, which represents God's Word, symbolized an ongoing positive relationship with God.

One of the dangers to this relationship is constant distractions: "He who received seed among the thorns is he who hears the word, and the cares of this world and the deceitfulness of riches choke the word, and he becomes unfruitful" (Matthew 13:22). The Sabbath ensures that the relationship with God does not get neglected.

In any friendship, however, loyalty plays a crucial role. The Sabbath reveals the loyalty that we have to God when earthly forces try to push against Sabbath observance. Revelation describes the most extreme version of this push: "A third angel followed them, saying with a loud voice, 'If anyone worships the beast and his image, and receives his mark on his forehead or on his hand, he himself shall also drink of the wine of the wrath of God' " (Revelation 14:9, 10). This warning shows that there will be a push to show loyalty to someone who is not God, and, of all the commandments, the Sabbath shows the most intimate loyalty to Him.

Apply It:

Visit an elderly person who is lonely.

Dig Deeper:

John 15:15; Exodus 16:28, 29; Ezekiel 22:26

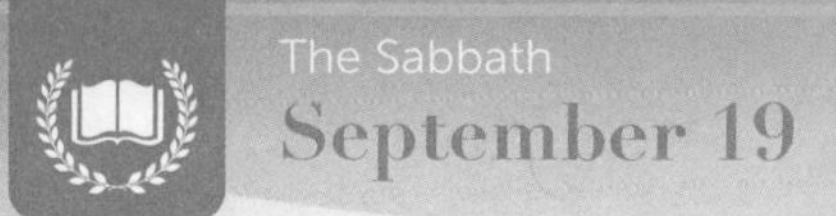

Resting in Faith

"He who has entered His rest has himself also ceased from his works as God did from His" (Hebrews 4:10).

Which nationalities work the longest hours? Well, to begin on the opposite end of the spectrum of 37 countries reviewed by the Employment Outlook report, the average work week for Germans is 28 hours. Other countries that enjoy lots of down time include the Netherlands, Norway, Denmark, and France. The hardest working country is Mexico, where the average citizen clocks in 43 hours a week. Costa Rica falls in second place, followed by South Korea, Greece, Chile, and Russia. The average work week in the United States is a little more than 34 hours.

Have you ever noticed the similarities between the language about the Sabbath at Creation and at the cross? Both speak of work *finished* and then *rest*. "Thus the heavens and the earth, and all the host of them, were finished" (Genesis 2:1). "[Jesus] said, 'It is finished!' And bowing His head, He gave up His spirit" (John 19:30). When God finished the work of making the world, He rested on the Sabbath. So also, when Jesus finished the work of redemption, He rested in the grave on the Sabbath.

The Sabbath symbolizes resting in the work of Christ, both in Creation and redemption. Far from being a legalistic form of righteousness by works, the true essence of Sabbath is stopping our work and remembering the work of Jesus for us: "He who has entered His rest has himself also ceased from his works as God did from His" (Hebrews 4:10). Sabbath reinforces the teaching of righteousness by faith!

God offered this spiritual rest to the literal nation of Israel. Though they failed as a people (not as individuals) to enter that rest, the Lord still offers this gift to all humanity. "There remains therefore a rest for the people of God" (Hebrews 4:9). Do you struggle with working too much? Then stop and enter God's gift of spiritual rest. "Today, if you will hear His voice, do not harden your hearts" (Hebrews 4:7).

Apply It:

Think of a time when you experienced refreshing peacefulness and rest. Where were you?

Dig Deeper:

Matthew 11:28; Hebrews 4:1–10; Revelation 14:11

Trading Spaces

"He shall speak pompous words against the Most High, shall persecute the saints of the Most High, and shall intend to change times and law" (Daniel 7:25).

A once popular home decorating show involved two sets of families "trading" the task of redecorating a room in a home. Neither could see the other's work until completion, and the result either wowed or worried the beneficiary.

It's one thing to trade remodeling assignments, but quite another to swap the sacred space of the Bible Sabbath for another day of the week. Yet this is what has happened over the course of centuries, and millions of Christians have been deceived as a result.

Let's remember: The Sabbath day was created, sanctified, and ordained by God back at the beginning of the world (Genesis 2:1–3). In Exodus 20, the command to rest from worldly labors on the seventh day of the week was literally carved in stone by God's finger.

The sad truth is that the devil hates the Sabbath. He hates all of the Ten Commandments and all of God's law, but while there are too many murders and thefts going on in the world—among other transgressions—the Sabbath poses a special problem.

By overturning, or changing, the day of worship, it's possible to introduce all sorts of doubt about the origins of life. Is it any wonder that so many professed Christians today, worshiping on a day not specified by God, also embrace some variation of evolution as an explanation of how we got here?

There is, also, a prophetic implication to the change of the day of rest noted in Daniel. By following the cult of *Sol Invictus*, pagans invested much in the "Day of the Sun." When Roman emperor Constantine embraced a form of Christianity, he brought that practice into his newfound religion to make it more palatable to other sun-worshipers.

In the future, the Bible says, church and state will unite to force a fake "day of rest" on people. The only solution is to "let God be true but every man a liar," as Paul wrote in Romans 3:4. Resist the go-along impulse and stand on God's Word!

Apply It:

Remember what the Sabbath means, what it commemorates, and Who created it.

Dig Deeper:

Exodus 20:8–11; Isaiah 66:23; Revelation 14:12

Fashionable Laws

"The mystery of lawlessness is already at work; only He who now restrains will do so until He is taken out of the way" (2 Thessalonians 2:7).

Fashions may come and go, but psychology still rules how we dress. Karen Pine, a research psychologist, shares how our clothes impact how we feel about ourselves in her book *Mind What You Wear*. For instance, people who dress like the boss are more likely to be promoted quicker. Women are twice as likely to wear jeans when depressed than when happy. She also discovered that patients put more trust in a doctor who wears a white coat.

Some people apparently view the seventh-day Sabbath as a changing fashion. They don't think twice about how God's holy day was "changed" by humans from Saturday to Sunday. The Bible predicted how this would happen through an earthly power that would "intend to change times and law" (Daniel 7:25).

The origin of Sunday observance as a Christian institution had its origin in "the mystery of lawlessness" (2 Thessalonians 2:7), which was already at work when Paul wrote. Daniel's vision revealed that a little horn power, represented as "a beast rising up out of the sea" (Revelation 13:1), "was given a mouth speaking great things and blasphemies" (verse 5).

Only one power within Christianity has claimed the prerogative to change times and laws. Around AD 1400, Petrus de Ancharano claimed that "the pope can modify divine law, since his power is not of man, but of God, and he acts in the place of God upon earth, with the fullest power of binding and losing his sheep."

John Eck, a defender of the Catholic religion, demonstrated this assertion when attacking Martin Luther during the Reformation. He challenged Luther on the observance of Sunday instead of the Bible Sabbath and claimed "the church has changed the Sabbath into Sunday on its own authority, on which you [Luther] have no Scripture."

God's law is not like changing fashions. David wrote, "The entirety of Your word is truth, and every one of Your righteous judgments endures forever" (Psalm 119:160).

Apply It:

Think of an outdated clothing fashion. How is God's law unlike changing styles of clothing?

Dig Deeper:

Daniel 7:23–27; Matthew 7:24–29; Revelation 13:1–10

Wild Horses

*"Those from among you shall build the old waste places;
you shall raise up the foundations of many generations;
and you shall be called the Repairer of the Breach,
the Restorer of Streets to Dwell In" (Isaiah 58:12).*

A piece of land owned by the Wales Wild Land Foundation will be restored by wild Konik horses. These horses eat purple moor grass, which prevents native plants from growing. By eating the unwanted plants, the horses will be opening the way for bilberry and heather to populate the area again.

God's people have always worked to restore the world's relationship with God. This is done by asking people who have never worshiped God to keep the Sabbath. It is also done by calling on those who used to keep the Sabbath to restore their commitment to God.

The prophet Isaiah records both kinds of Sabbath restoration in his prophecy. In a chapter dedicated to the Jewish ministry to Gentile non-believers, he first speaks of the centrality of the Sabbath in people's conversion: "The sons of the foreigner who join themselves to the Lord, to serve Him, and to love the name of the Lord, to be His servants—everyone who keeps from defiling the Sabbath, and holds fast My covenant" (Isaiah 56:6). These new Sabbathkeepers will receive the blessings of the relationship with God along with seasoned believers.

Later in his prophetic book, Isaiah speaks of the second kind of Sabbath restoration: its renewal among those who have abandoned it. After speaking of the restoration of a breach in a wall he explains what the wall metaphor means: "If you turn away your foot from the Sabbath, from doing your pleasure on My holy day, and call the Sabbath a delight, the holy day of the Lord honorable, and shall honor Him, not doing your own ways, nor finding your own pleasure, nor speaking your own words" (Isaiah 58:13). Like building up a broken wall, the Sabbath will be restored.

■ Apply It:

Use the Sabbath to work with, and witness to, those who are environmentally conscious.

■ Dig Deeper:

Isaiah 56:1, 2; Revelation 14:6–12; Revelation 14:9

Remembering the Day

"Remember the Sabbath day, to keep it holy" (Exodus 20:8).

A British survey reveals that almost half of men do not know the date of their wedding anniversary. Men under 25 were most forgetful, while a third of men over 55 can't remember. On the other hand, 63 percent of women remember the date and only three percent admit to having forgotten their anniversary.

Remembering an anniversary means more than just telling your spouse, "I remembered." It means doing something, like buying flowers or taking her out to eat at a romantic restaurant. It's interesting that out of all the Ten Commandments, only one begins with the word "remember" (Exodus 20:8). Maybe it's because God knew how easy it is for people to forget.

To remember the Sabbath means that we will think about it during the week and make preparations to observe it in a holy way pleasing to God. It means to turn away "from doing your pleasure on My holy day" (Isaiah 58:13) and "not doing your own ways, nor finding your own pleasure, nor speaking your own words."

One way we can honor the Sabbath is by stopping our secular work. "Six days you shall labor and do all your work, but the seventh day is the Sabbath of the Lord your God. In it you shall do no work" (Exodus 20:9, 10). We don't please God by focusing on our own secular interests, conversations, sports, and business work. It would be like taking your sweetheart out to eat and looking at your smartphone the whole time.

The Sabbath is a day of delight and should enhance our relationship with God and one another. We follow Christ's example when we worship on the Sabbath (Mark 1:21), when we fellowship with others (Luke 14:1), when we spend time outdoors (Mark 2:23), and when we alleviate pain and suffering in others (John 5:1–15).

When the Sabbath begins on Friday evening at sundown (Genesis 1:5 and Mark 1:32), remember to gather your family and prayerfully welcome God's holy day and invite Jesus as your welcome guest.

Apply It:

Think of one special way you could remember the Sabbath and welcome the day of rest.

Dig Deeper:

Exodus 16:23; Nehemiah 13:15–22; Mark 15:42

Stewardship

21

Far More than Money

"Do you not know that your body is the temple of the Holy Spirit who is in you, whom you have from God, and you are not your own? For you were bought at a price; therefore glorify God in your body and in your spirit, which are God's" (1 Corinthians 6:19).

For more than fifty years, John Wanamaker was a prominent name in American households. He was the "merchant prince," creating great department stores in Philadelphia and New York City, the first of their kind. He served as Postmaster General, controlling the nation's primary communications network. And he was an active Christian, working with evangelists such as Dwight L. Moody.

But Moody bemoaned Wanamaker's business achievements, even though they helped fund Moody's evangelism. The revivalist thought Wanamaker's considerable business acumen could better serve God if the merchant became a ministerial aide to Moody.

But Wanamaker resisted. He believed that making money and funding Christian work was as valid a means of stewardship as being in full-time service.

We can't judge Wanamaker's heart, but it's possible to suggest the mogul was onto something. He built his business into one of the great enterprises of his day, and he did so in part because he wanted to not only help finance Christian outreach, but also to bring a bit of more faithful living to the people his stores served.

In short, Wanamaker's view of stewardship encompassed his whole life, and it was reflected in what he did and where his money went.

You may not have the wealth of a Wanamaker—or you might be even more accomplished in business. But the responsibility of being a good steward remains: God has given us our talents, our abilities, our possessions, and, yes, our very lives. As we read in James 1:17, "Every good gift and every perfect gift is from above."

We are responsible to live in such a way that we do our best with what He has given us. That is stewardship—and it involves far more than money!

Apply It:

Consider everything that God has given you—treasure, time, talents—and ask yourself if you are managing these in the way He would have you do so.

Dig Deeper:

Genesis 1:1; Psalm 24:1; 1 Chronicles 29:12

The Most Valuable Model

"You shall love the Lord your God with all your heart, with all your soul, and with all your strength" (Deuteronomy 6:5).

Which automobile in the United States has the highest overall insurance cost? *24/7 Wall Street* reviewed data on insurance claims made by make and model and determined that the annual average insurance paid on a Tesla Model S four-door electric 4WD topped the list at $1,540.63. Next in line is the Mercedes-Benz S class four-door LWB 2WD and then the Mitsubishi Lancer 2WD. The cheapest car to insure is the Subaru Outback 4WD with Eyesight. Large or midsize luxury vehicles tend to be more expensive to insure and small to midsize SUVs tend to be cheaper to insure.

More valuable than an automobile is the gift of our bodies—given to us by the Lord to be cared for and used to glorify God. Stewardship involves responsibility for our whole being. Jesus affirmed this to a lawyer who questioned Him regarding eternal life. He quoted, "You shall love the Lord your God with all your heart, with all your soul, with all your strength" (Luke 10:27).

It is a privilege as a Christian to develop your physical and mental powers to the best of your ability. Personal care for our health is meant to exalt the Lord and not ourselves. "Therefore, whether you eat or drink, or whatever you do, do all to the glory of God" (1 Corinthians 10:31). Good stewardship of our bodies also permits us to bring happiness to others, as the Bible teaches, "You shall love your neighbor as yourself" (Leviticus 19:18).

Even our God-given abilities are to be properly used in service to the Lord and to others. A person can focus their talents on exalting themselves or burying their gifts in self-pity or false humility. But true servants acknowledge the Master and invest their gifts for building up God's kingdom. To these it will someday be said, "Well done, good and faithful servant; you have been faithful over a few things, I will make you ruler over many things. Enter into the joy of your lord" (Matthew 25:23).

Apply It:

Do you spend more time caring for your car than your own body?

Dig Deeper:

Matthew 25:14–30; Romans 12:1, 2; Philippians 4:13

Healthy Savings

"God blessed them, and God said to them, 'Be fruitful and multiply; fill the earth and subdue it; have dominion over the fish of the sea, over the birds of the air, and over every living thing that moves on the earth' " (Genesis 1:28).

A recent study confirmed that a single blood test is sufficient to diagnose type 2 diabetes. The researchers who conducted the study are hoping that their discovery will save patients the extra time and money that it takes to be tested twice. Those with the disease will also receive an earlier treatment, preventing further health complications.

God has given people time and strength for moneymaking and responsibilities (Proverbs 10:22). The fulfillment of these duties was intended to bring people happiness for "whatever you do in word or deed, do all in the name of the Lord Jesus, giving thanks to God the Father through Him" (Colossians 3:17). There is joy in caring for God's possessions.

When Jesus was on earth, He demonstrated the type of life that people were intended to live by using His time wisely. From an early age, He realized His duty to God and did it even when His parents did not expect it: "He said to them, 'Why did you seek Me? Did you not know that I must be about My Father's business?' " (Luke 2:49).

In addition to the wise use of time, people have been advised to use their money wisely. By spending their energy and money on worthy causes, such as helping the poor or spreading the good news, Jesus' followers show that they understand where their strength comes from.

The principle is most clearly stated in the writings of Moses: "You shall remember the Lord your God, for it is He who gives you power to get wealth, that He may establish His covenant which He swore to your fathers, as it is this day" (Deuteronomy 8:18). This principle shows that our physical and emotional health comes from God. Therefore, even our best efforts at moneymaking cannot get off the ground without Him. When this is clearly understood, people tend to be more careful with the use of their resources.

Apply It:

Spend your resources on a cause you have not supported before.

Dig Deeper:

James 1:17; Genesis 2:15; Ephesians 5:16

It Belongs to God

" 'Bring all the tithes into the storehouse, that there may be food in My house, and try Me now in this,' says the L*ORD of hosts, 'If I will not open for you the windows of heaven and pour out for you such blessing that there will not be room enough to receive it' "* (Malachi 3:10).

It was just another work day for Bismark Mensah, a Walmart employee from Federal Way, Washington. As he collected shopping carts in the parking lot, he found an envelope containing $20,000 cash. Without hesitation, Bismark chased down the car of the customer who had dropped it, returning every dollar. The money was to be for a down payment on a new house. Mensah turned down a reward for his good deed.

It's tempting to keep something that doesn't belong to you, but it happens all the time—with God's money. When the Lord confronted His people and asked them, "Will a man rob God? Yet you have robbed Me!" (Malachi 3:8), they replied, "In what way have we robbed You?" The Lord told them, "In tithes and offerings."

The Bible teaches that one-tenth of all material things acquired belong to God. Scripture says, "All the tithe of the land, whether of the seed of the land or of the fruit of the tree, is the LORD's. It is holy to the LORD" (Leviticus 27:30). The Hebrew word for tithe simply means one-tenth. "Concerning the tithe of the herd or the flock, of whatever passes under the rod, the tenth one shall be holy to the LORD" (verse 32).

Abraham paid tithe to Melchizedek, the priest of "God Most High" (Genesis 14:20). Jacob made a vow to the Lord, "Of all that You give me I will surely give a tenth to You" (Genesis 28:22). God commanded the nation of Israel to return tithe (Numbers 18:24, 26, 28) and Jesus affirmed the practice of tithing (Matthew 23:23).

Tithing is a blessing, for it acknowledges God as the owner of all things. Why not return what belongs to Him?

Apply It:

Have you ever found something valuable and tried to return it to its owner?

Dig Deeper:

Deuteronomy 12:6, 11, 17; Malachi 3:8–12; 1 Corinthians 9:11–14

With a Grateful Heart

"Thanks be to God for His indescribable gift!" (2 Corinthians 9:15).

John Tay was a man seized by an idea: The people of Pitcairn Island, a tiny rock in the South Pacific inhabited by survivors of the *HMS Bounty*'s famous mutiny, and their descendants, had studied their way into the truth of Sabbath keeping and other Bible doctrines. But they needed to be baptized. No pastor was available to do the job.

Tay's idea? Collect a special offering from church members in North America. This he did, appealing to members of Sabbath School classes across the land. Children especially were anxious to donate to the project. The campaign to build the schooner named *Pitcairn* was the start of sacrificial giving by church members on behalf of world missions outreach.

Giving an offering, a donation apart from the tithe God has already claimed on our income (Malachi 3:10), shows a willingness to support the church's mission to spread the gospel around the world (Matthew 28:19).

But it also signifies something more: It shows that the giver's heart is in the right place—putting the work of God above temporal pleasures and personal concerns. We are to take care of our households (1 Timothy 5:8), yes, but we are also to work to proclaim the Word and serve our neighbors, across the street or across the oceans, with the love of Christ.

Where we give our offerings is an intensely personal decision, one best made with sincere prayer and great thoughtfulness. The decision to give offerings, wherever and whenever possible, should become an instinctual one. A Christian thinker once told friends to "obey the generous impulse." May God give us that attitude as well!

Apply It:

We are the recipients of so many blessings from God. Let's remember that giving to His work and His people is often the least we can do to say "thanks."

Dig Deeper:

Exodus 36:2–7; 2 Chronicles 24:4–13; Luke 12:48

Embezzling Heaven

"You are cursed with a curse, for you have robbed Me, even this whole nation" (Malachi 3:9).

Employees deserve to be reimbursed for company expenses paid out of their own pocket. But David Smith, a former Quest Diagnostics manager, found a way to get reimbursed for much more—$1.2 million to be exact. Smith set up fake companies, created fake invoices, and turned in fake expense reports for payments that he supposedly made to companies on Quest's behalf.

The FBI finally caught up with Smith, who was sentenced to five years in prison. How was he nabbed? Besides making up fake companies, the addresses he created for them didn't match up. One fake company address was actually an entrance ramp to a freeway in Tampa.

It's one thing to steal from a company, but can you imagine trying to rob God? The Bible explains the results of unfaithfulness in returning tithes and giving offerings: "You are cursed with a curse, for you have robbed Me, even this whole nation" (Malachi 3:9). Such strong language referred to a majority of God's people.

In an unusual invitation, God asks His people to "bring all the tithes into the storehouse" (verse 10) and adds, "try Me now in this." What follows is a promise of unusual proportions: "If I will not open for you the windows of heaven and pour out for you such blessing that there will not be room enough to receive it" (v. 10).

The joyful results of obedience don't end there for faithful tithe payers. "I will rebuke the devourer for your sakes, so that he will not destroy the fruit of your ground, nor shall the vine fail to bear fruit for you in the field" (v. 11). And there's more: "All nations will call you blessed, for you will be a delightful land" (v. 12).

In a world where "taking" is thought to bring abundance, heaven teaches, "Give, and it will be given to you: good measure, pressed down, shaken together, and running over will be put into your bosom. For with the same measure that you use, it will be measured back to you" (Luke 6:38).

■ Apply It:

Have you ever tested God in tithes and offerings?

■ Dig Deeper:

Leviticus 26:3–5; Nehemiah 10:37–39; Malachi 2:2

September 30

Everyone Benefits

"This gospel of the kingdom will be preached in all the world as a witness to all the nations, and then the end will come" (Matthew 24:14).

The percentage of companies that allow employees to bring their dog to work has risen to 8 percent, up from 3 percent in 2013. This may be because bringing dogs to work brings comfort to the owner and other employees, while providing the opportunity for the interaction of people who might otherwise not collaborate.

While there are downsides to bringing a dog to work, there are virtually no downsides to being a good steward. Those who use their resources to help others benefit from that giving by knowing that they are helping Jesus. He explained this point when He stated: "The King will answer and say to them, 'Assuredly, I say to you, inasmuch as you did it to one of the least of these My brethren, you did it to Me' " (Matthew 25:40).

Although God may not want us to focus only on the blessings we receive by being good stewards, we know that we have the promise of affirmation when we take care of the needs of others.

Additionally, we can focus on the true benefits that others can receive from us. Those who live in wealthy countries, or who have the blessing of owning a car, can be considered rich in one sense. When Paul was addressing the rich, he conveyed a command that emphasized the centrality of generosity: "Let them do good, that they be rich in good works, ready to give, willing to share" (1 Timothy 6:18).

The habit of generosity is not only an example to unbelievers, but also has the potential of funding evangelism and missionary work. In this way, stewardship can help the giver, the receiver, and the mission of the church. In turn, the mission of the church is closely tied to the return of Jesus, who will not return before the gospel has reached every corner of the world.

■ Apply It:

Make a new friend by discussing one another's pets.

■ Dig Deeper:

Luke 12:15; Galatians 5:24; 1 Timothy 6:19

Christian Behavior

22

Keeping in Balance

"I beseech you therefore, brethren, by the mercies of God, that you present your bodies a living sacrifice, holy, acceptable to God, which is your reasonable service" (Romans 12:1).

It's tough to stay in balance, especially if you're trying to conquer a four-inch wide balance beam. Seven-time Olympic medalist Shannon Miller admits she has fallen off more times than she can count. "I've split, bonked it, scraped it, pounded it, bounced off it. I've landed on my head, my hip, my thigh, my ribs, and just about every other body part."

But along the way, she has learned a thing or two about keeping balanced. For instance, a gymnast must remember that maintaining balance depends on the body being square in line above the center of the beam. That means keeping thighs together, arms narrow, and shoulders squared.

It's easy for people to lose their spiritual balance and fall off the narrow road to the kingdom of heaven—especially in the area of Christian behavior. There are two extremes we fall into. The first is attempting to keep rules as a means of salvation. Of this, Paul warns, "You have become estranged from Christ, you who attempt to be justified by law; you have fallen from grace" (Galatians 5:4).

The other extreme is concluding that since works cannot save, they don't matter at all. Paul also warned of this extreme too: "You, brethren, have been called to liberty; only do not use liberty as an opportunity for the flesh, but through love serve one another" (Galatians 5:13). In essence, both views will cause you to slip off the beam.

The best way to stay in balance in our Christian behavior is by "looking unto Jesus, the author and finisher of our faith" (Hebrews 12:2). While our behavior and spirituality are closely connected, we can never earn our salvation by doing good works. Instead, Christian behavior is the natural result of standing squarely in Christ.

Apply It:

Do a contest with your kids or friends and see who can stand on one foot the longest. What might you learn from this exercise about being balanced in your Christian walk?

Dig Deeper:

Matthew 7:13; John 17:15, 16; Ephesians 4:1

Not Your Own

"Do you not know that your body is the temple of the Holy Spirit who is in you, whom you have from God, and you are not your own?" (1 Corinthians 6:19).

The next time you want to make an excuse for not going to the gym, consider Ester van den Hoven of Loma Linda, California. She's 93 and goes to an exercise class that lasts for 60 minutes three times a week!

Explaining her longevity to the "Thrillist" website, Ester said, "Be optimistic, be outgoing, try to live a stressless life and laugh easily. Oh, and stay away from the sugar."

It might not surprise you that Ester has embraced the Bible's teachings about caring for the body as a temple of God's Spirit. In fact, there are so many health-conscious Christians in and around Loma Linda that *National Geographic* magazine dubbed the town America's only "Blue Zone," where people often live to 100 years old—seven to 10 years on average longer than most Americans.

Instead of adopting a "YOLO" ("You Only Live Once") approach to health that suggests, among other things, "you can sleep when you're dead," fixing one's thoughts on living to glorify God can give you more happy years on earth, more chances to make memories, and to experience all the good things that life has to offer.

Christ was interested in the health of people when He was on this earth. The Bible says that the Savior not only taught the gospel, but He also personally touched people's physical lives. "Jesus went about all Galilee, teaching in their synagogues, preaching the gospel of the kingdom, and healing all kinds of sickness and all kinds of disease among the people" (Matthew 4:23).

Maybe Ester van den Hoven is on the right track—and maybe, just maybe, we should all follow in her footsteps!

Apply It:

Take a close look at your lifestyle and see where you might be able to do better in caring for the "temple" God has given you.

Dig Deeper:

1 Corinthians 3:16; John 10:10; 3 John 2

Exercise with Endurance

"Since we are surrounded by so great a cloud of witnesses, let us lay aside every weight, and the sin which so easily ensnares us, and let us run with endurance the race that is set before us" (Hebrews 12:1).

He is considered the greatest sprinter of all time. Usain Bolt is an eight-time Olympic gold medalist who won the 100 m, 200 m, and 4 x 100 m relay at three consecutive Olympic Games. The six-foot five-inch Jamaican, nicknamed "Lightning Bolt," gained worldwide fame at the 2008 Beijing Olympics for his double sprint victory in world record times. On May 17, 2009, he ran the 100 m in Manchester, United Kingdom, in 8.70 seconds, the fastest time ever—that's 25.71 mph!

You don't need to be an Olympic champion to get the exercise your body needs. In fact, there are many ways to get regular exercise that will increase your energy, relieve stress, give you healthier skin, help control your weight, improve your digestion, reduce depression, and lower your risk for heart disease and cancer.

The Bible warns against the lack of exercise and inactivity. "Go to the ant, you sluggard! Consider her ways and be wise, which, having no captain, overseer or ruler, provides her supplies in the summer, and gathers her food in the harvest. How long will you slumber, O sluggard? When will you rise from your sleep? A little sleep, a little slumber, a little folding of the hands to sleep—so shall your poverty come on you like a prowler" (Proverbs 6:6–11).

God gave Adam and Eve the gift of exercise in the open air when they cared for their first garden home. "The Lord God took the man and put him in the garden of Eden to tend and keep it" (Genesis 2:15). You might even say that Jesus set an example of personal exercise by walking the roads of Palestine during His years of ministry.

The apostle Paul illustrated the Christian life as a running race to be tackled with "endurance." Physical exercise helps clear the mind and increases our spiritual stamina.

Apply It:

Develop a habit of taking a brisk walk in the open air every day of the week.

Dig Deeper:

Genesis 3:19; Proverbs 14:23; 1 Corinthians 9:27

Brighten Your Day

"Then God said, 'Let there be light'; and there was light" (Genesis 1:3).

Scientists in China have completed a study on the benefits of sunlight to mice. They found that mice that were exposed to the equivalent of 30 minutes of sunlight had increased memory and motor functions compared to the mice who did not experience sunlight. This study provides hope that the same effects may occur in humans.

God's creation of light on earth plays a central role in the preparation of the planet for life. In other places in the Bible, light is directly associated with life. The psalmist expresses this relation by connecting light with salvation from death: "You have delivered my soul from death. Have You not kept my feet from falling, that I may walk before God in the light of the living?" (Psalm 56:13).

Solomon spoke of the pleasant experience of light, showing that light is also connected to happiness: "Truly the light is sweet, and it is pleasant for the eyes to behold the sun" (Ecclesiastes 11:7). Most people in the world have abundant access to sunlight and its benefits. This means that they can become healthier in their body and mood by spending a moderate amount of time in the sun.

Although the Bible is not explicit in speaking of the health benefits of the sunlight, it hints at the essential nature of light for health. These hints should make Christians receptive to scientific studies that speak of the health benefits of the simple and natural activity of spending time in the sun.

As a result of the scientific confirmation of the benefits of the sun, Christians have the responsibility to protect their God-given health. By preserving their health, Christians can be a blessing to others. Although it may sound funny to think of spending time in the sun as a responsibility, the duties of healthy living show us that God's commands for the Christian are pleasant.

Apply It:

Spend 15 minutes in the sun.

Dig Deeper:

Isaiah 30:26; John 1:4; Psalm 136:7, 8

Water Is Life

"Whoever drinks of the water that I shall give him will never thirst. But the water that I shall give him will become in him a fountain of water springing up into everlasting life" (John 4:14).

If you've been exercising hard and feel the need for a refreshing beverage, there are plenty of options—but many are high in sugar and caffeine. That's why nothing compares to nature's best drink: water. It's the best choice for your body. Since your body is continuously losing water, proper hydration is essential for your survival.

Dehydration is a medical term that describes your body not getting enough water. You need about eight glasses of water each day to be properly hydrated; water makes up about 60 percent of your body weight (75 percent for children). Your brain is made up of about 80 percent water and sufficient amounts of this simple, pure liquid actually helps you to think more clearly.

Water creates the best environment for your blood to flow smoothly, helps regulate your blood pressure, and promotes vascular health. One research study revealed that men who drank five or more glasses of water each day had a 54 percent less risk of having a heart attack than those who drank two or less glasses of water a day.

Drinking proper amounts of water can also help you lose weight. It's been shown that those who drink a couple of eight-ounce glasses of water about a half an hour before eating actually eat about 75 fewer calories at a meal. So, if you're thirsty, don't grab coffee or a soda. Drink deeply of the liquid created by your Maker for bringing life to your body.

Jesus used water to illustrate the message of salvation. To the Samaritan woman at the well who was searching for hope, He explained, "The water that I shall give him will become in him a fountain of water springing up into everlasting life" (John 4:14). And to those who are parched, Christ said, "I will give of the fountain of the water of life freely to him who thirsts" (Revelation 21:6).

Apply It:

Set a goal this week to drink between 6 and 8 cups of water each day.

Dig Deeper:

2 Samuel 23:15; Proverbs 5:15; John 4:1–26

Take a Deep Breath

"The Lord *God planted a garden eastward in Eden, and there He put the man whom He had formed"* (Genesis 2:8).

Fresh air is a gift from God. Studies show that when we get away from polluted air and breathe in fresh outdoor air, wonderful things happen to our bodies—from reduced stress and anxiety to increased energy, clearer thinking, lower blood pressure, and improved digestion. Fresh air also enhances our immune system to help protect us from disease.

In fact, researchers have identified phytoncides—special chemicals that are released into the air by plants to protect them from insects and disease—as helpful to human immune systems. When we breathe in the phytoncides, our natural killer cells (NK cells) are stimulated, increasing in population and activity. These cells are powerful fighters, defending our bodies against a variety of diseases. And even spending a weekend outdoors among the trees can result in enhanced NK protection for over a month.

When God designed Eden for the original humans, He added plants and "made every tree grow that is pleasant to the sight and good for food" (Genesis 2:9). God landscaped our world with plants and trees not only for visual appeal and for food, but also to help keep us healthy by playing a role in cleaning the air.

Spending time in the fresh air helps us not only physically and mentally, but also spiritually. With clearer minds and healthier bodies, we can more easily grasp the spiritual truths vital to our salvation. With increased energy, we can be more "zealous for good works" (Titus 2:14).

In the purest breath ever taken by mankind, God "breathed into his nostrils the breath of life; and man became a living being" (Genesis 2:7). Sadly, our progenitors compromised this gift when they chose to sin, but Jesus bought back eternal life for our race.

Today, Christ wants to breathe into our hearts the breath of new life through our relationship with Him. Will you allow Him to breathe into you this new life today?

Apply It:

Sometime this week, step outside and thank God for the fresh air and for the new life He breathes into your heart.

Dig Deeper:

John 20:22; Job 33:4; Acts 17:25

Stepping Down

"Wine is a mocker, strong drink is a brawler, and whoever is led astray by it is not wise" (Proverbs 20:1).

Prized by Swiss painters for centuries, Mount Niesen in Switzerland is breathtaking. But what will really take your breath away—literally—is the 11,674 steps (a world-record stairway) up the side of the mountain. When a funicular railway was built on the steep slope in 1910 to carry visitors to the top, a set of stairs was also added next to the grinding 65-percent gradient. Taking the stairs up to the top of the 7,700-foot peak is akin to climbing the Statue of Liberty 33 times.

There is another set of stairs that millions walk *down* every year, a descent that leads them into the pit of hell. Alcohol is one of the most widely used drugs in the world and has devastated families for centuries. It has led to broken homes, caused accidental deaths, and put many into poverty. Untold numbers have been led astray. "There is a way that seems right to a man, but its end is the way of death" (Proverbs 14:12).

The Bible warns us about the use of alcoholic beverages. The apostle Paul warned, "Do not be drunk with wine, in which is dissipation; but be filled with the Spirit" (Ephesians 5:18) and admonished us to "walk properly, as in the day, not in revelry and drunkenness" (Romans 13:13). Peter likewise encouraged Christians to turn away from "our past lifetime in doing the will of the Gentiles—when we walked in ... drunkenness" (1 Peter 4:3).

The downward steps of alcoholism are marked by sobering statistics. Around 88,000 people die each year in the United States from excessive alcohol use. It is the third-leading lifestyle-related cause of death in the nation. Up to 40 percent of all hospital beds in America are being used to treat health conditions related to drinking alcohol.

Don't be led down the path of alcoholism toward destruction. It is a slippery slope that your weakened willpower cannot stop.

■ Apply It:

Do you know someone struggling with alcoholism? Stop and pray for them right now.

■ Dig Deeper:

Proverbs 23:29–35; Proverbs 31:4, 5; Galatians 5:19–21

Take Five—or More!

"Be still, and know that I am God" (Psalm 46:10).

You might have to put in a little extra time on the job to keep customers happy in your business, but be glad you don't have the schedule of the late Miwa Sado, a 31-year-old journalist for Japan's NHK public broadcasting network.

Ms. Sado succumbed after logging an incredible 159 hours of overtime—equal to nearly four 40-hour workweeks of extra time—in one month in 2013. A labor panel listed *karoshi*—a Japanese word meaning "death from overwork"—as the cause of her demise.

Her story might also suggest that God unquestionably knew what He was doing way back in Genesis 2:1–3 when He set apart a day of rest. God, of course, wasn't tired, but He wanted to set an example for His creation.

That theme echoes throughout Scripture. When the Israelites observed the Sabbath command and rested, they were close to God and prospered. When they ignored the Sabbath, things were more perilous, sometimes disastrously so. (See Nehemiah 13:15–22.)

In the New Testament, we see that Jesus continued this great concern, once telling His disciples, " 'Come aside by yourselves to a deserted place and rest a while.' For there were many coming and going, and they did not even have time to eat" (Mark 6:31).

In this one verse, we get a template, a pattern, for personal re-creation. Come apart from the world and its busyness. If you don't have access to a "deserted place," try to find a nearby park, or even some quiet time somewhere at home. (Pro tip: turn off the smartphone.) And rest "a while." It doesn't have to be days or weeks. Just take a break, and ask God to refresh you as you do it.

Of the many gifts God has given us, the Sabbath is a day that not only reminds us of our spiritual rest in Christ, but it's also a day of physical peace and rest that we should never neglect.

Apply It:

As you plan your week, consider where, and when, and how you can take advantage of rest.

Dig Deeper:

Exodus 20:10; Psalm 55:6; Hebrews 4:9

Transforming Our Minds

"We all, with unveiled face, beholding as in a mirror the glory of the Lord, are being transformed into the same image from glory to glory, just as by the Spirit of the Lord" (2 Corinthians 3:18).

Which is better for your brain? Reading a book or watching TV? Which of these two activities enhances your relationships? Which more effectively lowers your stress? Which develops your frontal lobe? Hands down, research continues to uncover the long-term benefits of reading.

It keeps your mind alert, while watching TV tends to encourage your brain to be passive. Reading has actually been shown to delay cognitive decline in elderly people, and those who regularly read are less likely to have Alzheimer's. Six minutes of reading can also reduce stress levels by 68 percent, according to researchers at the University of Sussex.

One study found that mothers who read to their children had much better communication with them. The interaction of asking their child questions was much higher than while sitting and watching an educational TV program. Parents who read to their children tend to more carefully choose books with values important to them versus parents who allow their children to watch TV programs while monitoring the content.

The Bible explains how "beholding" transforms us into the very image of what we spend time observing (2 Corinthians 3:18). If we watch movies that portray lying, stealing, cheating, drinking, drugging, and pre-marital or extra-marital sex, it bends our thoughts and behaviors in that direction. While media can be used for good, the Christian will be cautious about their choices because television and movies make a huge impact on one's life.

The apostle Paul outlines a simple plan for keeping a handle on media: "Whatever things are true, whatever things are noble, whatever things are just, whatever things are pure, whatever things are lovely, whatever things are of good report, if there is any virtue and if there is anything praiseworthy—meditate on these things" (Philippians 4:8).

Apply It:

If you currently do not read much, find a good book and determine to fill your mind by reading literature with high values.

Dig Deeper:

Psalm 101:3; 1 Corinthians 15:33; Matthew 5:29

Pure Words

"Beloved, I beg you as sojourners and pilgrims, abstain from fleshly lusts which war against the soul" (1 Peter 2:11).

In a study conducted in 2017, researcher Mark Bannister found that 75 percent of the songs that became top hits had explicit lyrics. This rise in popular songs with graphic words is extremely dramatic when considering that it is an 833 percent increase since the year 2001.

Lyrics are considered explicit when they refer to sex, violence, or other subjects without an appropriate amount of metaphorical veiling. This means that if lyrics alone are considered, there are fewer popular songs that are appropriate for Christian consumption today than in previous years.

Much of the popular music that has been produced in recent years encourages or glorifies lust or violence. In other words, this type of music directly conflicts with the type of lifestyle that Christians were intended to live. The apostle Paul warned Christians against imitating the behavior of the society around them: "Let us walk properly, as in the day, not in revelry and drunkenness, not in lewdness and lust, not in strife and envy. But put on the Lord Jesus Christ, and make no provision for the flesh, to fulfill its lusts" (Romans 13:13, 14).

Music can powerfully engage our emotions, which means it can also be used to encourage good decisions. The same can be said of reading materials. There are plenty of websites, magazines, and books that can inspire us to live useful and loving lives. Although it may, at times, be difficult to discern whether a song or a book helps or hinders our Christian walk, we can trust the guidance of God.

He has given us an abundance of principles upon which to base our decisions. Whether we are choosing music or books, we can decide what is worthy of our attention by comparing it to the standard God has set: "The fruit of the Spirit is in all goodness, righteousness, and truth" (Ephesians 5:9).

Apply It:

Do an extra five minutes of research before your next media purchase.

Dig Deeper:

2 Corinthians 6:15–18; 1 John 2:15–17; James 4:4

Your Irreplaceable Body

"Whether you eat or drink, or whatever you do, do all to the glory of God" (1 Corinthians 10:31).

Nutrition is a critical component in the care of horses. Like humans, horses only have one stomach and use microbial fermentation to break down the grass and hay they consume. A horse's digestive system is delicate and can easily be upset by rapid changes in feed. Horses need clean, high-quality feed that is given at regular intervals. They are sensitive to molds and toxins and should not be fed lawn clippings.

Sadly, some people spend far more time and money on the nutritional needs of a horse or a championship dog than on their own bodies. Though God has created us with irreplaceable physical bodies, people will invest thousands in properly caring for pets while neglecting their own health. High-quality food is purchased for their beloved animals while owners eat junk food and drink sodas that ruin the body.

God gave Adam and Eve the ideal diet in the very beginning: "See, I have given you every herb that yields seed which is on the face of all the earth, and every tree whose fruit yields seed; to you it shall be for food" (Genesis 1:29). After the fall, "the herb [plants] of the field" (Genesis 3:18) were added. This heaven-ordained diet made up of grains, fruits, nuts, and vegetables offers the best nutritional ingredients to maintain excellent health.

While the Bible does not condemn the eating of certain meats, the original diet was a balanced vegetarian plan. Science has not only confirmed the benefits of a plant-based diet, but it reveals the increase in disease among those who eat animal products. There is also an increase in atherosclerosis, cancer, kidney disorders, osteoporosis, and trichinosis among meat eaters.

There are also indications that a vegetarian diet will be the standard in the new earth: "The wolf and the lamb shall feed together, the lion shall eat straw like the ox" (Isaiah 65:25).

Apply It:

Think of one type of food that you feel convicted to quit eating and toss it out.

Dig Deeper:

Isaiah 11:7; Daniel 1:8; Acts 10:12–14

Clean and Unclean

"The swine is unclean for you, because it has cloven hooves, yet does not chew the cud; you shall not eat their flesh" (Deuteronomy 14:8).

When the pastor of one of America's largest megachurches says Christians need to cut out unclean foods, such as swine and shrimp, that gets notice.

And that's exactly what Joel Osteen—whose Lakewood Church in Houston, Texas, draws 50,000 people each week—did a few years ago. He carefully explained why unclean foods were classified that way by God, that their digestive systems didn't fully process what they ate, and that what they ate was, as he said, "kinda gross."

But you don't need to know who Joel Osteen is to learn what God suggests as the ideal diet. His preference is found in Genesis 1:29: "I have given you every herb that yields seed which is on the face of all the earth, and every tree whose fruit yields seed; to you it shall be for food."

That's the ideal—a plant-based diet is, by its very nature, clean. But if someone feels they must eat meat, God says to restrict the diet to those He deems acceptable. The Lord carefully gave His people guidelines in Leviticus 11 and Deuteronomy 14 to distinguish between clean and unclean animals.

When you stop and think about it, the command makes sense: God made the animals people try to eat—and He made the people who try to eat them! Wouldn't it follow that God knows what's best for the people He created?

Again, a plant-based diet is the ideal, both for good health and to be good stewards of the earth we inhabit. As our example shows, just about anyone who reads the Bible can clearly see the reasoning behind God's prohibition of unclean foods. The question remains though: Will we obey?

Apply It:

We need food not just to sustain life, but also to stay healthy. Review God's dietary counsel and see if you need to make some changes.

Dig Deeper:

Genesis 7:2, 3; Genesis 9:3–5; Leviticus 11

Inward Adornment

"Do not let your adornment be merely outward—arranging the hair, wearing gold, or putting on fine apparel—rather let it be the hidden person of the heart, with the incorruptible beauty of a gentle and quiet spirit, which is very precious in the sight of God" (1 Peter 3:3, 4).

The Tarkhan dress is the oldest known piece of clothing. It was discovered in 1913 in an ancient Egyptian cemetery about 30 miles from Cairo. However, its significance wasn't understood until 1977, when it was cleaned and properly examined. It was found turned inside out and showed signs of wear. The garment dates from the First Dynasty, around 3,000 BC. It is made of linen—the earliest-known textile fabric used for clothing, featuring tightly pleated sleeves and a yoke stitched to a skirt. The dress is on display at the Petrie Museum of Egyptian Archaeology in London.

Actually, the first piece of clothing for humans is described in the Bible. After the first pair sinned, "for Adam and his wife the LORD God made tunics of skin, and clothed them" (Genesis 3:21). Appropriate dress is not an afterthought in the Word of God. Principles of simplicity, modesty, practicality, health, and attractiveness are found in Scripture and guide us in choosing proper clothing.

For instance, a Christian will not detract from the beauty of a godly character with styles that arouse the "the lust of the flesh, the lust of the eyes, and the pride of life" (1 John 2:16). The apostle Paul explained how Christians should practice economy and avoid "gold or pearls or costly clothing" (1 Timothy 2:9). Even one's health should be taken into consideration when choosing clothes that are appropriate for work and for seasonal changes.

Christians recognize that one's natural beauty should be enhanced by their character since transient fashions have no value in God's eyes. What is most precious in heaven's eyes cannot wear out, for it is "the incorruptible beauty of a gentle and quiet spirit" (1 Peter 3:4).

Apply It:

Look through your wardrobe and ask yourself, "Do these clothes lift up God's standards of simplicity, modesty, economy, practicality, health, and spiritual beauty?"

Dig Deeper:

Exodus 33:5, 6; Matthew 6:25–33; 1 Peter 3:1–4

Smart Goodness

"The wind blows where it wishes, and you hear the sound of it, but cannot tell where it comes from and where it goes. So is everyone who is born of the Spirit" (John 3:8).

During the past few years, a movement called "effective altruism" has emerged. Proponents of it apply strategies to do the most amount of good. Sometimes this involves art enthusiasts funding eye surgeries for children. A lifetime of seeing art becomes more valuable than buying a single painting.

All of the standards of Christian behavior can be boiled down to positive principles. However, God intended that we would not only make decisions based on strategy but also on our response to Him. When Christians first realize that Jesus has saved them, there is usually a dramatic shift in behavior and attitude. Often, this is because the person is responding with gratitude for their salvation.

Paul described this shift as a new creation: "If anyone is in Christ, he is a new creation; old things have passed away; behold, all things have become new" (2 Corinthians 5:17). This means that the attention shifts away from selfish pursuits and toward the service of love.

While this service is usually more dramatic at the beginning of the Christian life, God has promised to continue influencing us positively throughout our lives. As a result of the influence of the Spirit of God, our behavior reflects positive character traits: "love, joy, peace, longsuffering, kindness, goodness, faithfulness, gentleness, self-control" (Galatians 5:22, 23).

These character traits are seen when the Christian sets a good example, gets involved in spreading the gospel, expresses praise to God, or collaborates with diverse people. When these pursuits fill up the life, they push out the negative behaviors that used to compete for our attention. Although the absence of negative behavior may be praiseworthy, it is positive service for others that becomes the primary attraction in the life of a Christian.

Apply It:

Think of just one way you could make your service for Christ more strategic.

Dig Deeper:

Philippians 2:5; 1 Corinthians 2:16; Psalm 63:2–5

Marriage and the Family

23

In His Image

"God said, 'Let Us make man in Our image, according to Our likeness. ...' So God created man in His own image; in the image of God He created him; male and female He created them" (Genesis 1:26, 27).

If you take a starfish of a certain genera and break off one of its arms, that arm will grow into a new starfish. This reproductive process is called autotomy and happens naturally when, over the period of one hour, a detached arm, called a "comet," separates from the main body. The damaged tissue heals in about ten days, and a new arm grows within a few months. However, many of these broken-off arms do not survive.

Several types of worms are also able to reproduce on their own. The California blackworm (or mudworm) has both male and female reproductive parts and can even reproduce if they are broken apart. Each part can become a new worm. But unlike worms, bacteria, strawberry plants, or freshwater cnidarians, producing new humans requires a father and mother.

In the beginning, God created humans as male and female. Both were created in His image, according to God's "likeness." The word "man" used in Genesis 1:26 does not refer only to males, but to both males and females. In the same way that the Father, Son, and Spirit make up "God," so also male and female together make up "man" or humankind.

God could have propagated human life on earth through asexual reproduction, but His plan was to have a husband and wife come together to create children. After Adam was created, he recognized that he was alone. God then said, "It is not good that man should be alone; I will make him a helper comparable to him" (Genesis 2:18). Eve complemented Adam and was similar in some ways, yet unique in others. She stood beside him as his equal in worth, but was not identical in person.

Imagine how incomplete our world would be if it were made up of only males or females, men or women, boys or girls.

Apply It:

Can you think of another plant or animal that can reproduce asexually?

Dig Deeper:

Genesis 2:15–24; 1 Corinthians 11:8; Galatians 3:28

What God Ordained, Man Can't Change

"A man shall leave his father and mother and be joined to his wife, and they shall become one flesh" (Genesis 2:24).

The Bible is clear: Marriage is intended to be the union of one man and one woman. They are to so intermingle that they become "one flesh."

But marriage is a process. The first part involves *leaving*. Each partner in the new marriage must maintain a respectful separation from their parents. Circumstances at times may require a newlywed couple to live with one set of parents for a period of time. And it may become necessary to care for the parent of a given spouse at some point. But however physically near one's in-laws or one's own parents might be, there must be lines of demarcation to preserve the new marriage.

Being "joined" to each other suggests a commitment far beyond the "starter marriage" idea floated a few years ago. "Divorce" shouldn't enter the marriage vocabulary—except in the most critical and desperate of circumstances, such as abuse.

When a couple participates in a marriage ceremony, the officiant will ask God to bless and sanctify the union. Often, you'll hear these words from Matthew 19:6 in the ceremony: "What God has joined together, let not man separate."

And when God, in Genesis, says the two "shall become one flesh," more than mere sexual intimacy is involved. It means a blending of hearts, minds, and even wills to produce a bond so strong that the world's temptations and lures cannot break it.

The God-ordained vision of marriage is a tall order, to be sure. But those who are devoted to its attainment, and ask the Creator of marriage for His help, are well positioned to attain it.

Apply It:

If you're married, ask God to make you into the kind of spouse He wants you to be. If you are single and searching, consider the definition of marriage God has ordained, and ask Him to make you ready for the person He has in mind for you!

Dig Deeper:

Proverbs 2:16, 17; Amos 3:3; Hebrews 13:4

October 17

Walking Together

"Can two walk together, unless they are agreed?" (Amos 3:3).

Children occasionally get lost in the woods, but by following some basic rules, their chances for survival can increase. For instance, search-and-rescue teams encourage children to stay in one place and not wander. Meandering makes it more difficult to track a child and increases their chance of falling and hurting themselves.

Another rule is to keep warm, find a cozy waiting place (but not a hiding place), and never lie on bare ground. The cold ground can rob precious heat from one's body. Build a mattress with branches, moss, or leaves. And never eat anything you are not sure of. Most important, stay together if you are with someone else or a pet. If it is cold outside, being together keeps you warm.

God created humans to enjoy companionship. Solomon said, "Two are better than one, because they have a good reward for their labor" (Ecclesiastes 4:9). This is especially true in the marriage relationship. But walking together means being of one mind and spirit. That's why God warned the Israelites not to intermarry with the neighboring nations, "for they will turn your sons away from following Me, to serve other gods" (Deuteronomy 7:4).

The apostle Paul repeated this principle: "Do not be unequally yoked together with unbelievers. For what fellowship has righteousness with lawlessness? And what communion has light with darkness? And what accord has Christ with Belial? Or what part has a believer with an unbeliever? And what agreement has the temple of God with idols?" (2 Corinthians 6:14–16).

Becoming "one flesh" (Mark 10:8) means more than the union of physical intimacy. It is based upon two people being loyal to one another, proclaiming a willingness to stay together, even in difficult circumstances. It requires an unselfish love that will not give up, a love that "bears all things, believes all things, hopes all things, endures all things" (1 Corinthians 13:7).

A successful union of two lives also requires sharing lives, possessions, thinking, joys, and even sufferings. If a couple ever gets lost—physically or emotionally—those who survive best stay together.

Apply It:

Have you ever gotten lost when you were alone? What was it like?

Dig Deeper:

Joshua 23:11–13; Ruth 1:16, 17; Ecclesiastes 4:9–12

Quality Union

"Let your fountain be blessed, and rejoice with the wife of your youth" (Proverbs 5:18).

A study conducted in 2016 found that married couples find more satisfaction in their relationships when they had high-quality sexual encounters. This was compared to married couples who had sex more frequently but were less happy with the quality.

The Bible promotes quality sexual encounters within marriage. This is perhaps clearest in the Song of Solomon. There the descriptions of intimacy are not vulgar. Instead, they express the elegance of a loving union that is protected by the marriage covenant. One example of the joyful, physical expression of love is found in the exclamations that begin the song: "Let him kiss me with the kisses of his mouth—for your love is better than wine" (Song of Solomon 1:2).

It is clear that the two main contributors to this song have a profound respect for one another. Their interactions are characterized by warmth, kindness, and consideration. This suggests that their intimacy is driven by a sincere and pure love for one another. The result is a poetic experience.

The poetry of the Song of Solomon uses garden imagery that is reminiscent of the first garden. Soon after God created Eve, the first pair is recorded as having achieved a comfortable intimacy: "Therefore a man shall leave his father and mother and be joined to his wife, and they shall become one flesh" (Genesis 2:24). This was according to God's original design.

Although God could have described His design of marriage only in terms of fruitful procreation, as He did in Genesis 1, He went a step further and spoke of the marriage bond in physical terms. Certainly the bond between husband and wife extends beyond sex. However, the joy of sex becomes one of the expressions of a holy and emotional attachment.

Apply It:

If you are married, try to replicate a Song of Solomon experience with your spouse.

Dig Deeper:

Proverbs 5:19; Genesis 4:1; Hebrews 13:4

October 19

The Greatest Love

"God demonstrates His own love toward us, in that while we were still sinners, Christ died for us" (Romans 5:8).

In December 1917, Vince Coleman was working as a dispatcher in a harbor-side train station in Halifax, Nova Scotia, when two ships collided nearby and caught fire. One of them, a French munitions ship packed with high explosives, drifted toward the pier, which was only a short distance away.

Coleman and his coworker, realizing a loaded passenger train was soon to arrive, contacted another station to stop it. Both men then left the station, but Coleman returned and continued sending out telegraph messages to warn away other trains—until he was killed by the explosion. It was evident from his final message that he understood he would lose his life as a result.

It's unusual for someone to be willing to give his or her life to save someone else. As the Bible puts it in Romans 5:7, "Scarcely for a righteous man will one die; yet perhaps for a good man someone would even dare to die." Yet Scripture goes on to say that Jesus died for those in rebellion against Him, His very enemies, because of His love toward us.

Biblical love—also known as *agape* love—is the highest form of love. This is the giving, self-sacrificing love with which God loves us. "Greater love has no one than this, than to lay down one's life for his friends" (John 15:13).

Although the relationship between a husband and wife generally involves several kinds of love, it is *agape* love that gives marriage its foundation. This selfless kind of love is described in 1 Corinthians 13:4–8: "Love suffers long and is kind; love does not envy; love does not parade itself, is not puffed up; does not behave rudely, does not seek its own, is not provoked, thinks no evil; does not rejoice in iniquity, but rejoices in the truth; bears all things, believes all things, hopes all things, endures all things. Love never fails."

We can't generate this unstoppable love on our own. We can make a choice to love unconditionally, but only our continuous connection with God enables our success.

Apply It:

What person in your life most exemplifies *agape* love?

Dig Deeper:

John 15:12; Galatians 5:14; Matthew 5:44

Battling Change

"Let each one of you in particular so love his own wife as himself, and let the wife see that she respects her husband" (Ephesians 5:33).

Talking to a spouse about an object of interest can be a request for a response. Researchers at the University of Washington found that spouses who responded positively toward these requests 87 percent of the time were still married after six years. In contrast, those who responded positively only 33 percent of the time were divorced by the sixth year.

God designed that marriage would be a union of love. However, there was a noticeable change in Adam and Eve's relationship after they disobeyed God. Before they sinned, Adam dwelt on the unity in the relationship when he spoke of Eve: He said, "This is now bone of my bones and flesh of my flesh; she shall be called Woman, because she was taken out of Man" (Genesis 2:23).

After sin came in, Adam blamed Eve for his disobedience—showing that he was ready to ignore their unity. At that point, God stepped in to provide a principle that had the potential of alleviating some of the tension in the marriage.

He told Eve, "I will greatly multiply your sorrow and your conception; in pain you shall bring forth children; your desire shall be for your husband, and he shall rule over you" (Genesis 3:16). Although many regard this as a curse, it is important to note that the only thing that God actually cursed immediately after the entrance of sin was the ground. This suggests that God was providing a way for the couple to retain unity.

Other parts of the Bible, such as Ephesians 5, explain that this submission involves respect and occurs in a relationship in which the husband loves the wife. When other passages are brought to bear on God's principle of submission, it shows that He was not promoting the abuses that merely perpetuate the selfishness that began with sin.

Apply It:

Learn a new way to show love and respect in your family.

Dig Deeper:

Song of Solomon 7:10; Colossians 3:18, 19; Ephesians 5:22–32

The Chambers of Death

"You shall not commit adultery" (Exodus 20:14).

Married couples who regularly attend worship services together are the least likely to break the seventh commandment. That's the conclusion of the General Social Surveys and the Family Research Council. Adults in "always-intact marriages" who weekly go to some type of religious service have an unfaithfulness rate of 7.7 percent, while those who never attend worship have a 15.3 percent rate of committing adultery. For those who are previously married or separated or divorced, the rate is 23.3 percent for those who worship weekly and 33.8 percent for those who never worship.

God knew that the stain of adultery and fornication would tear marriages to pieces. By keeping the Lord first in the marital relationship and following His commandments, the joy and harmony of this sacred union would be preserved. "This is the will of God, your sanctification: that you should abstain from sexual immorality" (1 Thessalonians 4:3).

This Bible verse stands in sharp contrast to the flexible "tolerance" views accepted in society between "consenting adults." Statistics vary, but the vast majority of Americans do not wait until marriage to have intimate relations. Yet the Scriptures plainly state, "Fornication and all uncleanness or covetousness, let it not even be named among you, as is fitting for saints" (Ephesians 5:3).

Even apart from the Bible, many have come to recognize the far-reaching effects of premarital and extramarital sex. Such acts defraud the legitimate partner and can harm people physically, emotionally, financially, legally, and socially. Extended family can be hurt and children wounded, and dishonesty and lies almost always hover over such affairs.

God wants to protect you from "the works of the flesh ... which are: adultery, fornication, uncleanness, lewdness" (Galatians 5:19). The seventh commandment was not given to withhold something good from you, but to keep you from "descending to the chambers of death" (Proverbs 7:27).

Apply It:

Think of a couple who are experiencing marital difficulties or may even be divorced. Stop and pray for them right now.

Dig Deeper:

Leviticus 20:10–12; Proverbs 6:24–32; 1 Corinthians 6:9, 13, 18

Don't Go There!

"You have heard that it was said to those of old, 'You shall not commit adultery.' But I say to you that whoever looks at a woman to lust for her has already committed adultery with her in his heart" (Matthew 5:27, 28).

In 1976, a reporter for the *Los Angeles Times*, Robert Scheer, obtained an interview with Jimmy Carter, then a state governor and a U.S. presidential candidate. Carter's image as a strait-laced, Baptist Sunday School teacher was such that many religious Americans swooned over the prospect of having a pious Christian in the White House.

Carter's blunt admission to Scheer—who published the story in, of all places, *Playboy* magazine—made global headlines: The candidate admitted that he had "lusted" in his heart, despite having been faithful to his wife.

In the more than forty years since Carter's bombshell, American society has seen all sorts of, well, unimaginable behavior credited to presidents from both parties. And, sadly, there are many people on either side of the aisle who are willing to overlook moral failures if their political agenda is advanced.

Of course, this isn't God's standard for marriage, for "the body is not for sexual immorality" (1 Corinthians 6:13). "Adultery in the heart" can be as much a poison as fornication itself. The culture that was stunned by Carter's admission is now so seemingly blasé about impure thoughts that television and movie comedies are often built around those thoughts. The "loyal sidekick" in such presentations may weakly caution the soon-to-be-erring friend, "Don't even go there," but the plot will contain the unexpressed hope that the person does, indeed, "go there."

If ever there was a "counterculture" movement to which Christians are called, it's the one where we are called to abandon, to run from, the very thought of such sins: "Flee sexual immorality," we're told in 1 Corinthians 6:18. Those are words to live by!

Apply It:

Ask God to keep your heart, your mind, and your marriage (if you are married) pure. He will gladly answer that prayer!

Dig Deeper:

Psalm 119:11; Job 31:1; 1 Corinthians 10:13

October 23

Authentic from Above

"They are no longer two but one flesh. Therefore what God has joined together, let not man separate" (Matthew 19:6).

In 2017, some lawyers reported that it was becoming increasingly difficult for immigrants to become permanent U.S. residents after marrying American citizens. Immigration officers, who have to ensure a marriage is an authentic union not based merely on a desire to become a citizen, sometimes go to great lengths in their evaluations. For instance, before granting residency to the immigrant spouse, officers may park outside the home of an applicant to see if the couple actually lives together.

God intended every marriage to be authentic and assured couples that the authenticity would come from Him. This means that even marriages that were entered into for less than honorable motives can be held together by God. For this reason, when marriages seem to be at risk, Jesus' statements on marriage imply that the union is worth fighting for.

In His explanation concerning the sin that is connected to divorce, Jesus called for a deeper loyalty: "I say to you, whoever divorces his wife, except for sexual immorality, and marries another, commits adultery; and whoever marries her who is divorced commits adultery" (Matthew 19:9). Although this statement may sound stern, it was not intended as a demand for blind obedience.

On the contrary, just before making this statement, Jesus explained that He wanted couples to experience the kind of marital bond that took place before sin: "Moses, because of the hardness of your hearts, permitted you to divorce your wives, but from the beginning it was not so" (Matthew 19:8). Jesus was implying that married couples should be striving for the original design in marriage.

Although sin is the source of many marital difficulties, Jesus came to save us from our sins. In contrast to the hard-hearted, our escape from sin can be described as the reception of a soft heart that appreciates the beautiful gift and design of marriage.

Apply It:

Spend a few hours with a couple that rely on God for their success in marriage.

Dig Deeper:

Mark 10:7–9; Matthew 5:32; Ephesians 4:2, 3

Compassion Over Fear

"On some have compassion, making a distinction" (Jude 1:22).

Six people were rescued from a burning boat off the coast of Florida in 2018. The rescuers were not acquainted with them. However, they were willing to risk the danger of being close to the flames in order to bring them to safety.

God has asked Christians to be compassionate to all people. Unfortunately, many Christians have responded to the LGBTQ community with fear and hostility. Those who respond this way often use the Bible's condemnation of homosexuality as a justification for their attitude.

However, the Bible's prohibition of homosexual relationships and practices does not negate its primary message of salvation. In other words, Christians are called to respond to the LGBTQ community with as much compassion and concern as they afford to any other sinful human, Christians included.

The apostle Paul made it clear that he did not condone homosexuality: "Do you not know that the unrighteous will not inherit the kingdom of God? Do not be deceived. Neither fornicators, nor idolaters, nor adulterers, nor homosexuals, nor sodomites, nor thieves, nor covetous, nor drunkards, nor revilers, nor extortioners will inherit the kingdom of God" (1 Corinthians 6:9, 10).

Notice that this list includes the common sin of covetousness. This suggests that we should be ready to minister to every kind of sinner, while remembering that every sin can prevent people from entering the kingdom. Paul's response should give everyone on this list hope: "Such were some of you. But you were washed, but you were sanctified, but you were justified in the name of the Lord Jesus and by the Spirit of our God" (1 Corinthians 6:11).

One way to define a redemptive attitude is to consider how people have guided us to Jesus and away from our sins. Chances are, we made some of our best decisions in response to a caring friend.

Apply It:

Have a friendly conversation with a member of the LGBTQ community.

Dig Deeper:

John 8:11; Romans 3:23; Matthew 19:4–6

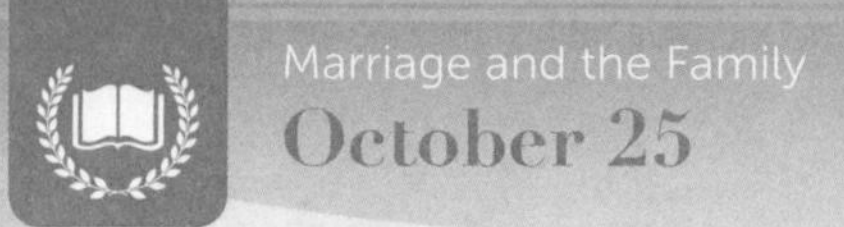

October 25

True Fatherhood

"Fathers, do not provoke your children, lest they become discouraged" (Colossians 3:21).

Maybe you've heard something like this: "Any man can have a child, but it takes a real man to be a father."

That's biologically true, of course, and socially correct. Whether or not the people involved are believers, the duty of raising children includes the active, continual, involved relationship of the father, whenever and wherever possible. (The children of those fathers who have either deserted a family or who have died need support from other family members and neighbors.)

In the Christian setting, the need for fathers who are responsible and actively involved in their children's lives is even greater. Children carefully observe and remember how their parents, perhaps especially their fathers, model Jesus' example to them. In instance after instance, pastors and teachers often hear from those who have deserted the faith because the father in the home acted one way in a congregation but quite differently at home.

Fathers have what is called a "priestly responsibility" in the home (Colossians 3:18–21). The father becomes, as Ephesians 5:23–28 notes, a type of Christ in the family. Note the distinction here: Fathers are a *type* of Christ; they are not Christ Himself, of course.

Knowing this responsibility should help fathers exercise Christlike leadership in the family. If we ask ourselves not only *what* Jesus would do, but also *how* He would do it, we can have a greater assurance that our parenting will more closely reflect the One we say we serve.

Apply It:

If you still have children at home, remember the fatherly responsibility you have to show Christlikeness in your actions. And if your children have grown, they're still your kids and still need leadership that reflects the love of Jesus. His mercies are new *every* morning!

Dig Deeper:

Genesis 18:19; Proverbs 20:7; Ephesians 6:4

Brave and Protective

"Hear the instruction of your father, and do not forsake the law of your mother" (Proverbs 1:8).

It started out as a fun and relaxing mother-daughter outing, as Valeh Levy surfed with Sydney, her 15-year-old daughter, off New Smyrna Beach in Florida. But as they paddled their surfboards side by side, gearing up to catch another wave, suddenly Sydney was jerked off her board and pulled under the water by a shark. Although she was able to get back on her board, it happened again.

Catching a glimpse of the ominous dark shape below, Valeh realized what was happening. Determined to save her child, she sprang into action, grabbing her daughter by the shoulders, wrestling her from the shark's jaws, and dragging her onto the front of her surfboard. With the shark circling them, they screamed for help and were assisted by other surfers. Although her foot and ankle required surgery, Sydney's life was saved by her mother's brave actions.

Mothers today face somewhat analogous challenges as a predator of souls circles their children, hoping to drag them down and injure them, "seeking whom he may devour" (1 Peter 5:8). Worldly mothers have little defense against these kinds of attacks on their kids, but a Christian mother knows her strength and wisdom come from God. "With Him are wisdom and strength, He has counsel and understanding" (Job 12:13).

Filled with courage from above, a Christian mother will fight tenaciously for the souls of her children and grasp promises from God, such as Isaiah 41:10: "Fear not, for I am with you; be not dismayed, for I am your God. I will strengthen you, yes, I will help you, I will uphold you with My righteous right hand.' " She will put her trust in the Lord and rely on His guidance, while striving to shape their characters. With gentle persuasiveness, she will consistently point them to Jesus and help them to choose the path that leads to eternal life.

Apply It:

Think of three ways your mother helped shape your life for the better.

Dig Deeper:

Proverbs 22:6; Deuteronomy 6:6–8; Proverbs 31:10–31

Raising Godly Children

"What great nation is there that has such statutes and righteous judgments as are in all this law? ... Only take heed to yourself, and diligently keep yourself, lest you forget the things your eyes have seen, and lest they depart from your heart all the days of your life. And teach them to your children and your grandchildren" (Deuteronomy 4:8, 9).

Probably everyone has observed, at some time, a child imitating an adult—and it can be quite entertaining to watch. Research shows that young children and even infants around the globe actually over-imitate adults in performing a task, meaning that they observe and then copycat adults' actions, even if the actions are unnecessary or useless.

One study, using containers with toys inside, demonstrated that even when children were instructed not to perform actions that were unnecessary in order to open the containers, they continued to copy what they had seen an adult do. If that included unnecessary steps, the kids would dutifully copy those steps.

God has given parents an incredible responsibility in raising children. Kids depend on their parents, look up to them, and predictably mimic them. With such a powerful influence, parents need to seriously consider their role in their children's lives.

Except for their relationship with God and their spouse, parents should make their children top priority. Kids need a constant supply of nurturing love, security, and consistency from their parents. They need to be guided into obedience, good values, and respect for authority. "Correct your son, and he will give you rest; yes, he will give delight to your soul" (Proverbs 29:17).

Yet it's essential that discipline always be loving. "Do not provoke your children to wrath, but bring them up in the training and admonition of the Lord" (Ephesians 6:4).

When parents raise kids in a faithful and conscientious manner, teaching them to love the Lord above all else, they can confidently grasp the wonderful promise: "Train up a child in the way he should go, and when he is old he will not depart from it" (Proverbs 22:6).

■ Apply It:

How are you using the influence God has given you to bless the children in your life?

■ Dig Deeper:

2 Timothy 3:16; Deuteronomy 6:6, 7; Colossians 3:21

An Extended Family? Yes!

"When I am old and grayheaded, O God, do not forsake me, until I declare Your strength to this generation, Your power to everyone who is to come" (Psalm 71:18).

Some of the best people you'll ever consider family might not even come from your bloodline. They might be sitting next to you in church!

We are commanded to care for our families, as Paul declared in 1 Timothy 5:8: "If anyone does not provide for his own, and especially for those of his household, he has denied the faith and is worse than an unbeliever."

But we also have the opportunity—especially if we're unmarried—to show that love and kindness to others in the church circle. The "seasoned citizens" among us may be especially lonely if their spouse has passed away, and they'd give just about anything to have fellowship with you.

That single parent juggling work, children, and a church schedule might be praying even now for someone to take an interest in their situation, and to offer both a word of encouragement as well as a helping hand. Could you be the answer to their prayer?

The list goes on, of course: single adults, college students in town for a brief period, others serving their country in the military or public service. All these people may be in your community—and your congregation—far from their families and hometowns.

If we're supposed to show hospitality to strangers, how much more should we open our hearts, and our doors, to those who are in the family of faith? After all, we hope to share heaven with these people—why not let heaven begin right now?

Apply It:

Ask God to reveal to you people who are in need of your gifts. And when He does, respond!

Dig Deeper:

Exodus 22:22; Proverbs 23:10; Isaiah 1:17

Christ's Ministry in the Heavenly Sanctuary

24

Where God Dwells

"We have such a High Priest, who is seated at the right hand of the throne of the Majesty in the heavens, a Minister of the sanctuary and of the true tabernacle which the Lord erected, and not man" (Hebrews 8:1, 2).

Perhaps the most disputed piece of real estate on our planet is the area known as the Temple Mount in Jerusalem. It's the one bit of territory not directly controlled by the state of Israel; an Islamic trust known as the "Waqf" is in charge. To keep tensions from boiling over, Jews are prohibited from praying on the mount, even though it is the site of their ancient temple. It is only at the Western Wall, at the bottom of one side of the Temple Mount, that Jews are allowed to pray.

It's easy to understand the affection that Jews, Muslims, and Christians have for this sacred space. It is believed that this is the ancient Mount Moriah where Abraham offered to sacrifice Isaac. Christians revere it as a place where Jesus walked, taught, healed—and the place from which He chased the money changers. Muslims believe it is where Mohammed ascended to heaven.

But for Christians, what is left of the Temple Mount is of less significance than the sanctuary in heaven. The earthly sanctuary was just a type of the place where God Himself dwells, and where Jesus, today, is ministering on our behalf.

Everything in the earthly sanctuary was a copy of that which was found in the heavenly one. "It was necessary that the copies of the things in the heavens should be purified with these, but the heavenly things themselves with better sacrifices than these. For Christ has not entered the holy places made with hands, which are copies of the true, but into heaven itself, now to appear in the presence of God for us" (Hebrews 9:23, 24).

How wonderful to know that whoever may control the mound of earth where man's most disputed real estate is located, there's no dispute over who controls the heavenly Sanctuary!

Apply It:

How comforting is it to know that there's a sanctuary in heaven where God dwells and Jesus ministers on your behalf?

Dig Deeper:

Exodus 25:9, 40; Micah 1:2, 3; Revelation 9:13

Distortion Solution

"It was symbolic for the present time in which both gifts and sacrifices are offered which cannot make him who performed the service perfect in regard to the conscience" (Hebrews 9:9).

Psychologists have discovered that people change their definitions when they see fewer examples of them. In a study, participants saw groups of colored dots and were asked to choose the purple ones. They had to repeat this process 200 times before they were shown pictures with increasingly scarce purple dots. Even when offered money to choose only purple dots, they began to choose blue dots and call them purple.

God knew that sin would distort our ability to understand His plan of salvation. In order to help us get a picture of the plan, He instructed Moses to make a sanctuary that would show His saving work on earth and in heaven.

The sacrifices in the sanctuary service taught the people that He would send someone to die on behalf of every person. John the Baptist understood that it was not the sacrificed animals that brought the people salvation, but rather the Man that the animals represented: "John saw Jesus coming toward him, and said, 'Behold! The Lamb of God who takes away the sin of the world!' " (John 1:29).

Each household had to bring its own sacrifice so every family member would understand that it was their sin that was responsible for the death of the coming Messiah. However, only one man would have to die in order to make everyone righteous—and that death would take place only once: "So Christ was offered once to bear the sins of many. To those who eagerly wait for Him He will appear a second time, apart from sin, for salvation" (Hebrews 9:28).

Although the sacrifices pointed forward to a single death, they revealed the penalty of sin, the assurance of forgiveness, and the promise of a transformed life. This system helped reveal the depth of love that would resolve the sin problem.

Apply It:

Build a sanctuary model that you can show your friends.

Dig Deeper:

Romans 6:23; Isaiah 53:6; Hebrews 9:26, 27

Daily Reconciliation

"There is one God and one Mediator between God and men, the Man Christ Jesus" (1 Timothy 2:5).

The bottlenose dolphins that live off the coast of Bermuda dive up to 1,000 meters looking for prey. This ability is unique when compared to dolphins that live closer to the shore and only go down about ten meters. Physiologists have found that this deep diving is made possible by the presence of 25 percent more red blood cells.

Jesus' blood is the reason we have access to the Father and to heaven. His blood reminds us of His spotless life and the death that was caused by our sin. It is because of His sacrifice that Jesus is able to continually administer salvation from the heavenly Sanctuary.

The earthly priests transferred sin to the sanctuary using the blood of animals. Jesus' ministry in the heavenly sanctuary involves the Father's acceptance of Christ's life on our behalf. This can happen because of what Christ did on earth: "He made Him who knew no sin to be sin for us, that we might become the righteousness of God in Him" (2 Corinthians 5:21).

Receiving the righteousness of God involves the forgiveness of our offenses and meager attempts at self-justification. It also involves giving us the power to overcome the temptations we are currently experiencing: "Let us therefore come boldly to the throne of grace, that we may obtain mercy and find grace to help in time of need" (Hebrews 4:16). Jesus' presence in heaven assures us of our forgiveness, provides power over temptations, and reminds us that He can empathize with us.

When Jesus was on earth, He had to endure difficult temptations. Now that He's in heaven representing us, we know that the power He sends us is rooted in His empathy for our struggles. Although this whole process seems particularly intricate, it is so essential that it happens every day in the Sanctuary.

Apply It:

Do something kind for someone that hurt you in the past.

Dig Deeper:

Leviticus 4:35; Hebrews 8:1, 2; Hebrews 7:25

Preparing a Place for Us

"I go to prepare a place for you" (John 14:2).

In examining the ministry of Jesus in the heavenly Sanctuary, John 14:2—which Christians traditionally regard as talking about Jesus' preparation of an eternal home for those who follow Him—might seem out of place.

Yes, this verse talks about heaven. But might it also suggest, however subtly, the work Jesus is performing in the Most Holy Place of the sanctuary right now?

Think of what the Hebrew high priest did on the annual Day of Atonement, still called Yom Kippur by Jews today. The high priest entered the Most Holy Place, sprinkled the blood of the sacrifice on the Ark of the Covenant, and prefigured the sacrifice of Jesus, whose blood would cover the sins of all humanity.

Could it not be said that the sprinkling of the blood by the high priest "prepared" the sanctuary for another year of ministry? "He shall make atonement for the Holy Place, because of the uncleanness of the children of Israel, and because of their transgressions, for all their sins; and so he shall do for the tabernacle of meeting which remains among them in the midst of their uncleanness" (Leviticus 16:16). Was that priest not going ahead of the Israelites to make a way for them to come to God?

Jesus, now in heaven, is our Mediator. He sees those who belong to Him and pleads on their behalf. That is why we don't need to fear the judgment, because Jesus is arguing our case. He is reminding all of heaven that His blood was already poured out for our sins. All we need to do is accept that sacrifice.

Yes, friend, Jesus has indeed gone to "prepare a place" for us. Part of that preparation is the eradication of sin for all time, something foreshadowed by His ministry in the Most Holy Place.

Apply It:

It's always a good time to meditate on what Jesus is doing on our behalf—and to offer a prayer of thanks for His ministry for us!

Dig Deeper:

Leviticus 16:30–33; Hebrews 6:19, 20; Hebrews 9:12

Azazel

"Aaron shall cast lots for the two goats: one lot for the Lord *and the other lot for the scapegoat"* (Leviticus 16:8).

In today's world—especially given the influence of drama in the cinema and on television—it's easy to imagine a "scapegoat" as just being a simple person. Either it's someone truly guilty or, more likely, an innocent person framed for a set of wrong actions or circumstances but who is vindicated in the later part of the story.

By contrast, the scapegoat in the Bible, known as Azazel, was not selected in error. He represents Satan, of whom Jesus said, "I saw Satan fall like lightning from heaven" (Luke 10:18). He became the chief adversary of God and of all believers. The Azazel goat is sent into the wilderness once the sins of the people are, symbolically, placed on its head.

This in no way suggests that the Azazel goat—or Satan, who is bound after the Second Coming and the judgment—*atones* for the sins of all. That is given to the Lord's goat, in the sanctuary application, and to Jesus during His life on earth and death on the cross. Jesus, and He alone, has paid the *complete* price and made the *total* atonement for our sins, and the sins of all who have ever, or will ever, live. It is, of course, up to each individual to accept Christ's sacrifice so that they may be saved.

The Azazel goat is a symbol of Satan, the adversary of whom Peter warned, "Be sober, be vigilant; because your adversary the devil walks about like a roaring lion, seeking whom he may devour" (1 Peter 5:8). The Bible says that this opponent of God's people will see a sad, eternal end when he will be "cast into the lake of fire and brimstone" (Revelation 20:10).

Apply It:

As we consider God's use of the Azazel goat as a type of Satan, whose ultimate destruction is assured, let's give thanks for Jesus' redemptive sacrifice on our behalf.

Dig Deeper:

Leviticus 16:20; Hebrews 9:22; Revelation 20:2, 3

Perfect Security

"That in the dispensation of the fullness of the times He might gather together in one all things in Christ, both which are in heaven and which are on earth—in Him" (Ephesians 1:10).

A pilot program at Quantas Airlines allows certain passengers to pass check points using their face as their passport and boarding pass. The airline plans to use biometric technology for all passengers at check-in, during bag drop-off, to provide lounge access, and for boarding.

The three phases of the judgment will ensure that the universe is a place where security is no longer an issue. During the first phase of the judgment, the angels witness Christ's investigation into those who claim to be His followers. This phase was foreshadowed by the removal of sin from the sanctuary on the Day of Atonement: "He shall make atonement for the Holy Place, because of the uncleanness of the children of Israel, and because of their transgressions, for all their sins; and so he shall do for the tabernacle of meeting which remains among them in the midst of their uncleanness" (Leviticus 16:16).

The second phase of the judgment provides the righteous a thousand years in heaven to look into the evidence that the wicked have rejected salvation: "I saw thrones, and they sat on them, and judgment was committed to them. Then I saw the souls of those who had been beheaded for their witness to Jesus and for the word of God, who had not worshiped the beast or his image, and had not received his mark on their foreheads or on their hands. And they lived and reigned with Christ for a thousand years" (Revelation 20:4).

The final phase of the judgment is the destruction of the wicked after the thousand years. Just as the scapegoat was led into the wilderness where it would die, so Satan cannot harass God's people during the second phase and dies in the third phase.

Apply It:

Befriend someone you have not met before.

Dig Deeper:

1 Corinthians 6:1–3; Revelation 20:11–15; Matthew 25:31–46

Clean Happiness

"According to the law almost all things are purified with blood, and without shedding of blood there is no remission" (Hebrews 9:22).

A group of researchers in Philadelphia planted grass and trees and cleaned up empty lots in different parts of the city. They also tracked the mental health of people in the neighborhoods where they provided the change. When compared to other neighborhoods, those who were poor and had seen the changes reported a 70 percent decrease in mental health problems.

God has a plan to permanently clean up our record of sin. When our sins are blotted out, we are deemed ready for eternal life. Those who claimed to be Christians but were actually persecuting God's people will also be considered, and their decision to reject a life of harmony with God will be respected.

In the sanctuary that was set up by Moses and the Israelites, the yearly service pointed forward to the time of final cleansing. On the Day of Atonement, all of the sins that had been symbolically transferred to the sanctuary were cleansed by the blood of a goat. That goat represented Christ. It would take Christ's blood to clean the record of sins in heaven: "It was necessary that the copies of the things in the heavens should be purified with these, but the heavenly things themselves with better sacrifices than these" (Hebrews 9:23).

Because the record of sins is affected by the ceremonies of that day, it also means that a judgment takes place. In other words, the decisions that are made concerning the heavenly books are a ruling of the heavenly court. This point is especially clear in Daniel's vision: "A fiery stream issued and came forth from before Him. A thousand thousands ministered to Him; ten thousand times ten thousand stood before Him. The court was seated, and the books were opened" (Daniel 7:10).

This judgment deals with self-proclaimed Christians and reveals the fake and the real.

Apply It:

Clean up a section of your neighborhood.

Dig Deeper:

Revelation 22:12; Revelation 12:10; Luke 20:35

When Will Judgment Happen?

"He came near where I stood, and when he came I was afraid and fell on my face; but he said to me, 'Understand, son of man, that the vision refers to the time of the end' " (Daniel 8:17).

In the year 1033, people around the world expected Jesus to return. That year, they reasoned, would signify the passing of a thousand years since the crucifixion and resurrection, and surely the Lord would come back for His own by then! (And if you are tempted to do the same, remember Jesus' words in Matthew 24:36, that "no one" knows the "day and hour" of Christ's return.)

But just because the world doesn't come stamped with a specific expiration date does not mean it's impossible to discern the "signs of the times" (Matthew 16:3).

One key factor is the presence of Rome at both ends of Jesus' ministry. While the Savior was on earth, it was the pagan Roman Empire that captured and killed Him. Jesus gave up His life to atone for our sins, yes, but it was through the agency of the Roman state that this took place.

Daniel identifies Rome as the "little horn" that will persecute the saints. And Rome is still a religious-civil power, one that has sought "to change times and law" (Daniel 7:25) and one that has interposed a manmade system of religion that puts other sinful humans in the role of mediator—a role belonging to Christ alone.

This final Rome will also seek to compel obedience to its religion by aligning with worldly governments. Those who resist will face intense pressure to revert, and if they continue to resist, they will be confronted with the very real possibility of martyrdom.

These will indeed be perilous times for millions of God's faithful, the ones called a "remnant" people (Romans 9:27). But Jesus promised "he who endures to the end shall be saved" (Matthew 24:13). Now, then, is the time to study and pray, so that you'll be ready for that great and terrible day.

Apply It:

Jesus told his followers to "watch" (Mark 13:37). Keep looking out—and always keep looking up!

Dig Deeper:

Daniel 8:9; Daniel 8:12; Hebrews 7:25

A Ministry of Restoration

"I heard a man's voice ... who called, and said, 'Gabriel, make this man understand the vision.' So he came near where I stood, and when he came I was afraid and fell on my face; but he said to me, 'Understand, son of man, that the vision refers to the time of the end' " (Daniel 8:16, 17).

Perhaps one of the most intriguing and most disputed passages of Scripture comes immediately after the verse quoted above. Daniel 9, in which the famous "seventy weeks" are described, has spawned virtual libraries on the question of what the time periods of the 70 weeks—which represent 490 days/years—actually mean, along with the subsequent 1,810 days/years. Together, they comprise the 2,300 days/years spoken of in Daniel 8:14.

It is long past time thoughtful readers have the actual meaning presented. The end of the 70 weeks marked the end of Christ's life on earth, His sacrifice for our sins. This period was "cut off" as we read in the original Hebrew of Daniel 9:24. The cutting off was a division of that time period from the rest of the 2,300 years, which culminated in the year 1844.

The key to understanding why 1844 is so important comes in part from knowing what did not happen that year. Although many sincere believers felt Christ would return at that time, the "Great Disappointment" that followed led to the understanding—by a few at first, and then by many of the Millerite believers—that what happened was not a return to earth, but rather the commencement of the final phase of Christ's heavenly ministry.

This restoration of truth is important for all those who wish to be ready for His Second Advent. Understanding what Christ is doing now, and that He is preparing for a soon return, will help those who desire to be among the wise who are ready when the shout goes out: "Behold, the bridegroom is coming!" (Matthew 25:6).

■ Apply It:

Read over Daniel 8 and 9 and consider what an awesome responsibility carrying and understanding this vision entails. Pray for your understanding of this vital message!

■ Dig Deeper:

Daniel 8; Daniel 9; Matthew 25:1–13

Exoneration of Love

"Through his cunning he shall cause deceit to prosper under his rule; and he shall exalt himself in his heart. He shall destroy many in their prosperity. He shall even rise against the Prince of princes; but he shall be broken without human means" (Daniel 8:25).

After serving 21 years in prison for a murder in 1988, Jacques Rivera was exonerated by a jury who found that three detectives had framed him. The jurors also awarded Rivera $17 million as compensation for his traumatic experience. The decision was made after the only witness in the case changed his story.

Both God and His people have been accused of being responsible for much, if not all, of the evil in this world. However, the day is coming when they will be vindicated before the universe.

God will be vindicated even as the little horn power attempts to eclipse His ministry in the heavenly sanctuary. When that ministry is open for the whole world to see, God's character is seen as loving. This will undo Satan's attacks through the little horn power. That moment of vindication is a long-awaited event: "I heard a holy one speaking; and another holy one said to that certain one who was speaking, 'How long will the vision be, concerning the daily sacrifices and the transgression of desolation, the giving of both the sanctuary and the host to be trampled underfoot?' " (Daniel 8:13).

The people of God will also be vindicated in the face of accusations of the little horn power. This takes place during the same judgment: "Until the Ancient of Days came, and a judgment was made in favor of the saints of the Most High, and the time came for the saints to possess the kingdom" (Daniel 7:22). It is Christ's death that empowers His work in the heavenly sanctuary and reveals His love. At the end of time, God will exonerate those who have been proclaiming His true character of love to all by word and example.

Apply It:

Redirect a conversation that is becoming gossip.

Dig Deeper:

Matthew 10:32; Luke 12:8, 9; Revelation 3:5

November 8

Non-threatening

"Who is he who condemns? It is Christ who died, and furthermore is also risen, who is even at the right hand of God, who also makes intercession for us" (Romans 8:34).

People in the fashion and technology industries have been creating fake Instagram personalities. These models often look so perfect that they elicit responses of doubt concerning their authenticity. Nevertheless, followers actually follow these human creations.

God knows who His true followers are. However, He provides the investigative judgment in order to make a distinction for the onlooking universe. It's a time for discerning between those who have falsely worn the Christian label and those who have decided to genuinely follow Jesus. Ultimately, the latter will not be threatened by the judgment that takes place before the Second Coming.

Jesus explained that the church would have false believers up until His Second Coming. He illustrated it through a parable in which tares, or weeds, represent those who claim to be disciples but are not. The wheat represents Christ's true followers. When the suggestion is made that the weeds be pulled out, the farmer responds: "Let both grow together until the harvest, and at the time of harvest I will say to the reapers, 'First gather together the tares and bind them in bundles to burn them, but gather the wheat into my barn' " (Matthew 13:30).

Sometimes it may seem simple for us to discern the real Christian from the fake, like in the area of good deeds. Those who are actively involved in proclaiming the gospel or helping the poor appear to be in an authentic relationship with God. However, Christ explained that this is not always an accurate test: "Many will say to Me in that day, 'Lord, Lord, have we not prophesied in Your name, cast out demons in Your name, and done many wonders in Your name?' " (Matthew 7:22).

Apply It:

Have you ever struggled with hypocrisy in an area of your life? Pray for God to help you be a genuine Christian.

Dig Deeper:

Matthew 7:23; Daniel 7:9, 10; 1 John 2:1

Quick Focus

"Fear God and give glory to Him, for the hour of His judgment has come; and worship Him who made heaven and earth, the sea and springs of water" (Revelation 14:7).

Homeowners are often insured and prepared for worst-case scenarios, such as fires or burglaries. However, in a four-year time span, the average homeowner claimed almost $10,000 in water damage. This suggests that most homeowners are unprepared for floods, leaks, and water heater malfunctions.

God intended His people to spread the message of the gospel with a sufficient amount of urgency. This urgency is necessary because the judgment of those who declare their fidelity to Christ has already begun. At the same time, those who have been believers for many years are asked to open their hearts to the repentance God provides.

There are millions who have not yet had the opportunity to prepare for the Second Coming. However, the followers of Christ have been called to reach them with the news of salvation: "The Lord has commanded us: 'I have set you as a light to the Gentiles, that you should be for salvation to the ends of the earth' " (Acts 13:47). The news of salvation should be framed by the judgment of the church. In other words, new believers need to know that God intends to prepare them to be identified as true Christians by every creature in the universe.

Those who are currently spreading the message can model heartfelt preparation to new believers. During the ceremony that foreshadowed the day of judgment on God's people, the Israelites were instructed to fast, deny themselves, and repent: "The tenth day of this seventh month shall be the Day of Atonement. It shall be a holy convocation for you; you shall afflict your souls, and offer an offering made by fire to the Lord" (Leviticus 23:27).

This heart-searching is an openness to the cleansing work of the Holy Spirit in all believers.

Apply It:

Take an hour-long break from electronic devices.

Dig Deeper:

Mark 13:33; Hebrews 4:14–16; Acts 5:31

The Second Coming of Christ

25

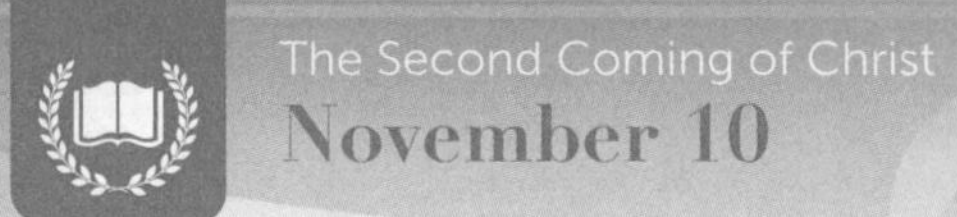

The Speed of His Return

"Behold, I am coming quickly" (Revelation 22:12).

Speed is relative. When early pioneers crossed the Great American Desert in search of gold, they rode in wagons pulled by oxen. It took about five months to travel from Rhode Island to California. But with the arrival of the transcontinental railroad, a trip from Omaha to Sacramento took under five days. Now you can fly that same distance in less than five hours! In 1850, a trip across the United States in 83 hours would seem unbelievably fast. On the other hand, a five-month trip over that same distance today would seem incredibly slow.

Physicists also tell us that motion is relative to the observer. If you watch a speedboat traveling at 25 miles per hour while you are standing on the shore a quarter mile away, it will appear to be going slower than if it passes ten feet in front of you. As we stand closer to the coming of Christ, the signs of His coming will intensify.

There is a difference between those who await Jesus' coming and those who are caught unaware. People who pay no attention to the signs of the times may know that someday the world will end, but if their focus is on other things, they will be surprised when that day comes. That's what Jesus meant when He stated, "If the master of the house had known what hour the thief would come, he would have watched and not allowed his house to be broken into" (Matthew 24:43).

In order to sharpen the prophetic outlook of these early believers, Peter explained, "Beloved, do not forget this one thing, that with the Lord one day is as a thousand years, and a thousand years as one day. The Lord is not slack concerning His promise, as some count slackness, but is longsuffering toward us, not willing that any should perish but that all should come to repentance" (2 Peter 3:8, 9). For those who search the prophecies of Scripture and look for the promise of His coming, the final events will happen with incredible speed.

Apply It:

What is the fastest speed you have ever traveled?

Dig Deeper:

Isaiah 25:9; 2 Peter 3:1–9; Revelation 22:20, 21

He's on His Way!

"Men of Galilee, why do you stand gazing up into heaven? This same Jesus, who was taken up from you into heaven, will so come in like manner as you saw Him go into heaven" (Acts 1:11).

Funerals are not happy events. For those who attended the April 2000 memorial services for H.M.S. Richards, Jr., the director of the *Voice of Prophecy* ministry and the son of its founder, the feeling of loss that his passing represented was especially harrowing.

At one point in the service, Harold's daughter, Mary Margaret, rose to speak. The child and grandchild of beloved preachers, her voice was clear, if trembling at times, when she described that which her father and grandfather so fervently believed: Soon, in the eastern sky, there would appear Jesus and thousands of angels returning for His people—those alive and those at rest in the grave.

That "blessed hope" (Titus 2:13) gripped her heart during those most painful hours of saying farewell to her father. That same hope has sustained millions of Christians through the centuries and resonates in hearts today.

For those struggling with the loss of a loved one, the promise of Christ's return is a solid rock to grasp amidst a torrent of despair. Death does not get the final say; God does: "O Death, where is your sting? O Hades, where is your victory?" (1 Corinthians 15:55).

We who believe know that Jesus came to the earth the first time, and we know that the First Advent ensures the Second Advent: "I will come again," He said in John 14:3. The last words of the Bible—Revelation 22:20—quote Jesus' enduring promise: "He who testifies to these things says, 'Surely I am coming quickly.' Amen. Even so, come, Lord Jesus!"

That's a hope we can hang on to during days of joy and days of sorrow. He's on His way!

Apply It:

H.M.S. Richards, Sr., who founded *Voice of Prophecy*, always ended his broadcasts with the call, "Have faith in God," regardless of circumstances. Today, keep that faith centered on Christ's promise!

Dig Deeper:

2 Peter 3:13; Psalm 50:3–5; Hebrews 9:26, 28

Unmistakably Heard

"The trumpet will sound, and the dead will be raised incorruptible, and we shall be changed" (1 Corinthians 15:52).

The Chrysler air raid sirens, built as official warning alarms for U.S. cities in 1952, are so loud that a normal person would be deafened standing within 200 feet of one during operation. The sirens are powered by Hemi engines and can discharge 2,610 cubic feet of air per second. They are so powerful that a piece of paper placed in front of the siren would spontaneously ignite.

Much louder than the Chrysler air raid siren is the second coming of Christ. Because "false christs and false prophets will rise and show great signs and wonders to deceive, if possible, even the elect" (Matthew 24:24), Jesus gave true signs of His soon return. Not only will "every eye" see Him (Revelation 1:7), but Paul explains, "The Lord Himself will descend from heaven with a shout, with the voice of an archangel, and with the trumpet of God. And the dead in Christ will rise first" (1 Thessalonians 4:16). The sounds accompanying Jesus' return will be heard by the living and the dead!

Jesus will return "in the glory of His Father with His angels" (Matthew 16:27) to gather all believers. "He will send His angels with a great sound of a trumpet, and they will gather together His elect from the four winds, from one end of heaven to the other" (Matthew 24:31).

Not only will God's children see and hear Christ's coming, but the wicked will also behold His return. "The sign of the Son of Man will appear in heaven, and then all the tribes of the earth will mourn, and they will see the Son of Man coming on the clouds of heaven with power and great glory" (Matthew 24:30).

If anyone tells you that Jesus has secretly returned to the earth and has been seen and heard only by a select few, don't be deceived. Christ warned, "If anyone says to you, 'Look, here is the Christ! Or 'There!' do not believe it" (Matthew 24:23). Not even the world's loudest siren will compare to the sound of Jesus' return.

Apply It:

What's the loudest sound you have ever heard?

Dig Deeper:

Matthew 24:27; Luke 24:36–43; Acts 1:11

Unnatural Prediction

"Behold, He is coming with clouds, and every eye will see Him, even they who pierced Him. And all the tribes of the earth will mourn because of Him. Even so, Amen" (Revelation 1:7).

Universities and corporations are developing artificial intelligence programs that can help predict power outages due to natural disasters. So far, IBM's program has been able to predict power outages with 70 percent accuracy with as much advance warning as 72 hours.

The faithful people of God will be able to recognize the nearness of Christ's coming with some degree of accuracy. However, unbelievers will be caught off guard. This is because even if a computer program could predict the nearness of Christ's return, many people would not believe the prediction.

Thus, those who are faithful to God will have a much better approximation of the Second Coming than the wicked. The Bible describes the surprise of the wicked when the unexpected return takes place: "You yourselves know perfectly that the day of the Lord so comes as a thief in the night" (1 Thessalonians 5:2).

Although the return of Christ will come as a surprise, all people will witness this event because it will be more cataclysmic than every natural disaster that has taken place. Jesus compared His return to the worldwide flood recorded in Genesis. By making this comparison, He implied that the faithful could not remain ignorant of an event as earth-shattering as His coming. The Bible says the antediluvians "did not know until the flood came and took them all away, so also will the coming of the Son of Man be" (Matthew 24:39).

Just as when Noah preached about the coming flood, most who hear won't be aware of the significance of the signs of the end. However, the righteous will realize that their preparation for that event requires more than just storing up emergency supplies. For them, their relationship with God will be the paramount form of preparation.

Apply It:

Use the news of a natural disaster to speak of the Second Coming.

Dig Deeper:

1 Thessalonians 5:4–6; Matthew 24:43; Daniel 2:44

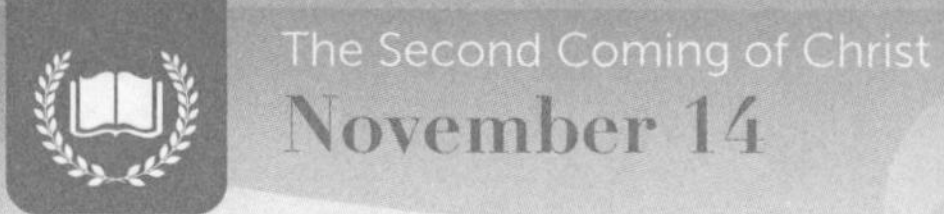

The Glorious Welcome

"Looking for the blessed hope and glorious appearing of our great God and Savior Jesus Christ" (Titus 2:13).

Protocol for visits to the United States by a head of state from another country are strictly followed. The high expressions of friendly relations during these visits are characterized by an emphasis on official public ceremonies. Depending on the rank of the visitor, the customary length of stay ranges from three to four days.

The first activity in welcoming heads of state is the flight line ceremony. Visitors typically arrive by aircraft at Joint Base Andrews, where a ground crew moves stairs into position and a red carpet is unrolled. A military cordon flanks both sides of the red carpet and a welcoming committee stands ready to greet the visitors. As the arrivals walk down the stairs, the U.S. Air Force Band performs *Arrival Fanfare Number One*. At the bottom of the stairs stands an American schoolchild holding a bouquet of flowers to greet them.

Only a select few can be part of a U.S. welcoming party, but when Christ returns, every believer who has ever lived—regardless of age, gender, education, economic status, or race—will joyfully participate in the coming of the King of kings. At the sound of the trumpet, "the dead in Christ will rise first" (1 Thessalonians 4:16). These resurrected children of God are united with their loved ones and sing, "O Death, where is your sting? O Hades, where is your victory?" (1 Corinthians 15:55).

After the dead in Christ rise from their graves with new bodies, the living believers are changed and also receive immortal bodies. "This corruptible must put on incorruption, and this mortal must put on immortality" (1 Corinthians 15:53). Both groups of believers together turn to greet their loving Savior. "We who are alive and remain shall be caught up together with them in the clouds to meet the Lord in the air. And thus we shall always be with the Lord" (1 Thessalonians 4:17).

May each of us strive to be part of this welcoming committee!

Apply It:

Have you ever had the privilege of greeting an official dignitary?

Dig Deeper:

Isaiah 25:9; Matthew 25:32–34; Mark 13:27

The Signs of the Times

"The sun will be darkened, and the moon will not give its light; the stars of heaven will fall, and the powers in the heavens will be shaken" (Mark 13:24, 25).

It's not just the heavens that are shaken at the end of time: Jesus told His disciples that at the close of history, "There will be famines, pestilences, and earthquakes in various places. All these are the beginning of sorrows" (Matthew 24:7, 8).

The world today is filled with uncertainty; the destruction taking place across North America alone is sobering: In 2017, Hurricanes Harvey, Maria, and Irma, were responsible for hundreds of deaths and billions in property damage.

The nation of Japan suffered a devastating episode in 2011 when the Fukushima earthquake unleased nuclear power plant radiation and resulted in a thousand deaths. In 2018, their government predicted higher probabilities of major quakes in Hokkaido and parts of the Pacific coast.

Earthquakes are also being felt in England and Scotland, while in Oklahoma, hydraulic fracturing—used to push natural gas from underground deposits—is being linked to a substantial increase in seismic activity in a state previously "calm" in terms of earthquakes. Man's inhumanity to the planet he was given to care for is reaping, it seems, a whirlwind of consequences.

The rise in natural disasters points toward the climax of world history. Scripture clearly promises that "the beginnings of sorrows" (Mark 13:8) will include an earth reacting to centuries of abuse and neglect. Other phenomena over the decades—such as the 1833 meteoric shower in which an average of 60,000 meteors per hour fell from the heavens (see Revelation 6:13)—offer continuing testimony that a time of shaking, "like the shaking of an olive tree" (Isaiah 24:13), is at hand.

Christians rely on the Bible, and not The Weather Channel, to tell us of the "end of the age" (Matthew 24:3). But we should note the signs in the heavens, on the earth, and under its surface—"for the time is near" (Revelation 1:3).

Apply It:

Do not fear the phenomena around you, but praise God that His Word is true. Jesus is coming again, and the signs of His return are everywhere!

Dig Deeper:

Matthew 24:21, 22; Luke 21:28–31; Revelation 6:12

Into All the World

"This gospel of the kingdom will be preached in all the world as a witness to all the nations, and then the end will come" (Matthew 24:14).

The growth of Scripture translation and publication since 1800 has been explosive. Since Johann Gutenberg first printed the Bible with moveable type over five centuries ago, God's Word has been advancing rapidly around the world. At the beginning of the 19th century, Bibles were available in just 68 languages. Today, the complete Bible has been translated into 670 languages, with portions of it available in 3,312 languages.

The distribution of the Bible in the last century is equally mind boggling. While it's not possible to obtain exact statistics, one Bible society estimates that around six billion Bibles were printed between 1815 and 1992.

Spreading the gospel through the written Word in our time is a fulfillment of Jesus' prophetic statement that the "gospel ... will be preached in all the world" (Matthew 24:14). Christ did not predict that all the world would accept the gospel, but that all would have an opportunity to hear or read the truth. The work of evangelism by humans, who cooperate with heavenly agencies, will speed up the coming of the Lord. Peter admonished, "What manner of persons ought you to be in holy conduct and godliness, looking for and hastening the coming of the day of God" (2 Peter 3:11, 12).

We live in a time when instantaneous global communication is a reality. The advancement from clay tablets to the printed page took thousands of years, whereas in less than one hundred years, we have witnessed the discovery of the telegraph, radio broadcasting, telephones, computers, satellites, the Internet, smartphones, texting, social media, and more. All of these are being used to spread the good news.

God encouraged Israel, "Enlarge the place of your tent, and let them stretch out the curtains of your dwellings; do not spare; lengthen your cords, and strengthen your stakes" (Isaiah 54:2). What are you willing to sacrifice in order to enlarge your impact for Christ?

Apply It:

What is your favorite form of communication? Now use it to share the good news!

Dig Deeper:

Daniel 12:4; Acts 17:31; Revelation 14:6, 7

Political Religion

"I saw one of his heads as if it had been mortally wounded, and his deadly wound was healed. And all the world marveled and followed the beast" (Revelation 13:3).

In early 2018, Pope Francis was seen as favorable by more than 60 percent of American adults. While this was less than the popularity of Pope John Paul II, who had an approval rating of over 75 percent, the respect and influence of the papacy as a whole continues to remain strong enough to garner respect from a large majority of Americans.

These statistics are significant when considering that the papacy had lost much of its power during the 19th century and did not regain its popularity until the late 1970s. The decline and rebirth of the papacy was foretold in the prophecies of the apostle John. Using the symbol of a beast, John spoke in Revelation 13:3 of how a religious and political power would die out but then regain its power.

The apostle Paul also spoke of this power as gaining its strength just before the second coming of Christ. Although he was not speaking of any particular pope or Catholic person, Paul was clear that a religious institution that did not receive its power from God would be used by the enemy of God: "The coming of the lawless one is according to the working of Satan, with all power, signs, and lying wonders" (2 Thessalonians 2:9).

John confirms that a religious-political power would become the means for forced worship. Although this persecution has not yet begun, prophecy states that, among other things, a death decree will be used to compel worship: "He was granted power to give breath to the image of the beast, that the image of the beast should both speak and cause as many as would not worship the image of the beast to be killed" (Revelation 13:15).

Unless a religious institution refrains from using the state power, it will be fulfilling at least one of the prophecies of John.

Apply It:

Use your vote to advocate for religious liberty.

Dig Deeper:

Revelation 16:13, 14; Revelation 13:13, 14; Revelation 14:12

Lawlessness Abounds

"Because lawlessness will abound, the love of many will grow cold" (Matthew 24:12).

Which are the most dangerous cities in the United States? Looking only at those cities with a population of at least 200,000, the top ones for violent crime include Detroit, St. Louis, Memphis, Baltimore, Kansas City, Cleveland, Milwaukee, Oakland, and Stockton. Four categories were used to define violent crimes: murder and non-negligent manslaughter; forcible rape; robbery; and aggravated assault. With 1,930 incidents, California led the pack for total number of murders in the United States in 2016. A total of 17,250 murders were reported that year for the entire country.

As contempt for God's law increases, so do the numbers of rapes, murders, robberies, and other violent crimes. Jesus predicted that neglect for the law of God would lead to cold-heartedness. The essence of following God's law is found in self-sacrificing love for others, just the opposite of violent crime. "Love does no harm to a neighbor; therefore love is the fulfillment of the law" (Romans 13:10).

Conditions on our planet will only get worse as we move closer to the second coming of Christ. Paul predicted, "Know this, that in the last days perilous times will come: For men will be lovers of themselves, lovers of money, boasters, proud, blasphemers, disobedient to parents, unthankful, unholy, unloving, unforgiving, slanderers, without self-control, brutal, despisers of good, traitors, headstrong, haughty, lovers of pleasure rather than lovers of God, having a form of godliness but denying its power" (2 Timothy 3:1–5).

Within 35 days in 2017, two of the five deadliest mass shootings in U.S. history took place. Locations stained with blood are popping up everywhere—even a small church in rural Texas, where 26 people were shot down. A gunman opened fire from a Las Vegas resort into a crowd in October 2017, killing 58 and injuring more than 500. It is the deadliest shooting in modern U.S. history.

The sobering signs we see should cause us to follow the apostle Paul's counsel to "examine yourselves as to whether you are in the faith" (2 Corinthians 13:5).

Apply It:

Have you observed an increase in lawlessness in your own community in the past few years?

Dig Deeper:

Matthew 24:21, 22; Luke 21:25; 1 Timothy 4:1, 2

A Violent End

"Nation will rise against nation, and kingdom against kingdom. And there will be great earthquakes in various places, and famines and pestilences; and there will be fearful sights and great signs from heaven" (Luke 21:10, 11).

For 73 years, starting in 1945, the United Nations has been viewed by many people around the globe as humanity's best hope for peace.

And while a third major world war has been prevented, the hundreds of conflicts and regional wars since the end of World War II, also in 1945, have resulted in the deaths of millions of people—some estimates at ten million and up.

There appears to be no end in sight. The famous Doomsday Clock of the Bulletin of the Atomic Scientists was set at "two minutes to midnight" in January 2018, one of its closest settings ever. ("Midnight" would mean nuclear holocaust.) "To call the world nuclear situation dire is to understate the danger—and its immediacy," the scientists said in their annual statement.

The wars we've seen—and will see in the years ahead—are the outgrowth of the Great Controversy between Christ and Satan. The adversary "knows that he has a short time" (Revelation 12:12) and is throwing everything possible against those waiting for Christ's return, regardless of how much such strife will hurt innocent men, women, and children. Daniel tells us "there shall be a time of trouble, such as never was since there was a nation" (Daniel 12:1), yet God's people "shall be delivered."

Believers in Christ will be concerned for themselves, their families, and their neighbors, of course. But this is also a time to rejoice, for Jesus said, "When these things begin to happen, look up and lift up your heads, because your redemption draws near" (Luke 21:28).

Apply It:

Share the good news—that Jesus is coming again and that He can make anyone ready for that return—with someone who needs to hear it today.

Dig Deeper:

Mark 13:7, 8; Matthew 25:6; Isaiah 25:9

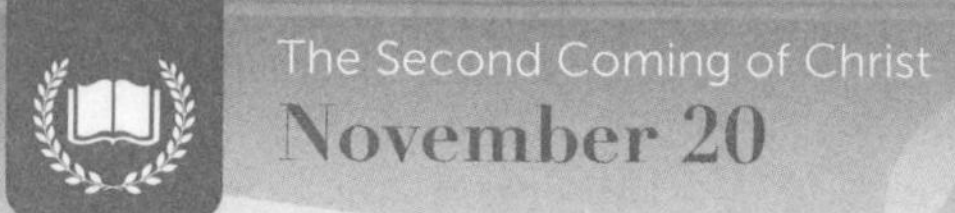

Always Ready

"Therefore you also be ready, for the Son of Man is coming at an hour you do not expect" (Matthew 24:44).

Are you looking to make your house burglar proof? One security consultant, who knows how burglars think since he used to be one, gives these practical tips for outfoxing thieves: Never advertise the fact that you have a pet because it will let burglars know that you do not have motion-sensitive detectors. And be wary of installing cat flaps, as they make your doors easier to kick in.

Another tip is to keep your valuables out of sight. If you are selling your home online and display a lot of pictures, be careful what you show. It might provide a tempting smorgasbord of valuables for burglars to steal. Better locks, security cameras, outdoor lighting, and less shrubbery close to your home are other ways to avoid being caught unawares.

For those who are unprepared for the second coming of Jesus, His return will come like "a thief in the night" (1 Thessalonians 5:2). Christ warned, "Know this, that if the master of the house had known what hour the thief would come, he would have watched and not allowed his house to be broken into" (Matthew 24:43). There is no better way to catch a thief than to watch for one!

Of course, Jesus is not comparing Himself to a robber: "The thief does not come except to steal, and to kill, and to destroy. I have come that they may have life, and that they may have it more abundantly" (John 10:10). Rather, Christ compares the unexpected coming of a thief to those who are not ready for His return.

Those who are prepared for the Second Coming are expecting His return and are watching. "Watch therefore, for you do not know what hour your Lord is coming" (Matthew 24:42). They do not know the exact time of His return: "Of that day and hour no one knows, not even the angels of heaven, but My Father only" (Matthew 24:36). But signs tell them that it is near.

Apply It:

Has a thief ever broken into your home and stolen goods?

Dig Deeper:

Matthew 7:22, 23; Matthew 25:1–13; Hebrews 9:28

Continuity

"Know therefore and understand, that from the going forth of the command to restore and build Jerusalem until Messiah the Prince, there shall be seven weeks and sixty-two weeks; the street shall be built again, and the wall, even in troublesome times" (Daniel 9:25).

What do filmmakers, artists, and scientists have in common? They are all likely to have one major hot streak during their careers. This means that for a certain period in their lives, they exceed their average success at selling paintings or being quoted. These were the findings of a study that looked at hot streaks in tens of thousands of careers.

The time prophecy of Daniel chapter 9 reveals that God had a streak of time planned for the fulfillment of His covenant with Israel. Many people have assumed that the final week of this prophecy is still in the future because they believe that the antichrist is spoken of in the final week: "After the sixty-two weeks Messiah shall be cut off, but not for Himself; and the people of the prince who is to come shall destroy the city and the sanctuary. The end of it shall be with a flood, and till the end of the war desolations are determined" (Daniel 9:26).

However, the prince in this verse is the Messiah, as can be seen in the phrase "Messiah the Prince" in verse 25. This is also consistent with the centrality of the Messiah in verse 27: "He shall confirm a covenant with many for one week; but in the middle of the week He shall bring an end to sacrifice and offering. And on the wing of abominations shall be one who makes desolate, even until the consummation, which is determined, is poured out on the desolate" (Daniel 9:27).

Without the antichrist in this passage, there is no reason to speculate about a secret rapture before the Second Coming. Instead, the prophecy shows that Jesus' death fulfilled the covenant.

Apply It:

Work toward a hot streak in spreading the gospel.

Dig Deeper:

Matthew 28:20; 1 Thessalonians 4:16, 17; Matthew 24:27

Resilience

"Teaching them to observe all things that I have commanded you; and lo, I am with you always, even to the end of the age" (Matthew 28:20).

After twelve boys and an adult were rescued from a cave in Thailand after two stressful weeks, mental health experts discussed whether the ordeal they experienced would lead to long-term distress. Psychologists believe that the boys will recover if they had plenty of support and accountability from loved ones.

The most traumatic of all human experiences will take place just before the Second Coming. However, God's people will have the presence of Christ with them and will be able to endure the trials.

Many Christians believe that these tribulations last for seven years, and they have welcomed the teaching that a secret rapture will remove them from the earth before the trials. However, the Bible does not specify the length of time for the trials.

The mistaken idea that the righteous would be taken to heaven before the final events is sometimes forced into Paul's writings when he says, "Jesus who delivers us from the wrath to come" (1 Thessalonians 1:10). The "wrath to come" is often interpreted as the trials that will be experienced just before the second coming of Christ.

However, in his second letter to the same group of believers, Paul explained what he meant by the wrath to come: "To give you who are troubled rest with us when the Lord Jesus is revealed from heaven with His mighty angels, in flaming fire taking vengeance on those who do not know God, and on those who do not obey the gospel of our Lord Jesus Christ" (2 Thessalonians 1:7, 8).

Paul was saying that the wrath the righteous would avoid would be the death that the wicked will experience at the Second Coming. In both passages, he was encouraging the righteous to anticipate deliverance after the tribulation.

Just as God delivered His people through the plagues that fell upon Egypt, so will the Lord carry His people *through* the final plagues that will fall upon the earth just before Jesus returns.

Apply It:

Talk to someone who has overcome a traumatic experience.

Dig Deeper:

John 17:15; 2 Peter 2:9; Matthew 24:9

Death and Resurrection

26

Stay Away!

"Samuel had died, and all Israel had lamented for him and buried him in Ramah, in his own city. And Saul had put the mediums and the spiritists out of the land" (1 Samuel 28:3).

King Saul was in dire straits. The imposing Philistine army had gathered to attack his nation, and his smaller, fewer troops were simply no match. In desperate need of counsel, Saul sought to contact the beloved prophet Samuel, who had died.

The king visited a medium in a nearby town, begging the witch, "Bring up Samuel for me" (1 Samuel 28:11). After the medium uttered some enchantments, an apparition claiming to be Samuel appeared. The ghost gave the king a devastating message, and the next day his three sons were killed in battle. Discouraged and heartbroken, Saul fell on his sword and died.

Who really spoke to Saul? Was it truly the ghostly form of the prophet of God—or someone else altogether? The key to understanding this story is found at the beginning of the chapter, which explains that "Saul had put the mediums and the spiritists out of the land" (1 Samuel 28:3). Why did the Bible writer make this statement?

God gave explicit instructions to Israel about attempts to contact the dead. The Lord told Moses, "You shall not permit a sorceress to live" (Exodus 22:18). Furthermore, God instructed, "Give no regard to mediums and familiar spirits; do not seek after them, to be defiled by them" (Leviticus 19:31). Even more pointedly, the Lord said, "There shall not be found among you anyone who makes his son or his daughter pass through the fire, or one who practices witchcraft, or a soothsayer, or one who interprets omens, or a sorcerer, or one who conjures spells, or a medium, or a spiritist, or one who calls up the dead" (Deuteronomy 18:10, 11).

As we will see in this section, the reason God commanded His people to not attempt to consult the dead is because "the dead know nothing" (Ecclesiastes 9:5). We tread on dangerous ground when we disobey God.

Apply It:

Have you ever seen an advertisement for someone who claims they can contact the dead?

Dig Deeper:

Leviticus 20:27; 1 Samuel 28:3–25; Isaiah 8:19

The Oldest Lie

"The serpent said to the woman, 'You will not surely die' " (Genesis 3:4).

Perhaps you've heard someone say, "That's the oldest lie in the book." Can you guess where this expression comes from? Most likely, it refers back to the third chapter of Genesis, where the serpent (a.k.a. Satan) tries to convince Eve that what God promised won't come to pass.

But God's Word is true. He was serious when He told Adam, in Genesis 2:16, 17, "Of every tree of the garden you may freely eat; but of the tree of the knowledge of good and evil you shall not eat, for in the day that you eat of it you shall surely die." Satan's lies, found in those first verses of Genesis 3, really are "the oldest lie in the book"—that is, in the Bible.

Yet today, millions and millions of people believe the same thing. They imagine that they can sin and not face eternal death, but rather some kind of continuous life that won't be all that bad. Inconvenient, sure, but we'll have plenty of friends in "that other place" to keep us company.

No. A thousand times, no! Only God is immortal. Ever since the first pair believed the lie in Genesis 3, humankind's immortality—conditioned on accepting, obeying, and following God—was revoked. The fate of those who do not accept Christ, who reject Him and the salvation He offers, will be a permanent, unconscious, eternal separation from God; it will be a true and lasting death, delivered at the judgment seat of Christ.

And between the time our earthly life ends and that final judgment begins, there is, well, nothing. Ecclesiastes 9:5 is unambiguous: "The living know that they will die; but the dead know nothing, and they have no more reward, for the memory of them is forgotten."

We are not immortal beings—not, that is, without Christ's sacrifice being received by us as our way to salvation and eternal life. Any other notion is just the oldest lie in the book being repeated.

Apply It:

Be sure to carefully examine what the Bible says about mortal life, eternal life, and what we can expect without Christ—and what awaits those who trust Him!

Dig Deeper:

1 Timothy 6:16; Job 14:2; Colossians 1:16, 17

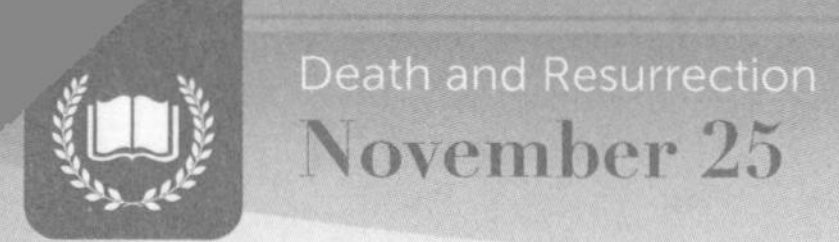

November 25

One-Hundred Percent Fatal

"The wages of sin is death, but the gift of God is eternal life in Christ Jesus" (Romans 6:23).

Which contagious diseases are the deadliest? Well, it depends. You can look at the fatality rate (the number of deaths per number of cases) or you can count the number of deaths in total caused by a disease. With proper medical treatment, the fatality rate for many illnesses drops dramatically—as is the case with tuberculosis and malaria.

At 1.6 million deaths, the deadliest disease by death toll is HIV/AIDS. However, new medical therapies have dramatically increased the life expectancy for those with the disease. One disease, if left untreated, has a 100-percent fatality rate—rabies. About 55,000 people die each year from it, primarily in Asia and Africa.

Sin is like rabies, but you don't need to get bitten by a dog to become infected with sin. Unfortunately, it is passed on to every human born on this planet. As the apostle Paul explained, "Through one man sin entered the world, and death through sin, and thus death spread to all men, because all sinned" (Romans 5:12).

When Adam and Eve sinned, God prevented them from eating from the tree of life so that they could not eat and "live forever" (Genesis 3:22). The gift of living eternally, called immortality, was based on the condition of obedience to God's laws. It is only by the mercy of God that our first parents did not immediately die.

Though each of us is born mortal, we may receive immortality through our Savior, for "the gift of God is eternal life in Christ Jesus our Lord" (Romans 6:23). The Bible gives us hope. "For as in Adam all die, even so in Christ all shall be made alive" (1 Corinthians 15:22). Without Christ, the virus of sin is 100 percent fatal. But divine love has provided a vaccination that promises perfect success: "God so loved the world that He gave His only begotten Son, that whoever believes in Him should not perish but have everlasting life" (John 3:16).

Apply It:

When did you last attend a funeral or memorial service and wish that death would forever end?

Dig Deeper:

Genesis 3:19; John 5:28, 29; 2 Timothy 1:10

An Eternal Gift

"We shall not all sleep, but we shall all be changed—in a moment, in the twinkling of an eye, at the last trumpet. For the trumpet will sound, and the dead will be raised incorruptible, and we shall be changed. For this corruptible must put on incorruption, and this mortal must put on immortality" (1 Corinthians 15:51–53).

The United Gifts to Minors Act (UGMA) and United Transfers to Minors Act (UTMA) allow for custodial accounts that are sometimes used by parents and grandparents to transfer financial gifts to minors when they reach a certain age. Once the account is set up, any assets added to the account become the possession of the minor—but it can only be used when he or she reaches the required age, usually 21.

People who set up these accounts often come to regret their decision, since there are no conditions besides age and no spending restraints, and many 21-year-olds lack the wisdom and maturity to handle a sizeable chunk of wealth. Yet these types of accounts have, in many other cases, proven to be a blessing to the young person receiving them.

Similarly, God's gift of eternal life belongs to us at the time that we receive Christ. The apostle John wrote that "God has given us eternal life, and this life is in His Son. He who has the Son has life; he who does not have the Son of God does not have life" (1 John 5:11, 12).

John goes on to say that he has written this for believers so they can know they "have eternal life" (verse 13). If you belong to Christ, you are part of the family of God and the eternal life account has been set up in your name. It belongs to you. But the actual realization of the gift will only come at the appointed time—on the day of Jesus' return when He will give "eternal life to those who by patient continuance in doing good seek for glory, honor, and immortality" (Romans 2:7).

Apply It:

Thank Jesus today for His incomprehensible gift of eternal life.

Dig Deeper:

Daniel 12:2; 1 John 2:25; Mark 10:29, 30

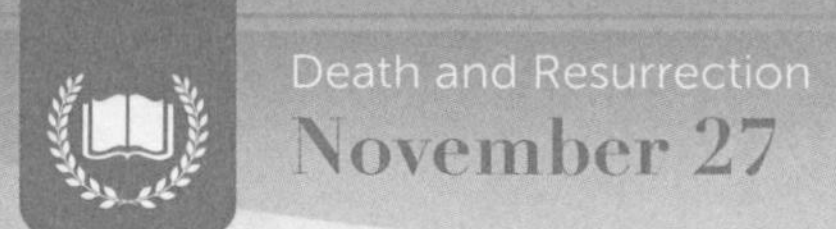

November 27

Preserved to Live

"Consider and hear me, O Lord my God; enlighten my eyes, lest I sleep the sleep of death" (Psalm 13:3).

In the summer of 2018, the deadly Carr wildfire of Northern California burned through many structures along Highway 299. However, firefighters were able to spare Old Shasta, an historic state park. Much like the park, a restored blacksmith shop in its deserted town of Shasta City preserves the area's history even though it is no longer a commercial establishment.

The Bible teaches that when people die, they are no longer a part of conscious activity. However, this does not mean that they are destroyed forever. God has a plan to resurrect and recompense both the righteous and the wicked. For this reason, the death that every human faces is often described using the metaphor of sleep.

On the one hand, this metaphor would have been problematic for the Sadducees, who believed that death was a permanent state. However, the apostle Paul made it clear that the metaphor of sleep included the anticipation of an awakening: "If we believe that Jesus died and rose again, even so God will bring with Him those who sleep in Jesus" (1 Thessalonians 4:14).

On the other hand, the sleep metaphor should have created problems for those who believed that death involved a conscious state. This is because the Bible describes death as an unconsciousness state: "The living know that they will die; but the dead know nothing, and they have no more reward, for the memory of them is forgotten" (Ecclesiastes 9:5).

The sleep metaphor, which is prevalent all throughout the Bible, need not discourage anyone because it suggests that the moment of awakening seems to follow almost immediately after the moment of drifting off. This means that the time spent in the grave will not feel long—even if it means that the dead are not resurrected for hundreds of years.

Because of the promise of resurrection, we can now associate one of our most terrible enemies with the blessing of a deep slumber.

Apply It:

Visit someone who is grieving a loss.

Dig Deeper:

Daniel 12:2; Matthew 9:24; John 11:11

We Are But Dust

"In the sweat of your face you shall eat bread till you return to the ground, for out of it you were taken; for dust you are, and to dust you shall return" (Genesis 3:19).

For ages, people have been trying to rid their households of dust. From the woman in Jesus' parable of the lost coin who swept her house to the challenges of floating dust in the International Space Station, dust is everywhere. Each year, the average household collects 40 pounds of dust made up of pollen, hair, textile fibers, soil minerals, and dead skin!

Not all dust is bad. The largest source of atmospheric dust is the Sahara Desert. It blows 770 million tons of dust across the Atlantic to South America, where it fertilizes the ocean and the Amazon rainforest. This dust impacts the air temperature, ground cooling, and rainfall levels.

The Bible tells us that God "formed man of the dust of the ground" (Genesis 2:7). Abraham humbly admitted when talking with God, "Indeed now, I who am but dust and ashes have taken it upon myself to speak to the Lord" (Genesis 18:27). Fortunately, by God's grace, "He raises the poor from the dust and lifts the beggar from the ash heap" (1 Samuel 2:8).

It should come as no surprise that when we die, we return to dust. God explained to Adam, "For dust you are, and to dust you shall return" (Genesis 3:19). When humans were created, a body made of dust was combined with the breath of life to produce a living being. At death, the inverse takes place: the body returns to the ground and the breath of life returns to God. "His spirit departs, he returns to the earth; in that very day his plans perish" (Psalm 146:4).

The soul does not exist apart from the body; it is not a conscious entity. There is no Bible verse that suggests some part of us lives beyond death. Rather, Scriptures plainly teach, "The soul who sins shall die" (Ezekiel 18:20). Until the resurrection, all who die return to dust.

Apply It:

What have you found to be the most effective way to get rid of dust?

Dig Deeper:

Psalm 8:3–5; Ecclesiastes 12:7; Isaiah 26:19

Sleep Tight

"What man can live and not see death? Can he deliver his life from the power of the grave?" (Psalm 89:48).

Where do people go when they die? In the nation of Ghana, it's believed that you might continue your career or some other aspect of life at your passing. Many there opt for "fantasy coffins" built to resemble a lion, an athletic shoe, or an airplane.

There's a big demand for fantasy coffins in the capital city of Accra, but less so in the rural countryside. Local residents can pay as little as $1,000 (U.S.) for such a container; overseas customers wanting the very best can spend as much as $15,000.

But there's a funny thing about those fantasy coffins—or any other coffin, for that matter. Each and every coffin ends up in the same place: a grave.

Sheol is the Hebrew word for grave, and it often appears transliterated in Bible verses. In almost every instance, *sheol* is defined as the final stop for a person. There's no purgatory, no heavenly "waiting room," no place for the dearly departed to go. When God saved David from his enemies, he recalled how "the sorrows of Sheol surrounded me; the snares of death confronted me" (2 Samuel 22:6).

Almost every person who has ever died is in *sheol* awaiting "the resurrection of life" or "the resurrection of condemnation" (John 5:29). Those whose bodies have deteriorated into dust or whose bodies were somehow destroyed by fire or other circumstance are also awaiting the resurrection, because God has a memory of each one (Job 14:13).

When you're dead, you're dead, and your body awaits God's verdict. That's why it's vital to receive Jesus as Savior during your lifetime. After death, there's no opportunity to change your mind (John 5:24).

But for those who trust in Christ, there's great news about the future. As Paul said in 1 Corinthians 15:55, "O Death, where is your sting? O Hades, where is your victory?"

Apply It:

If someone tells you there is conscious life after death, ask God to let you know whether this is a moment to share the Bible's truth about the grave.

Dig Deeper:

Genesis 37:35; Acts 2:27, 31; Revelation 20:13

Borrowed Life

"The Lord God formed man of the dust of the ground and breathed into his nostrils the breath of life; and man became a living being" (Genesis 2:7).

Public libraries are now loaning out audiobooks through an app called Libby. Although these audiobooks are digital recordings, they are treated like physical copies. This means that there is a limit to how many people can borrow them at any one time.

God gives each person the breath of life, and that breath returns to God at death. However, unlike audiobooks, the Bible verses that speak of the spirit, or breath, treat it as a kind of life force. In other words, the life force is not a conscious or perceiving identity. Instead, it is the power that God infused into Adam's lifeless body to bring him to life for the first time.

In the Old Testament, the Hebrew word that is translated "breath" in the Creation account is translated "spirit" at other times. In addition, Solomon gave a clue as to the meaning of the human spirit. He explained that it is something that came from God and returns to Him at death: "The dust will return to the earth as it was, and the spirit will return to God who gave it" (Ecclesiastes 12:7). Because the Bible does not teach that people's conscious identities were with God before they were born, there is no reason to think that the spirit in this passage is something other than a life-giving force.

Additionally, Solomon explains that animal spirits may go to a different place after death: "Who knows the spirit of the sons of men, which goes upward, and the spirit of the animal, which goes down to the earth?" (Ecclesiastes 3:21). This difference between the location of animal and human spirits after death also suggests that spirits are not conscious identities. Otherwise, Solomon would be teaching that people and animals are in different places after death. However, there is no verse in the Bible that suggests this.

Apply It:

Return something that you've borrowed.

Dig Deeper:

Ecclesiastes 3:19, 20; Psalm 146:4; Job 33:4

December 1

The Biggest Liar

"You will not surely die" (Genesis 3:4).

If you think you're good at telling lies, you just might qualify to enter an annual competition in England called the World's Biggest Liar. From around the world, competitors gather and have five minutes to tell the biggest and most convincing lie they can. No props or scripts can be used, and politicians and lawyers are excluded since they are deemed too skilled at telling "porkies."

History is riddled with notorious liars, including Richard Nixon, Charles Ponzi, and P.T. Barnum. But nobody can top the list like Satan himself, whom Jesus called "a liar and the father of it" (John 8:44). His biggest and most convincing lie was the one he told Eve at the tree of knowledge of good and evil. Even though God told Adam and Eve that if they ate from that tree they would "surely die" (Genesis 2:17), the couple chose to believe the devil's tale.

The single lie that sinful man is immortal has laid the foundation for the deceptive belief of Spiritualism—a movement based on the notion that the spirits of the dead roam the earth. This unbiblical teaching has swept millions into thinking they can communicate with the dead, even though the Bible says that the "soul who sins shall die" (Ezekiel 18:20).

Sadly, this twisted teaching was imported into the Christian faith through pagan philosophy—especially from Plato—during a time when the church was deep in apostasy. Today, the belief that the dead are conscious has paved the way for Christians to accept Spiritualism. After all, if the dead are alive and in the presence of God, why would they not come back to earth as ministering spirits?

The Bible not only exposes spiritualism as false but forbids anyone from trying to communicate with the dead (Leviticus 19:31). Jesus repeatedly dealt with "evil spirits" (Luke 7:21), and John the revelator tells how in the last days the "spirits of demons" will perform signs (Revelation 16:14).

Only as we stay close to the Word of God can we avoid being deceived by evil spirits that pretend to be spirits from heaven.

Apply It:

Think of a time you believed a lie. How did it affect your life?

Dig Deeper:

Deuteronomy 18:10, 11; Acts 19:12; Revelation 12:9

On the Other Side?

"I saw three unclean spirits like frogs coming out of the mouth of the dragon, out of the mouth of the beast, and out of the mouth of the false prophet. For they are spirits of demons, performing signs" (Revelation 16:13, 14).

It once was said that the key to publishing a bestselling book was to either write a biography of Abraham Lincoln, a story about a doctor, or a book about dogs. Presumably, a book about Lincoln's doctor's dog would be a guaranteed winner!

Today, however, there's another surefire way to hit the bestseller lists: write a book about how you (or, better still, your young child) died, went to heaven, and returned to life. The happier the descriptions about life "over there" you can throw in, the better. At least one Hollywood movie, *Heaven Is for Real*, hit the silver screens after a book of the same name sold millions of copies.

But all is not floating on a cloud in the realm of afterlife memoirs. In 2015, a major Christian publisher withdrew *The Boy Who Came Back from Heaven* after its protagonist, Alex Malarkey, said he had not returned from a celestial sojourn in 2004.

In an uncertain world like our own, people want something to cling to in the face of death and its loss and separation. Books detailing an afterlife, television shows featuring "conversations" with the dead, and people offering to connect you with a departed loved one—all these will increase as the end draws near. (See 1 John 4:1.)

Don't be deceived, however. The dead "know nothing" (Ecclesiastes 9:5) and can't communicate with the living. That's one reason why it's important to, as much as possible, maintain close relationships with loved ones while they're still with us.

Apply It:

People will offer ways to connect with those "on the other side." Do not be taken in by the notion; remain sure of what God has said.

Dig Deeper:

Psalm 146:4; Revelation 3:5; Revelation 16:13, 14

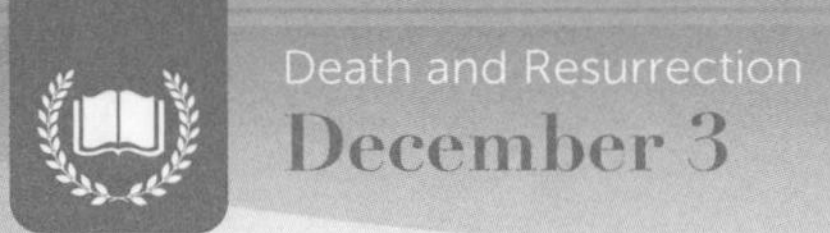

Revival Precedent

"Blessed be the God and Father of our Lord Jesus Christ, who according to His abundant mercy has begotten us again to a living hope through the resurrection of Jesus Christ from the dead" (1 Peter 1:3).

A team of Russian scientists is claiming that they brought to life roundworms that had been frozen for thousands of years. Although some in the scientific community are skeptical, this is not the first time that roundworms have survived being frozen for an extended period of time. The previous record for reviving a dormant roundworm was 39 years.

Jesus' resurrection was not just an awakening from a dormant state. On the contrary, Jesus' side had been pierced to guarantee His death. It is His resurrection from complete death that gives every Christian hope for their own resurrection. (See 1 Corinthians 15:20.)

To prevent any confusion about His resurrection, Jesus made it abundantly clear that He was not a spirit when He came to them in His resurrected body: "Behold My hands and My feet, that it is I Myself. Handle Me and see, for a spirit does not have flesh and bones as you see I have" (Luke 24:39). Jesus knew that some believed the dead returned to the living without a body, and He did not want to perpetuate that belief.

He also understood that if His resurrection was not completely authentic, it would cast doubt on the possibility of another human being raised. The apostle Paul explicitly made this point when he spoke of the implications of believing Christ was still in the grave: "Then also those who have fallen asleep in Christ have perished" (1 Corinthians 15:18). In other words, he was saying that the Christian's hope in the resurrection is based on Christ having gone through the grave before us.

In response to this wonderful hope, the disciples were motivated to proclaim salvation from sin and death "to all the nations" (Matthew 24:14). Because they knew that Jesus had conquered death, they could offer that victory to everyone.

Apply It:

Together with a friend, pray for spiritual revival in your church.

Dig Deeper:

Job 14:13–15; Job 19:25–29; Psalm 49:15

Not the Same

"I have hope in God, which they themselves also accept, that there will be a resurrection of the dead, both of the just and the unjust" (Acts 24:15).

Identical twins are identical, right? Wrong. With the increase of fertility treatments, the number of twins born in the United States rose to 76 percent over the past thirty years. More twins are born in Massachusetts than in any other state, with 4.5 twins for every 100 live births. The increase in twins has raised discussions about how similar identical twins really are.

Yes, many sets of identical twins invent their own language. No, identical twins may not always have the exact same genetics. Even though they share the same DNA, twins do not have identical fingerprints. In fact, mirror image identical twins have reverse asymmetric features, which means one may be right-handed and the other left-handed. Their hair whorls may swirl in the opposite direction, and they may have birthmarks on the opposite sides of their body.

The Bible teaches that there are two resurrections and that they are not the same. Yes, in both resurrections, people will come back to life, but from that point on they are very different experiences. Jesus taught, "Do not marvel at this; for the hour is coming in which all who are in the graves will hear His voice and come forth—those who have done good, to the resurrection of life, and those who have done evil, to the resurrection of condemnation" (John 5:28, 29).

The first resurrection takes place at the Second Coming, in which the righteous dead are raised from the grave (1 Thessalonians 4:16). The second resurrection takes place at the end of the thousand years. "The rest of the dead did not live again until the thousand years were finished" (Revelation 20:5). Those who are raised in the first resurrection are called "blessed" and "over such the second death has no power" (Revelation 20:6).

God takes "no pleasure in the death of one who dies" (Ezekiel 18:32) and pleads with all to "turn and live," for these two resurrections are not identical.

Apply It:

Are you a twin or do you know a set of twins? Are they really identical in every way?

Dig Deeper:

1 Corinthians 15:22, 23; Philippians 3:21; Revelation 20:6

December 5

Conquering Evil

"There was a man in their synagogue with an unclean spirit. And he cried out, saying, 'Let us alone! What have we to do with You, Jesus of Nazareth? Did You come to destroy us? I know who You are—the Holy One of God' " (Mark 1:23, 24).

If you believe you are being harassed by an evil spirit, whether in the form of subtle but ongoing temptations, actual harassment, or even possession, is there anything you can do to overcome it? We find the answer by looking at the life of Christ.

Jesus often encountered evil spirits. Notice His response: "Jesus rebuked him, saying, 'Be quiet, and come out of him!' And when the unclean spirit had convulsed him and cried out with a loud voice, he came out of him" (Mark 1:25, 26). Christ did not spend a long time conversing with demons. He simply commanded them to flee. Witnesses to the event said, "With authority He commands even the unclean spirits, and they obey Him" (verse 27).

If you are under attack by evil spirits, call upon God in the name of Jesus Christ for help. Draw as close to Him as you can by praying, repenting of your sins, reading His Word, and praising Him through worship and song. You can find special strength and encouragement in such Scriptures as Proverbs 3:23–26 and 2 Timothy 1:7. When you find yourself spiritually weak and ready to give in, go back to the well of Bible truth and His promises to be refreshed again and again. And if you feel you need special help from a spiritual leader, you can also request special prayer and anointing at your church.

Finally, and most important, take time every day to put on the armor of God, remembering that "we do not wrestle against flesh and blood, but against principalities, against powers, against the rulers of the darkness of this age, against spiritual hosts of wickedness in the heavenly places" (Ephesians 6:12). We should "put on the whole armor of God" (verse 11) to combat these powers and to be a light for others.

Apply It:

Have you ever encountered the presence of evil?

Dig Deeper:

Psalm 56:3; Ephesians 6:10–20; 1 John 4:4

The Millennium and the End of Sin

27

Hitting the Pause Button

"He laid hold of the dragon, that serpent of old, who is the Devil and Satan, and bound him for a thousand years" (Revelation 20:2).

At the turn of the millennium, software that helped run maximum security prisons in Australia could have failed catastrophically on January 1, 2000. Although major problems were averted, some technical support workers explained that much of their success was because problems were rooted out early enough.

God has a fail-proof plan for preventing Satan from influencing people during the thousand years after the second coming of Christ. When Jesus comes, all unsaved humans are destroyed by the brightness of His coming. This means that Satan cannot tempt them into more sin, and those who are living have been resurrected and taken to heaven: "But the rest of the dead did not live again until the thousand years were finished. This is the first resurrection. Blessed and holy is he who has part in the first resurrection. Over such the second death has no power, but they shall be priests of God and of Christ, and shall reign with Him a thousand years" (Revelation 20:5, 6). Here, John is explaining the millennium by jumping back and forth on the timeline.

John then lists only one explanation for the meaning of the binding of Satan to the destroyed earth: "He cast him into the bottomless pit, and shut him up, and set a seal on him, so that he should deceive the nations no more till the thousand years were finished. But after these things he must be released for a little while" (Revelation 20:3). Heaven's strategy for dealing with Satan was unveiled so that everyone would know God's thorough plan to abolish evil in the universe.

Apply It:

Encourage someone who is fearful or losing hope in God.

Dig Deeper:

Revelation 20:1; Revelation 19:11–21; Revelation 16:13

Ignored Warnings

"Son of man, I have made you a watchman for the house of Israel; therefore hear a word from My mouth, and give them warning from Me" (Ezekiel 3:17).

They can stretch across many miles of ocean, reach heights of more than a hundred feet, and travel as fast as a jetliner. Tsunamis are often deadly ocean waves created by a sudden disturbance of the sea by landslides, earthquakes, volcanic eruptions, and even meteorites. When tsunamis hit a shoreline, their devastating force is often unexpected since many residents ignore warnings.

On December 26, 2004, more than 230,000 people were killed, 500,000 injured, and 1.7 million left homeless after a 9.2-magnitude earthquake created a tsunami that impacted 14 countries in Asia and Africa. The event remains one of the deadliest natural disasters in recorded human history. The death toll could have been less had early warnings been heeded.

Jesus compared His return to the flood that destroyed the world in Noah's time. "As the days of Noah were, so also will the coming of the Son of Man be. For as in the days before the flood, they were eating and drinking, marrying and giving in marriage, until the day that Noah entered the ark, and did not know until the flood came and took them all away, so also will the coming of the Son of Man be" (Matthew 24:37–39).

Another depiction of the Second Coming shows the Savior riding on a white horse and striking the nations of the world. When the beast and the false prophet are slain, the rest of Satan's followers will die and none will remain, for "the rest were killed with the sword which proceeded from the mouth of Him who sat on the horse" (Revelation 19:21).

The same devastating scene is described by Isaiah, who said, "Behold, the Lord comes out of His place to punish the inhabitants of the earth for their iniquity; the earth will also disclose her blood, and will no more cover her slain" (Isaiah 26:21). Oh, that people would have heeded the repeated warnings given by God's servants!

Apply It:

Have you ever been caught unawares by a storm? Were warning signals given?

Dig Deeper:

Proverbs 16:18; Matthew 10:28; Luke 21:28

Adversary No More

"All who knew you among the peoples are astonished at you; you have become a horror, and shall be no more forever" (Ezekiel 28:19).

While the story of a daring prison escape might make for good drama, the real-world consequences don't end after a 90-minute performance. Just ask Joyce Mitchell, a onetime civilian employee working at a tailor shop in a New York State prison.

Mitchell was arrested after she helped two convicted murderers, Richard Matt and David Sweat, tunnel their way out of prison. She smuggled in hacksaw blades and other tools that helped the two escape. Matt was killed by state troopers; Sweat was captured and now spends 23 hours a day in a prison cell. Their helper may not be released before 2022.

Unlike the toughest jails in America, Satan's binding on earth will be unbreakable. The adversary will be in an "abyss" where he will have nothing to do and no one to corrupt.

The proud accuser of God's people will be "a horror," as Ezekiel declared of the king of Tyre. Like that ruler, Satan "shall be no more forever" and will have no influence in the new heavens and earth.

Just as the scapegoat was led into the wilderness (Leviticus 16:8–10), so Satan shall be led into that abyss. The Bible says, "I saw an angel coming down from heaven, having the key to the bottomless pit and a great chain in his hand. He laid hold of the dragon, that serpent of old, who is the Devil and Satan, and bound him for a thousand years; and he cast him into the bottomless pit, and shut him up, and set a seal on him, so that he should deceive the nations no more till the thousand years were finished" (Revelation 20:1–3).

What a day that will be! No discord, no conflict, no hatred between nations! Put your salvation in Jesus' hands so that you can see it happen.

Apply It:

Satan cannot escape his fate, but you can avoid eternal destruction. If you haven't yet asked Christ into your heart, do so right now.

Dig Deeper:

Leviticus 16:21, 22; John 12:31; 2 Peter 2:4

A Time to Celebrate and Reign

"The kingdom and dominion, and the greatness of the kingdoms under the whole heaven, shall be given to the people, the saints of the Most High" (Daniel 7:27).

What's your idea of a great house? A four-story Los Angeles abode that went on the market in 2017 boasts 38,000 square feet, 12 bedrooms, and 21 bathrooms. It has a bowling alley, three kitchens, a home theater, an 85-foot infinity pool, and dozens of other luxury features. It originally listed for a "mere" $250 million. Purchasing fantasy homes like this has become a trend among some billionaires.

But however opulent and breathtaking earthy mansions are, they will never hold a candle to the perfect homes Jesus has prepared for those who love Him. (See John 14:1–3.) When our Redeemer takes His people to heaven directly after the first resurrection, they will burst out in a song of gratitude—not primarily for dwellings, but for their deliverance.

To finally be free from sin and suffering and, most of all, to be with the One who gave Himself for them, will overwhelm the redeemed with joy. The Bible says they will "sing the song of Moses, the servant of God, and the song of the Lamb, saying: 'Great and marvelous are Your works, Lord God Almighty! Just and true are Your ways, O King of the saints!' " (Revelation 15:3).

According to Revelation, the saved will even reign with Christ! "He who overcomes, and keeps My works until the end, to him I will give power over the nations" (Revelation 2:26). And Revelation 20:6 confirms, "Blessed and holy is he who has part in the first resurrection. Over such the second death has no power, but they shall be priests of God and of Christ, and shall reign with Him a thousand years."

Although the righteous will be in heaven during the thousand years, and the unsaved will be dead, God's people will reign with Him in the sense that they will be actively involved in the judgment of the wicked.

Apply It:

In what ways will our heavenly homes far outshine any homes on earth today?

Dig Deeper:

2 Timothy 2:11, 12; Revelation 3:21; Daniel 7:18

No Ethical Dilemmas

"Do you not know that the saints will judge the world? And if the world will be judged by you, are you unworthy to judge the smallest matters?" (1 Corinthians 6:2).

The Chinese government launched a "social credit system" that assigns a number to every citizen. This number is calculated based on the credit score, behavior, preferences, and friends of Chinese citizens. This system will reward some for good citizenship and punish others.

Most people in the West cringe at the thought of passing judgment on the preferences of others. However, they probably feel comfortable with assessing behavior that is clearly criminal.

God's ability to transform sinners and instill them with wisdom reinforces His plan for human involvement in reviewing the judgments He has passed: "I saw thrones, and they sat on them, and judgment was committed to them. Then I saw the souls of those who had been beheaded for their witness to Jesus and for the word of God, who had not worshiped the beast or his image, and had not received his mark on their foreheads or on their hands. And they lived and reigned with Christ for a thousand years" (Revelation 20:4).

While it may seem obvious that demons are committing grievous sins, the apostle Paul explained that the task of judging angels should give us pause: "Do you not know that we shall judge angels? How much more, things that pertain to this life?" (1 Corinthians 6:3). In other words, if we can be trusted with something as important as judging angels, we should be able to judge the comparatively small disputes that arise between believers.

Along with his angels, Satan will have time to think about his own mistakes during his distraction-free millennium. Most important, the entire judgment process assures God's followers of His fairness in dealing with wicked humans who had merely appeared to be heaven-bound. God wants to be certain that we trust Him and His decisions.

Apply It:

Ask God for wisdom concerning a dispute between believers.

Dig Deeper:

2 Peter 2:4; Jude 1:6; John 7:24

No Escape

"When the thousand years have expired, Satan will be released from his prison" (Revelation 20:7).

It's been called the greatest death-row escape in history. Few can top the Mecklenberg Six—a group of condemned killers who simply walked out through the prison's doors. The six were facing the Virginia electric chair when they made their daring escape on May 31, 1984.

After they studied the complacent procedures of correctional officers, one of the inmates overpowered a guard and released all of the locks in the housing unit. Inmates stole uniforms, put on riot helmets, and claimed to be removing a bomb, which was actually a TV covered with a blanket. They then made their way to a waiting van and drove out of the prison. However, all six were eventually recaptured and executed.

But there is a greater escape that will take place at the end of the millennium when Christ returns with the redeemed to the earth. "The rest of the dead" (Revelation 20:5), that is, the wicked, will be resurrected, allowing Satan to once more "go out to deceive the nations which are in the four corners of the earth" (Revelation 20:8).

Christ and His people will descend to the earth to end the great battle, to execute the millennial judgment, and to purify the earth in order to set up His eternal kingdom. Then Jesus will truly be recognized as "King over all the earth" (Zechariah 14:9).

Satan's final deception is to inspire the wicked to surround "the camp of the saints and the beloved city" (Revelation 20:9). Evildoers who refused to accept the invitation to enter heaven through the grace of Jesus now try to enter by force, but "fire came down from God out of heaven and devoured them" (verse 9).

The great (but temporary) escape of Satan and his followers has not changed the hearts of the wicked. Instead, the same thoughts of evil that followed them into the grave remain with them as they stand before God and the Holy City. Their final effort to attack the city vindicates the character of God.

Apply It:

Have you ever visited a prison? How did it feel to be behind locked gates?

Dig Deeper:

Isaiah 14:12–15; Galatians 3:22; Revelation 20:1–15

Justice at Last

"We must all appear before the judgment seat of Christ, that each one may receive the things done in the body, according to what he has done, whether good or bad" (2 Corinthians 5:10).

A pastor from years gone by once retold the story from a church he shepherded in Kentucky. There, the son of a hardscrabble farm family committed a financial crime and went before a judge, who asked the defendant whether or not he was guilty. The boy replied, "Guilty, your honor."

Because it was the young man's first offense, the judge gave the criminal a suspended sentence. The pastor said that the young man cleaned up his act and lived on the right side of the law ever since.

But the pastor remembered the exchange between the defendant and his worldly judge, and wrote, "When you look into the face of God, and He asks you that simple question, 'Are you guilty or are you not guilty?,' you can't help but reply—you have to reply, you have no other choice but to reply—'Lord, I'm guilty.' "

There's no escaping your appointment before God, the Eternal Judge. Everyone who has ever lived, everyone living right now, and everyone who shall live until the moment of Christ's return will face a judgment. It will come as a surprise to many, happening after Satan is unbound at the end of the millennium and as he and his forces attempt to attack the city of God.

As the opponents gather, God sets up "a great white throne" (Revelation 20:11). From there, the final judgment will be carried out. Those who are not alive at Christ's return will be resurrected to learn their fate.

The judgment is intended to inform each person of a verdict and show, once and for all, that God is just. Everyone will have the same response: "[T]hat at the name of Jesus every knee should bow, of those in heaven, and of those on earth, and of those under the earth, and that every tongue should confess that Jesus Christ is Lord" (Philippians 2:10, 11).

Apply It:

Have you ever stood before an earthly judge? How did it feel?

Dig Deeper:

Revelation 20:12; Luke 13:28; Isaiah 45:22, 23

Limited Fuel

"They went up on the breadth of the earth and surrounded the camp of the saints and the beloved city. And fire came down from God out of heaven and devoured them" (Revelation 20:9).

The Mendocino Complex Fire, which sparked in July 2018, is considered the largest blaze in California's history. It surrounded a large part of Clear Lake, a natural body of freshwater and the largest of its kind in the state.

When God executes judgment at the end of the millennium, the event will resemble a lake of wildfire over the entire earth. While this massive end to evil is a response to sin, some have tried to add more to the story, claiming that the wicked will receive some kind of eternal life in order for their punishment to continue forever. However, the God described in the Bible would never allow such an atrocity. Instead, the wicked are described as being completely "devoured" by the fire (Revelation 20:9).

There are three words in the Bible translated as "hell." Two of them, *sheol* (Hebrew) and *Hades* (Greek), describe the grave—the place of the unconscious dead. The third, *Gehenna* (Greek "geena," Valley of Hinnom), comes from the place where rebellious Israelites burned their children to the god Molech. The Creator promised that punishment would be carried out against those cruel parents: "The corpses of this people will be food for the birds of the heaven and for the beasts of the earth. And no one will frighten them away" (Jeremiah 7:33).

When Jesus warned against "geenna," it had this shameful association: "Do not fear those who kill the body but cannot kill the soul. But rather fear Him who is able to destroy both soul and body in hell (*geenna*)" (Matthew 10:28). Yes, even the worst of sinners die a bodily, eternal death at the end of the millennium.

Apply It:

What was the most difficult punishment you ever experienced in your life?

Dig Deeper:

2 Peter 3:7; Isaiah 34:8; Isaiah 28:21

Everlasting Fire

"His winnowing fan is in His hand, and He will thoroughly clean out His threshing floor, and gather His wheat into the barn; but He will burn up the chaff with unquenchable fire" (Matthew 3:12).

An unstoppable wall of fire rampaged through Chicago on the evening of October 8, 1871. For three days, the Great Chicago Fire raged, killing more than 300 people and destroying over three square miles of the city. The city's prominent use of wood for buildings and sidewalks, combined with only an inch of rain between July 4 and October 9, created the perfect conditions for carrying flying embers around the city.

The initial response of the Chicago fire department's 185 firefighters was quick, but they ended up going in the wrong direction. When the blaze jumped the South Branch of the Chicago River, the enormous amount of heat created a fire whirl that drove the flames high and far. When the city's waterworks went up in flames, the city's water mains went dry, making it impossible to stop the blaze. In the end, more than $222 million in property was destroyed. The county coroner could not give an exact number of deaths because some of the victims were incinerated and left no remains.

When Christ described the fate of the wicked, He said they would burn with "unquenchable fire" (Matthew 3:12). This punishment is called the "everlasting fire" (Matthew 18:8) and "eternal fire" (Jude 1:7). While many believe sinners will never stop burning, the Greek word *ainos* is a relative term and its meaning is determined by the object it modifies. For instance, the reference in Jude is to the fires that completely destroyed Sodom and Gomorrah. Those cities do not burn to this day; instead, the results are eternal.

When Jesus said of the wicked, "Depart from Me, you cursed, into the everlasting fire prepared for the devil and his angels" (Matthew 25:41), He meant the effects of this unquenchable fire will be everlasting and that only ashes would remain (Malachi 4:1–3).

Apply It:

Do you have a fire extinguisher in your home? If not, go out and purchase one.

Dig Deeper:

Jeremiah 17:27; 2 Peter 2:6; Hebrews 6:2

A Lasting Punishment—That Ends

"When the wicked spring up like grass, and when all the workers of iniquity flourish, it is that they may be destroyed forever" (Psalm 92:7).

It's a staple of cartoons and sermon illustrations: the sinner "roasting" over the flames of eternal torment. But does the Bible really teach that the wicked will be punished again and again? Will the wages of sin actually be a hellish "Groundhog Day," in which the unrepentant are tormented without end? In a word, no. Paul, in Romans 6:23, famously declared that death is the actual wages of sin.

Why punish the unrepentant? To demonstrate to the universe, including Satan and his fellow fallen angels, that there is ultimate justice and that the justice is fair. Everyone will see when and how they had an opportunity to follow God—and where they forsook those chances.

"But," you say, "verse after verse talks about punishment and torment lasting forever and ever." Yes, there are verses that say that, but what is the *context* of "forever"? As other verses tell us, it isn't an endless cycle of punishment. Rather, if one is "destroyed forever," that's how long the results of the punishment will last: that is, forever.

Make no mistake: Those who are not transformed at the resurrection, those who have not accepted Christ, will not rise with everlasting bodies. We read in 1 Corinthians 15:53, "This corruptible must put on incorruption, and this mortal must put on immortality." If we haven't "put on immortality," we simply don't have it.

In the Old Testament, we learn God's final plan for evildoers: " 'You shall trample the wicked, for they shall be ashes under the soles of your feet, on the day that I do this,' says the LORD of hosts" (Malachi 4:3). If words mean anything, then this passage assures that those whom God punishes will cease to exist.

The good news is that the vilest sinner can be made clean by coming to Jesus. Then, instead of a punishment that lasts forever, an eternal paradise awaits!

Apply It:

Look through the Bible references for "forever"—from Genesis to Revelation—and study their context.

Dig Deeper:

Revelation 14:11; Isaiah 34:9, 10; Malachi 4:1

The Punishment Fits

"That servant who knew his master's will, and did not prepare himself or do according to his will, shall be beaten with many stripes" (Luke 12:47).

A number of thought leaders have spoken about the dangers of being involved in public shaming on social media. The problem is not that people write cruel remarks or threats. Instead, it is the compounded responses that come in the form of clicking a "like" button to show agreement with a criticism. When thousands of people do this, the target of criticism can feel crushed.

This trend reveals that people have trouble measuring out the appropriate punishment. Knowing this, Jesus explained that it is better for us to try and reconcile with our enemies than to get revenge: "When you go with your adversary to the magistrate, make every effort along the way to settle with him, lest he drag you to the judge, the judge deliver you to the officer, and the officer throw you into prison" (Luke 12:58).

Additionally, He made it clear that His method of vengeance is superior to ours. To illustrate this point, Jesus gave the example of wicked servants who do not follow the master's will because he is on a journey and seems to be delayed in his return. When the master returns, each wicked servant is punished according to the gravity of the action committed.

Furthermore, the punishments are based on the amount of knowledge that each servant had concerning right and wrong: "But he who did not know, yet committed things deserving of stripes, shall be beaten with few. For everyone to whom much is given, from him much will be required; and to whom much has been committed, of him they will ask the more" (Luke 12:48). In other words, wrong actions done in ignorance will be treated with less severity.

This principle of fair punishment will be applied in the final punishment of sin.

Apply It:

Try to reconcile quickly in your next conflict.

Dig Deeper:

Romans 12:19; Hebrews 10:29; 2 Corinthians 2:5–7

A Colossal Cleaning

"The day of the Lord will come as a thief in the night, in which the heavens will pass away with a great noise, and the elements will melt with fervent heat; both the earth and the works that are in it will be burned up" (2 Peter 3:10).

It's not the most pleasant subject, but when a job has to be done, it has to be done. So—what's the best toilet bowl cleaner on the market? Instead of providing a list of products, here is what many people say they want from a cleanser: It cleans with a single flush; it tackles the toughest stains; it prevents the build-up of toilet rings; it kills most germs; it eliminates odors; it has no harsh fumes; and it's safe for plumbing and septic systems.

Is all that too much to ask?

There's a much bigger cleaning job that will take place at the end of the millennium, when God tackles the work of removing all sin from the universe. The apostle Peter explains that the cleaning agent used by the Lord is fire: "The elements will melt with fervent heat; both the earth and the works that are in it will be burned up" (2 Peter 3:10).

Every impurity of sin will be eliminated by the fire that destroys the wicked. From the ashes of what is left over, God will create "a new heaven and a new earth, for the first heaven and the first earth had passed away" (Revelation 21:1). Even better still, "God will wipe away every tear from their eyes; there shall be no more death, nor sorrow, nor crying. There shall be no more pain, for the former things have passed away" (verse 4).

For those who desire to walk in the New Jerusalem, a cleansing work must include asking Christ to remove sin from the heart. In light of the coming judgment, Peter concludes, "Therefore, since all these things will be dissolved, what manner of persons ought you to be in holy conduct and godliness?" (2 Peter 3:11).

Apply It:

What does your favorite household cleaner teach you about getting rid of sin?

Dig Deeper:

1 John 1:9; 2 Peter 3:10–13; Revelation 21:1–8

Is Satan Immortal?

"I brought fire from your midst; it devoured you, and I turned you to ashes upon the earth in the sight of all who saw you" (Ezekiel 28:18).

Is Satan immortal? The Bible states that God "alone has immortality" (1 Timothy 6:13–16). This means that no creature possesses immortality. As a created angel, this fact applies to Satan, formerly known as Lucifer, who once held the highest position among the angels.

Also, the Bible directly states that "the soul who sins shall die" (Ezekiel 18:20). *Nephesh*, the Hebrew word from which we get the word "soul," includes the meaning of "creature" and "living being." So this verse applies not only to human beings, but also to angels. Not only has Satan sinned, he is the originator of sin. Jesus said to wicked religious leaders, "You are of your father the devil. ... He was a murderer from the beginning, and does not stand in the truth" (John 8:44). Since Satan is a living being, and since he is the originator of sin, he will certainly experience the consequence of sin, which is death. After all, the "wages of sin is death" (Romans 6:23).

Jesus spoke of "the everlasting fire prepared for the devil and his angels" (Matthew 25:41). Does this mean that Satan will burn forever in eternal misery? There is a Bible passage that explains both parts of the question. God, speaking to Satan, said, "By the abundance of your trading you became filled with violence within, and you sinned; therefore I cast you as a profane thing out of the mountain of God; and I destroyed you, O covering cherub. ... I brought fire from your midst; it devoured you, and I turned you to ashes upon the earth in the sight of all who saw you" (Ezekiel 28:16–18).

Is Satan immortal? God said that Satan would be devoured. Will Satan burn forever in hellfire? God said that in the sight of everyone, Satan will be turned to ashes.

Apply It:

How does it make you feel to know Satan will die one day?

Dig Deeper:

Isaiah 14:12–21; 1 Corinthians 15:51–55; 1 Timothy 1:17

The New Earth

28

Tangible Reality

"We, according to His promise, look for new heavens and a new earth in which righteousness dwells" (2 Peter 3:13).

Imagine walking down the street in Hiroshima on a beautiful summer morning when, far above, you hear the sound of a lone plane. Then suddenly, a brilliant flash of light overwhelms you, followed by a giant blast, which knocks down entire buildings. This is what a group of Japanese high school students has painstakingly produced in a virtual reality (VR) experience that mimics one of the atomic bombs dropped on Japan in 1945.

VR is a computer-generated immersive experience that combines auditory, visual, and other stimulus. People typically don headsets with screens that allow them to "look around" an artificial world. VR is most commonly used in gaming and 3D cinema, but it is also being used in medicine, education, the military, flight simulators, and driver training.

It's a common belief among many Christians that heaven will not be a tangible place where we enjoy touching, tasting, seeing, smelling, and hearing things for real. A false picture of the hereafter is even presented in the media, portraying the saints floating on clouds and playing harps—sort of an outdated VR experience. But the Bible paints the heavenly Canaan in far more vivid terms.

When John "saw a new heaven and a new earth" (Revelation 21:1), the very concept of a "new" earth implies a world much like our own, but without the damage caused by sin. In reality, when God first created our world—with real trees, grass, animals, fish, birds, water, sky, and people—and called it "good" (Genesis 1:3, 9, 12, 18, etc.), it was not some virtual environment for Adam and Eve.

When God destroys sin and makes a "new" earth, it is *this* earth that will be made new—renewed and recreated to its original state before sin made its ugly stain upon our world. After "the earth and the works that are in it will be burned up" (2 Peter 3:10), God will make the earth fresh again, a tangible reality that we will enjoy forever.

Apply It:

What tangible experience do you look forward to in the earth made new?

Dig Deeper:

Isaiah 11:6–9; 2 Peter 3:10–13; Revelation 21:1–3

Transparent Light

"When you pray, say: Our Father in heaven, hallowed be Your name. Your kingdom come. Your will be done on earth as it is in heaven" (Luke 11:2).

During massive anti-corruption protests in Romania in 2018, a symbol of honesty was developed. Protestors used the flashlight function on their cell phones to show their discontent with government corruption. By shining the lights, they made a statement against the darkness of grafting.

The New Jerusalem will be the brightest and most transparent city in the history of our world. This literal brightness will be welcomed by the righteous, who do not need to rely on darkness for secretive and dishonest ploys.

During His ministry, Jesus encouraged His disciples to pray for the coming of the kingdom of God to this earth (Luke 11:2). John prophesied of the moment when all their prayers would be answered in a literal way: the descent of the New Jerusalem to the planet (Revelation 21:2).

Unlike most cities, our home in paradise will be the location of an eternity of fairness based on love. While many large cities are currently associated with pollution, the New Jerusalem will be resplendent with the glory of God: "The city had no need of the sun or of the moon to shine in it, for the glory of God illuminated it. The Lamb is its light" (Revelation 21:23). John uses the spiritual and physical presence of light to draw our attention to the just practices of the King of the new earth.

Although the writer may have been focused on the importance of beauty in the New Jerusalem, there is also a sense of honesty and openness in the material from which it is made: "The construction of its wall was of jasper; and the city was pure gold, like clear glass" (Revelation 21:18). This kind of forthcoming atmosphere is the perfect home for the honest!

Apply It:

Take an opportunity for honesty that will benefit someone else.

Dig Deeper:

Revelation 21:9, 11; Revelation 21:24, 25; Revelation 22:1

December 21

Feeling at Home

"Let not your heart be troubled; you believe in God, believe also in Me. In My Father's house are many mansions; if it were not so, I would have told you. I go to prepare a place for you" (John 14:1, 2).

How do you make visitors feel at home? Luxury hotels compete to provide a comfortable environment that makes guests want to come back. What do they have that you could also supply for guests in your own home? First of all, provide friends and family with a comfortable bed—not a foam pad or a sofa that's too short. And make sure you put crisp, clean sheets on the bed. Set on the nightstand a clock radio and maybe a bottle of water with a glass.

Provide a quiet place for guests to escape to. Furnish the room with a relaxing chair, a reading nook with a few great books and magazines, and a reading lamp. Eliminate clutter and make the guest room free of stuff in the way. Have some bare tabletops, empty drawers, and closet space available. And if you really want to go the extra mile, have a few cozy robes and slippers waiting.

Do you know that God is working to provide the perfect home for you? But in the heavenly land, you will not be a temporary guest. Jesus said, "I go to prepare a place *for you*" (John 14:2, emphasis supplied). You will not be overnight company, for Christ said, "If I go and prepare a place for you, I will come again and receive you to Myself; that where I am, there you may be also" (verse 3). The apostle Paul said that when Christ comes and we rise to meet Him in the air, "we shall always be with the Lord" (1 Thessalonians 4:17).

Not only will we have a home in "the city" (Hebrews 11:10), but we will "inherit the earth" (Matthew 5:5). It's a place we'll never want to leave.

Apply It:

Where have you most felt at home?

Dig Deeper:

Psalm 37:9; Isaiah 65:21; Revelation 21:3

Floating on a Cloud? Not Likely!

"[The Lamb has] made us kings and priests to our God; and we shall reign on the earth" (Revelation 5:10).

Those of a certain age will recall television cartoons in which, on occasion, a character "dies." They're then shown floating on a cloud, dressed in a white robe, and plucking the strings of a harp.

Hollywood—among others—has often depicted the "next life" as a time of ease and freedom from work. No punching a time clock, no fighting commuters on the train or the freeway—just floating around all day enjoying things.

As we study what the Bible says, however, this idyllic picture isn't easily found. The new earth will be different from what we know today, a world made right, in the manner God wanted the earth to remain after He created humanity. It will be what Eden was before the fall, a true paradise.

But it won't be a place of idleness. The redeemed will have "work" to do, although not the kind of arduous labor many face today. We'll "build houses and inhabit them," as Isaiah 65:21 declares, though in a world made new, such work won't have the same toil it does now.

Yes, we'll spend time gathered around God's throne, praising Him not only for His goodness, but also for His kindness in redeeming us to live in this place (Revelation 15:3, 4). We'll share our stories throughout the universe, answering the questions on how we obeyed God and found innumerable blessings in doing so.

Not every detail of our future existence is spelled out in the Bible's discussion of the new earth. Surely some pleasant surprises await. (See 1 Corinthians 2:9!) However, the implications of Scripture are clear: a paradise awaits in which we will have gardens to dress, homes to occupy, and very happy work to do—forever!

Apply It:

Read what the Bible says about the rewards prepared for the saved and thank God for touching your life.

Dig Deeper:

Genesis 1:28–31; Matthew 5:5; Revelation 22:3–5

Fellowship Forever

"Now we see in a mirror, dimly, but then face to face. Now I know in part, but then I shall know just as I also am known" (1 Corinthians 13:12).

Imagine not being able to recognize other people, even your loved ones, by looking at their faces. Sadly, this neurological disorder, called prosopagnosia (from the Greek words for "face" and "lack of knowledge") has affected about 2.5 percent of the population. "Face blindness" can be acquired from a brain injury or people can be born with it.

No lasting remedies have been found for prosopagnosia, though people can use "piecemeal" recognition to identify others—for instance, by clothing, hair color, body shape, and voice. Because face recognition is an important identifying feature of our memory, prosopagnosics not only are challenged to keep track of people, but struggle to socialize with others in normal ways.

At the coming of Christ, the righteous are promised new minds and bodies (1 Corinthians 15:53). But some have wondered if our loved ones will be able to recognize us when we are glorified and given new bodies at the resurrection.

We can be grateful that everyone in God's kingdom will be able to recognize others, not only their loved ones, but even the saints of old (Matthew 8:11). After Christ's resurrection, the disciples had no problem recognizing Him. Mary recognized His voice (John 20:11–16). Some disciples even recognized Jesus by His manner of breaking bread. Luke says, "Then their eyes were opened and they knew Him" (Luke 24:31).

God created humans to be in relationship. The Bible says, "God is love" (1 John 4:8)—and love does not live in a vacuum. The health of the church, the body of Christ, is fostered by fellowship with heaven (1 Corinthians 1:9) and with other believers. Heaven will be glorious, not just because we will be in communion with God, but because of the sweet and harmonious relationships we will experience with others.

Apply It:

Besides Jesus, who do you most look forward to seeing in heaven?

Dig Deeper:

Genesis 32:30; Exodus 33:11; Revelation 22:4

A Superior Gift

"In Your presence is fullness of joy; at Your right hand are pleasures forevermore" (Psalm 16:11).

Some researchers believe that loneliness has become an epidemic in America, with studies showing that roughly half the population is scoring high on the loneliness scale. Loneliness affects more than just mental health; those who are lonely are often more likely to suffer from many types of chronic disease. In fact, a former U.S. Surgeon General estimated that being isolated socially is as harmful to the body as being obese or smoking fifteen cigarettes a day.

When the first human, Adam, looked at all the animals, he must have felt a pang of loneliness, for "there was not found a helper comparable to him" (Genesis 2:20). But the first marriage solved Adam's problem. With his new helper by his side, he no longer felt lonely.

A good marriage is a wonderful gift from God. It can be a great blessing. So many things in our world can cause us to experience isolation or other negative emotions, but having someone with which to share the challenges and joys of life can give one courage.

Jesus said that after His people are resurrected at His coming, "they neither marry nor are given in marriage, but are like angels of God in heaven" (Matthew 22:30). While we're not entirely sure what this means for those who are already married, we know there will be no loneliness in paradise. Friends will be everywhere, and no one will feel unloved. That doesn't mean we won't have special friends.

God's Word assures us that "no good thing will He withhold from those who walk uprightly" (Psalm 84:11). While marriage may be a thing of the past, we can be sure that our compassionate Lord will care for every need and will provide us with something far superior in the world to come.

Apply It:

If you are married, tell your spouse how much he or she is appreciated.

Dig Deeper:

1 Corinthians 2:9; Acts 2:28; Revelation 21:4

Service Learning

"In the middle of its street, and on either side of the river, was the tree of life, which bore twelve fruits, each tree yielding its fruit every month. The leaves of the tree were for the healing of the nations" (Revelation 22:2).

Several years ago, New York University started raising money for an endowment fund that would provide free tuition for all of their medical students. After students had already made plans to pay for their own tuition, the school made the surprise announcement.

God has a tuition-free plan for every one of His followers on the new earth (Romans 6:23). He desires His children to continue learning throughout eternity. In order to ensure this, Jesus paid the cost with His own blood. God can now provide everything that the righteous need to develop and grow in their understanding of His wisdom.

This is especially true of the study of the plan of salvation. During their time on earth, Christ's followers have been set back in their understanding of salvation. This is partly because of health problems and physical limitations that sin has brought upon them. However, the Bible speaks about the complete healing of the righteous in the New Jerusalem: "The inhabitant will not say, 'I am sick'; the people who dwell in it will be forgiven their iniquity" (Isaiah 33:24). With fresh minds, the redeemed will study their redemption.

The physical recovery from sin will also afford God's people the opportunity to serve Him in many ways. Although serving others has often been considered a difficult work, labor on the new earth will be a pleasant expression of love: "There shall be no more curse, but the throne of God and of the Lamb shall be in it, and His servants shall serve Him" (Revelation 22:3). Although the Bible does not specify the details of this service, it is clear that Christ's followers will desire to imitate their Master in experiencing the joy of service.

The atmosphere of learning through service in heaven will enhance interpersonal harmony for eternity. Now is a good time to practice such giving that will prepare us for life on the new earth!

Apply It:

Learn something that will improve your service to others.

Dig Deeper:

Matthew 20:28; Isaiah 66:23; 1 Peter 1:12

No More Night

"God will wipe away every tear from their eyes; there shall be no more death, nor sorrow, nor crying. There shall be no more pain, for the former things have passed away" (Revelation 21:4).

"No More Night" is a favorite hymn of many that tells of a time when the pain and suffering of this life will be gone forever: "No more night/No more pain/No more tears/Never crying again/And praises to the great I Am/We will live in the light of the risen Lamb!"

It turns out that's a pretty good summary of what to expect in the new earth, which God has in store for those who follow Him. Death, sorrow, crying, pain—all the elements of the curse brought on by the rebellion in Eden—will be eliminated when God creates "a new heaven and a new earth" (Revelation 21:1).

That promise alone should make us long for this new world. Anyone who has lost a loved one or has endured a chronic illness or disability will appreciate the prospect of a world without pain, a world devoid of tears.

Perhaps the most tragic lesson of history has been human inhumanity to our fellow humans—men, women, and children. From the wars and massacres recorded in the Bible, through the epidemics, battles, and genocides of centuries gone by, to the tragic record of the last hundred years, there are abundant examples of barbarism.

Those whose hearts ache daily over the loss of a loved one will have those wounds eternally mended. And those whose bodies were broken by disease or disability will be made whole and young and vigorous.

In Isaiah 65:17, we're promised that "the former shall not be remembered or come to mind," meaning the sufferings of this life will not be etched into our memory banks forever. When we are made new by God, we will have hearts full of joy and gratitude. The old will have passed, never to be recalled.

What a day that will be!

Apply It:

Whatever you're facing in life today—or have faced so far—remember that there is a bright, happy tomorrow ahead of you, in which God will heal every hurt!

Dig Deeper:

Isaiah 65:16; Revelation 21:8; Revelation 22:15

An Incentive to Endure

"Do not lose heart. Even though our outward man is perishing, yet the inward man is being renewed day by day. For our light affliction, which is but for a moment, is working for us a far more exceeding and eternal weight of glory" (2 Corinthians 4:16, 17).

One of the most grueling sporting events in the United States is The Race Across America—a cross-continental, 3,000-mile bike race from the Pacific to the Atlantic. You can race solo or go in teams of two, four, or eight members who alternate turns riding. The race must be completed in 12 days, meaning solo riders may only catch 90 minutes of sleep per day while sitting in the saddle for about 20 hours each day. Sleep deprivation can cause hallucinations, so support crews must monitor riders.

In our race toward the heavenly finish line, we can become weighed down with the cares of this life. The apostle Paul knew this well: "We are hard-pressed on every side, yet not crushed; we are perplexed, but not in despair; persecuted, but not forsaken; struck down, but not destroyed" (2 Corinthians 4:8, 9).

Christ set us an example of looking ahead in order to endure the present. "Therefore we also, since we are surrounded by so great a cloud of witnesses, let us lay aside every weight, and the sin which so easily ensnares us, and let us run with endurance the race that is set before us, looking unto Jesus, the author and finisher of our faith, who for the joy that was set before Him endured the cross, despising the shame, and has sat down at the right hand of the throne of God" (Hebrews 12:1, 2).

There is nothing wrong with desiring the glories of heaven. Jesus said, "Rejoice and be exceedingly glad, for great is your reward in heaven" (Matthew 5:12). Even Moses considered "the reproach of Christ greater riches than the treasures in Egypt; for he looked to the reward" (Hebrews 11:26). So instead of racing for a medal, consider the gift of heaven, "a far more exceeding and eternal weight of glory" (2 Corinthians 4:17).

Apply It:

Have you ever won a race?

Dig Deeper:

Matthew 10:22; Luke 6:23; 1 Corinthians 3:14

Microscopic Harmony

"I have no pleasure in the death of the wicked, but that the wicked turn from his way and live. Turn, turn from your evil ways! For why should you die, O house of Israel?" (Ezekiel 33:11).

Health officials once believed that measles had been completely wiped out by the year 2000. However, the disease resurfaced, and by 2017 there were 118 cases. This is unsettling because measles can have complications that kill some children or cause permanent damage, such as deafness.

The evils that are seen in this world are often blamed on God. This leads many people to reject God, misunderstanding His true character. In order to correct the distorted picture of His nature, God has been doing everything He can to show His love.

Jesus predicted that His death on the cross would draw people to Him: "I, if I am lifted up from the earth, will draw all peoples to Myself" (John 12:32). If the glimpse of God's love was enough to draw all people to Jesus, how much more will we be drawn after evil is completely vanquished? Although we received a flood of insight into God's character when Jesus died on the cross, we will be able to understand it so much better without the distortions of evil in the natural world.

This is partly because nature will be recreated according to its original design. Diseases, disasters, and the attack of predators will be eliminated: "The wolf and the lamb shall feed together, the lion shall eat straw like the ox, and dust shall be the serpent's food. They shall not hurt nor destroy in all My holy mountain" (Isaiah 65:25). Although the Bible does not specify the details of what nature will be like, we know that it will reflect a loving God.

Do you look forward to the new earth, a land that will lack even microscopic predators like measles?

Apply It:

Pray especially for sick acquaintances in the coming weeks.

Dig Deeper:

Isaiah 11:7–9; Exodus 34:6, 7; Isaiah 51:3

On and On and On . . .

"In My Father's house are many mansions; if it were not so, I would have told you. I go to prepare a place for you. And if I go and prepare a place for you, I will come again and receive you to Myself; that where I am, there you may be also" (John 14:2, 3).

A noted Christian preacher told the story of a vacation once gifted to him, a stay on one of the Hawaiian islands—complete with the most luxurious accommodations imaginable.

Food was copious, fresh, and appetizing. Towels appeared, it seemed, before being requested. And throughout the hotel, an army of employees stood by ready to open a door as he approached.

As he recalled it, he even wondered, "Is this heaven? It sure seems like it!"

Life in our new earth, the paradise promised to the believer, will be far more grand than any resort. "Eye has not seen, nor ear heard, nor have entered into the heart of man the things which God has prepared for those who love Him" (1 Corinthians 2:9).

Perhaps the greatest feature, however, is the infinite nature of this new life. Vacations eventually come to an end, just as our more pedestrian holidays have a conclusion. After that time away, we re-enter the routines of daily life.

In tomorrow's world, in the earth made new, there will be no need for "re-entry." Everything will continue without end. Happiness will endure. Joy will be everlasting. And the redeemed will never grow old, never lose their vitality, and never die—"the voice of weeping shall no longer be heard in her" (Isaiah 65:19).

As we read in Scripture, "The kingdoms of this world have become the kingdoms of our Lord and of His Christ, and He shall reign forever and ever!" (Revelation 11:15). It will be a new world order, to borrow a phrase, but one of peace, plenty, and healing for all!

Apply It:

Share this wonderful good news with a friend, a coworker, a neighbor: God is coming to make a new earth, and each of us has the chance to be there, if we would only trust in Jesus!

Dig Deeper:

Daniel 2:44; Daniel 7:27; Revelation 5:13

Every Tear Dried

"God will wipe away every tear from their eyes" (Revelation 21:4).

Tears are not all bad. The salty fluid that pours out of the lacrimal glands in your eyes is full of helpful protein, water, mucus, and oil that serve more than one purpose. Basal tears are always present in your eyes to keep them from drying out. Reflex tears protect the eyes from harsh irritants like smoke, onions, or dusty wind.

Even crying has its benefits. Emotional tears are common when people suffer loss. Some scientists believe that having a good cry can actually rid the body of toxins. While reflex tears contain about 98 percent water, emotional tears have several chemicals, including hormones, that indicate high levels of stress and even an endorphin that helps to reduce pain and improve mood.

The Bible says that in heaven, "God will wipe away every tear from [our] eyes" (Revelation 21:4). What type of tears will these be? Perhaps they are tears of grief since the rest of the verse says, "There shall be no more death, nor sorrow, nor crying. There shall be no more pain, for the former things have passed away." Not all pain is caused by a physical trauma. Some pain comes from grieving the loss of a loved one.

Some wonder how heaven can be a happy place when the saved think of loved ones who are lost. We know God promises to wipe away our tears. When the redeemed stand in the New Jerusalem, they will be surrounded by the beauties of the new earth and the pain of their losses and tragedies will fade. The Bible says, "Behold, I create new heavens and a new earth; and the former shall not be remembered or come to mind" (Isaiah 65:17).

During the millennium, as the saints review the lives of all the saved and lost, there certainly will be tears shed over missing loved ones who are not in the kingdom. But there will come a time when those final emotional tears will be wiped away by God! What a tender and compassionate heavenly Father we have.

Apply It:

When did you last grieve the loss of a loved one and shed tears?

Dig Deeper:

Psalm 30:5; John 11:35; 1 Thessalonians 4:13

December 31

You Can't Take It with You

"Flesh and blood cannot inherit the kingdom of God; nor does corruption inherit incorruption" (1 Corinthians 15:50).

How would you like to inherit $14.4 billion? That's what Laurene Powell Jobs collected as the widow of Apple cofounder Steve Jobs. She inherited his wealth and assets, which included shares of Apple stock and a 7.3 percent stake in The Walt Disney Company—which tripled in value after Steve's death in 2011, making up more than $12 billion of her net worth. But just like with her husband, when Laurene dies, as the saying goes, "You can't take it with you."

Some people have read 1 Corinthians 15:50 and concluded that the kingdom of heaven is a fanciful, ethereal place full of wispy clouds, ghosts, and illusory beings that float around all day. If "flesh and blood cannot inherit the kingdom of God," then how can the redeemed be flesh-and-bone people?

To understand what the apostle Paul means by "flesh and blood," we need to look at the context of this passage. Just a few verses earlier, he explains how our resurrected bodies will be different from our present bodies. "So also is the resurrection of the dead. The body is sown in corruption, it is raised in incorruption" (verse 42). He later adds, "For this corruptible must put on incorruption, and this mortal must put on immortality" (verse 53).

Sin changed our bodies and our very natures. Therefore, when we enter the paradise of Eden restored, our bodies will be changed so that we can fully enjoy the perfection of heaven. "Flesh and blood" is a figure of speech referring to the human body on this earth (see Matthew 16:17). Christ, in His resurrected body, declared that He was truly "flesh and bones" (Luke 24:39).

Flesh and blood refers to our corruptible bodies on earth. When Jesus comes, He will "transform our lowly body that it may be conformed to His glorious body" (Philippians 3:21). When thinking of our old, earthly bodies, we'll be glad to leave them behind.

Apply It:

What one thing do you look forward to leaving behind when you go to heaven?

Dig Deeper:

1 Corinthians 15:35–58; Galatians 1:16, 17; Ephesians 6:12